Ichi
1974

D0723755

DISCARDED

Selected Readings on
MODERN JAPANESE SOCIETY

Editors:
George K. Yamamoto
University of Hawaii
Tsuyoshi Ishida
Hiroshima Institute of Technology

McCutchan Publishing Corporation
2526 Grove Street
Berkeley, California 94704

Copyright © 1971
by
George K. Yamamoto
and
Tsuyoshi Ishida

Library of Congress Cat. Card Number 72-146314
Standard Book Number 0-8211-0803-4

CONTENTS

PREFACE

Scarcely a century out of feudalism, Japan is now one of the leading industrial nations of the world. Her population has tripled during the last hundred years but the present relatively low rate of annual growth in numbers is like that of the industrialized West. A rising standard of living has accompanied an increasing concentration of the people in large urban centers, an expanding technological-commercial occupational structure, and a blurring of the stratification system by increased social mobility.

The vast change in organization and operation of the economy, accelerated since defeat in World War II and subsequent recovery, was initiated many decades earlier. The seeming anomaly of an industrialized Asian society that began its move toward economic modernization long before the middle of the twentieth century has impelled many a student of modern society to attempt explanations of this obtrusive fact. Others have focused their efforts on describing and assessing the changes in—and frequently the durability of—traditional aspects of social organization in Japanese life in the wake and in the midst of economic development.

The articles in this collection were selected to give a quick but probing look at the gains, dislocations, accommodations, and altered or persistent perspectives and practices that are the social consequences or accompaniments of the economic modernization process, and to acquaint readers with examples of the interest writers have shown in accounting for the emergence of Japan as an industrialized nation.

The first selections, in the order of their appearance, focus their attention on marriage, the family, and related national population trends; the extension of familistic relationships into social spheres beyond the family, and a special instance of this ritual kinship system in the world of professional *sumo;* authoritarian values in a changing political environment, and a hypothesis of stress-reducing factors in a constraining, collectivity-oriented society. The next articles move from this focus on the small group, interpersonal relations, and the psychological effects of traditional culture on individuals, to delineations of social class relations in rural settings, including the plight of the largest "racial minority" in Japan, the outcastes; types of urban centers, their associated class structures, and popular evaluations of occupations; aspects of educational, political, and religious institutions on the contemporary scene. The last few works provide a sample of modest efforts to explain the generation of motivation, the skills utilized, and the tempo of movement in the development of modern Japan.

Several criteria were used for selecting these particular articles. Each selection may be regarded as either a descriptive-interpretive essay or a research report informed by social science conceptual frameworks and theoretical concerns. All but three of these writings are available only in the periodicals in which they originally appeared. All the selections are republished here in their original form in full (except for abridgment of some footnotes in a few articles), to maintain the unity of each selection as a complete product of its author and to permit students to assess the perspective and method of study of the writer as well as the content information he conveys. Although the historical setting of the articles is not confined to the period following World War II, they were all first published in the recent past.

The editors wish to thank those students in our classes whose comments on these and many more assigned readings have aided us in the selection process. We also wish to give special thanks to Mr. Shiro Saito of the University of Hawaii Library for his kind help in tracking down elusive material.

George K. Yamamoto
University of Hawaii

Tsuyoshi Ishida
Hiroshima Institute of Technology

THE GO-BETWEEN IN A DEVELOPING SOCIETY:
THE CASE OF THE JAPANESE MARRIAGE ARRANGER

Ezra Vogel

The most common conceptual model for analyzing acculturation or modern-ization posits a pre-existing social organization which is upset by new patterns, causing disruptions which continue until the new patterns are firmly implanted. While this model has obvious utility, it sometimes obscures the fact that special institutional forms may take on crucial importance during the transition stage and operate with relatively little disruption until replaced by other institutional forms at a later time.

The present article examines one such institutional form in Japan, a country which has made the transition to industrialization fairly smoothly and rapidly. Various explanations have been given for the very rapid and successful industrializa-tion of Japan: the compatibility between the pre-industrial and industrial value systems, the well-organized and integrated central government, the availability of second sons in a primogeniture kinship system, the level of economic development before modernization, and the industrious nature of Japanese people. While, in a single historical case where various factors are intertwined, it is impossible to isolate any single cause, nevertheless it may be shown how special intermediary institutional forms also operated to ease the transition.

One of the crucial problems in an industrializing society is making available a mobile supply of workers and a mobile supply of appropriate brides. In Japan, this mobility was mediated by go-betweens who had some particularistic ties to the group from which a person came and the group to which he was going. The use of the go-between operated in such a way as to safeguard the member who was moving and both the group from which he came and the group to which he was going. It served to safeguard the group from which he came because, in effect, the mobile person was required to go through channels before moving. There was not an open labor market, so that there was no widespread threat that members might suddenly leave nor did group members threaten insubordination. Because a potentially mobile person needed the help of members of his group in achieving a new placement, he could not afford to alienate them. Similarly, by going through personal connections, the group which was taking in a new member could be assured of his loyalty and devotion, and the mobile person was assured of kind treatment at the hands of the new group. Often loyalty and personal connections were symbolized in a ritual kinship relationship with either the go-between or certain people in the new organization becoming, in effect, a ritual parent. If problems arose, the go-between who had made the original arrangements was available to work them out. Although placement occurred in the context of

Vogel — *From Human Organization, Vol. 20, No. 3, (Fall, 1961), pp. 112-120. Reprinted by permission of The Society for Applied Anthropology and the author.

personal connections, a large number of objective considerations also governed who was to be placed where.

While the use of go-betweens in Japan has a very long history, it appears to have taken on a special importance in the period of rapid industrialization for placement of group members, and the pattern remains very important today. However, as the labor and marriage markets gradually become freer and the participants themselves have more opportunity for shopping around independently, the need for such go-betweens is beginning to decline.

The present study examines the role of the marriage go-between *(nakohdo)* who still continues to be an important figure in a large number of marriages in Japan.[1] There are endless variations in the nakohdo's roles and in how much he may be involved in arranging a particular match, but, in general, he has some responsibility in introducing prospective spouses, carrying on investigations and negotiations for the marriage, officiating at the marriage, and assuming an ill-defined responsibility for the welfare of the young couple after marriage. For his services the nakohdo is rewarded by presents and loyalty from the young couple and his family, and general respect from the community. In rare cases, he is a semi-professional, receiving money payments or fairly large presents for his services.

While the nakohdo is generally considered old-fashioned and even "feudalistic" by many Japanese themselves, in fact, use of the nakohdo became widespread only toward the end, or after the end, of the feudal period,[2] and in certain localities was used for the first time only in the twentieth century. While, for ideological reasons there is some tendency among modern Japanese to regard the nakohdo as a rapidly disappearing phenomenon left over in the most feudalistic parts of Japan, it is still widespread throughout Japan, in urban as well as in rural areas, although the nakohdo may have more importance in introducing in cities and for carrying on negotiations in rural areas.[3] While, in accord with the popular public image, the author's middle-class informants argued that it is rare in the lower classes, the lower-class informants gave sufficient evidence to show that it is widespread among lower classes as well, particularly in rural areas. It is difficult to estimate exactly how many marriages are now arranged by a nakohdo. In a national opinion survey conducted in 1952, it was found that approximately 60 percent of couples then married had used a go-between in arranging their marriage, but unfortunately the data were not analyzed by year of marriage.[4] One way of estimating the prevalence of the nakohdo is through the prevalence of marriages involving *miai* (meetings especially arranged by a go-between to introduce the couple and sometimes their respective families[5]). Of the cases seen in domestic courts in 1956 (total 13,733 cases), about 70 percent had miai, and in no prefecture was the percentage below 65 percent[6]). In a 1958 survey of Tokyo area middle-class apartments where the average length of marriage was about four years, roughly one-third of the couples had had a miai and, when the data were analyzed by length of marriage, there was no indication of a decline in the use of the miai.[7] Since these apartment dwellers are among the more modern groups in Japanese society, it would seem reasonable to accept the view of expert informants who estimated the number of current arranged marriages to be about half of all marriages in Japan. The present paper is concerned only with marriages as "arranged," but a large proportion of marriages which are not "arranged" use a variety of friends to perform various small go-between tasks, all of which would otherwise be performed by a single nakohdo. Nearly all marriages have a formal nakohdo at the ceremony,[8] and often friends or relatives are asked to make introductions, to convey messages between the parties, or to make investigations concerning the other parties. Private detective agencies are widely used for investigations and specialized private and public institutions are used for introductions.[9]

Despite the widespread use of the nakohdo, most Japanese, especially the young people, are ideologically opposed to the nakohdo. In one Tokyo area survey, only 26 percent of those polled thought that the nakohdo should continue to be used to help arrange marriages.[10] In the mass media, the nakohdo is presented as a terribly old-fashioned, untrustworthy and often comic character.[11] Parents objecting to their child's desire to find his own spouse do not do so on ideological grounds, but on practical grounds, i.e., the proposed spouse may not be good enough, may not be reliable, etc. Even the nakohdo has no ideological objection to "love marriages," and several proudly told of their own children's love marriages. This gap between an ideology strongly against the nakohdo and the actual use of the nakohdo is something recognized by Japanese scholars and the popular press as well.[12] The widespread use of the nakohdo suggests that he is still performing a significant function, despite ideological objections, and this article attempts to examine this function.

The data for this study were obtained through exploratory interviews with large numbers of informants and through focused interviews of two hours or more with twenty-eight nakohdo. Only those nakohdo were included who had performed actual negotiations preceding marriage and who were considered nakohdo by themselves and the parties concerned. The largest single group, members of the woman's club of one of the large wards of Tokyo, was selected by the coordinator of the clubs on the basis of having the most experience as nakohdo. The other nakohdo were selected because they had different types of clients. Nakohdo interviewed lived in several different geographical areas, fishing and farming villages, and represented upper, middle, and lower classes. While most were professional, some were semi-professional.

The Activities of the Nakohdo

The nakohdo who performs the actual work leading to marriage is generally a person of middle age or above who is respected in his community. In the urban middle classes, the nakohdo who does the real work of arranging is generally a woman,[13] but in the lower-class and rural areas, it is often a man, and often a husband and wife act together as a nakohdo couple. There is a Japanese proverb which says that everyone should serve as a nakohdo three times in his life, and the nakohdo regards his work as a public service. While the ordinary person may serve as a nakohdo two or three times in his life, some semi-professional nakohdos have performed as many as several hundred matches. With rare exceptions, the nakohdo takes great pride and pleasure in his work, but he does not actively seek work and serves only when requested. The nakohdo has an enormous devotion to his task, is very identified with his work, is proud of his successes and troubled by his failures to conclude satisfactory marriage arrangements.[14]

In order for the nakohdo to make effective introductions, it is important for him to be well known *(kao ga hiroi)* and to have suitable contacts. No particular training is required and, in most cases, the nakohdo had his first experience through a request to locate a spouse by a very close friend or relative, and since he happened to know an appropriate person, he made the necessary arrangements. After that, the nakohdo developed a reputation for his ability to successfully conclude matches and was approached by other people with similar requests. Frankness, honesty, tactfulness, and loyalty are considered the main virtues of the nakohdo, and the author's impression was that they tended to embody these characteristics.

For convenience, the activities of the nakohdo may be classified as: 1) introducing, 2) negotiating, and 3) ceremonializing.[15]

Introducing

The early stages of the introduction process are clearly subordinated to the personal relationships of the parties concerned. It is usually the girl's mother who first makes a social visit to the nakohdo, and, as part of a social visit, she will incidently mention that her son or daughter is approaching marriageable age. If she does not already know the nakohdo, she will use another informal go-between who does know the nakohdo, and they can make a social visit to the nakohdo together. This situation is clearly defined as one of no commitment, and the basic information can be gathered, and the nakohdo can decide whether or not to make a commitment to the case. The party to the introduction can decide whether or not to use a nakohdo without in any way disturbing the social relationships involved. What is casually mentioned can be casually dropped.

If the nakohdo decides to accept the potential bride's picture and a brief background history, he may do so with the minimum commitment of merely looking around for a possible match. He will also do his looking around within the context of personal relations, asking friends about potential candidates. One of the preferred modes is for one nakohdo to vouch for his party and to use a friend as a second nakohdo to vouch for the other party. At this early stage, before the parties are actually introduced, there may be extensive visiting back and forth between the nakohdo and the two parties, making further investigations where necessary. In some rural areas, the nakohdo may ask the mother of the bride to take her for a walk so the potential man can look her over, and, while the bride suspects what is happening, she is regarded as not knowing, thus preserving the opportunity for making judgments without commitment. In any case, before the miai, many factors about the spouse may be considered and decided without any great feeling of pressure to decide in one direction or another.

The offical introduction is usually conducted at the miai in a meeting of the nakohdo, the potential bride and groom, and sometimes representatives of each family. This is generally regarded already as a serious commitment involving public recognition, and a party refused feels a blow to his prestige and status, to say nothing of the time and energy commitments involved. There are clearly limitations on the number of miai one may have in addition to the problems of time and expense: A reputation for refusing would make other parties hesitant to accept a miai, a nakohdo whose miai ended in failure may feel rebuffed and not attempt another miai if he thinks his party unreasonable, and, as a potential spouse gets older, he has less opportunity for finding a good partner. Because of the seriousness of the formal meeting at the miai, the parties concerned are not likely to attempt a miai unless they feel that there is a serious chance of success, and they will do a large part of the investigating and decision-making before the miai.

Despite the seriousness of the miai, it is clear that there is an opportunity for decision after the miai, and it is not uncommon for a person to have several miai before marriage. The opportunity for decision-making after the miai is preciously guarded by playing down the seriousness of the miai, simplifying the miai itself, and keeping the atmosphere light and pleasant. In some cases the parties even maintain that the meeting is not a real miai but only a little get-together. Although the parties do not want the atmosphere to become so light that the other party is not taking its responsibility seriously, at a conscious level they do want the atmosphere very light, and the nakohdo must strike a delicate balance between serious talk with a light casualness which will permit the possibility for decision-making afterwards without serious embarrassment to either party.

In recent years, there has been an attempt even to enlarge the scope of free decisions after the miai. While the attempt to define the miai as just a chance to meet someone else has not succeeded, the young people are given considerable chance to talk and make independent decisions both during and after the miai. An attempt is ordinarily made to give the couple a chance to talk alone, as is evidenced by the standard joke about the nakohdo who spends a long time in the bathroom during the miai. Young people, particularly those ideologically opposed to miai marriages, are now making an effort to discuss things frankly with a prospective spouse and arrangements are usually made for the young couple to meet alone several times after the miai before making a decision about marriage.

The crucial elements of the decision about marriage have to do with objective status factors such as the relative social standing of the two families, present and potential economic earning power of the husband, appearance and refinements of the bride, all of which can be investigated by the nakohdo before the miai. To some extent, the miai is crucial in telling whether the parties concerned seem to get along well together, but this getting along is vaguely defined, and, because of this vagueness, there is ordinarily elaborate preparation for the miai to insure that everything goes smoothly, with resulting attention to and tension about great numbers of details.[16] In the discussions between nakohdo and the party concerned, or even in discussions between the parents and child in one party, it is difficult to describe the characteristics of the mood, and often attention is given to such characteristics as skin defects, posture, tone of voice, and the like. In any case, these impressions are very carefully weighed, along with the more objective information obtained before the miai in making a decision about marriage.

Negotiating

Ordinarily the most time-consuming job of the nakohdo is in the negotiations between the two families. The amount of time required varies from a single visit or telephone call to each side, to a major proportion of the nakohdo's time for many months. In general, in the cases where the men do most of the negotiating, as in lower-class groups and certain rural areas, the negotiations tend to be briefer and more businesslike. Where women do much of the negotiation the process is often combined with social visiting, and, in some cases, the marriage arrangements are at least ostensibly subordinated to this visiting.

In cases where negotiations are most prolonged, the mothers of the prospective mates are the ones who discuss problems in greatest detail with the nakohdo. However, the nakohdo generally insists on getting the approval of the young people concerned from the very beginning, since without it, there will be great difficulty in making a successful match, and the mother often becomes a go-between carrying messages between her own family and the nakohdo. Despite the nakohdo's defensive denials to the contrary, there is no doubt that the nakohdo and parents may heavily influence decisions, but the child is ordinarily brought into discussions at all stages of negotiation, and, if at any point he firmly disapproves, negotiations are broken off, and such cases are not unusual. Particularly in rural areas, the fathers seem to have an important part in negotiations also, and in most places, even if the nakohdo does not speak to the father directly, it is expected that the mother will speak to him and get his general approval for her activities, although she may not discuss all the details with him and may even select which things to talk over with him, depending on how she wishes the negotiations to proceed. In some cases, the nakohdo will meet with mother and the prospective spouse, and in other cases she may meet with both parents, or with other members of the family.

One of the major duties of the nakohdo is to serve as guarantor for the other party and to conduct all the investigations necessary to establish the position of the other party. Precisely what things are thought most desirable varies greatly depending on the interests and desires of the people concerned but, at a minimum, they wish to establish that the other family has a good reputation and social position, is not descendent from an outcaste family, does not have cases of mental illness, serious physical illness, or crime which would affect the family line. The bride's side wishes to establish that the prospective groom is capable of continuously supporting her in the style she would like, and that he is sufficiently healthy so that he will be able to work regularly and is not likely to leave her a widow at a young age. The groom's side wishes to establish that the prospective bride is in good health, will be able to work hard, is pretty, gentle, and mild in disposition. It is important that the bride be a virgin, and the groom should not be the kind of person who would waste his money on alcohol and women after marriage. The extent to which one can demand these characteristics in the spouse depends in large part, of course, on the extent to which one is considered desirable.

The methods which the nakohdo will use to investigate are designed to obtain this required information. A minimum of information about family residences is contained in the public family records *(koseki)*. Using this information, it is usually possible to trace back whether the opposite family lived in a neighborhood which was inhabited by outcastes. This is getting increasingly difficult to establish by such simple methods as, in many cases, the outcaste residences are not always in separate neighborhoods. If there is any serious doubt about whether or not one was a member of an outcaste family, however, it may be necessary to visit a family's original home, and trace back various other kinds of records. The general status and reputation of a family is usually established by visits to the family's original home, and this will usually include questions about mental illness, serious physical illness which might be hereditary, and crime. In general, the nakohdo felt that the neighbors would be quite truthful in expressing their opinion because of the importance of making a good match. However, the neighbor's opinion is often colored by his general pattern of relationships with the family, and if there is any grudge in the neighborhood and the nakohdo happens to go to a neighbor who has a grudge, he may get a very distorted picture. For this reason, each family ordinarily makes an effort to maintain very good relationships with neighbors not only because they feel it is pleasant, but because it may make a very real difference in whether they will be considered desirable at the time of marriage.

If certain questionable things about a party's reputation develop, it will then be necessary to investigate this in detail. There is a certain strategy involved, however, in not investigating the family in too much detail too early in the game, because the neighbors get curious about the potential marriage, and this would make it more difficult to break off negotiations, since it would be embarrassing to the refused party. One pursues the investigation in accord with the degree of commitment of the parties at that particular time. Because of the problem involved in assessing the subtle details about a family's reputation, a nakohdo prefers to continue working through friends since she can rely on their information without arousing neighbors and without having serious doubts about the validity of her information. She pursues the areas which seem most problematic in meeting the desired standards. If the groom-to-be has a degree from a good university and a respectable white-collar job with a well-known firm, there will probably not be any further need to investigate his occupational career, except for a routine check-up by the nakohdo at the groom's company to make sure that he is considered competent, reliable, and that he will continue to be promoted. The nakohdo will usually talk directly with the groom's superiors or, in a very large company, the personnel department, and since this is expected, the nakohdo is respectfully received, and given the desired information. However, in case the husband did not graduate from a good university, it may be necessary to investigate his school record in more detail in order to judge his competence. If the groom is not an employee in a large company, then his future is considered much more dubious so that a nakohdo is likely to investigate his bank account, the amount of goods he is likely to receive through inheritance, and to gather whatever evidence on his skill and connections would be useful in estimating his future financial success. Usually, the investigating process is one in which the nakohdo continually checks back with the family concerned. If the family has more doubts, it is generally the duty of the nakohdo to investigate in more detail the problems brought up by the family.

If the family still has doubts, they may decide to hire a private detective to supplement the investigation made by the nakohdo. Ordinarily, the family pays directly for the private detective if he is used, but the nakohdo may also decide to employ the detective, if he himself has doubts about his own material. Private detectives seem to be used very rarely in rural areas, but fairly often in cities. In some cases, the large private detective organizations may be used to gather routine information in other parts of Japan if it is inconvenient for the nakohdo to make a trip to investigate such things himself and if reliable personal contacts are lacking in this locality. The request by the family for the use of a private detective is ordinarily regarded as a reflection that the nakohdo has not turned up sufficiently reliable information, and the nakohdo generally disapproves of using a private detective and is a bit skeptical of their results even if he himself may advise the family to use a detective to clear up a particular point. The main reason the nakohdo gives for the dislike of detectives is that they are not very reliable, making reports sound definite when, in fact, there is insufficient evidence, and there are many stories in the common folklore giving support for these doubts.

While each nakohdo insisted that he himself was very frank and truthful in relating bad as well as good points, he spoke of exaggerations other nakohdo make, a characteristic which is the focus of public suspicion.[17] There is doubtless an element of truth in the tendency for the nakohdo to exaggerate, a tendency which stems from the enormous involvement the nakohdo has in the success of his work and loyalty to his party. To the extent that he receives prestige for his work, it is in terms of his ability to conclude a successful match, and the techniques for attaining this are, in many ways, analogous to the techniques of salesmanship. In the large majority of cases, however, the nakohdo has some personal relationship with the parties concerned and expects to continue this personal relationship long after marriage so this fact places serious limits on the extent to which the nakohdo can distort to make a match.

The Bargaining Process

Much of the bargaining process depends on assessing the relative position of the parties. Aside from the general qualifications which need to be investigated, there are a number of other factors which determine the bargaining situation. One is the sex-ratio of eligibles. For example, immediately after the war, when the number of eligible women was much higher than that of men, the nakohdo had hosts of applications from eligible girls. In some cases, a girl's mother would even present the girl's picture in different places simultaneously, a practice which nakohdo invariably try to discourage, since it can lead to many complications in making arrangements. It is felt that the man's side should initiate proposals for miai, but particularly in the immediate post-war period, the girl's side was using every indirect approach possible to invite a proposal. In this period, because of the sex-ratio, it was common for a girl of higher social standing to arrange a marriage with a man of somewhat lower standing.

The relative bargaining position of the parties is also determined by particular Japanese values regarding marriage. For example, a girl past 23 or 24 is regarded as fairly old for marriage, and in the ordinary case it is difficult for her to find a spouse of appropriate social status when she is much beyond this age. As a result, many young girls who, until 20 or 21 are insistent on a love marriage, turn to the nakohdo at this age for fear it may soon be too late. Indeed, the nakohdo usually has an overly plentiful supply of girls in the upper age brackets. Also when a girl is 18 or 19, her family may have very high standards of what the other party should be like, but, as the girl gets older, these conditions gradually are lowered. Indeed, when asked how to handle the problem of a girl's family making difficult demands, the nakohdo's answer was very simple: "wait." The demands will gradually lessen. Also the child whose father died when he was young is at a considerable disadvantage in terms of Japanese values. It is assumed that his disciplinary training is inadequate and that his family will be in a somewhat more difficult financial situation. Hence, the nakohdo similarly has an over-supply of pictures of prospective spouses whose fathers died when they were young, and this, too, is reflected in their bargaining position.

The relative position of the two parties determines not only the eventual selection but the process of negotiation.[18] The party which is most anxious to make the match must often wait for some time until the other party has made a decision, and it is the job of the nakohdo to convince the reluctant party. Because it is ordinarily understood that a party will not start another negotiation until one has been completely settled, this poses a serious problem if one party stalls, especially in the case of a girl in the upper age brackets since time is very precious. In this case, the nakohdo tries to force a quicker decision on the part of the reluctant family and urges them to be very frank. If however, the reluctant party refuses to make a decision, and the other party is very much interested in the reluctant party, they may wait as much as several months. On such occasions, the nakohdo may be called on to make estimates of the willingness of the other party and predictions about the eventual decisions, a weighty responsibility indeed. Often, indefinite stalling appears to be used as a polite way of refusal. The stalled party becomes very anxious, its pride is wounded, and, in such a case, the nakohdo tries to have a frank talk with the reluctant party to determine intentions and, if it is a refusal, the reluctant party will probably give the nakohdo an acceptable explanation as to the reason, usually a particular recognizable defect of the opposite party. Although the nakohdo may have an even closer relationship with the refused party, he does not necessarily tell the reason since it may be embarrassing or discouraging to the refused party. He may offer an invented reason (as, for example, that the year of births were not appropriate according to the almanac predictions) or he may give no reason. Usually, the reason is clear to the refused party, i.e., that the other party hopes for a match with a higher-status family, and the refused party will not ask to know the reason if the nakohdo does not give it.

Living Arrangements

While the decision about whether to proceed or not is the most crucial set of negotiations for the nakohdo, there are a series of secondary considerations regarding the wedding and living arrangements for the young couple. In many cases, these discussions are crucial for the decision-making process. For example, in the urban middle class, the girl's family may refuse the young man if he insists on bringing his widowed mother to live with him after marriage. The eldest son, or an only son, with a widowed mother is one of the most difficult cases for the nakohdo to handle as the widowed mother will keep finding reasons why the proposed girl is unsuitable, and the girl's family will probably refuse to have the mother brought along. One nakohdo, with over twenty successful matches, said that she would refuse to deal with such a case unless the mother would agree to live separately. In the rural areas, there is presently considerable difficulty for the eldest son in finding a bride willing to live on the farm with him and his family, since most girls would prefer the easier life of marriage to a "salary man" who does not live with his mother. In order for him to get a bride, it may require various concessions about vacation time for the bride, provision of material property for her, and may involve getting a girl of slightly lower status. Ordinarily, the bride brings a certain amount of furniture with her at marriage, paid for by her family, but usually the groom's family presents a monetary gift at the time of decision to marry which helps to pay for the furniture later furnished by the bride, and the extent of these amounts are usually negotiated through a nakohdo. The total amount spent depends largely on the status of the families concerned, and although the exact proportion varies from area to area, it is generally fairly set within any particular social-class group in a given area. The specifics of time and place are usually decided by fairly standardized formulae. For example, the date of the wedding is usually set by deciding in what general season the parties wish to marry, and often the nakohdo will check the almanac to find a lucky day at that time of year. The young people do not regard this as actually bringing good luck, but as a custom or as a concession to the wishes of their elders.

After the miai, the young couple may decide whether to go ahead with the wedding, but, in the several hundred cases handled by these nakohdo, there were few cases in which a decision was made against marriage after the miai because the young couple did not get along well. But, through dating between the miai and marriage, one can obtain the new ideal which combines the traditional opposites; one can have an arranged marriage which is a "love marriage."

Ceremonializing

Even in the case in which the introduction and negotiations were conducted without a nakohdo, a *tanomare nakohdo* is especially requested for the ceremony to supply social sanction. Ordinarily, the requirements for ceremonializing require a very high-status couple. The ideal is for the husband to select, as ceremonial nakohdo, the person most likely to help him in his occupational future in order to cement this bond, and the superior obliges, feeling more certain of the continued loyalty of the young man. However, for the purposes of negotiations, it is usually wise not to have such a high-status nakohdo, since it involves more pressure to follow his advice regardless of the opinion of the parties concerned, and because it may also be difficult to express frank objections, criticism, and to request more information with a nakohdo of much higher status, especially with an employer. But, if one asks one person to be negotiator, it becomes embarrassing to ask another couple for the ceremony. This problem can be handled in several ways. If a high-status person is very close to the family, then one can be frank with him, and he may be used at the ceremony even in place of the employer, especially if the husband is employed in a less paternalistic organization. Another way, which has many advantages, is to have a widow serve as the negotiator. Since the ceremony requires a couple, there is no problem of embarrassment about asking a couple of higher status to perform as the nakohdo for the ceremony, and the negotiator and the couple can work together very nicely at the ceremony. In certain rural areas with a more tight-knit social structure, there may be no real alternatives in selecting a nakohdo since it will be virtually prescribed by the social structure.

The young couple may reward the nakohdo with a present, perhaps purchased on their honeymoon trip, and occasional presents at New Year's in later years, especially the first few years of marriage. In the lower classes the nakohdo may be rewarded with a cash sum equivalent to a certain percentage of the engagement gift. While the couple may occasionally visit the nakohdo after marriage, and it is vaguely understood that one may call on the nakohdo for help, the couple rarely does so. It is difficult to estimate how much difference the employer's serving as a nakohdo makes for the employee's future success or security, but, in general, it does not appear too great as a distinct variable. An employee who gets along well with his boss already tends to choose him as a nakohdo. The most important area in which the couple returns to the nakohdo is in the area of marital problems. In general, where a nakohdo has performed a large number of successful cases or lives at some distance from the couple or is of quite high status, the nakohdo simply reported that everything has gone fine for his couples and that the couples never came to him with problems. However, in the cases in which the nakohdo lives very near to the couples and there is easy access, particularly in rural villages, the nakohdo reports that the couple will come frequently to discuss marital problems, although the problems are not necessarily of a serious nature. In such cases, where the nakohdo may be called on frequently, even for relatively minor problems, there was much more responsibility for the nakohdo, and he was much less enthusiastic about being a nakohdo.

Discussion and Conclusion

There are two general features of the role of the nakohdo which deserve special mention. The first is that, although the nakohdo operates through particularistic relationships, through personal connections with both parties, the use of the nakohdo not only permits, but tends to maximize, universalistic considerations in the decision-making process. At virtually every step in the process, the nakohdo is used in a way which increases rather than decreases the opportunity of making a universalistic decision, given the values regarding marriage. The nakohdo is originally chosen by the family because, of persons available to a family, he is felt to provide access to the widest number of opportunities for a good match. The investigation process is conducted by the nakohdo in order to provide as accurate information as possible about those characteristics considered most important. The nature of the items to be investigated and the interests of the parties make it impossible for the two parties to talk over frankly every possible kind of difficulty in detail, but the nakohdo is able, because of his particular status, to investigate such matters. Yet the nature of the items to be investigated requires an unusually high degree of confidence in the investigator, and, by virtue of the nakohdo's position of respect and prominence in the community and his personal relationship with the parties concerned, a high degree of confidence can be placed in his findings.

As shown above, the bargaining position of the two parties and the negotiating process depends basically on their relative assets in terms of the value system, and the nakohdo acts to free rather than to bind the decision-making process. One block to the free negotiating process is the understanding that each party should be negotiating with only one party at a time, but this restriction is accepted regardless of the nakohdo's presence, and the nakohdo helps break through this block by insisting on quicker decisions in case negotiations lag unreasonably. By insisting on frankness and offering an opportunity for communication of real feelings, it is possible to carry through negotiations fairly quickly and, if necessary, to begin negotiations with another party. The nakohdo's interest in making a successful match and the family's desire to please the nakohdo, who is doing so much for them, constitute the greatest danger for distorting the decision-making process. Yet the fact that he expects to have continued relationships with the parties after the marriage and will be held partly responsible for difficulties places strict limits on the amount to which he can distort the essential factors and tends to lead to decisions which are made with the hope that they will be most satisfactory to the parties concerned.

While, in the United States, there is a much greater opportunity for meeting potential spouses and for testing out adjustment through dating, in Japan, the nakohdo offers an even more universalistic basis for frank investigation of the opposite party. In the United States, objective characteristics of the couple to be married are subordinated to the personal relationship between the partners, and this limits direct investigation of bank accounts, inheritance intentions, job prospects, neighborhood reputation, and the like.[19] In Japan, the existence of the nakohdo makes it possible to consider all the qualifications very frankly and directly without damaging the relationship between the two parties. This same general characteristic would seem to apply to the use of the go-between in other segments of Japanese society. In the labor market, the consumption market, and in political relationships as well, it may be possible to make relatively rational decisions through personal relationships. This is not just because a balance of personal interests may lead to more universalistic decisions, but because the go-between creates sufficient distance between parties to permit universalistic decisions. This has implications beyond the topic of marriage and may help to explain the ability of Japan to modernize in line with rational considerations of industrialization even without radical disorganization of existing personal relationships. Using go-betweens, it is often possible to make rational decisions within the context of a society which is still dominated by personal ties.

While this system probably does not permit as universalistic a basis of decision as a much more open market, nevertheless, without disrupting the local ties, it has been able to achieve a reasonable approximation to the universalistic characteristics of a more open market. The use of the go-between permits a kind of detachment which makes it possible to have a relatively objective investigation.

Because of this detachment permitted by the go-between, it is possible to use the go-between for a wide range of problems other than personnel placement. The go-between's role as a mediator is extremely crucial and this concept, rather than the concept of two warring sides, tends to characterize Japanese legal transactions, for example. If delicate negotiations of any kind are required, it becomes possible to work them out in a fairly neutral setting without serious loss of face. The value of using third persons for planned social change, for foreigners working with Japanese when negotiations are delicate, can hardly be overestimated.

The second general comment concerns the existence of the go-between as a functional alternative to dating in modern industrialized society. With the possible exception of European Jews, no other industrialized society has marriage-arranging in large segments of the population. Part of this explanation would seem to lie in the fact that Japanese society is still rather tightly structured and that movement is still channeled through personal relationships.

Through institutions like the nakohdo, Japan has been able to mitigate the disruptions caused by rapid social change, and the success of these institutions, in turn, in coping with the societal problems has slowed down social change. The nakohdo's success in smoothing the transition has undoubtedly meant that traditional patterns of social organization have been able to persist in the face of industrialization far longer than they would have had there been no such institutions to mediate the process of industrialization. While the nakohdo is becoming somewhat less important as the market situation becomes freer, the nakohdo remains important partly because of the ability of the nakohdo to adjust to new conditions. The go-between system has had no trouble in adapting to the fact that young people have been given increased opportunity to have an important say in the decision, that they have some chance for dating, and that they have an increased opportunity to meet members of the opposite sex before marriage. But, at the same time, that he has adjusted to the increasing relative power of children, he makes sure that the parents' wishes are also considered and thus he serves an integrative function for the family.

It is probably true, as modern young Japanese hope, that the nakohdo is weakening in power and the family-based criteria are becoming less important than the compatibility of the couple itself, but, until youth is much more emancipated, the nakohdo will be useful in integrating the parents' wishes and the youth's wishes and in providing opportunities for matches for those who otherwise would not get married. There are certain characteristics of Japanese national character which fit in with the use of the nakohdo,[20] but, in addition, the nakohdo is likely to have an important role for some time to come, unless structural changes occur in Japanese society which would vastly increase the opportunities for young people to meet each other and to make reliable decisions about marriage which would be satisfactory to themselves and to their families.

FOOTNOTES

1. Very brief descriptions of the nakohdo, in the context of specific Japanese communities may be found in Ronald Dore, *City Life in Japan; A Study of a Tokyo Ward,* Routledge and Kegan Paul, London, 1958; John Embree, *A Japanese Village: Suye Mura,* Kegan Paul, Trench, Trubner, and Co., Ltd., London, 1946; Edward Norbeck, *Takashima: A Japanese Fishing Community,* University of Utah Press, Salt Lake City, 1954; Robert J. Smith and John B. Cornell, *Two Japanese Villages,* The University of Michigan Press, Ann Arbor, Mich., Center for Japanese Studies, Occasional Papers No. 5, 1956. A first-rate novel, now available in English, centers around marriage arranging in an upper-class Kansei area family a few decades ago. Edward Seidensticker (trans.), Junichiro Tanizaki's *The Makioka Sisters,* Alfred Knopf, New York, 1957.

It may be noted that the nakohdo is also an unusually valuable informant about other affairs in the community because of his intimate knowledge of various families. While, because of the confidential relationship to his families, the nakohdo may be unwilling to reveal certain details about the families, he is an extremely valuable informant about informal patterns in a community, especially about affairs relating to families.

2. Kunio Yanagida, "Nakohdo oyobi Seken" (Nakohdo and Society), *Kon'in no Hanashi,* Iwanami Shoten, Tokyo, 1948, pp. 159-201. Yanagida argues that, in early feudal days in which collateral groups were more important than the *ie* (family), social control over marriage was exerted by youth groupings and by the adults in charge of the youth groupings. As *ie* became stronger, conflicts between *ie* and youth groups over marriage arranging developed, and gradually *ie* took over by using a nakohdo who served the *ie's* interests and placated the youth groups by giving them various rewards and inviting them to marriage ceremonies, thus explaining the great size of wedding celebrations. Even if Yanagida's argument was not completely accurate historically, it is accurate in explaining the functional relationship of *ie,* nakohdo, and age groups, especially in rural Japan. Yanagida argues that this development of the role of the nakohdo began in upper-class groups and filtered down to other social groups only in the later feudal days.

3. Takashi Koyama, *Gendai Kazoku no Kenkyuu* (A Study of the Contemporary Family), Kobundoo, Tokyo, 1960.

In a recent sampling only 31.9 percent of modern middle-class Tokyo apartment dwellers used a nakohdo to make the proposal, compared to 59.6 percent of mountain villagers a few hours away from Tokyo. But the introduction function of the nakohdo was slightly more important in the city, since many rural marriages are made with childhood acquaintances. In this study, 55.4 percent of apartment dwellers were introduced to each other as prospective spouses compared with 52.3 percent in mountain villages.

4. UNESCO *Tsuushin,* "Kazoku seido ni okeru hoken isei ni tsuite no choosa," (Research on the Feudal Remains of the Family System), No. 49 (February 5, 1953), pp. 313-326.

5. While there is a very high correlation between existence of a miai and a nakohdo, the function of the nakohdo at the miai may be almost merely cermonial. Also there may be go-betweens even though there are no miai. Also, it should be noted that a decrease in the number of miai does not necessarily indicate the increasing freedom of people to choose partners themselves. In some rural areas, where one marries a person he has lived near, it is not usually felt necessary for a miai to occur whether it is the person himself or the parents who make the decision about marriage. Often only the rural upper class used a nakohdo, since they had to select spouses from other communities. In some remote rural areas, it had been a common practice for spouses to meet for the first time at their wedding. Hence, in such a place, having a miai is a step toward increasing the freedom among the young people to make their own decision.

6. *Shihoo Tookei Nenpoo, 3. Kajihen* (Annual Report of Judicial Statistics. 3. Family Cases), General Secretariat, Supreme Court, Japan. It is impossible to assess whether or not cases with a go-between were more or less likely to go to the family court. Arguments could be made for both sides of the question, and there is no clear reason to suspect that this estimate is greatly different from cases not referred to the family court.

7. This is from the research of Professor Robert Blood in Tokyo, as yet unpublished.

8. In their formal ceremonial role, the go-betweens are called *baishakunin* and, in case they are requested to serve only for the ceremony, without responsibility for previous negotiations, they are referred to as *tanomare nakohdo.*

9. In one case, well-known in the Japanese popular press, a Professor Hidaka of Tokyo University has regular tea parties for prospective spouses to meet, in which he assumes, somewhat indirectly, the role of introducer. He has introduced several hundred couples who later married. There are similar parties on a small scale in other places in Japan, and, compared to parties of single people in America, the purpose of matrimony is less thinly disguised.

Public consultation centers are not yet available all over the country and they are not widely used. In Tokyo, most of the wards have such centers, as does the Tokyo City government which established its center 25 years ago. These centers take responsibility not only for introductions but counseling for marriage. In 1956, the Tokyo City government's *Kekkon Sodanjo* (Marriage Consultation Center) had active cases of 1256 men and 2355 women. It is estimated by the director that over ten percent of these cases are successfully matched through the center, although the figure may be much higher because of unreported marriages.

In one case of a semi-professional nakohdo interviewed by the author, the nakohdo and her husband were formerly private detectives. When her husband died, she felt that she could no longer do general detective work by herself, so she devoted herself exclusively to marriage arranging. However, she charges no fee, although she receives a more than sufficient supply of presents. The use of private detectives to investigate families prior to marriage is rather common and may be used with or without a nakohdo.

10. This survey of Tokyo was conducted in 1953 by the National Public Opinion research center. It is reported in Takeyoshi Kawashima, *Kekkon* (Marriage), Iwanami Shoten, 1954. In some rural areas, there are many who still defend the nakohdo on ideological grounds, but this number is rapidly decreasing.

11. In one movie seen by the author, for example, the audience roared as the nakohdo kept repeating, "Now I'm going to tell you the real truth. . ." An example of the popular press is a story of one private marriage introduction place which paid certain attractive people to sit in as parties to miai, even though they had no interest in marriage, in order to collect fees from the other party. Another anecdote tells of an attractive couple who held parties to introduce single boys and girls, but the boys at the parties doted on the young wife, the girls on the young husband, to the pleasure of the couple, but the boys and girls remained single. Taiko Nirabayashi, "Kekkon Sodanjo" (Marriage Consultation Centers), *Mainichi,* May 22, 1960.

12. Kawashima, *op. cit.* This is a contradiction often noted in the popular press. For example, *Asahi Evening News,* October 10, 1959 for an English version.

13. Yanagida argues that, while historically women served as nakohdo before men, women's social contacts tend to be more limited and men were used as nakohdo to broaden the range of possible contacts. (Yanagida, *op. cit.*) In general, women tend to carry on the detailed work of negotiation, while men tend to perform the more formal activities.

14. Because he generally has high status relative to the parties concerned and because all communication must be channeled through him, he does not suffer from the effects of cross pressures as do, for example, factory foremen or army sergeants in the mediating function.

15. This classification is similar to that of Kawashima who omits the role of introducing.

16. The enormous concern about these details and the resulting embarrassments are reflected in the story of the country girl who, in order to behave properly, follows exactly everything the nakohdo does, including spilling a couple of peas onto the table, which is then repeated down the line by all the other guests.

17. The Japanese term "nakohdo guchi" is universally known and often used to describe talk which is so exaggerated as to be misleading.

18. Although it involves two families and not just two people and the way of exploiting is different, the bargaining has many of the features of dating and rating. Willard Waller, "The Rating and Dating Complex," *American Sociological Review,* II (Dec., 1937), 727-734.

19. Of course, there are limitations on this personal love relationship in the United States, but less so than in many other countries. See William J. Goode, "The Theoretical Importance of Love," *American Sociological Review,* XXIV (1959), 38-47. Of course, even in Western

countries, there may be fringe movements employing marriage arrangers. For example, Karl Miles Wallace, "An Experiment in Scientific Matchmaking," *Marriage and Family Living,* XXI (1959), 342-348.

20. In intensive cases, studies being conducted by Suzanne H. and Ezra Vogel through the National Institute of Mental Health in Ichikawa-shi, Japan, it appears that there is a tendency for many Japanese children to be very dependent on other people's decisions and to be reluctant to make their own. This same idea is explored more systematically through the wide-scale use of projective tests in Japan and is reported by George De Vos, "The Relation of Guilt to Achievement and Arranged Marriage Among the Japanese," *Psychiatry,* XXIII (1960), 287-301.

ATTITUDES TOWARD ARRANGED MARRIAGES
IN RURAL JAPAN

Hiroshi Wagatsuma and George De Vos

The following paper is a methodical exercise on the use of projective techniques in measuring attitudinal aspects of social change. We are indirectly examining the effects of legal change of marriage laws as related to value attitudes in local settings. This study can be considered an example applying Culture and Personality methods to the effects of legal reforms on a culture.

—Marriage shall be based only on the mutual consent of both sexes and it shall be maintained through mutual cooperation with the equal rights of husband and wife as a basis—

(From the post-war Constitution of Japan, Article 24)

Introduction

Up until the end of World War II, the traditional family system *(kazoku-seido)* had long been considered a bulwark of Japanese society. Confucian ethical ideas supporting a patrilineal, patriarchal family structure constituted the core values of the Japanese culture and were the source of justification for legal regulations governing and regulating behavior in all avenues of life. Since World War II, influence of Western ideas with their emphasis on individual rather than family orientation in the choice of occupation as well as a marriage partner have received legal support in the post-war Constitution and its orientation toward Western liberal democracy. There is considerable evidence of changes taking place in Japanese values concerning personal and public relationships, particularly in urban areas. This paper reports a study measuring the changing attitudes in a particular rural setting as pertains to marriage by the use of psychological techniques.

Generally, throughout the Tokugawa feudal period (1603-1868) the Confucian ethic as a self-conscious guide for behavior was limited mostly to the *samurai* (warrior) class and big landowners and rich merchants. Differential emphasis on hierarchal social relations, as well as Confucian ethical values, seems always to have followed lines of social class. Among town residents of the lower social strata and among rural peasants, many of whom were little affected by Confucianism, familial relations and all other interpersonal relations seem to have been more egalitarian and more intimate than those prescribed for the Confucian family. It was with the establishment of a strong centralized Meiji government that the Confucian ethical values permeated the farming and plebian classes more generally as an internalized system of moral constraint rather than as an enforced legal code imposed by the dominant social group.

Wagatsuma/DeVos — *From Human Organization,* Vol. 21, No. 8, (Fall, 1962), pp. 187-200. Reprinted by permission of The Society for Applied Anthropology and the authors. Material also appears in modified form in Chapter 2 of *Socialization for Achievement: Essay on the Cultural Psychology of the Japanese* by George DeVos, published by the University of California Press, 1971.

With the dissolution of the Tokugawa feudal regime in 1868, the Confucian doctrines, the backbone of the feudal regime, for a time lost their support in official sanctions. However, after a short period of active policy of imitating Western customs and way of life *(bun-mei kai-ka,* civilization and enlightenment), the Meiji government decided to readopt the Confucian ethics as the basis for a general system of national moral education to be taught in the centralized compulsory school system that had been established. Under the system of sanctions espoused by the government, the nation and family became the supreme good. Personal choice in marriage, which had been quite customary among people of lower social strata in towns and country, came to be more generally viewed as a disruptive act, rebellious against both family and nation. Only an arranged marriage came to be considered proper; other forms of marriage were looked upon as barbaric or backward.

Not only were the Confucian value ideas emphatically taught in the schools throughout the nation, but also various institutional aspects of the patriarchal family system, with the Confucian feudal values as its background, were supported by the offical legal codes. Continuity of the family system revolved around legally codified primogeniture, the powerful right of the family head *(ko-shu)* over his family members (his rights to give consent or disapproval to an individual entering his family, to establish the place of residence of his family members, to give consent or disapproval of a marriage of his family members, and to expel any family member who did not observe these duties, etc.), and the legal inferiority (or being a legal minor) of women (a wife's obligation to obtain her husband's consent to all legal acts of importance, to have her husband manage her property, etc.).

In such a Confucian-feudal pattern (as it is often the case with a patriarchal and patrilineal society), marriage was considered not primarily for the sake of those who marry, but for the interest of the family concerned. Continuity of "house" and prosperity of the lineage were dominant preoccupations. Hence transmission of family name and property were essential criteria in marriage choice.

Marriage by law was primarily the matter of a person (usually a bride) leaving her family and entering that of her husband.[1] Accordingly, it was provided that the consent of the family head was necessary for the marriage of members of his family.[2] A boy under the age of 30 and a girl under 25 could not legally marry without the consent of his (or her) parents. In keeping with these legal provisions, the general value attitudes considered a love marriage *(ren-ai kekkon)* as something improper, indecent, "egoistic," or something similar to an extramarital affair in Western Christian moral codes. To be "proper," a marriage needed to be "arranged" by parents and other elder members of the families concerned.[3]

In the post-World War II revision of the Japanese civil code, which was the natural consequence of the revision of the Japanese Constitution, legal support for the traditional family system was all but abolished. Men and women over the age of 20 can now legally marry without the consent of parents. The new Constitution explicitly states that a marriage should be based upon the mutual consent of both parties and be maintained through mutual cooperation with equal rights for both husband and wife. New laws were enacted with regard to individual dignity and equality of the sexes in choice of spouse, property rights, choice of domicile, and other matters pertaining to marriage and the family. Along with the general endeavor to "democratize" family relationships and people's thoughts generally, there appeared numerous writings, speeches, and lectures by more liberal Japanese encouraging young people to think of their marriage as a matter of their own responsibility.[4]

Some changes in expressed attitudes toward marriage have become apparent, especially in cities. For instance, Steiner quoted in his article interesting figures from Statistics of the Population Research Office of the Welfare Ministry, 1948. According to these statistics, the number of so-called "love" marriages in the pre-war period were approximately 10 percent of the total number of marriages in the Tokyo "uptown" area *(yamanote,* a middle- and upper-class residential area) and 15.3 percent in the "downtown" area *(shita-machi,* an area of industrial and commercial activities with mainly lower-class residences). In the post-war period, the numbers of "love" marriages reported increased to 37.8 percent in the yamanote area and to 40 percent in the shita-machi area.[5] Similar but less radical increases were observed also in farming and mountain villages in Saitama Prefecture near Tokyo. These figures, it must be noted, are from the area in Japan most subject to Western influence.

Another study offering supporting evidence of this post-war change is found, for instance, in the results of a more widely dispersed opinion survey conducted by the Japanese National Public Research Institute in connection with UNESCO research on the post-war Japanese Youth.[6] A total of 2,671 people from various urban and rural areas were asked, along with a series of other questions,

Do you think that the choice of a husband or a wife is a matter of the person's concern or for his (or her) family?

Taking the age groups of most frequent marriage in the urban areas (between 25 and 29 years of age) and in the rural areas (between 20 and 24), 53 percent of the city group (a total of 153 men and women) answered so as to show preference for marriage as a matter of individual concern. Of this group 31 percent gave intermediate opinions, and only 12 percent expressed the opinion that marriage should be a matter of exclusive family concern. Of the total of 255 men and women in the rural group, 47 percent considered marriage as exclusively an individual matter, 39 percent had intermediate opinions, and 13 percent express the opinion that marriage should be a family matter exclusively. If this survey is any reflection of actual attitudes generally, it would seem that marriage arranged by families from the standpoint of family concern only is no longer in favor with more than a small minority either in the urban or rural areas. Other results in the same survey show that individuals over 30 years of age are more liable to suggest attitudes involving some sort of compromise solution. See Table 1.

TABLE 1*
Attitudes toward marriage as predominant for the
individual or for the family

Age group	Number of subjects	For "family" exclusively	Intermediate opinions	For "individual" exclusively	No opinion
Urban					
16-19	139	17	24	51	8
20-24	145	10	36	49	5
25-29	153	12	31	53	5
30-over	604	14	39	45	2
Rural					
16-19	200	15	30	49	8
20-24	255	13	39	47	1
25-29	224	15	36	47	2
30-over	954	14	47	38	3
Whole Sample	2,671	14	39	44	3

*Modified from Table 50, page 183, Jean Stoetzel, *Without the Chrysanthemum and the Sword.* Columbia University Press, New York, 1955.

More recently in his survey on the Japanese youth's attitudes toward marriage and family, Professor Baber collected responses from more than 4,000 university and high school students of city, town and village upbringing.[7] Among numerous questions he used there are eleven items pertinent to the problem of marriage and mate-selection. On the whole their responses indicate more "progressive" attitudes than the above-mentioned results obtained by the Japanese National Public Research Institute. For instance, on the question of whose interest should come first in the choice of a husband or wife, 98.3 percent of boys and 98.8 percent of girls considered the young couple's interest rather than their families' should come first. No significant differences are found by university or high school, or by city, town, or village upbringing. When asked if they considered the "love match" *(ren-ai kekkon)* to be the ideal method in the choice of a husband or wife, four-fifths of the boys and nearly three-fourths of the girls believed the love match to be the ideal method. See Table 2.

TABLE 2*
Attitudes toward "Love Match"–Question: Do you
consider the love match in the choice of a husband
or wife to be the ideal method?

Boys				Girls			
University		High School		University		High School	
Yes	No	Yes	No	Yes	No	Yes	No
76.6	23.4	83.6	16.4	75.2	24.8	67.3	32.7
					N = 4,946		

*Modified from Table 21, page 65, Ray Baber, *Youth Looks at Marriage and the Family,* Tokyo, 1958.

When the parents disapprove of the girl their son wants to marry, the boys and the girls, both of university and high school, are overwhelmingly agreed (approximately 85 percent) that the son's will should prevail, with a relatively small difference between urban and rural youth. When the parents disapprove of the young man their daughter wants to marry, over 70 percent of the boys and the girls believed the daughter's will should prevail although some respondents became less sure of themselves when a daughter rather than a son was the case. See Tables 3 and 4.

TABLE 3*
Attitudes toward Parental Disapproval–Question: When
the parents disapprove of the girl their son wants to
marry, whose will should prevail–the parents'
or the son's?

Boys				Girls			
University		High School		University		High School	
Parents'	Son's	Parents'	Son's	Parents'	Son's	Parents'	Son's
13.5	86.5	14.6	85.4	11.6	88.4	16.8	83.2

*Modified from Table 19, page 62. Baber, *op. cit.*

TABLE 4*
Attitudes toward Parental Disapproval–Question: When
the parents disapprove of the young man their daughter
wants to marry, whose will should prevail–the parents'
or the daughter's?

Boys				Girls			
University		High School		University		High School	
Parents'	Daughter's	Parents'	Daughter's	Parents'	Daughter's	Parents'	Daughter's
26.0	74.0	26.5	73.5	17.2	82.8	29.0	71.0

*Modified from Table 20, page 63, Baber, *op. cit.*

These results do seem to indicate that the majority of young Japanese students consider the marriage should be primarily for the sake of the young couple and their will should not be thwarted by their parents' opinion or by their families' interest. However, it is still the contention of the authors that these surveys are somewhat misleading, for there is an obvious behavioral lag between attitudinal avowals of acceptance of personal choice in marriage as being more important than family consideration and actual marriage practices. Even Baber's students, who are seemingly very "pro-love match" on the general problem as we saw, become much less so when the question is on a more "realistic" basis; being asked which method of choosing a marriage partner they think will be used *in their own case,* about 40 percent of the boys and only less than 20 percent of the girls answered that they will make the choice themselves. Although only a minority expects their parents to make the choice, more than half of the boys and two-thirds of the girls think that their parents and they will make the choice together. It is difficult to tell exactly what is meant by this answer. It may be that they want to find the future husband or wife themselves and yet need their parents' support for their marriage, or they will not blindly accept their parents' choice but talk with them and accept it only when they find the candidate agreeable. It probably means both. In any case, it should be noteworthy that these young students subscribe to a "love match" *in principle* and are of a "progressive" opinion in regard to the general problem of marriage, but when it becomes their own problem many of them reveal dependency on their parents in some way or other and would not so defiantly veto parental choice.

In actuality, arranged marriages do continue to be made even by individuals who express preference for a marriage of personal choice. Why is there this discrepancy? One obvious answer is the effect of social pressure exerted by family and community on the individual. There can be no argument against the effect of such pressures.[8] A less obvious consideration is one we would like to document from indirect evidence taken from projective test materials obtained in a farming village; namely, there is a "psychological lag" in internalized sanctions. An arranged marriage is psychologically easier for many individuals. Free choice in marriage very often involves rebellious attitudes toward parents and guilt feelings may be aroused in making such an attempt.

Attitudes Toward Marriage Revealed in
Projective Test Materials in a Farming Village

The materials analyzed in the present report are a small segment of a large body of data gathered in an interdisciplinary survey conducted in Japan from 1953 to 1955.[9] The present report concerns itself only with the results obtained on two projective tests in a single farming community. In this village of 24 households, 85 percent of the individuals were contacted and tested with at least two of the various testing devices and opinion scales used. Sixty individuals over 18 years of age were given one of two alternate forms of the Problem Situation Tests discussed below. This plan allowed for alternate forms of related items and a larger total number of possible situations. Eighty-one individuals over 12 years of age were given one of three sets of Thematic Apperception Test Cards. This plan again allowed sampling with 18 cards, 12 of which were given to each individual so that two-thirds of the sample cards were included in each testing situation. The Problem Situation Test used was modified from the "Insight Test" developed by Dr. Helen D. Sargent.[10] The Thematic Apperception Test used was the Marui-De Vos Japanese modification of the standard Murray Thematic Apperception Test. These two tests differ from one another in the type of information elicited, giving different levels of insight; namely, the PST tending to reveal conscious attitudes, and the TAT, more implicitly held values. From the variations between the respective data, it is possible to discuss some discrepancies between conscious avowal of values and the expression of less consciously controlled perceptions of what an implementation of these values would entail for the individual acting in accordance with them. The Problem Situation Test overlaps to some extent with opinion survey type data whereas the TAT provides a dimension not yet reported for Japan; namely, the often unconscious structuring of values within the context of spontaneous perceptions of social situations. Cultural practices such as marriage are not often analyzed from a psychological standpoint based on this type of objective data. This paper provides an opportunity to show the significance of such data as a means of understanding the relationships between certain aspects of personality and cultural change.

Analysis of Problem Situations
Test Results Obtained in Niiike[11]

The Problem Situations Test materials collected in the farming village, Niiike, reflect attitudes seemingly similar to those reported in the previously mentioned reports. A majority of Niiike residents tend to show attitudes accepting the idea of love marriage when they are assessed by an opinion test type of method. However, greater discrepancy between men and women was revealed in our results than in the previous surveys. The results in this particular village are somewhat more conservative than the previous reports, but we anticipate that the yet uncompleted city material will show a more liberal direction.[12]

A) *Attitude Toward Marriage for Repayment of Family Obligation.*

One item used in the Problem Situation Test given to Niiike residents was structured to ascertain attitudes toward a hypothetical situation wherein a person was expected to marry an individual so as to pay back *"on"* (obligations) incurred by the parents. It is worded as follows:

A man's [or woman's, in the alternate form given to women] parents were habitually indebted to an individual for help. One day this individual asks the parents to accept his daughter as a bride for their son. The parents are very happy. What does this person do?

The answers to this item differ markedly with age and sex (see Table 5). Of the 14

TABLE 5
ANSWERS TO QUESTION I

Question: A man's parents were habitually indebted to an individual for help. One day he asked the parents to accept his daughter as a bride for their son. (Or, he asked for their daughter as a wife for his son.) The parents of the man (or woman) are very happy about the request. What would he (or she) do?

Age Group	a (18–24)	y (25–34)	m (35–49)	o (50–64)	s (65 +)	Tot. M	Tot. W
Men (Form A)	3	3	4	3	1	14	
Women (Form A)	5	2	5	2	2		16

		Tot. M	Tot. W
I.	He (or she) does not marry	5	2
	1. because he does not like the other person		1a
	2. because he already has a lover and dislikes the other person	1a	
	3. because one should marry according to one's own will	3ays	
	4. because it is better to give things as thanks for receiving help	1o	
	5. because he is ashamed		1a
II.	He (or she) marries if the other person is suitable	3	0
	1. because one should marry for one's self and not for parents or family or obligation	3ymo	
III.	He (or she) will investigate	0	1
	1. because marriage is a lifelong decision		1y
IV.	He (or she) will marry	6	12
	1. because of obligation	3amo	5mmmos
	2. because of setting the parents at ease		6aymmos
	3. because he has had the will to marry	1m	
	4. because he finds the other person suitable	2ym	1a
V.	Rejection	0	1
			1a

TABLE 6
ANSWERS TO QUESTION II

Question: A man wants to marry a girl whom he loves (or who loves him), but he cannot support both his mother and wife.

Age Group	a (18–24)	y (25–34)	m (35–49)	o (50–64)	s (65 +)	Tot. M	Tot. W
Men (Form A)	3	3	4	3	1	14	
Women (Form A)	5	2	5	2	2		16

		Tot. M	Tot. W
I.	He will marry	5	6
	A. Marry and work		
	1. because they would like to marry	4aymo	2ms
	2. in order to get security in life		2 yo
	3. in order to support the mother and live happily		1a
	B. Marry and live separately from mother		1m
	1. because he loves the girl	1o	
	2. no reason		
II.	He will delay marriage	4	0
	1. because they cannot live now	2ay	
	2. in order to complete the duty of supporting mother	1m	
	3. no reason	1y	
III.	He will not marry	5	8
	1. because it is difficult financially	4ammo	5mmmos
	2. it is financially difficult and also she understands it	1s	
	3. because he is bad who can't support the mother and himself		1a
	4. because his mother's eyes are strange (anger? jealousy?)		1a
	5. no reason		1a
IV.	He is distressed	0	1
			1y
V.	Rejection	0	1
			1a

men and 16 women tested, five men and two women rejected the idea of such a marriage completely. Six men and 12 women accepted the idea of marriage while three men and one woman hedged in one way or another. One young woman rejected the item completely in a manner that strongly suggested intense internal conflict over answering. Only three (all over age 35) of the six men suggesting marriage accepted the idea of marriage for obligation. Their replies, as well, as those of five women, explained that the person's family owed much to the other family, and therefore he or she must return the favor of the parents.

In the younger age group of women more indication of possible conflict over the idea of marriage under such circumstances was noted. Two of the seven of the younger age group agreed with the idea, one rejected the idea completely, one said she "disliked" the other person, and one stated no action but said that the person felt shame. Nevertheless, only one younger woman directly expressed concern over the fact that marriage is a lifelong decision. *Not a single woman* objected to such a marriage as a matter of principle.

While only three men, including an adolescent, directly accepted such a marriage for obligation, one notes in the answers given by others of the men a great deal of hedging by means of expressing qualification tending in the direction of acceptance of such a marriage. Two men said that they would marry because the other person is "suitable," and three stated that they would marry *if* the other person is suitable and *not* for family obligation. Four other men brought out the principle that marriage should be a matter of decision in accordance with one's own will, but one of these stated immediately that he supposed that he would marry in the proposed situation "because he had the will to marry." The other three men more forthrightly rejected the marriage idea as stated in a direct manner. It is obvious that the men were more often concerned with matters of abstract principle whereas the women were not.

This item brings out a type of difference between sexes noted in all the psychological and opinion material obtained in Niiike village; namely, that the women are definitely more prone to submit themselves to the older, traditional values. The adolescent girls show trouble in relation to these values, but there is no tendency among them to phrase their concern in terms of newer concepts or principles of individualism. The men in their hesitancy, their qualifications, demonstrate that they are in certain instances caught in a dilemma between a sense of obligation and gratitude toward the parents (or a feeling of submissiveness) and a respect for individualism. As a group they appreciate the value of self-will in their behavior, seeing it as a more important value than passive submission to obligation. Yet, one notes beneath this evaluation of self-will and the surface of masculine activity an underlying submission to pressure in terms of traditional expectations.

B) *Attitudes Concerning Priority of Duty to Mother or Wife.*
   Another item used was,

A man who loves a girl (or a man whom a girl loves) wants to marry her, but he cannot support both his mother and wife. What would he do?

Of the replies given by 14 men and 16 women, approximately one-third of both sexes suggest marriage; nine out of 11 who give this answer suggested that the wife also could work (see Table 6). Only two, however, mentioned the possibility of living separately from the mother. One-third of the men and one-half of the women gave up the idea of marriage. Among these, the larger group represented were those men and women between 35 and 50 years of age, who generally stated it was "too difficult to live," in a rather resigned tone. Four other men suggested some postponement of marriage. No women, however, considered delaying a satisfactory solution. It is obvious from the answers that women are more conscious of age as a factor in marriageability than are men.

In general, in the content of their answers to this item, the men seem more concerned with love relationships. The women are more directly aware of economic pressures and indirectly concerned with the primacy of the obligation to the mother. Solving this supposed dilemma by having both men and women work is certainly not lacking in the replies of either sex, however. The fact that this is a farming village where women are expected to work probably makes such a solution more consciously available as a way out than might be found in the yet unanalyzed urban samples.

C) *Attitudes Concerning Love Versus Parental Opposition.*
    Another item used was,

A man is loved by a girl who is below him in wealth and social position. Reciprocating the love, he, too, wants to marry her. He talks to his parents about it, but they are against the idea. What would he do?

This item is an attempt to test the strength of attitudes about a love marriage as opposed to parental opposition and social status (see Table 7). More women than men dutifully submitted to the parents' wishes or feelings. Of the 14 men and 15 women tested, two men and six women directly gave up the idea of marriage. An additional three of each sex still hoped to gain the parents' consent by further discussion. In contrast, nine of 14 men and six of 15 women said that the man (or woman) should marry. It is noteworthy that six men gave mutual love as the dominant reason for marriage in this instance. Women focused somewhat more on the problems of "social position" in their answers. Four women stated that the man *would* marry because social position is *not* important. Two men stated directly that marriage should be made freely. As a reason for not marrying, undutifulness to the parents (one man), anticipated trouble (one man and three women), and the importance of parents and house *(Ie)* (one woman) were mentioned as reasons.

Another item tested was related to the previous one, as follows:

A man is engaged to be married to a girl whom he loves. However, when he introduced the girl to his parents, one of them raises strong objections. What does he do?

The wording of this item emphasizing strong parental objections to a marriage again had more effect on women than on men (see Table 8). Only four (one-fourth) of the women but six (over one-third) of the men would marry counter to parental wishes. Of nine persons seeing an individual marrying in this circumstance, two thought it necessary to mention a counter obligation to the fiancee. Another cited the mother as having given agreement. Only one woman mentioned love as the chief incentive in going through with the marriage. More men than women showed the additional persistence of trying to talk to the parents further in order to gain cooperation. One man suggested the use of an investigator or marriage broker to

TABLE 7
ANSWERS TO QUESTION III

Question: A man is loved by a girl who is "below" him in wealth and social position. Reciprocating the love, he wants to marry her. He talks to his parents about it, but they are against the idea.

Age Group	a (18–24)	y (25–34)	m (35–49)	o (50–64)	s (65 +)	Tot. M	Tot. W.
Men (Form A)	3	3	4	3	1	14	
Women (Form B)	1	3	6	4	1		15

		Tot. M	Tot. W.
I.	He will marry	9	6
	1. for himself		1m
	2. because social position is not important		4ammo
	3. because he loves her	6aymms	1o
	4. because marriage should be made freely	2yo	
	5. because social position is not important and if necessary he will leave home and marry	1a	
II.	He will make efforts to marry	3	3
	1. ask parents to permit him	3moa	2yy
	2. ask a mediator		1o
III.	He will not marry	2	6
	1. because marriage results in undutifulness to parents	1o	
	2. because some trouble may happen in the future	1y	3ymo
	3. because the parents are right		1m
	4. because the impulse of the moment will not keep them together too long		1m
	5. because parental will and house are important		1s

TABLE 8
ANSWERS TO QUESTION IV

Question: A man is engaged to be married to a girl whom he loves. However, when he introduced her to his parents, one of them raised a strong objection.

Age Group	a (18–24)	y (25–34)	m (35–49)	o (50–64)	s (65 +)	Tot. M	Tot. W
Men (Form B)	3	3	3	3	3	15	
Women (Form A)	5	2	5	2	2		16

		Tot. M	Tot. W
I.	He will marry	6	4
	1. because they have been close for a long time	1o	1m
	2. in order to keep a promise to marry	1m	1m
	3. because it is OK if they love each other		1a
	4. because his mother agrees		1a
	5. because the marriage is their own concern	2ao	
	6. because his fiancee is beautiful	1a	
	7. no reason	1y	
II.	He will talk further with his parent	4	2
	1. in order to persuade parent	1m	
	2. because it is better to get agreement	1a	
	3. because if he does so, he can marry		1a
	4. because he thinks the parent will agree finally		1y
	5. he will wait until he receives agreement	1s	
	6. ask the parent to investigate about her, as he has confidence in her	1m	
III.	He will not marry	3	8
	1. for the parent	1s	
	2. because it is bad to be scolded by father		1m
	3. because he loves his father much more than his fiancee		1s
	4. for the peace of his home		1o
	5. because it is not necessary to marry against the parent	1y	
	6. because it is not allowed in Japan	1s	
	7. because he thinks of his relatives		1m
	8. because of the opposition		2ao
	9. because there are many men in the world		2ay
IV.	Distressed	2	2

convince the parents that this marriage selection was a proper one (the use of the intermediary would make it more proper). Counting two cases which expressed only distressed emotional reaction and no solution, ten of 16 (roughly 2/3) women tested compared with three of 14 (roughly 1/5) men would give up their marriage plans.

Combining the results of the last two questions which are directly concerned with problems of marriage in which love is involved versus parental will, one sees that in 31 women tested with either one or the other of these two items, 14 clearly submitted to parental objections and would not marry, five persisted in attempting to gain acceptance, and 10 stated that the person would marry (see Table 9). Of 29 men, five submitted, seven attempted to gain approval, and fifteen stated that a man would marry in such circumstances. In other words, the men interviewed put greater stress on assertive behavior than did the women. It is interesting to compare the relatively greater amount of approval of a free marriage on the prior question with the answer on the latter one where the statement has a parent taking a stronger attitude of disapproval. This might suggest that the closer the problem is phrased in terms of direct opposition by parents, the less certain an individual becomes of making a marriage for love. Furthermore, the prior question, by bringing in the idea of social status, may have weakened the focus for some on the parental opposition mentioned in this item. The people of the village, which is fairly homogeneous in regard to social status and wealth, are probably less concerned with wealth and social status in regard to marriage than with parental approval or disapproval, whether the basis of approval or disapproval be the social status or some other factor.

TABLE 9

Answers to Two Questions Testing the Relative Strength of Attitudes
about a Love Marriage as Opposed to Parental Objections

	Q. III		Q. IV.		Q. III & IV	
	men	women	men	women	men	women
He (she) will marry	9	6	6	4	15	10
He (she) will try to persuade parents	3	3	4	2	7	5
He (she) will give up marriage	2	6	3	8	5	14
He (she) will be depressed or sad			2	2	2	2
Total	14	15	15	16	29	31

In summary, Chart 1 shows the value attitudes of each age group revealed by their answers to the four questions we have considered in this paper. The attitudes are classified into four categories: individualistic orientation, intermediate orientation, family orientation, and rejection of the item, or emotional reaction as a residual category. Individualistic orientation includes the answers which express the general idea that one's marriage should be made according to one's will, for one's future happiness, and that one should not give up marriage for purposes of conforming to parental wishes or to other familial and societal pressures. Family orientation includes the answers which reveal the opinion that family concern and parents' will should be given priority in regard to one's marriage. The intermediate orientation includes those items in which some attempt is made to reconcile these two opposing factors. The relative strength of each orientation is shown by what percentage of the total answers is found within each age group. One notes that women of almost all ages tend to show a lower percentage of answers with an individualistic orientation than do the men. The women of ages 25-34 show the highest proportion of attempts to conciliate the two positions; whereas, men between 35 and 49 are next highest. Women above 35 show very strong trends toward taking attitudes of familial priority.

Underlying Attitudes of Niiike Villagers Toward
Marriage as Revealed by TAT Stories

It is interesting to compare the above results with the more indirectly, less consciously controlled attitudes expressed in answers to the Thematic Apperception Test. This test procedure evokes attitudes that are expressed implicitly in the context of stories given to a series of pictures. In these stories we find less evidence in the rural village which supports the presence of any meaningful change of attitudes from adherence to family obligation in marriage toward more individualistic choice. From the type of stories told in Niiike to the Thematic Apperception Test pictures, one can readily infer not only that a free, love marriage is an unreal possibility for most of the villagers, but also that there are definite internalized sanctions in a good number of the villagers against considering a love marriage. In the total of 807 Thematic Apperception Test stories collected from the villagers, 42 stories (roughly five percent) were concerned with or had some explicit reference to a marriage situation.

These stories were found in eleven of the eighteen TAT pictures used. This wide range of distribution shows that the stories concerning a marriage situation were not concentrated on any specific card but resulted from a variety of pictorial stimuli. Stories concerning marriage situations were not specific to either sex or to any age group considered. These stories could be classified for purposes of analysis into three groups: 1) stories in which there is mention of arranged type marriage or in which parents are shown as protagonists to the marriage situation (13 stories); 2) stories involving a "love" marriage, depicting children as protagonists (24 stories); 3) a miscellany of unclassified stories too ambiguous or tangential to be placed in either of the two above classifications (5 stories).

As shown in Table 10, women are more prone to give stories of arranged marriage than are men. Ten out of 20 of their stories are so concerned, compared with only three out of 22 of the stories given by men. Men, conversely, in their fantasy are more concerned with problems of initiative versus compliance in a marriage choice. Nine arranged marriage stories (three by men and six by women) are positively toned with no indication of any tension. In these stories either the parents are depicted as helping their children in marriage arrangement or the child is accepting of the parents' initiative. For example:

Picture JM7M, man, age 59
Well . . . each one is a man? From the hair style, one is a woman, isn't she? . . . This looks like a husband and a wife. I would say that they are discussing their son's marriage. Yes, in the future they will find a very good wife for their son.

Picture J6M, man, age 17
This is a mother and this is her son. They are going out somewhere. They are

going out to see the son's prospective bride . . .

The go-between, *nakohdo,* is usually an important figure in an arranged marriage. In one story response to the same picture as the previous story, the protagonist is a go-between:

Picture J6M, woman, age 37
This is a story of a marriage arrangement. This woman is a go-between. She is arranging a marriage for this man. They are going to meet with the prospective bride . . .

TABLE 10
TAT Stories Concerning Marriage Circumstances
in Niiike*

	Men	Women	Total
Total Stories Concerning Marriage	22	20	42
Stories about Arranged Marriage	3	10	13
no tension	3	6	9
with tension	0	3	3
indefinite	0	1	1
Stories about Love Marriage	15	9	24
no tension	1	1	2
with tension	14	8	22
(eventual conformity to family pressure)	(2)	(0)	(2)
(conflict without outcome)	(4)	(3)	(7)
(successful persistence)	(3)	(0)	(3)
(eventual failure of love marriage)	(5)	(5)	(10)
Others	4	1	5

*Total stories given to TAT in Niiike (807).

Not all the stories of arranged marriage are without tension. Three stories given by younger women contain some expression of tension in the human relationships involved. In one of them given by a 14-year old girl, a daughter eventually conforms to her mother's wish and accepts an arranged marriage:

Picture J7F, woman, age 14
When a daughter and her mother are talking after supper, an acquaintance calls on them. He seems to be her fiance. The daughter herself, however, did not know that he was to be her fiance because her mother had decided this on her own authority, without informing the daughter. In the past they used to read books. The mother used to teach her daughter, I suppose . . . [?] . . . The mother will persuade her daughter that she will have to marry the man. The daughter . . . she will obey her mother, although she is very sad and it is "painful" for her.

In another story given by a teen-age girl there is a successful rejection of arranged

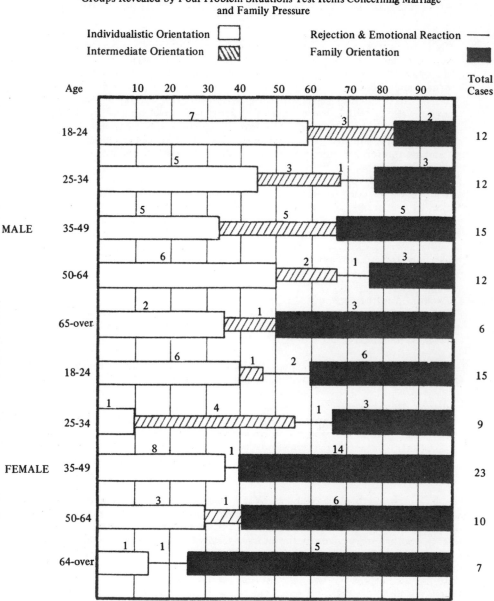

CHART 1
Individualistic, Intermediate, and Family Orientation of Different Age and Sex
Groups Revealed by Four Problem Situations Test Items Concerning Marriage
and Family Pressure

Individualistic Orientation

Intermediate Orientation

Rejection & Emotional Reaction ——

Family Orientation

marriage wherein a son rejects his father's wish to marry him to a certain girl, leaves home, and establishes himself. He then marries a girl of his own choice. This story in contrast to its relative prevalence in American TAT stories is extremely rare in Niiike village.

Picture J7M, woman, age 17
This man is a company employee, about 27 or 28 years old. His father is very stubborn and conservative. The father told him to marry a lady whom he does not like. He does not agree with his father, so they are against each other, and the father tells him to leave home since he does not obey his father. He is going to leave home. He will live for himself. He will work hard and . . well . . . well . . . well . . . he will get a high position and live in great comfort and will get married with a favorite person and live happily . . . When he has a child and lives a harmonious life, his father comes to understand his thinking and forgives him. Everything will then be worked out well.

Tension and conflict are far more characteristic of the 24 stories given by individuals of all ages in which a love marriage expressly appears. Only in two stories, by a man over 65 and a teen-age girl, in which personal choice of a mate is involved, does one find stories free of some expression of tension. In 12 of these 24 stories concerning free marriage, the focus is on a conflict between a child's desire to marry a person of his own choice and parental opposition. In these stories a large proportion (seven stories) do not spontaneously depict any resolution. For example:

Picture J4, woman, age 62
This man looks angry . . . this is his lover. The man is looking at something . . . at the picture of his parents. His parents are opposed to his marrying his lover, so he is angry.

In certain of these stories the person when questioned by an examiner gives an optimistic ending, but usually without much conviction:

Picture 3M, man, age 46
Well . . . this is a girl, I guess . . . She is sad, is heartbroken. She could not have her wish . . . It seems that she loves someone and wants to marry him. She asked her parents for permission, but they refused, having a different opinion. She is sad . . . [future?] Well, she will marry him anyway, I guess, won't she?

The lack of strength of conviction about opposing parents is displayed in another such story where, after stating upon further questioning that a man eventually married according to his own choice, the respondent finds it easier to substitute quickly another story wherein the mother reproves the son over spending money. The respondent thus turns from considering the consequences of the previous story and in an alternative one ends on a note of passivity, with the mother envisioned as a protagonist reproving wrong behavior on the part of the son. This sort of sequence in the story-telling suggests the operation of underlying guilt feelings:

Picture J6M, man, age 57
Humph . . . this man looks serious . . . This is . . . this son had a love affair

and consulted his mother about his marriage, I guess . . . His mother has a different opinion . . . She does not agree with her son. I wonder . . . [future?] He will marry the girl of his own choice against his mother's opinion. That's all. There is one more interpretation. It seems that the son was reproved by his mother for spending too much money . . . That's all.

There are three stories, all given by men 35-50 years of age, in which a child does persist through parental opposition to the conclusion of a successful marriage choice. It is this particular age group that throughout the psychological material in the survey generally conveyed in the strongest fashion the value of initiative in personal behavior. However, it is also in this same age group that one finds the largest number of stories of an unsuccessful love marriage as discussed below. In stories of successful opposition to parental opinions, three out of four stories see a young *man* as succeeding. In stories of submission the tendency is the converse; the heroine is usually a young *woman* who submits. Hence, there is some indication of a tendency to perceive some men as sufficiently strong willed to attain a love marriage. However, young women are seen more characteristically prone to be submissive:

Picture 3M, man, age 42
The girl is sad. She is sorry. She could not have her wish . . . She wanted to marry someone, but her parents did not allow her . . . She will eventually give up and submit to her parents' will.

There are ten stories classified as failure of a love marriage, eight of which directly depict tensions between the marriage partners. Conversely, there is not a story in the entire sample referring to tension between spouses whose marriage was an arranged one.

The stories of failure of love marriage have a moralistic tone, depicting what dire events happen when a couple marries for love. For example:

Picture J4, woman, age 29
This is a husband and this is his wife. They married for love, but the husband is now addicted to drink. He has a mistress. He is quarrelling with someone in a tavern. His wife tries to stop him, but she cannot stop him.

Picture J5, woman, age 65
This is a wife. She is seeing off . . . seeing off her husband, who is bad. He is going out . . . going out to do gambling or to his mistress . . . to do something bad . . . His wife is seeing him off. She cannot do anything about it . . . they married for love, but things do not go well . . .

Picture J13, man, age 26
This is a certain couple. The wife's attitude is very bad. I think when the husband came back late at night from his office she is lying down slovenly, without going to meet him. Her husband now grieves over his marriage, with such a woman . . . Judging from the husband's attitude, he cannot stand her any longer . . . Unless he gets divorced. [Does he divorce her?] He will do so in the future . . . As for the past, it seems that they loved each other and did a *ren-ai kekkon* (love marriage).

Picture J13, man, age 35
Well, this is . . . well, this man and woman married for love. The woman was a cafe waitress and married the man for love, but they have not lived happily, so the man repents the marriage very much. Well, this man used to be a very good man, but he was seduced by the waitress and lost his self-control and at last he had sexual relationships with her. Afterwards, he becomes afraid and he has to think over their marriage. If their married life had any future at all, I hope they will maintain some better stability but if this woman does not want to do so, he needs to think over their marriage, I suppose.

The above stories definitely show that there is some feeling that a love marriage is somehow illicit and can come to no good. These stories of a failure in a love marriage reveal strong feelings of disapproval and/or guilt on a deeper level toward actualizing a love marriage by depicting miserable situations and the unhappiness of a man or woman who married for love. It almost sounds as if you will find your mate unsuited if you marry for love. In fact, this idea that if you marry for love on an individualistic basis, you will find your mate unsuited is generally held by those people with a strong, traditional value orientation. However, the feeling of disapproval and possible guilt toward a free love marriage may be due not only to the internalization of old values but also to more unconscious psychological factors involving the strong unresolved attachments to parents and such character traits as passivity. These psychological conditions also contribute heavily to the lack of inner strength for independence or autonomy, which in terms of cultural values has always been identified with rebellious wishes. The following story in rather extreme form depicts remorse and repentance for parental opposition which is not readily duplicated on a conscious level in Western thinking:

Picture J13, woman, age 22
He got married for love with a woman in spite of opposition by his parents. While they were first married they lived happily but recently he reflects on his marriage and the manner in which he pushed his way through his parents' opposition . . . He wishes his present wife would not exist . . . He attempts to push away the feelings of blame within his mind. One night on the way home he buys some insect poison and gives it to his wife to drink and she dies. What he has done weighs on his mind. He gives himself up to the police. He trustfully told his story to them. He reflects on how wicked he has been in the past. He completes his prison term and faces the future with serious intent.

In the other stories, love seemingly is "punished" by death of the beloved person:

Picture J6F, man, age 41
They are father and daughter. The daughter is sitting on the chair in her room. Father is looking in and she is turning around to face him. He is very thoughtful of his daughter and as she is just about of age for marriage, he wants to suggest that she marry a certain man he has selected. But she has a lover and does not want to marry the man her father suggests. The father is trying to read her face though he does not know about the existence of the lover. He brought up the subject a few times before, but the daughter showed

no interest. Today, also . . . A smile is absent in her face. The father talks about the subject again, but he fails to persuade her, so finally he gives in and agrees to her marrying her lover. Being grateful to the father for his consent, the daughter acts very kindly toward him after her marriage. The husband and the wife get along very affectionately also, but her father dies suddenly of apoplexy. The father was not her real father; he did not have children, so he adopted her and accepted her husband as his son-in-law, but he died . . . He died just at the time when a baby was born to the couple.

Picture J6F, woman, age 22
The parents of this girl were brought up in families strongly marked with feudal atmosphere—the kind of family scarcely found in present time, so they were very feudal and strict. The daughter could not stand her parents. She had to meet her lover in secret. She will see her lover today as usual without her parents knowing it, but by accident her father came to find out about it. She was caught by her father on the spot. When she returned home her father rebuked her severely for it, but she could not give up her lover. In spite of her parents' strong objections, she married him. [future?] The couple wanted to establish a happy home when they marry, but probably she will lose her husband. He will die and she will have a miserable life.

In analyzing these stories, a punitive meaning can readily be attributed to the death involved. One may assume that although a respondent first puts into words an unconscious wish for a love marriage, he himself, on a deeper level, disapproves it, and then punishes the hero or heroine by causing the death of the beloved person to follow the rebellious act.[13]

One may summarize the TAT evidence by saying that when people of Niiike village explicitly depict an arranged marriage situation in TAT pictures, they tend to take an accepting attitude toward such a marriage. On the other hand, a number of individuals are prone to see love marriage as something that leads to a certain type of conflict between partners or as something which is guilt-provoking and difficult to accomplish, however consciously or unconsciously they may wish for it.

Discussion

Present attitudes toward marriage in Japan are by no means invariant or simple in nature. To understand the complexity of cultural practices in modern changing Japan in regard to marriage or in other areas of life, it is necessary to examine attitudes in depth in both a cultural-historical sense as well as in a psychological one.

A cultural-historical analysis of rural groups would be concerned with consequent changes in attitudes and practices in specific rural areas which occur with changes in centers of social and political dominance. In Japan in recent times one notes, for example, in many rural communities[14] the permeation of Confucianist ethics concerning the nature of the family, influencing marriage practices and helping define what is "proper" in marriage among rural villagers. These values are now again more recently being modified by changes in modern post-war Japan. Processes of urbanization and industrialization along lines found in Western societies are very much in evidence on the modern urban Japanese scene. Evidence of these influences backed by recent post-war changes in legal sanctions is not lacking in rural villages as well.

Approached psychologically, the acculturative processes involved show different rates of change between attitude and behavior. Some previously deeply internalized values about marriage and family obligation can at times be consciously disavowed, but remain as inner constraints that prevent behavioral implementation of newer values by many young people who would like to adopt a different way of life. To demonstrate the working of these inner psychological processes is not, however, to dispute the determinant influences of overall cultural and economic forces on acculturation generally.[15]

Nevertheless opinion survey methods based on direct questioning and tabulation of the proportion of individuals affirming one idea or other by themselves are insufficient for gaining insight on questions as they effect the inner integration of values within the individual. Specifically this paper attempts to demonstrate on a small scale the efficacy of using psychological test data as part of a survey technique. By utilizing psychological tests that reveal attitudes indirectly as well as directly, we have shown an apparent difference between consciously stimulated attitudes and the indirect appearance of attitudes in the context of spontaneous stories depicting interaction in primary relationships. The P.S.T. (Problem Situation Test) data are more in line with the results of direct opinion survey results than are the less self-conscious expressions of attitudes in the context of TAT (Thematic Apperception Test) stories.

In the particular village reported, internalized sanctions which function in relation to marriage choice are inferentially more related to previous dominant cultural attitudes than to newer consciously accepted values. This phenomenon can be considered as a manifestation of what might be termed "psychological lag." A concept of "psychological lag" in the persistence of internalized sanctions is of central issue in applying a culture and personality frame of reference to an understanding of attitude change in any acculturation process. It may help explain the nature of personal inner discord of an individual when older and newer attitudes are both present without as yet being resolved. Santayana, through the characters in his book, *The Last Puritan,* brought out that American culture, although seemingly having left the older Puritan tradition behind, still manifests in many individuals a lurking residue of emotional constraint. The premise that life is to be for the pursuit of happiness seems sometimes to run into inner restraints that help to explain America's proneness toward a work ethic. Somehow many Americans are not as free to pursue happiness as they would like to believe themselves free to do. The same sort of lag is found in Japanese attitudes toward family life. In many Japanese there is an avowed value of being able to be "free" in a love relationship, but also at the same time a curious inability to implement this value in a successful way behaviorally. In one sense, this dilemma concerning the potential tragedy of loving is not new in Japanese culture. Love romances usually ending unhappily have for generations been enormously popular in Japan. Benedict made this point when she wrote that the Japanese had made things extraordinarily difficult for themselves by idealizing love matches in fiction but forbidding them in reality. What is different now, however, is the fact that the government and to a certain extent the society generally is avowedly committed to a "new Japan"—a Japan relating herself to Western traditions of equality and individual self-determination.

The psychological test data presented in this paper only hint at some of the complexities of the relationship between the internalization of older standards and the avowal of new ones. We believe, however, that we have presented by means of concrete evidence from two psychological test techniques some disparity between conscious and apparently less conscious attitudes in a rural Japanese village in regard to acculturative changes in attitudes toward marriage.

FOOTNOTES

1. In families without a suitable male heir, adoption of an adult "son" (*yoshi*) who takes the name of his wife's parents is a very common practice, especially in business and professional groups. The practice of adult adoption of a *yoshi* insures the continuation of a business or profession in the hands of an individual who has demonstrated abilities in families where an actual son is not present or does not prove adequate.

After marriage usually a bride's name was changed to that of her husband, but this did not happen simply as a result of marrying him. Legally, she first entered her groom's family, and becoming a member of the family, she took the name of this family. Thus, her family name became the same as that of her husband (Article 788, 746).

2. Marriage registration without the consent of the family head was sometimes accepted by the county office, but if a family member married without consent, the family head was still legally authorized to punish the member by expelling the person from the family (*ri-seki*) or by refusing the person after divorce to re-enter his family (*fuku-seki kyo-zetsu*).

3. There seem to have been, however, always deviations from this general value attitude. In the first place, in the country and among urban lower social strata, many marriages were initiated by the individual's personal choice, although "arrangements" for the sake of formality were increasingly prevalent after Meiji. Secondly, even in the marriages arranged by parents, there have always been cases in which young people were given a veto right to the proposed marriage, thus having opportunities to express passively at least some element of choice. Further, there have always been a relatively small group of parents, who, in arranging marriages for their children, were—or thought they were—more concerned with the happiness of their children than with the interests of their family. This type of attitude often considered the marriage not as primarily for the sake of the families concerned; rather arrangement by parents was considered a necessary procedure since young people were seen as not being experienced or mature enough to choose their own marital spouse properly and reasonably; hence, the parents had to take the responsibility in finding a suitable partner for their benefit. And also in many communities in remote country areas and especially many fishing villages, where the indoctrination with Confucian values was less operative than in cities and farming villages, people's attitudes toward marriage remained freer and marriage based upon individual choice and love was more frequent. For instance, see George De Vos and Hiroshi Wagatsuma, "Variations in Value Attitudes Related to Women's Status in Japanese Rural Villages," *American Anthropologist,* LXIII, No. 6 (1961), 1204-1230.

4. As for the post-war change in Japanese civil codes, see Kurt Steiner, "Postwar Changes in the Japanese Civil Codes," *Washington Law Review,* XXV (1950), 286-312; Sakae Wagatsuma, "Democratization of the Family Relations in Japan," *ibid.,* 405-426.

5. These statistics do not necessarily represent the number of love marriages there were in actuality before or after the war. They reveal only what proportion of people report the fashionable or approved form. One may doubt whether anything like 40 percent of Tokyo marriages in the period reported here were in fact love matches.

6. Jean Stoetzel, *Without the Chrysanthemum and the Sword—A Study of the Attitudes of Youth in Post-War Japan,* UNESCO—Columbia University Press, New York, 1955.

7. Ray E. Baber, *Youth Looks at Marriage and the Family: A Study of Changing Japanese Attitudes,* International Christian University Press, Tokyo, 1958.

8. One indirect form of negative community sanctions is the simple lack of informal or casual social opportunities to mix with socially appropriate members of the opposite sex. Opportunity even in Tokyo to attend the type of parties familiar to Western adolescents or young adults is extremely rare. In large cities like Tokyo and Osaka some intellectual and socially known middle-aged couples sponsor the parties of young people, offering their houses

and giving various advice. *Hidaka* parties, named after a university professor who first started it on a fairly large scale, are popular in Tokyo and the rate of marriage resulting is high. Such examples, however, are conspicuous by being rare.

9. This large scale survey used opinion schedules and projective techniques in three rural villages and two cities of central Honshu. The survey field work was completed in August 1955. The over-all city sample of 2,760 individuals over 18 years of age was obtained by using area tracts laid out by the national census in the cities of Okayama and Nagoya. A predetermined number of each household sample in the survey was contacted for several interviews. Occupation and education of the individuals in the survey were checked against the national census figures of 1950.

Three villages were selected for their representative nature, and more or less blanket sampling was used. A total of 435 rural inhabitants was contacted. In one farming village in southcentral Honshu in Okayama Prefecture, 73 percent of the individuals (85 individuals in 24 households) were contacted. In one mountain village *buraku* near the border of Nagano in Aichi Prefecture in mountainous central Honshu, 151 individuals (100 percent of those over 18 in 42 households) were contacted. In a fishing village on an island in Atsuma Bay, 57 percent of the population over 18 (264 individuals out of 166 households) were contacted.

These individuals in the city and village samples were all interviewed with social background schedules and opinion scales. In turn, a more limited number of individuals in the samples were approached with projective tests. In the cities, a total of approximately 400 Rorschachs, 600 Insight Tests (herein described), 600 Thematic Apperception Tests, and 200 Figure Drawings were given. In the villages, a total of 267 Rorschachs, 214 Insight Tests, 259 Thematic Apperception Tests, and 125 Figure Drawings were obtained. The projective testing was administered by specially trained psychology students. Each had a considerable supervised practice before testing individuals in the survey sample.

10. Helen D. Sargent, *The Insight Test; A Verbal Projective Test for Personality Study* (The Menninger Clinic Monograph Series, No. 10). Grune and Stratton, New York, 1953.

11. Niiike is a *buraku* (hamlet) located on the lower slopes of a hill, an ancient burial mound, some 20 miles west of Okayama city in Okayama Prefecture. It is situated about 400 meters north of the highway running between the two cities of Okayama and Kurashiki, separated from other *buraku* by fields, but not isolated. It is an agricultural village of 24 households and 133 people, of which 49 are farmers, 12 office workers and 69 women and children. Life depends primarily upon the paddy field, which for the most part yields a winter dry grain crop (barley and wheat) in addition to the summer rice. Niiike has also some upland dry fields for a varied vegetable and fruit production. The villagers also plant a kind of rush (*i-gusa*) annually and each family weaves these grasses into *tatami-omote,* between the periods of heaviest labor demand, as a subsidiary money crop. The people of Niiike are relatively well off as farmers go in Japan, especially if compared with the northeastern section of the country. For further information for a general study in Niiike, see R. K. Beardsley, *et. al.* (eds.), *Village Japan,* University of Chicago Press, Chicago, 1959.

12. Exact statistical results on the various opinion schedules used are soon to be published by the Human Relations Research Group in a series of reports. For a complete analysis of the Problem Situation Test used in the Niiike village, see "Social Values and Primary Relationships in a Japanese Village," *Occasional Papers,* Center for Japanese Studies, University of Michigan, preparation for publication.

13. Such attribution of punitive meanings of death seems to be a characteristic tendency in certain Japanese stories. In a few other TAT stories not concerned with marriage, parents sometimes die when the hero of the story does something wrong. For instance, a son becomes delinquent; a parent is worried, becomes ill, and dies. The stories of parental death following a child's bad behavior, therefore, suggest the parent is "punishing" the child by dying. A parent's dying is not only the punishment of the child but more often the final control over the child, breaking his resistance to obeying the parental plan. For further discussion of this mechanism in relation to guilt in Japanese culture, see George De Vos, "The Relation of Guilt toward Parents to Achievement and Arranged Marriage Among the Japanese," *Psychiatry,* XXIII, No. 3, (August, 1960). It has been observed that a not uncommon device used by a parent to force his

child to conclude an arranged marriage is to feign poor health and to plead with his child to "make him happy and ease his lot." Although he may suspect the subterfuge, few Japanese youths are strong enough to resist *this* form of pressure, George De Vos and Hiroshi Wagatsuma, "Psycho-cultural Significance of Concern Over Death and Illness among Rural Japanese," *International Journal of Social Psychiatry,* V, No. 1 (Summer 1959), 5-19.

14. Behavioral opinion and psychological evidence from a fishing village studied with the same methods as the farming village not cited in this paper but noted elsewhere (George De Vos and Hiroshi Wagatsuma, "Value Attitudes Relating to Women's Status in Two Japanese Rural Communities," *American Anthropologist, op. cit.*) suggests that a fishing village, Sakunoshima, was much less influenced to internalized Confucianist ethic than was true for the farming village. In line with these findings the attitudes toward love marriage invertly revealed on the TAT for this village show a contrasting optimism concerning the possibility for successful love marriages. This village was seemingly freer from direct feudal influences and consequently shows less difficulty in accepting present-day liberal attitudes. Work with this data has not been completed, but the contrast with the farming village is clear. Norbeck's monograph on a Japanese fishing village, Takashima (Edward Norbeck, *Takashima—A Japanese Fishing Community,* University of Utah Press, Salt Lake City, 1954), similarly gives evidence of the recency of the practice of arranged marriage, suggesting the coming in of the practice through the compulsory education of the last generation made other forms of marriage seem "improper."

15. One must also take into account effective community sanctions that would prevent behavior not approved by the dominant members of the group.

POPULATION CONTROL IN JAPAN:
A MIRACLE OR SECULAR TREND?

John Y. Takeshita

Japan's population grew beyond 93 million in 1960. This represented a 250 per cent increase since the turn of the century and 35 per cent just since the beginning of the last war. The density of her population increased from 299 per square mile in 1900 to 658 per square mile in 1960.[1] Crowded on an island no larger than the State of Montana is a population that ranks in size only behind such territorially expansive countries in China, India, U.S.S.R., the United States, Indonesia, and Pakistan. And yet today these comparative figures do not necessarily portend for Japan a disastrous future as they may have, say a decade ago. It is true that her population will probably increase beyond 100 million within the coming decade, but this prospect is no longer viewed with alarm. If there is alarm, it comes instead from the real possibility of population decline before the end of the present century if current trends in vital rates continue. Indeed, the demographic situation of Japan is so incredibly favorable for her immediate, if not also long-term, prospect that its emergence has inspired more than one observer to characterize it as miraculous. The "miracle" has specific reference to the amount and rapidity of fertility reduction that has occurred just since the baby boom years of 1947, 1948, and 1949.

The crude birth rate was reduced from 34 in 1947 to 17 in 1960, a 50 percent reduction in slightly over a decade.[2] The decline has continued in the recent years even with a progressive rise in marriage rate since 1957. The fertility of Japanese women has been curtailed so much that in 1958 for the first time in the history of modern Japan the net reproduction rate fell below unity.[3]

The population has continued to increase, of course, because mortality too has gone down considerably since the last war. The crude death rate dropped from above 14 in 1947 to below 8 in 1960. But the annual rate of increase has declined steadily as fertility has been reduced at a faster rate than mortality, which even shows signs of having come close to the minimum.[4] The population that was increasing at above 2 per cent per year just after the war is now increasing at less than 1 per cent a year. If current trends continue, Japan's population will hit a peak at about 113 million in the 1990's and thereafter decline.

One other consequence of the rapid but differential rates of decline in fertility and mortality has been the drastic change in the age structure of Japan's population. The change has been from a wide-base, pyramid-like structure to a narrow-base, arrowhead-like structure. The proportion of children has decreased as the proportion of adults has increased. The upshot of this structural change has been the reduction of the burden of support of the dependent population (say,

Takeshita — *From Marriage and Family Living,* February 1963, pp. 44-52. Reprinted by permission of The National Council on Family Relations and the author.

under 15 and 65 and over) by the productive segment in the ages 15-64. While it is true that the improvement in mortality has resulted in greater longevity and a steady increase in the proportion of the aged, this increase has not been large enough to offset the decrease in the proportion of the childhood population due to rapid decline in fertility and to raise the total dependency load.[5] In contrast to her recent past, the age structure of Japan's population today is one that is favorable to rapid improvement of her economy.

Whether facilitated by the recent demographic changes or not, Japan is today enjoying an unprecedented economic boom. The survivors of the bumper crop of babies born in the immediate postwar period are now entering the labor market but without the difficulties of employment they were anticipated to encounter. If the current trend in the demand for labor continues, the shrinkage in the ranks of new entrants to the labor force as a result of the decline in fertility since 1950 will produce a worker's market or, more hopefully, a spur to more efficient utilization of the existing labor force.[6]

Thirty-three per cent of the working force in 1960 were still in the primary industries. As high as this rate is, it represents a 15 percentage-point decline just since 1950. Her population continues to move from the rural to the industrial prefectures and to the largest cities for employment in the secondary and the tertiary industries. During 1955 and 1960 when the country's population increased by 4.6 per cent the population in the largest cities increased by 17.5 per cent. These figures testify to the continued industrialization and urbanizing of Japan in spite of the severe setback suffered in the last war. In fact, postwar recovery has been so rapid that by 1959 the real per capital income was 150 per cent higher than it was in 1934-36. If Japan has problems, they are problems of adjustment to rapid industrialization and urbanization, and problems common to economies that depend on a favorable international market. They cannot be called *population* problems because the population factor no longer interferes with Japan's economic progress as it does, say, in India.

Much has been said about the role of national policies in the demographic changes that have occurred in Japan since the war. There were two Allied policies that had direct demographic effects. The decision to strip Japan of her territories acquired since the Sino-Japanese War (1894-95) and force the repatriation of Japanese settlers as well as armed personnel resulted in a net population increase of more than 3 million and a half just in 1946 and over 5 million during the entire Occupation period that ended in 1952. The return of young men and the reunion of families resulted also in a prodigious crop of babies in 1947, 1948, and 1949. The Occupation also inaugurated a vigorous public health program which served to reduce with the aid of antibiotics the traditionally high Japanese death rates from tuberculosis and other respiratory ailments. This program, later extended by the Japanese, also served to reduce the infant mortality rate just as the birth rate soared. The direct consequence of these Allied measures, unintended to be sure, was to effectuate a 15.2 per cent increase in population between 1945 and 1950, with an average annual rate of increase of 2.9 per cent!

In contrast, the effects of the much-publicized policies subsequently adopted by the Japanese government are at best uncertain. What is certain is that they were inspired by the very conditions brought on by the aforementioned occupation policies. The pressure of a suddenly inflated population on the war-ravaged economy was indeed acute. This manifested itself in the widespread resort to induced abortion, then illegal, by the women of Japan. It was then that the government, slow in comprehending the demographic implications of the Allied measures, was forced into taking some action. In 1948, it took hold of an existing National Eugenic Law and literally reversed its provisions to permit both sterilization and induced abortion for "large" families for health reasons and in the case of induced abortion for economic reasons as well.[7] The 1948 law was ostensibly for eugenic purposes as the name Eugenic Protection Law implies, but subsequent revisions in 1950 and 1952 revealed its true purpose—namely, to legalize induced abortion for whatever reason. Legal restrictions exist to the extent that the woman must indicate reasons of health or finance for obtaining an induced abortion. But the criteria are unspecified and the certified physician is his own screening, board, so that the applicant's intention, whatever it maybe, is sufficient cause for approval.

But even as the government acquiesced in permitting easy abortion, it embarked upon a program of family planning education to encourage the use of contraception in lieu of abortion. This program was first introduced as a health measure for individual mothers, but since 1954 it has become part of an integrated population policy from the point of view of national welfare. Individual and group guidance programs were initiated under the Ministry of Health and Welfare with the training and certification of nearly 30,000 nurses, midwives, and other health workers for such activities and the establishment of over 800 Eugenic Protection Consultation Centers throughout the country.

It is difficult to tell what part these programs have played in the recent diffusion of birth control practices among the Japanese. It is likely that the influences have been more indirect than direct. Together with the law that permits open sale, advertisement, and discussion of contraceptives, the Eugenic Protection Law and the government-sponsored family planning programs probably have served to make the means more readily accessible to those who become interested in fertility control for various individual reasons, or more generally helped to create in Japan a social milieu which makes fertility control more favorable now than ever before.

The Evidence of Diffusion of Birth
Control in the Postwar Years

The diffusion of birth control among the Japanese since the passage of the foregoing law and the inauguration of family planning programs has been documented in a unique series of national surveys undertaken by the Manichi Population Problems Research Council. Six surveys have been completed through 1961, although the final report of the last of these was not in the author's hand at this writing. These surveys and the reports prepared by one of the leading newspapers of Japan have no doubt served to publicize family planning among the people even as they document a "social experiment" in progress. While there is much to be desired in the ways in which the data have been analyzed, the findings do show significant trends in the diffusion of birth control among the Japanese as a whole.

The practice of contraception spread rapidly from 1950 to 1957. In 1950, only about one in five couples reported current use of contraception. By 1957 about two in five reported such use. Unaccountably, the diffusion has been much slower since 1957, the proportion of users increasing from 39.2 per cent in 1957 to 42.5 per cent in 1959 and remaining there in 1961. Opinions in favor of contraception exceeded the actual practice. Sixty-one per cent expressed favorable opinions in 1950, 67 per cent in 1955, and 74 per cent in 1959.

Contraception is increasingly used as a spacing device as well as a means to limit the number of children. This is evident in the progressive rise in the proportion of couples who begin use soon after marriage. In 1952, only 9 per cent began before the first child was born, 30 per cent before the second, 62 per cent before the third, and 83 per cent before the fourth. In 1959, as many as 17 per cent began before the first child, 42 per cent before the second, 73 per cent before the third, and 91 per cent before the fourth.

Both frequency of use and timing of use differ by socioeconomic status and residential status, although differences have narrowed in recent years. The better educated and the modern, high status workers not only are more frequently users but start use sooner after marriage than the less educated and the traditional, low status workers. Likewise, residents of urban communities are more likely users than the residents of rural communities, and start somewhat earlier as well.

By far, the most influential source of contraceptive knowledge among the Japanese has been the mass media—magazine, in particular. In 1959, 49 per cent reported the latter as their source of knowledge. The role of doctors, midwives, health centers and the like is not negligible but is far from equal to the publicity the government programs involving these people have received.

A finding difficult for the government to accept for sometime has been the repeated indication of an increase in the proportion of wives who have resorted to induced abortion—from 15 per cent in 1950 to as much as 41 per cent in 1961. What is more, induced abortion has been found to be more likely among past users of contraception rather than among non-users. In 1961, 54 per cent of the former but only 9 per cent of the latter reported having had at least one induced abortion. It is increasingly apparent that induced abortion among the Japanese for the most part is not an alternative but a supplementary means of birth control.

Numerous other studies by such agencies as the National Public Opinion Institute, the Ministry of Health and Welfare, and others—both public and private—merely corroborate these findings of the Mainichi surveys. However, one difficulty of interpretation common to these studies has to do with the following question: Is birth control a strictly postwar phenomenon among the Japanese or is this an illusion created by the timing of these studies (all after the war) and the publicity this topic has received in recent years? The prewar trends and patterns of differential in Japanese fertility suggest earlier acceptance of birth control by them than just since the war—and, it might be added for a reason.

Indirect Evidence of Birth Control
in Prewar Japan: The Changing
Pattern of Differential Fertility

Fertility decline among the Japanese became evident soon after modern census-taking was instituted in 1920. That this decline was due not only to delayed marriage but also to voluntary control was evident in the consistent decline in marital fertility in the prewar years. As a matter of fact, even in 1947 when the crude birth rate was nearly as high as it was in 1925, the age-specific birth rates showed significant declines in the older ages from those in 1925. The postwar baby boom, from which the recent decline is usually measured, was not due to a reversal in fertility pattern but, as suggested earlier, to the reunion of families and new marriages that presumably had been postponed during the war. Penrose, observing the changing fertility in Japan in the 1920's, wrote as early as in 1934:

. . . there is evidence that marriage age has advanced a little, and, what is more important, that the means have been available for voluntary limitation of births, while the emotional opposition to such limitation has greatly declined. There is nothing in the known fact inconsistent with the theory that what fall has already taken place in the fertility rate has been largely due to consciously practiced birth control." [8]

The decline was not uniform throughout the population. Some groups showed earlier decline than others. In fact, the pattern of differential fertility that emerged even before the war is consistent with the early phases of a three-stage cycle of socioeconomic differentials hypothesized for any industrializing country. According to this model, there is in the first stage either fairly uniform fertility in the different socioeconomic groups or a direct relationship between fertility and status. In the second stage, there emerges an inverse pattern as the influences producing reduction in fertility operate first and most effectively on the highest status group and with diminishing effectiveness at each lower level. Finally, fairly uniform rates or a direct relationship once again are obtained at a lower level of fertility, as the influences producing fertility reduction diffuse throughout the population from the highest to the lowest status.

The inverse pattern of socioeconomic differentials in Japanese fertility was evident in a 1940 national fertility study conducted by the Institute of Population Problems of the Ministry of Welfare. Significantly, data from this pioneer study suggest that the inverse pattern may have been a recent phenomenon associated with the advance in industrialization and urbanization as hypothesized in the model. Comparing the average number of live births (as of 1940) for selected occupations by economic level for two marital cohorts, 1910-19 and 1920-24, Honda found an inverse relation to income only among the modern occupations in the more recent cohort, as shown in Table I.[9] It is apparent from these figures that

TABLE 1
AVERAGE NUMBER OF LIVE BIRTHS IN 1940 FOR THE MARITAL COHORTS OF
1910-19 AND 1920-24 FOR SELECTED OCCUPATIONS BY ECONOMIC LEVEL
Monthly income*

Marital cohort	Total	Less than 100 yen	100 yen- 149 yen	150 yen- 299 yen	300 yen or more
			Bank and office workers		
1920-24	4.2	4.3	4.2	3.7	3.8
1910-19	4.3	4.0	4.3	4.4	4.5
			Factory workers		
1920-24	4.6	4.7	4.6	3.6	–
1910-19	5.4	5.4	5.5	5.7	–
			Amount of business tax paid*		
		Tax exempted	Less than 25 yen	25 yen- 49 yen	50 yen or more
			Urban proprietors		
1920-24	4.2	4.4	3.8	4.1	4.3
1910-19	4.6	4.6	4.5	4.7	4.6
			Rural proprietors		
1920-24	3.9	3.6	4.1	5.0	4.0
1910-19	4.4	4.3	4.4	4.0	5.2
			Farmers: size of landholding**		
		Under 5 tan	5 tan- 9 tan	1 cho- 1.9 cho	2 cho- 2.9 cho	3 cho or more
1920-24	4.9	4.6	4.7	5.2	5.3	6.1
1910-19	5.4	4.2	5.3	5.8	6.3	7.2

*The official rate of exchange in 1940 was about $0.25 to 1.00 yen.
**One tan is approximately 0.245 acre and 10 tan is equal to 1 cho.

the influences associated with the transition to the second stage began to take effect from about 1920, which coincides generally with the acceleration of industrial-urban growth in Japan that became evident about this time. That the inverse pattern by income is a new pattern is further suggested by the fact that such a pattern is absent in both marital cohorts among the proprietors and agricultural workers, who are in "traditional" occupations.

The direct relationship between economic level and fertility among some groups may be due in part to greater incidence of fecundity impairments at the lower than at the higher economic levels. This is suggested by the higher incidence of childless unions at the lower than at the higher economic levels in those occupations in which a direct pattern of differential fertility is found. Childlessness during a period in Japanese history that generally saw an emphasis on familism is interpreted as being largely involuntary. It is also possible that the lower fertility of the less affluent in the early part of the present century was due to greater resort to induced abortion and infanticide in response to the harsh conditions of life. With the improvements in levels of living that became evident in the 1920's there may have occurred a decreasing incidence of control by abortion and infanticide in the lower status groups and an increase in control by contraception in the higher status groups from a different kind of motive—namely, to achieve and maintain a style of life whose standards were being established among them. It is not without significance that public discussion of contraception became evident in the early 1920's, although it was subsequently suppressed by a pronatalist, militaristic government.

Even for 1952, a projection of the prevailing duration-of-marriage specific rates indicates persistence of the inverse pattern of differential only among the salaried, as Table II shows.[10]

TABLE 2
PROJECTED FERTILITY OF JAPANESE WOMEN BY HUSBAND'S OCCUPATION
BY ECONOMIC STATUS, ACCORDING TO 1952 DURATION-OF-MARRIAGE
SPECIFIC BIRTH RATES

Occupation	Total	Economic status*			
		Lower	Lower-Middle	Upper-Middle	Upper
Total	3.44	3.53	2.96	3.60	4.01
Salaried	2.88	3.22	2.70	2.86	2.62
Proprietors	3.25	3.38	3.18	3.26	3.55
Laborers	3.72	3.44	2.77	3.71	5.25
Agriculture and forestry	4.13	3.92	3.32	4.64	4.62

*By monthly expenditure.

A 1957 study shows results consistent with the projected trends in that an inverse pattern by income is distinctly evident among the urban clerical and manual workers.

In summary, what the fertility trend in Japan shows us is that the recent decline is an acceleration of a trend that had its beginning with the industrialization and urbanization of that country. The pattern of differential fertility that emerged in the prewar period is indicative of that influence. That pattern is one that could have been anticipated from the experience of the Western populations that had been industrialized and urbanized much earlier. Postwar studies in Japan show that fertility control has been more widely practiced by the very groups that have the lower fertility in the population. As a matter of fact, even the postwar patterns of decline and diffusion of control practices suggest long-term influences of industrialization and urbanization at work. Of course, we cannot ignore the economic difficulties of the immediate postwar period that undoubtedly accelerated the long-term trend and facilitated the use of induced abortion and sterilization as acceptable means of fertility control. What appears to have happened is that the collapse of the pronatalist government with its programs of enforced austerity resulted in a relatively uninhibited play of those forces inherent in industrialization and urbanization which have long been pushing back against the government's deliberate attempts to contain them.

Fertility Differences in the Osaka Area:
An Attempt at Interpretation

Data from a sample survey of 1433 married women under 45 years of age in Osaka, the second largest metropolitan area, undertaken in 1956 by the author afforded an opportunity to test the plausibility of the interpretation just presented.[11]

Consistent with actual national fertility trend in recent years, the expected family size[12] of the Osaka area couples was small, showing a convergence of values on the narrow range of two to four children. That the decline in fertility was still in progress was indicated by the fact that the expected size was smaller for the younger and the more recently married in the present group; which, representing a metropolitan population, stands in the vanguard of national decline. This is consistent with the fertility trend in Japan since the time of this investigation in 1956.

Low expectations in family size among some of the couples were in part due to fecundity impairments. More than a third of the couples were classified as sub-fecund by the criteria used. Furthermore, impaired fecundity accounted for nearly all of the expected childless or one-child unions. However, the general decline in fertility evident among these couples did not appear to be due to an increase in the incidence of difficulties of this sort. Certainly there was no evidence that sub-fecundity was more prevalent now than when family size was larger. The low expectations in family size resulted from an increase in the number of small and moderate size families at the expense of very large families rather than from an increase in childlessness.

This involves changes in values and norms about family size. The overwhelming majority of the Osaka area wives considered as ideal a family of from two to four children with emphasis on the smaller number of two or three, and most of them approved of doing something to control the number and spacing of their children to achieve such a small family ideal. That changes have occurred in these attitudes recently was suggested by the small but consistent differences that were evident by age and duration of marriage. The younger and the more recently married women preferred smaller families and more frequently approved of family limitation than the older women and those married earlier. The differences were large between those who reached adulthood before World War II and those who reached it later. The influence of the social climate of the times was implied.

Consistent with these attitudes and values, nearly three out of four had already used or intended to use some means of family limitation, be it contraception, induced abortion, or sterilization. Again, generational differences were evident. The younger and the more recently married were more likely to do something to control their births than the older women and those married earlier.

Induced abortion was more likely among those who used contraception than those who did not as was found in the Mainichi surveys for the nation as a whole. Its rate was highest among those who had had unwanted pregnancies during use of contraception. Still there were some who relied exclusively on induced abortion as their sole means to control births. However, the age differentials for exclusive reliance on induced abortion was exactly opposite in direction to the age differentials with respect to contraceptive use, whether supplemented by induced abortion or not. While contraception was the more likely means among the younger women, exclusive reliance on induced abortion was more likely among the older women. The pattern which includes contraception appeared to be the more modern one; the use of induced abortion alone appeared to be a more traditional pattern.

Users of contraception differed in the effectiveness and timing of their use. Compared with American couples, the Osaka area couples not only began their use of contraception later but were also less effective in their use in terms of their ability to avoid unwanted pregnancies. Even so the availability of induced abortion either as an alternative or as a supplementary technique of control would serve these couples rather effectively in the attainment of their small family goals. Thus, the final result would in fact be rather small families. Furthermore, the younger women were starting use sooner and were showing greater effectiveness in use than the older women.

Most significantly from the point of view of the present discussion, the direction of differences in the expected family size observed among the Osaka area couples was generally predictable from the hypothesis that fertility decline and values, attitudes, and control practices consistent with such decline are due to conditions brought on by industrialization and urbanization of Japan.

First of all, the analysis by income showed that its influence was negligible once occupation and education were held constant. There was, however, evidence that the pattern of differential fertility by income might currently be in flux. The age differentials suggested that the pattern might be shifting from a direct to an inverse one consistent with the transition model alluded to earlier.

Four variables were used to indicate the couple's involvement in the industrial-urban way of life: education, occupation, community background, and wife's labor force status. When each of these variables was considered singly in relation to the fertility variables, education showed the most consistent and the largest differences. Surprisingly, community background taken alone did not make much difference as far as fertility characteristics of these couples were concerned. Wife's working status showed influences only when her work experience was motivated by individualistic considerations (such as, working because she likes to rather than because she had to) or carried out in extra-familial contexts (i.e., employed by someone else presumably away from home). But most important of all, when education, occupation, and community background were considered jointly, the differences in fertility characteristics were more marked than when any one of these was considered alone. For our purposes, we considered those wives who had at least high school education, who had always lived in urban communities, and whose husbands were in white-collar occupations, as most involved in the industrial-urban way of life and therefore most "modern"; and those wives who had only primary education, who had lived in rural communities, and whose husbands were in either proprietary or blue-collar occupations, as least involved in the industrial-urban way of life and therefore least "modern", or most "traditional". Two intermediate types were distinguished by whether the wives had two or just one of the "modern" characteristics. As Table III shows, "modernity" is associated with lower fertility and the other fertility characteristics consistent with lower fertility except sub-fecundity and exclusive reliance on induced abortion. Sub-fecundity is less apparent in the groups with low fertility, and exclusive reliance on induced abortion is strongly associated with "traditionalism". These patterns generally held whether the wife was under or over 30 years of age.

TABLE 3
FERTILITY AND FAMILY PLANNING AMONG OSAKA AREA COUPLES BY SELECTED
SOCIOECONOMIC CHARACTERISTICS (1956)

Combination of wife's education, wife's community background, and husband's occupation	No. of couples	Percentage who have used or intend to use		Mean ideal family size	Percentage					Mean expected family size
		Percentage involuntarily sub-fecund			approving family limitation	who have used contraception	effective planners	either contraception, induced abortion, or sterilization	only induced abortion	
Total	1,433	32		2.92	83	38	9	73	23	2.97
High school+, indigenous urbanite, white-collar	222	28		2.78	92	54	13	80	15	2.70
Two of above	378	30		2.82	88	46	11	76	19	2.82
One of above	522	34		2.96	78	34	8	70	23	3.06
Elementary, rural migrant, proprietor or blue-collar	311	33		3.07	77	26	6	69	32	3.17

These findings from the Osaka area support the interpretation that while the postwar difficulties may have accelerated the diffusion of fertility control and decline, they have not changed the pattern of such diffusion most probably instigated and facilitated by advances in industrialization of Japanese economy and urbanization of her society.

Conclusions

The postwar legislations in Japan probably served to facilitate but not instigate the diffusion of fertility control in the population. Industrial-urban transformation of Japanese society was well advanced so that fertility decline anticipated by the theory of demographic transition was already occurring even while the prewar government was advocating and implementing pronatalist policies. The rapidity with which diffusion has progressed in recent years is not due so much to the effectiveness of government-sponsored programs of family planning as to the effectiveness of social transformation affecting family life brought on by accelerated industrialization and urbanization of Japan. What this implies is that family planning will diffuse throughout the rest of the population as industrial-urban influences diffuse and even if the sponsored programs remain ineffective as some critics believe they are.

It is also unlikely that induced abortion will fall out of fashion either by fiat or by popular choice. Most criticisms of the Eugenic Protection Law which legalized induced abortion have come from Western sources or from natives who are sensitive to Western criticisms. But the West is no longer unanimous in its stand against induced abortion. It is likely that the Japanese will continue to try contraception but upon failure do the next logical thing: have the fetus removed by artificial means. And they will do this probably with less and less criticism from home and abroad.

The Japanese will not stop having children. They will continue to have children but fewer of them and when they want them. To the extent that timing becomes an important factor, the crude birth rate is likely to fluctuate, rather than continue to decline, depending on whatever social and economic conditions affect the individual couples' decisions to have a child now or later.

Even as we make these generalizations on the basis of past studies and by speculation, we are made acutely aware of the need for further research along several lines. There is certainly need for a systematic analysis of the precise role of legislation in the diffusion of population control in Japan. If the Japanese experience is to be used as a model in now developing countries, the nature of that model must be clarified much more than it is at present. By the same token, there is need for evaluation of the effectiveness of the sponsored programs of family planning education and guidance currently in force as far as their total impact on the national trend is concerned. If indirect influences are significant, they should be specified.

A more thorough fact-finding study with respect to family size values, attitudes and practices of birth control, and actual fertility is needed to supplement the already available series of data such as provided by the Mainichi surveys. Research somewhat akin to that conducted by the author in the Osaka area needs to be extended to other areas and to the national scene. Such undertakings would add much to our knowledge about the relationship between a variety of important factors affecting fertility behavior now known only in tantalizing fragments. But more importantly, such studies should make explicit what the family size goals of the Japanese are coming to be and the factors that influence their timing of births. This knowledge will help Japanese demographers in making more realistic short-term projections, and the Japanese government and businesses that rely on such information.

One other kind of study that is sorely needed is that which focuses on the actual process of diffusion of family planning ideas, knowledge and practice. In the experiences of many populations, the Japanese included, there is a point in the diffusion process when the idea suddenly catches on and whether to do or not to do family planning is no longer strictly a choice that is individually made but socially expected. To learn how and when that shift occurs is immensely useful for birth control campaigns in countries where the practice is just starting. Parts in Japan where there is far less than universal acceptance of family planning would offer ideal places for studies of this kind.

FOOTNOTES

1. For a comprehensive study of Japan's past and present population, see Irene B. Taeuber, *Population of Japan,* Princeton: Princeton University Press, 1958.

2. Crude birth rates and crude death rates are in terms of 1,000 of the population per year. These and other statistics unless indicated otherwise are from a pamphlet, "Selected Statistics Indicating the Demographic Situation of Japan," published in 1961 by the Institute of Population Problems of the Ministry of Health and Welfare.

3. The rate was 0.96, which means that only 96 per cent of a cohort of women subject to the age-specific female birth and death rates prevailing in Japan in 1958 would be replaced by their daughters in the next generation.

4. As far as the crude rate is concerned. While there is considerable room for improvement

in the death rates in infancy and for specific causes in the various ages, these improvements are not likely to show up in the crude rate because Japan's population is "aging."

5. The expectation of life at birth for male increased from 59.6 according to the mortality risks of 1950-52 to 64.9 according to the mortality risks of 1959-60; and for female, it increased from 63.0 to 69.7 during this period. The proportion of persons 65 and over increased from 4.9 per cent in 1950 to 5.7 per cent in 1960.

6. There is hint that the upsurge of demand for labor in the urban areas in recent years has resulted in a shortage of labor on the farms, thus forcing unexpectedly rapid mechanization which met strong resistance in the past when labor was not only abundant but also redundant.

7. The National Eugenic Law was passed in 1940, modeled after a similar law in Nazi Germany. It was strictly eugenic in intent and while prescribing compulsory sterilization for "undesirables" generally proscribed induced abortion. See, Juitsu Kitaoka, *Jinko kajo to kanzen koyo (Over-population and full employment),* (Tokyo: Daiyamondosha, 1956), pp. 113.

8. E. F. Penrose, *Population Theories and Their Application, with Special Reference to Japan,* Stanford, Calif.: Stanford University Press, 1934, p. 108.

9. Adapted from data presented in Tatsuo Honda, "Sabetsu Shussanryoku ni tsuite (On differential fertility)" *Jinko mondai kenkyu,* 68 (June, 1957), p. 10.

10. Adapted from Table 34 in Tatsuo Honda, *Sengo nibon no jinko mondai (kaiteiban)* (Population problems in postwar Japan [revised edition]), Tokyo: Institute of Population Problems (1956), Ministry of Welfare, Research Monograph No. 114, pp. 66–67.

11. Yuzuru Takeshita, "Socioeconomic Correlates of Urban Fertility in Japan," Unpublished Ph.D. Dissertation, Department of Sociology, University of Michigan, 1962.

12. Expected family size refers to the number of children one expects to end up having by the time she is about 45 years of age. For a discussion of its reliability in estimating actual fertility as used in the U.S., see Arthur Campbell, P. K. Whelpton, and Richard F. Tomasson, "The Reliability of Birth Expectations of U.S. Wives," Paper read at the International Population Union Conference, September, 1961 (Mimeographed).

RITUAL KINSHIP IN JAPAN:
ITS VARIABILITY AND RESILIENCY

Harumi Befu

The first anthropological report on the formal ritual kinship institution in Japan was presented in Western language by Iwao Ishino (1953) in his case study of laborers' organization.[1] This was followed by a theoretical interpretation of some ritual kinship groups of Japan by Bennett and Despres (1960). The theoretical thinking presented in these works was amplified and further developed in Bennett and Ishino's *Paternalism in the Japanese Economy* (1963).[2] Other than these, there have not been any anthropological works in Western languages which are specifically addressed to the subject of Japanese ritual kinship.

Since before the last war, Japanese social scientists have been studying this institution, with a respectable amount of accumulated literature of excellent quality to their credit. The most recent systematic discussion of ritual kinship groups — mostly those of the underworld — was presented by Iwai (1963). What emerges from a survey of this literature is the variety of forms this institution takes in Japan, a variety about which we were not at all adequately informed through the few works already available in the West.

The purpose of this paper is first to summarize the essential features (which may be regarded as the defining criteria) of Japanese ritual kinship groups, and secondly, to outline the several variables or parameters of the ritual kinship institution in Japan in order to convey some idea of its variability. We shall discuss each variable separately with examples, and suggest whenever possible the bases for the variation along any given parameter. Thirdly, this paper will discuss the mode of integration of this institution in the Japanese society and attempt to predict in which sectors of the Japanese society ritual kinship system is likely to survive in the future. It will be shown that there are two bases of integration, one related to the defining features of the ritual kinship system and the other to the variability of the forms they take.

Before I discuss the essential features of the ritual kinship system in Japan, I would like to introduce the pair concepts of "instrumental" and "expressive" which, ultimately derived from Talcott Parsons, Ishino (1953: 704) and Bennett and Ishino (1963: 87) have used in their analysis of Japanese ritual kinship system. Instrumental activities, as applied to the ritual kinship groups refers to what the group is ostensibly organized for, the "business" of the group. It may be agriculture, mining, lumbering, construction, labor racketeering, gambling, *sumo* wrestling, organized crime, stevedoring, arts, crafts, politics or supernatural benefits. The groups which carry out these instrumental activities, however, are

Befu — *From Sociologus,* Vol. 14, No., (1964), pp. 150-169. Reprinted by permission.

organized to carry out other types of activities which tend to promote solidarity within the group and provide common value-orientation; and these types of activities, referred to as expressive acts, facilitate the attainment of the instrumental goal by the group. The expressive structure of a given group tends closely to parallel the instrumental structure of the group, but it is analytically different from it, and it is in the expressive structure that ritual kinship plays its part. These concepts are extremely useful for the analysis of the ritual kinship system and will be utilized in the discussion to follow. It will be seen that the structure of particular ritual kinship groups is closely adapted to the requirements of carrying out certain instrumental activities.

Essential Features

As the essential, or defining features of the ritual kinship system, we shall discuss the following five: (1) functional diffuseness and particularism, (2) hierarchical organization, (3) economic dependence, (4) solidarity, and (5) symbolic expressions as seen in the employment of ritual kinship terminology and other practices.

(1) *Functional diffuseness and particularism.* Interpersonal relations in any ritual kinship institution, by definition, resemble the kinship or family relation in one way or another in situations where no true kinship relation is ordinarily involved. Typically a ritual kinship group is a gemeinschaft organization, a primary group in which kinship organization of the society is used as the model. Among other things, this implies commitment to one's ritual kin, not because of some abstract or objective reasons, but simply because he is in ritual kinship relation with him. It also means that the sphere of interaction between fictive kin is not limited, say to work situations, but pervades throughout the whole life. In short, the relationship is particularistic and functionally diffuse.

(2) *Hierarchical organization.* There is always in Japanese ritual kinship groups a hierarchical organization of leadership and followership between members of a group. The most common such status relation is that between ritual father (commonly called *oyakata* or *oyabun*) and ritual child *(kokata* or *kobun).* Even ritual siblingship, a relation between two individuals who are both ritual children to a same ritual parent, is seldom an egalitarian relationship, but ordinarily recognizes seniority on the basis of the time of induction into the group. Only if they are initiated into the group at the same time are they strictly equal to one another. Such egalitarian relationship is decidedly secondary compared with the hierarchical organization in Japanese ritual kinship.

The vertical relationship is expressed in the right of the ritual parent to exercise control over his ritual children and in the duty of the latter to obey the former. Although normatively the authority of the ritual parent is said to be absolute, in practice the amount of his authority varies a great deal from one type of ritual kinship group to another. As an example of minimum authority, ritual kinship relation established at life crises of a person may be cited. (Mogami 1938, Yanagida 1937.) This type of ritual kinship was prevalent in rural Japan until a few decades ago, but has much declined in postwar years. At birth, for instance, the midwife becomes a ritual parent, called *toriageoya* ("delivery parent") to the new born baby, and the relationship continues for life, expressed in exchange of greetings and gift-giving. The ritual child is expected to consult his ritual parent for advice in times of trouble and respect her opinion, and he is supposed to visit her at New Year's and other ceremonial occasions to pay respect. Beyond these, however, the ritual child apparently has little obligation to the ritual parent. The same can be said of ritual kinship relations established at other life crises, such as naming, illness, puberty and marriage.

Examples of the opposite extreme are the miners' group (Oyama 1926, Matsushima 1950, 1954) and the street-stall merchants' group (Iwai 1953, 1954, 1963: 57—115) in which the authority of the ritual parent has been said to be "absolute". Although literature often has one believe that in these and some other ritual kinship groups "absolute" obedience is demanded of a ritual child, this is probably an overstatement. Such a claim is more an expression of the fact that a good ritual parent knows how much obedience he can expect and does not demand any more than being an expression of literal truth.

The amount of control a ritual parent gains over his ritual child seems to depend in part on the nature of the instrumental goal of the group. If the instrumental goal of the group has already been accomplished in the past, the authority of the ritual parent cannot be great. The reason why a "crisis" ritual parent does not have much power over his ritual child is that the instrumental act which binds the two, namely, carrying the ritual child through a life crisis, is an event which was accomplished in the past — at the time the ritual relationship was contracted. There is thus nothing at present or in the future which binds the two instrumentally.

If, on the other hand, there is some instrumental goal toward which the ritual kinship group is working, then the ritual parent gains at least some control over his ritual children. If the instrumental goal is primarily political, as in the underworld gang or ultra-rightist political groups, then of course, even without the expressive (i.e., ritual kinship) aspect of the group, the leader already has a great deal of power over his henchmen. Ritual kinship relation, that is the expressive structure, of these groups serves to reinforce the authority of the leader. If, on the other hand, the group is instrumentally oriented, not toward political ends, but primarily toward economic objectives, such as street-stall selling *(tekiya)* or agriculture, the ritual parent gains control to the degree that the economic resources are scarce and unavailable without joining some ritual kinship group. For example, a ritual parent of a group of street-stall merchants has a great deal of power because he and others like him control all the areas where stalls may be set up and thereby monopolize the occupation.

Somewhat different from power and control, though related to it, is the diffuse authority of the ritual parent in daily affairs. Ritual children are expected to consult him and seek his advice even for such matters as family quarrels or daughter's marriage. His advice in these affairs, which are clearly outside the group's instrumental activities, is generally respected and honored.

(3) *Economic dependence.* Another expressive function of the ritual kinship group is found in the economic sphere of life. Although economic dependence is reciprocal between the ritual parent and child, the preponderant dependence is by the ritual child on his ritual parent. It is important to point out that ritual kinship groups are very often organized in those strata of the society in which personal saving is almost nil and even day-to-day subsistence is rather precarious. Not only in illness of a ritual child himself, but at birth, illness, marriage, and death of his family members, a ritual parent is expected to carry some if not all of the financial burden. Here one strong motivation for a man to join a ritual kinship group lies in the economic benefit he expects to derive from membership in such a group.

The amount of economic support which the ritual parent is expected to dispense may be considerable. In certain parts of rural Japan, until before the last war, ritual kinship groups were organized in which a wealthy, main (or stem) family was ritual parent to its genealogically related branches established by junior sons as well as to unrelated families established by its former servants and others (Ariga 1938; Bennett and Ishino 1963: 201−223; Kitano 1940; Fukutake 1954: 42 to 76). (We shall discuss the superimposition of ritual kinship upon true kinship later.) When a junior son or a servant established a separate household, his house, house lot, household furnishings, possibly a year's supply of food, and a plot of farmland were often given as gifts by the ritual parent. The ritual parent in this example must be able not only to provide relatively small amounts of economic help from time to time, but also to expend a large portion of his wealth at the time new households are established and thus a new ritual child initiated.

While ritual children thus expect to receive economic favors from their ritual parent, the latter also expects economic services. Because ritual children are not economically well off, and certainly not as well off as their ritual parent, their economic services usually amount to providing free labor services. In ritual kinship groups of rural north Japan, as part of his expressive duty, a ritual child was expected to provide assistance without recompense at memorial service, funeral, wedding and other ceremonial occasions of his ritual parent's household. In miners' groups the ritual children were expected to support their ritual parent until his death after he became too weak to work in the mine and retired.

(4) *Solidarity*. In addition to the political and economic functions of the ritual kinship group, we must not forget the strong sense of solidarity which arises as a result of the functionally diffuse and particularistic relationship between members. This solidarity is perhaps best expressed in terms of the concept of *on*, or indebtedness—a concept so central to the Japanese culture. The concept of indebtedness has three major components. First, indebtedness is a one-way process: a superior bestows indebtedness *(on)* to his inferior and never the other way around. In the ritual kinship system a ritual child becomes indebted to his ritual parent for the economic support and innumerable kinds of other favors he receives in expressive spheres as well as for the guidance and training, if any, he receives in instrumental aspects. Second, this *on* is at least in theory unfathomable and therefore never fully returnable. However, third, one must try his best to return at least "one-ten-thousandth" of it (Benedict 1946: 114−132) through his loyalty and services. This concept of indebtedness provides a binding bond which is the basis of the ritual child's obligation to submit himself to his ritual parent's authority and avail himself for his services.

(5) *Symbolic expressions*. One of the most salient symbolic expressions of the ritual kinship system is the employment of terms of reference and/or address which are quasi-kinship and are distinguishable from true kinship terms. Some prefix or suffix is added to true kinship terms, by which addition one can recognize that the relationship denoted by the term is not real but ritual kinship (Ishino 1953: 697−698). For example, *-kata* and *-bun*, roughly meaning "status of" or "role of" are suffixes of common use, as in *oya-kata* ("ritual parent") or *ko-bun* ("ritual child"). Somewhat different examples are found in ritual kinship contracted at life crises, such as birth, naming, illness, puberty, and marriage. A prefix is generally added to the true kin terms to designate a ritual kin of this type. Thus, the midwife of an infant is its *toriage-oya* ("parent who delivers").

A detailed study of the actual usages of ritual terms is yet to be undertaken. In general, however, we may say that the usage follows the same rules as true kinship terms as discussed by Befu and Norbeck (1958) in that in address, individuals in superior status are called by kin terms whereas those in inferior positions are called by personal names. One major difference is that in ritual kinship terminology reference and address terms, when both exist for a given status, are the same, whereas in true kinship terminology they are generally different.

Although terms which can be clearly recognized as quasi-kinship are generally used among ritual kin, sometimes terms which are ordinarily used among true kin are also employed. For example, among the miners (Matsushima 1950: 64) the ritual father is called *otossan,* his wife *okkasan,* and ritual elder brother *anisan.* These are variant terms used in addressing, respectively, true father, mother, and elder brother. Similar examples of the use of "true" kinship terms in the context of ritual kinship among street-stall merchants are given by Iwai (1953: 49). These examples show that ritual kinship institution in Japan cannot be clearly separated from true kinship at least by means of terminology alone.

Another symbolic expression of the ritual kinship system is the initiation ceremony. The degree of elaboration and formalism of this ceremony varies from one type of ritual kinship group to another. But in most cases it involves exchange of *sake* drinks and taking of an oath to be ritual parent and child to one another. The ceremony, in elaborate cases, may be conducted in front of an altar for a guardian deity and with an intermediary, and some of the elements of the ceremony are taken from the wedding ceremony. (Bennett and Ishino 1963: 48–51; Ishino 1953: 703–704; Iwai 1963: 146–160.)

The solidarity of the ritual kinship group is also symbolized in the ritualized greetings known as *jingi* which ritual parent and child or members of different ritual kinship groups exchange with one another on special occasions (Iwai 1963: 261–271). These greetings which are peculiar to ritual kinship groups serve to separate them from the rest of the society and serve as a Durkheimian collective representation.

The five features of ritual kinship institution listed above may be regarded as its defining criteria. They define the expressive structure of the concrete group called ritual kinship. While sharing essentially the same expressive structure, ritual kinship groups differ in their instrumental goals from farming to wrestling to gambling, as mentioned above. Groups vary also in the degree to which one or the other of the two analytical structures is emphasized, a point which is discussed in great detail by Bennett and Despres (1960) and Bennett and Ishino (1963). For example these authors describe a group of a lumber dealer and his ritual children in which the lumber dealer takes advantage of his ritual children's ideological (i.e., expressive) commitment and obligation to accept his authority and exploit them for his personal gain without regards to the welfare of the ritual children. In this example, emphasis on the instrumental activity of the group is paramount while expressive structure is being exploited. On the other hand the instrumental activities of the group may be negligible while what keeps the group going is the expressive structure. Such is the case with the so-called "crisis" ritual kinship system.

Other Variables

While all ritual kinship groups have an expressive structure defined in terms of the above listed five features, they vary considerably in other respects. We shall examine some of the more important variables in the following and discuss them with illustrations. The variables to be discussed are: (1) unit of the group, (2) size of the group, (3) kinsmen in ritual kinship, (4) recruitment, and (5) training.

1. *Unit of the group.* Although ritual relation is always initially contracted between two or more individuals, because of the strong tendency in Japan to identify individuals with their families and to treat the family as the basic social unit (Beardsley 1951), ritual kinship is often organized with families as the basic units of the group. In such a case, members of a family tend to take on the same role and attitude as the principal individual through whom the ritual relation is contracted. Thus the wife and children of a man who is a ritual child are also ritual children to his ritual parent and to the latter's wife and children. This is the case, for example, with the ritual kinship groups in rural Japan (Hattori 1955; Kitano 1940).

In some groups, on the other hand, the individual remains the basic unit. Ritual kinship groups of miners are typically such groups. Among them, in fact, the provision for daily living in the group life is so adequate that miners claim that they do not need a family (Oyama 1926: 67). Other types of ritual kinship groups in which individuals are the units are those of labor gangs, street-stall merchants, sumo wrestlers, and geisha girls.

The point of distinction between the two types of units is that in the first type, in which the family is the basic unit, an individual without family *cannot* become a full-fledged constituent member, whereas in the second type, one *need not* have a family to be a constituent unit of the group. It is not denied that even in those groups whose unit is individual, a married member's wife and children also tend to take on the same role attitudes toward other members as he himself.

The basic unit tends to be the family when the instrumental activity of the group is one which is carried out by families rather than individuals. Farming is a prime example. On the other hand, the basic unit is generally the individual when the instrumental activity depends on the performance of the individual, and his family cannot directly contribute toward the instrumental goal. Mining or construction labor are good examples of this type.

2. *Size of the group.* A ritual kinship group in Japan always has one person or family at the top of its hierarchy, others (ritual children) taking inferior positions in the hierarchical organization. The size of the group, therefore, depends on the number of ritual children in it. (One modification to this formula will be introduced later.) A major determinant of the size of the group is the nature of instrumental activity it pursues. If the instrumental activity is such that the group, particularly the ritual parent, would not gain economically or politically by increasing the number of ritual children, the size of the group tends to remain small. The minimum limit is two, one ritual parent and one ritual child. This is the case with many of the "crisis" ritual kinships. "Crisis" ritual kinship is thus a dyadic relationship. Even if the same person is ritual parent to two or more ritual children, he and all his ritual children taken together do not constitute a single group. Instead, such a situation results in a series of dyadic relationships with one overlapping member.

If, on the other hand, the instrumental activities of the group can be carried out more effectively by a larger group, the size of the group tends to increase. For example, in the type of construction work which Ishino describes, if the work crew is too small, it may not be able to carry out the required work. The group then will tend to enlarge so that the work requirement can be accomplished.

While the group may tend to enlarge, there are two major factors which tend to mitigate against an indefinite increase in size. One factor has to do with the availability of resources and the other with what may be called the gemeinschaft requirement of the group. The ritual kinship group needs scarce resources in its instrumental and/or expressive activities. If, for example, the instrumental activity of the group involves imparting of a skill, such as sumo wrestling, from the ritual parent to child, the scarce resource is the time available to the ritual parent for training all his ritual children adequately. Among street-stall merchants, the ritual parent must have a large enough territory so that all his ritual children can support themselves by engaging in business within that territory. On the expressive side, if, for example, a ritual child falls ill and needs financial support for subsistence and medication without contributing to the instrumental end of the group, the ritual parent is expected to provide the necessary support. Naturally, the larger the number of ritual children, the greater the ritual parent's resources have to be. The ritual parent, then, cannot recruit more children than his resources would allow.

This limitation based on the limited amount of resources is modified, as Ishino points out (1953: 704—705), by the fact that a man's ritual children can in turn become ritual parents of others, the whole group thus becoming three generational. Through this process of generation, the group can further grow in size, provided that members of the second generation can acquire the necessary resources to establish themselves as ritual parents. When the resource is time, naturally each ritual child has as much of this resource as his ritual parent and can easily in turn become a ritual parent. If the required resource is farmland, on the other hand, a ritual child cannot so easily acquire additional land. His chance of acquiring a ritual child of his own, therefore, is less than if his critical resources are time and skill.

The second limitation to the size of a ritual kinship group — the gemeinschaft requirement — is based on the fact that the group must, in order to perform its expressive functions, remain small enough so that face-to-face intimacy can be maintained by sufficient amount of interaction among members, particularly between the ritual parent and children. The critical factor here, then, is the amount of time available for the ritual parent to establish and maintain a gemeinschaft relationship with all his ritual children. For this reason, although a group can grow in size indefinitely through the process of generation, when the size of the group becomes extremely large, the group tends to split into several segments, the point of segmentation being ritual brothers who have ritual children and grandchildren of their own — somewhat like a segmentary lineage system.

Typically the size of an unsegmented group is no more than twenty or thirty. Bennett and Ishino give a round figure of twenty as the maximum size (1963: 77). The ritual kinship group Nakamura (1959) reports from rural Tsushima has twenty-two members. Among miners, Oyama says (1926, 30 : 68) that a ritual parent has a maximum of about 15 ritual children. The two laborers' groups which Ishino discussed have nine and seven members, respectively.

3. *True kin in ritual kinship group.* It may seem strange that a ritual kinship relation may be superimposed on true kinship relations. For ritual kinship is supposed to perform the functions which true kinship does in situations where true kinship ties are absent. Yet, as we noted above, overlap of true and ritual kinship has been known to occur in rural Japan. Here, a number of farming families are organized into a ritual kinship group, the core of which is composed of patrilineally related families. According to Kitano (1940: 82), the most normal form of ritual kinship group in Yamanashi prefecture is for the main family of the *dozoku* (a corporate group of patrilineally related families) to be the ritual parent

and the branches to be the principal ritual children, to which are added as ritual children the branches established by servants and other totally unrelated families. These families not related to the core nontheless enjoy the rights and privileges almost equal to the genelogical branches of the main family.[3]

It may be noted here that in the core of the group, the ritual parent-child relationship does not necessarily coincide with father-son relationship, that is, the head of the ritual parent family is not always the father of the heads of the ritual child-branch families. For the genelogical connections between the main and branch families generally go many generations back. If a younger son has branched out in the present generation to set up a separate family, then and only then would the genealogical and ritual kinship relations coincide. Such a situation, however, is uncommon because as stated above, it is a major economic undertaking to establish a household for a ritual child, something which a ritual parent can afford to do only once or twice in his lifetime.

In contrast to the above groups in which genealogically related families constitute the core of a ritual kin group, there are others in which no two members are related genealogically. If there are kinsmen in such a group, this is only accidental. Absence of blood relatives in these groups is due to several factors. For one thing, these groups are organized in a social setting, such as in cities, where a large number of kinsmen are not concentrated. At the same time, availability of a number of different kinds of occupations one may go into reduces the chance that two kinsmen enter a same occupation and join a same ritual kin group. That the absence of true kinsmen is simply accidental is illustrated in one of Ishino's examples in which a ritual kinship group of laborers includes the ritual parent's true son, a younger brother and a brother-in-law (Ishino 1953: 702).

4. *Recruitment.* Although both Eisenstadt (1956: 90) in his generalized discussion of "ritualized personal relations" and Ishino (1953: 697) in his case study of a labor boss system regard ritual kinship to be voluntarily entered into, this is not necessarily the case in Japan. Especially when the basic unit of the group is the family, the relationship once established, tends to continue generation after generation. Such is the case with the ritual kinship groups of northern Japan mentioned above, where the status in the ritual kinship group is inherited from father to son. Thus the heir of a ritual child remains a ritual child of his father's ritual parent and of the latter's heir.

A somewhat different situation takes place in Yamanashi prefecture (Fukutake 1954: 208—242). Here, although the heir of a ritual child is supposed to remain a ritual child of his father's ritual parent, the heir need not continue the relationship if the latter has declined in economic power and is not likely to be able to perform his expected expressive functions for him. The heir in such a case would terminate the ritual kinship relation with his father's ritual parent and initiate a new relation with another who is better-to-do.

When the relationship is ascribed or inherited, there is a problem of retaining adequate competence among members to carry out the group's activities, particularly its instrumental activities. Instrumental activities engaged in by ritual kinship groups in which the status is inherited may be divided into two types. In one type the instrumental activity is so generalized, as in farming, that the question of competence seldom arises. The other kind of instrumental activity is highly specialized, as in arts. A genuine problem arises here when the son is not competent enough in the particular art to succeed to the family occupation. In such a case the problem is resolved, as I have discussed elsewhere (Befu 1962), by legally adopting one of the promising disciples as the heir of the family in favor of the own son. A more common solution for a group whose instrumental activity is highly specialized is to make the relationship attainable only through achievement, that is, only those who manifest competence in the particular instrumental activity are eligible for membership in the ritual kinship group. I do not imply that in generalized occupations the problem of competence never arises; it does for example if the only son is feeble-minded. And in such a case the problem is solved in the same way as in specialized occupations.

In groups such as the underworld gang, street-stall merchants, miners, geisha girls, etc., whose membership unit is the individual, the relationship tends to be contracted individually rather than inherited. Whether there are ritual kinship groups which prohibit genealogical succession of all positions in the group I do not know.

There are ritual kin groups, however, in which certain key positions in the group cannot be inherited by a true kin such as a son. An example are the street-stall merchants (Ishino 1953: 697). Among them, the ritual parent who controls a given territory and parcels portions of it out to his ritual children is forbidden to transmit his economic interests and his sphere of influence to his true son. At the motivational level, the rule against nepotism in this case is an attempt to guard strategic resources of the group which should be transmitted only to ritual children as a reward for years of hard work.

But there is an additional reason at the level of collectivity. If a group is to survive, a competent individual must fill the key, leadership position, and the group cannot afford to let the leader's affect, that is, his desire to have his son succeed him, interfere with this requirement. The nepotism rule, then, is an institutionalized means of insuring that the key position of the group will be succeeded to by a member of the group who was not only recruited on the basis of his qualifications but also has proved his competence by working up from the rank and file.

When the ritual kinship relation is voluntary, we can distinguish between two types of motivation behind one's entrance into such a pact: instrumental and expressive. There are certain occupations, e.g., organized crime, street-stall selling, sumo wrestling, etc., which are monopolized by one or another ritual kin group. No one who is not a member of some ritual kinship group can engage in these occupations. The underlying motivation for joining a ritual kin group here is the desire to engage in the business of the group; it is instrumental. Expressive benefits one receives are consequences of joining the group. There are other occupations, e.g., farming, which are not monopolized by ritual kinship groups and therefore can be engaged in without joining such a group. But one joins it in this case because of the advantages one sees in the expressive functions the group performs for its members. The underlying motivation here is expressive. Naturally these are ideally dichotomized types of motivation. Those who join for instrumental reasons must see expressive advantages of the group as well, and those who join for expressive reasons must also realize the instrumental advantage of the group.

5. *Training period.* Ritual kinship groups differ as to whether a training period is required before one is admitted as a full-fledged member. More accurately, whether training is required depends, not so much on the group as on the type of occupation pursued by the group. In some, such as farming in north Japan, mining and street-stall selling, and geisha girls, training is required. Formal initiation into the group may take some years after the training began, and is often marked with a formal ceremony. In other occupational groups, such as laborers, there is no formal

training prior to the initiation of the ritual relation. The significance of a training period may be analyzed from two points of view, expressive and instrumental. During the training period a novice learns not only the skills necessary for the instrumental activities of the group (which is the manifest reason for requiring a training period) but also internalizes at the same time the expressive value of the group, the authority of the ritual parent, the necessity to depend on him, etc. As a result, such a group tends to develop a much stronger solidarity, cohesiveness, than one which does not require any training period. A further consequence is that the training tends to foster conservatism − the more intensive and extended the training period, the stronger the conservatism − in the occupation pursued by the group. For methods and techniques used by the ritual parent are accepted as the only right way of pursuing the occupation.

Integration

A thesis I wish to advance in this paper is that ritual kinship in Japan is not something which clearly stands apart from the rest of the society but that in many ways it imperceptibly merges into it. In the discussion above, I have used only those examples in which the ritual kinship institution is clearly recognizable both by the use of quasi-kinship terms and by pronounced expressive qualities. In reality, however, it is not always possible clearly to distinguish ritual kinship groups from other kinds of groups. How real this difficulty is may be illustrated with the ritual kin groups of rural Japan, mentioned above from time to time, whose core consists of patrilineally related families but which include unrelated families. Social scientists call these groups *dozoku* and do not generally speak of them as ritual kinship groups in the same breath as, say the miners' groups or street-stall merchants' groups. They instead consider it is a modified form of true kinship group. My decision to include them in the category of ritual kinship groups was based on the fact that quasi-kinship terms are used in these groups and that some of the members are not true kin of the core, in addition to the manifestation of the expressive characteristics of this institution defined above. Argument as to whether such groups are modified true kinship groups or whether they are ritual kin groups is rather futile. What is important is that if we ignore the rather arbitrary requirement of the use of quasi-kinship terms, the distinction between the two becomes most difficult to discern, since in the Japanese mind a dozoku may have no, one, or a dozen unrelated families in it. In fact, the community Kitano investigated consisted of three groups which contained, respectively, fourteen, two and no unrelated families, in addition to the partrilineally related core families. Ritual kinship terms are used between the main family and its genealogical branches in all these groups. Thus a dozoku is a kinship group capable of incorporating unrelated families and employing ritual kinship terminology. Thus it becomes difficult to maintain a clear distinction between ritual kinship and true kinship.

If true and ritual kinship relations are hard to distinguish, so are ritual kinship and social relationships which are neither true nor ritual kinship. This is illustrated in Suginohara's case study (1953). In some communities in northern Hyogo prefecture near Kyoto, artisans, such as masons, carpenters, and gardeners, often have a ritual kinship relation with certain wealthy families. These artisans, in order to become ritual children, go through a formal initiatory ceremony. Thereafter ritual kinship terms are used toward one another and the familiar expressive organization in economic and political spheres is observed. But there are other artisans of the same occupations who, called *deiri*, do not have the ritual kinship relation to the client because the initiation ceremony has never been performed. They thus do not call one another by ritual kinship terms. But significantly, some of them have the same kind of expressive relation to the client as the latter's formally initiated ritual children. Here is a case, then, which is for all practical purposes, ritual kinship without the use of the proper terminology to distinguish it as such.

Bennett and Ishino's discussion of various types of laborers' groups corroborates with the view presented here that many social groups in Japan resemble the ideal typical ritual kinship groups as defined here in varying degrees. They call the most ideal typical form "labor boss system", a somewhat less ideal typical one "boss-henchman system", and the form least like the ideal type "patron-client system". (1963: 200.) These systems are differentiated on the basis of the extent to which relative emphasis is placed on the ideological values surrounding the expressive functions of the group and on the instrumental goal of the group. In the ideal typical system, there is an even balance between the two. In the boss-henchman system, the ideological system is exploited for the sake of achieving an instrumental goal. In the patron-client system also, the primary emphasis is on the instrumental activities but at the same time the ideological principles are attenuated.

Many traditional arts and crafts, such as music, tea ceremony, swordsmanship, and dance, also have an organization which manifests the characteristics of ritual kinship institution, except the fact that the formal use of ritual kinship terms is not observed. Nishiyama, who has analyzed a large number of schools of arts and crafts, states as one of the three characteristics of these groups that (1959: 26) "the master and disciples are organized into a quasi-family group . . ." The hierarchical relation between the master and disciples is rigidly maintained, and the master gains a considerable amount of power over his disciples, including the power to expel them from his school. In a Noh music school (Shimazaki 1953), to take a specific example, the training begins at about ten. For about ten years the student lives with the master and receives lessons while doing household chores. After he leaves the master's home, he is forever identified as a member of the master's school, and is dependent on him for economic assistance at such crises as wedding, child birth, illness and funeral. In short, there is no essential difference between these schools of arts and the institutionalized ritual kinship groups, even though explicit use of ritual kinship terms is not observed. Even organization of Buddhist temples of the Shinshu sect is likened by Morioka (1962) to the kinship organization of main and branch families. Olson's report (1963: 44—53) of a country temple also suggests the same kinship-like organization of a main temple and its branches in Noto Peninsula.

In the above examples of schools of arts and crafts and temple organization, there is an explicit recognition by the participants that their organization is quasi-kinship, even though there may not be any formalized use of kinship or quasi-kinship terms. To take a case which is a shade less kinship-like, we may discuss the professor-student relation in Japanese universities, particularly in graduate schools. Many, if not most students, by the time they enter the graduate school, are known as students of a particular professor. Such students are expected to accept the professor's theoretical point of view and defend and propagate it. They would consult their professor not only about academic problems but about personal affairs such as their marriage and financial problems. Professors are very often chosen as the formal *nakodo*, the man who officially unites the bride and groom in the wedding ceremony, thus becoming morally responsible for the success of the marriage. The professor regards it his personal responsibility to find a job for his students with far stronger moral compulsion than his American collegaues. Students, on the other hand, are expected to perform services for their professor far beyond what is expected as a student. In this professor-student relation, there is no declared compact, no ceremony to validate the relationship and no special use of ritual kinship terms, and the relationship isn't regarded only in a mild way as simulating the proto-type of the ritual kinship relation. Nonetheless, functionally diffuse the particularistic ties, hierarchical social relations and performance of economic services are as clearly seen here as in other examples cited above. Moreover, professors and students alike acknowledge the fact that their mutual relationship does contain elements of ritual kinship.

Examples can be multiplied indefinitely. But the point has been sufficiently made that groups which have all the characteristics of ritual kinship institution — which are, of course, ultimately derived from kinship institution — are innumerable in Japan. How easily the model of kinship is transferred can also be illustrated in the use of kinship terms. We have seen that although in most cases terms used in ritual kinship are clearly recognizable as quasi-kinship, in some groups terms of true kinship are employed without any modification. In addition, Norbeck and Befu (1958) have shown the prevalence of the use of true kinship terms in non-kinship situations which are clearly not ritual kinship in the institutionalized sense. Kin terms for grandparents, elder siblings of both sexes, uncle, and aunt are quite freely used toward non-kin in Japan.

Human relations characterized by hierarchical organization, particularism and functional diffuseness and accompanied by an expressive organization of economic and political functions are almost ubiquitous in Japan. Such relationships quickly develop in warying degrees between teacher and students, seniors and juniors in school, section head and his subordinates in a business firm, foreman and workers, and union boss and members. This is precisely because characteristics of the ritual kinship institution more or less characterize much of Japanese society. These characteristics, when intensified, crystalize into institutionalized ritual kinship accompanied by the use of quasi-kinship terms. Ritual kinship has such a prominent place in Japanese society that in the mind of ordinary Japanese, it is this institution, rather than the true kinship, which serves as the model for small-scale social organization. Japanese more readily think of small, face-to-face groups as having characteristics of *oyabun-kobun* (ritual kinship) than having those of true kinship.

The prevalence of the ritual kinship institution is not merely due to the fact that its functional characteristics are pervasive in the society. It is also due to the fact that this institution can take many different forms depending on the instrumental and other requirements of the group. It can be an organization of farm families if cooperation of families is required to accomplish the instrumental goal of the group; or it may be an organization of individuals. The size of the group, too, can adjust according to its instrumental needs from two to a maximum of over a hundred. It can be organized in a predominantly kinship setting, with kinsmen as its core, or in a setting which does not involve any kinsmen. The relationship may be hereditary in a stable rural setting, or it may be short-lived in a changing urban environment. The resiliency of the ritual kinship institution in Japan, then, lies not only in the fact that its functional characteristics are those of much of the society, but also in the fact that it has structural adaptability to varied instrumental requirements.

An important question arises as to the type of situation in which functional characteristics of the ritual kinship institution are likely to crystalize in Japan. That is, what are the conditions which give rise to the full-fledged form of ritual kinship group? The question may be phrased in terms of future prediction: In which sectors of the Japanese society is ritual kinship system, in the full-fledged form, likely to survive? The question may be answered by an examination of the characteristics of the Japanese ritual kinship. We have seen that hierarchical social organization and functionally diffuse and particularistic personal relations — which Bennett and Ishino summarize as "paternalism" — are some of the dominant features of the Japanese society as a whole and that these features as seen in ritual kinship groups are simply expressions of these societal values. Seen from this point of view, then, we may predict that ritual kinship will continue to exist as long as and to the extent to which these values prevail in Japan. As these values become deemphasized in Japan — for whatever reason — it will become difficult for ritual kinship groups to be organized with strong ideological backing of the society. If different sectors of the society (classes, rural vs. urban sectors, etc.) may be assumed to undergo value changes at different rates, then the ritual kinship system will be expected to remain in those sectors of the society which tend to lag behind in the ideological change.

There is another consideration which is essential in predicting the persistence of ritual kinship in Japan. We have noted economic dependence of ritual children on ritual parent as one of the essential features of ritual kinship. That is, one of the crucial functions of ritual kinship groups is that the ritual parent provides economic assistance to his ritual children when the latter is unable to provide it himself, such as in time of crises in the family when expenditure of large sums of money is required. From this point of view, then, we may predict that ritual kinship will tend to survive in those sectors of the society in which even the bare basic subsistence is hard to come by, as for example is true for the lower class rural and urban populations in Japan. As the general level of living standard and income level relative to necessary expenditure improves, as individuals become able to save for emergency expenditures, and as government measures, such as socialized medicine, which help economically impoverished segments of the populations spread, one would expect ritual kinship to decline, for there would not be any economic necessity for one to join a kinship group. And if these economic improvements are accompanied by attenuation in the paternalistic ideology of the society, not only would there not be any economic reasons to join a ritual kinship group, but there would not be any ideological basis to organize it.[4]

In sum, the future resiliency of the ritual kinship system will be a function of the continuity of those values of the society which support ritual kinship, and also a function of existence of economic deprivation.

FOOTNOTES

1. Norbeck and Befu (1958) have used the expression *fictive kinship* in reference to the use of true kinship terms toward persons who are not genealogically related or who are not related properly according to the usual meaning of the terms. Ishino (1953), on the other hand, has called *ritual kinship* those relations in which terms which are recognized as quasi-kinship are used generally toward nonkin. We shall follow the established convention in the present paper. This distinction, however, only indicates a general tendency and does not always hold. As we shall see, true kinship terms are sometimes used in the context of ritual kinship.

2. A brief descriptive discussion of various kinds of ritual kinship groups and results of opinion polls concerning attitudes of Japanese toward ritual kinship system are presented by Matsumoto (1960: 38–40).

3. I am referring to the type of ritual kinship group which was found in northeastern Japan in prewar days, as described by Ariga (1938), in which gifts of considerable economic value

went with the establishment of a ritual child's household. There are, to be sure, ritual kinship groups in other parts of Japan, e. g., Yamanashi prefecture (Hattori 1955), in which such gifts are not involved in contracting the relationship.

4. One reason for the success in socialized medicine in Japan may be sought in the very fact that the ideology supporting the ritual kinship system is in the decline and therefore that a great many Japanese would rather depend on impersonal government assistance than on a person to whom they would later incur personal control and obligation.

BIBLIOGRAPHY

Ariga, Kizaemon: Noson shakai no kenkyu (Studies in rural society). Tokyo, Kawade Shobo (1938).

Beardsley, Richard K.: The household in the status system of Japanese villages. University of Michigan Center for Japanese Studies. Occasional Papers 1:62–73 (1951).

Befu, Harumi: Corporate emphasis and patterns of descent in the Japanese family. *In* Japanese culture: its development and characteristics. Robert J. Smith and Richard K. Beardsley, eds. Viking Funk Publications in Anthropology No. 34 (1962).

Befu, Harumi and Edward *Norbeck:* Japanese usages of terms of relationship. Southwestern Journal of Anthropology 14:66–86 (1958).

Benedict, Ruth: The chrysanthemum and the sword: patterns of Japanese culture. Boston, Houghton Mifflin (1946).

Bennett, John W. and Leo A. *Depres*: Kinship and instrumental activities: a theoretical inquiry. American Anthropologist 62:254–267 (1960).

– and Iwao *Ishino*: Paternalism in the Japanese economy. Minneapolis,

Bennett, John W. and Iwao *Ishino*: Paternalism in the Japanese economy. Minneapolis, University of Minnesota Press (1963).

Eisenstadt, S. N.: Ritualized personal relations. Man art. 96 (1956).

Fukutake, Tadashi: Nihon noson shakai no kozo bunseki (Structural analysis of the Japanese rural society). Tokyo, Tokyo University Press (1954).

Hattori, Harunori: Honke bunke kankei to oyabun kobun kankei (The stem-branch relationship and the ritual kinship relationship). Yamanashi University Memoirs of the Faculty of Liberal Arts and Education 6:57–66 (1955)

Ishino, Iwao: The *oyabun-kobun*: a Japanese ritual kinship system. American Anthropologist 55:695–707 (1953).

Iwai, Hiroaki: Tekiya no jittai (The life of street-stall merchants). Shakaigaku Hyoron (Japanese Sociological Review) 1:41–60 (1953).

– Han-skakai shudan (Anti-social groups). *In* Nihon no shakai (Japanese society). Tadashi Fukutake ed. Tokyo, Yuhikaku (1954).

– Byori shudan no kozo: oyabun kobun shudan kenkyu (Structure of pathological groups: a study of ritual kinship groups), Tokyo, Seishin Shobo (1963).

Kitano, Seiichi: Koshu sanson no dozoku shoshiki to oyakata kokata kanko *(Dozoku* organization and the custom of ritual parent-child relations in the mountain villages of Koshu). Minzokugaku Numpo (Annual Report of the Ethnological Society) 2:41–95 (1940).

Matsumoto, Y. Scott: Contemporary Japan: the individual and the group, Transactions of the American Philosophical Society n.s. Vol.50, Pt.1 (1960).

Matsushima, Shizuo: Kozan ni mirareru oyabun kobun shudan no tokushitsu (Characterstics of ritual parent-child groups in mines). Shakaigaku Hyoron (Japanese Sociological Review) 1:61–67 (1950).

– Rodosha no shakai (Social groups among the laborers). *In* Nihon no shakai (Japanese society), Tadashi Fukutake ed. Tokyo, Yuhikaku (1954).

Mogami, T.: Oyakata kokata (Ritual parent-childhood). *In* Sanson seikatsu no kenkyu (Studies in mountain life), Kunio Yanagita ed. Tokyo, Minkan Densho no Kai (1938).

Morioka, Kiyomi: Shinshu kyodan to "ie" seido (The Shinshu sect and its "family" system). Tokyo, Sobunsha (1962).

Nakamura, Masao: Tsushima sonraku ni okeru dozoku oyakata kokata kankei no ichi shiryo

(Material on the *dozoku* and the ritual parent-child relationship in a village in Tsushima). *In* Ie: sono kozo bunseki (The family: its structural analysis), Yuzuru Okada and Seiichi Kitano eds. Tokyo, Sobunsha (1959).

Nishiyama, Matsunosuke: Iemoto no kenkyu (Studies in schools of arts). Tokyo, Koso Shobo (1959).

Olson, Lawrence: Dimensions of Japan. New York, American Universities Field Staff (1963).

Oyama, Hikoichi: Tomoko domei no kenkyu (A study of miners' organization). Shakaigaku Zasshi (Journal of Sociology) 29:66–75, 30:63–84 (1926).

Shimazaki, Minoru: Geino shakai to iemoto seido (The artists' society and organization of their schools). Shakaigaku Hyoron (Japanese Sociological Review) 12:131–156 (1953).

Suginohara, Juichi: Ta jima ni okeru oyakata kokata kankei no jittai (The ritual parent-child relationship in Tajima Province). Social Survey Report of the Research Institute of Humanistic Science No. 10 (1953).

Yanagita, Kunio: Oyakata kokata (Ritual parent-childhood). *In* Kazoku seido zenshu (Encyclopedia of the family system) Part I: Shironhen (History) Vol. III: Oyako (Parent-child). Tokyo, Kawade Shobo (1937).

FLEXIBILITY IN AN EXPRESSIVE INSTITUTION: *SUMO*

Ann Fischer

Sumo, the Japanese wrestling game which has survived for over a millenium, is remarkable for its flexibility and responsiveness to social change. This paper makes two main points, using *sumo* as an illustration. First, it attempts to describe how this essentially simple game, encrusted with ritual in the course of historical development, permits and rewards differences of individual styles in the performance of its ritual. Second, it points out the means by which the social organization of the sumo institution interweaves with that of the larger society, and how, as a result of these connecting threads, sumo maintains receptivity to change and modifies its rules. The two points demonstrate that, in spite of a heavy weight of ritual, an expressive institution may maintain flexibility by encouraging individual behavioral differences and by modifying rules in response to pressure from other social institutions.

An expressive institution, of which sumo is an example, may be defined as an institution primarily devoted to the expression of values, beliefs, styles, and emotions in contrast to those institutions primarily devoted to the biological functioning of the group. The Japanese have a plethora of such expressive activities—for example, tea ceremony, flower arrangements, and ink painting—and these activities are often practiced in organized groups.

It is not necessary in this paper to present a complete inventory of sumo rules and rituals nor an elaborate description of the social organization of the sumo institution. I have attempted, however, to provide enough detail to illustrate the general points outlined above.

The Sumo Match

The essential equipment for a sumo match is an earthen ring and a loin cloth for the wrestler. When a match is about to take place, two wrestlers enter the ring and assume a crouching "ready" position, facing each other. The wrestlers may choose to fight or not to fight at this time. If they do not fight, after glaring at each other for a time, they leave the ring and return to their stations. The ritual posturing may be repeated a number of times. Formerly, the length of time allowed top wrestlers for posturing was unlimited, but it is now set at four minutes for champions and scaled, according to rank, down to nothing for neophytes. When the time limit is reached, the wrestlers must fight whether they wish to do so or not.

Mastering the technique of the *tachiai*—the take-off from the crouching position—is very important, because a split-second advantage can mean the difference between victory and defeat. The posturing before the tachiai enables the

Fischer — *From The Southwestern Journal of Anthropology,* Vol. 22 No. 1, (1966), pp. 31-42. Reprinted by permission of the author and the publisher.

wrestler to seize the correct psychological moment for the attack as he judges it from the facial expression and bodily tension of his opponent.

To win the match a wrestler must either maneuver his opponent out of the ring or force him to touch the earthen floor with some part of his body. Kicking, hair pulling, punching with the fists, and shaking or clutching the part of the loin cloth covering the sexual organs are prohibited, but pushing, pulling, and using leverage are permissible; therefore, a heavy wrestler or a wrestler with certain other physical features has the advantage. The combination of long arms, a long torso, and relatively short legs keeps the wrestler stable and allows him to use more effective leverage against his enemy.

Although sumo matches may be conducted with the simplest equipment—and they are so conducted among Japanese farm children and in the Pacific islands formerly occupied by the Japanese—the matches which command national attention in Japan are held in a ceremonial manner, attended by much symbolic ritual detail. The meaning of some of these details is common knowledge; others are understood by only a few avid sumo fans or by historians interested in the sport. Much of the ritual is a result of the fact that sumo matches have a long history of association with the harvest and other festivals held in the local Shinto shrines of the farm villages.

In the grand tournaments, at present held six times a year in five major cities, the wrestlers wear a special loin cloth, *mawashi*. The mawashi of high-ranking wrestlers is of silk; lower-ranking men must wear cotton. The loin cloth is very long and wide and must be folded before it is passed between the wrestler's legs and wrapped a number of times around his waist. Two aprons, one of glue-stiffened strings (silk or cotton as the rank requires) and one elaborately decorated and used for the ceremonial march to the center of the arena, complete the attire of wrestlers below the rank of grand champion. The grand champions, the *yokozuna,* wear large stiffened ropes around their waists, tied behind in an elaborate ceremonial knot. Folded paper streamers, called *gohei,* are suspended from this rope. They are of the same step-design made by priests and used to shake over people or objects in purification rituals. Of these garments, only the loin cloth and string apron are worn during the actual wrestling.

In addition to these trappings, the sumo wrestler has a special hair arrangement. His hair is long, tied in a kind of pony tail, and pulled toward the front of the head. At its end, the tail is stiffened into a small fan-shaped arrangement. The higher-ranking wrestler's hair drops down slightly on the neck and fans out before the tail is tied and placed on the head, while low-ranking wrestlers pull the tail taut above the neck. There are some who say that this hair style prevents injury to the head; but perhaps, as most believe, its main function is its value as a trademark. Even during the Meiji reform, when other Japanese were forced to cut their hair, sumo wrestlers were allowed the privilege of keeping theirs long.

For the national tournaments the wrestling ring is greatly elaborated. The ring is placed on a square packed-clay mound surfaced with sand. At present the ring is about thirteen feet in diameter and is delimited by a border of rice-straw bales imbedded in the clay so as to protrude only a few inches from the surface. Above the mound a roof resembling that of a Shinto shrine is held by cables from the ceiling of the arena. In the past, posts at the four corners of the mound would have connected with the roof; but today four huge tassles, suspended from the roof, mark their former position. A cloth drape, decorated with the seal of the Sumo

Association, forms a square above the mound.

On each of the fifteen days of the sumo tournament, the meet begins by the entrance in single file of the participating wrestlers in ceremonial dress. Following this, the wrestlers are seated to the east and west of the ring, and a top-ranking champion (yokozuna) with a lesser champion on each side of him ascend the mound. At the edge of the ring the yokozuna stoops, bows, and with his arms extended, but downthrust, claps his hands and rubs his palms together. Then he moves forward to the center of the ring, turns to face his lieutenants, and clapping and rubbing his palms together, stamps the ring with his right foot in order to drive away any evil spirit which might be residing there. Abruptly, he extends his right arm directly to the right from his shoulder, and with a sudden twist of his wrist turns his palm forward for all to see that his hand contains no hidden weapons. After further stamping and clapping of palms the champion rejoins his lieutenants at the side of the mound, the umpire moves to the center, the yokozuna bows to him, and the three wrestlers leave the mound. If there are other yokozuna currently wrestling, each performs the above ceremony.

At the completion of these ceremonies the ring is sprinkled with water and smoothed with brooms by a crew of two or three men. One of these may double as a caller *(yobidashi)*. When the ring is adequately prepared, the caller moves to the center of the ring, flings open his folded fan, holds it to the east and calls the direction and then the name of the wrestler who will fight on the east side. Turning to the west, he calls "west" and the name of the opposing wrestler. Then, lowering his fan, he retires from the ring.

At this time, the referee *(giyoji)*, who has been standing facing the caller, steps toward the center of the ring. In one hand he holds a warrior's fan, from the handles of which two long silken cords terminate in colored tassels indicating his rank. The referee is arrayed in colorful kimono and *hakama* (trousers), tailored in priestly style and made of brilliantly decorated cloth. He wears a hat like that of a Shinto priest. The names of these garments—*eboshi* (hat) and *suo* (robes)—are the same as the terms used for the clothing of a priest. Holding his fan forward and facing the appropriate directions, the referee repeats the caller's procedure, calling the names of the opponents. The two wrestlers rise from their chairs, placed just off the mound, and ascend for the fight. After ritual stamping, mouth washing, and salt sprinkling for purification of fighter and ring, the match begins. At its conclusion the loser bows and leaves the ring, while the winner, who also bows, is acknowledged by a gesture from the referee with his fan.

Even though the sport and the elaborate ritual activity surrounding it have been much simplified in this description, it is easy to understand why the Japanese say that sumo ranks with *kabuki* as the most Japanese of their expressive institutions. There is no hint anywhere in the folklore surrounding the sport that it had other than a Japanese origin.

The rituals that have adhered to sumo over hundreds of years stress purity and goodness as requisite to success in the harvest and in the fight, but right conduct is also emphasized even in the face of defeat. The character of the wrestler, therefore, was, and is, extremely important. Today, a wrestler is judged by the manner in which he performs the prescribed rituals and by the manner in which he fights, wins, and loses. These styles of behavior as well as the appearance of a wrestler attract admirers in the audiences, and Japanese interpret them as favorable or unfavorable traits—reason enough to select a wrestler as a favorite or to dislike him.

The individual styles elaborated in performing the rituals add much human interest to sumo. For example, some of the top-ranking wrestlers have developed stereotyped ways of throwing the salt for purifying the ring before a match. One very fat wrestler, Wakachichibu, throws a huge fistful of salt into the ring with a vigorous flinging open of his palm. Dewanishiki, almost equally fat, takes a tiny pinch of salt between two fingers and tosses it unconcernedly into the air as he walks to the center of the ring. When these two are matched, the audience invariably laughs at the contrast.

The wrestlers may compulsively perform certain aspects of the ritual in the same manner they used on an especially successful day, and an audience appreciates and understands their superstitions. Wrestlers may have their stylized sumo names changed ceremonially a number of times to attract good luck; names of old champions are especially favored for this purpose, although many of these names are considered to be owned and may not be acquired at will. In addition, wrestlers acquire reputations for fair play, skill in maneuver, speed, cunning, and strategic planning as well as for being especially large, hairy, or handsome.

Referees and callers also become noted for their ritual performances. The style and skill with which they enact their roles bring promotions in rank and the privilege of conducting the matches of the higher-ranking champions. For example, like our auctioneers, a caller may become famous for his style of calling in ceremonial tones. Any participant who performs a ritual in an artistic manner receives approval.

A cultural antique, sumo is continually restyled by new generations. A large part of its popularity rests on the fact that the audince understands and enjoys the individualistic embellishments given the ritual and the fighting techniques by the wrestlers and the other performers, while at the same time the basic structures of the game and the rituals are maintained.

In addition to the variability of individual styles of behavior, the sumo institution has manifested flexibility in the rules of the game, the policies for scheduling and holding matches, and the institutional organization itself.

The Social Organization of Sumo

The familistic orientation characteristic of Japanese social organization, evidenced in ritual kinship patterns among occupational groups (Ishino 1953; Bennett and Ishino 1963), for example, is a significant element in their expressive institutions. The familistic orientation is also important in the social organization of sumo and plays a part in structuring the relationships of the wrestlers.

Established sumo groups tour the countryside between grand tournaments in order to discover and enlist new wrestlers. Recent recruits who have just started to let their hair grow are identified by their relatively shorter hair as "baby" wrestlers. The wrestler who discovers a promising neophyte becomes "older brother" to the neophyte, and the neophyte becomes his disciple, or "younger brother." A group of wrestlers are banded together by virture of these relationships as fictitious brothers into a *heya,* which may be translated as "room." Fictitious brothers, like real brothers, are not supposed to wrestle with each other. When a successful elder brother retires from wrestling, he may become a "parent" of his heya, if there is an opening, or he may, with the consent of the parent or parents, take his own disciples and form a new heya. Such a new "room" of wrestlers maintains a relationship with the heya from which it has separated. If the disciple of a champion forms a new heya while his mentor remains in the original heya, the relationship between the two heya formed as a result of the division is that of parent to child. Where two disciples of the same champion decide to split the heya, and each of them becomes a parent of one segment, the relationship between the two resulting heya is a brotherly one. Thus, as heya grow and divide a chain of related heya is created.

Neophytes are in a servant relationship to older brothers, who train them. They live in the heya, receiving room and board but no salaries, and for many years must adhere to a very strict training regime.

Since the neophytes live in the heya, and since they cannot afford to marry, a wrestler seldom takes a wife until he becomes a champion. The only woman closely associated with the heya is the wife of the parent, who acts as mother to the wrestlers. The champion who hopes to succeed the parent of the heya is likely to marry the daughter of the parent and to inherit the parent's name. Marriage to the parent's daughter might be called "pseudo incest," since in this case not only do children of the same "parent" marry, but the groom assumes the identity of the bride's father by receiving his name at a special ceremony. This practice of naming is a common arrangement in Japan when a family lacks a male heir and adopts a daughter's husband as heir.

Most of the business of the collective sumo world is conducted by the Sumo Association, which is made up of the parents of the various heya and a few successful men from other areas of Japanese life. There are 105 shares in the Sumo Association, and these may be purchased from former owners by a wrestler who becomes a parent. The possibility of becoming a member of the Sumo Association depends upon the availability of shares for sale. The Association regulates relationships between heya, controls arrangements for tournaments, controls payments to personnel, and elects individuals to fill important roles such as referee, judge, or announcer. Judges are usually chosen from parents of the heya, but referees and announcers have internal group regulations of their own, and these roles tend to be hereditary.

It is clear that sumo social organization is analogous to family organization in Japan. The similarity of the processes by which branch families and *sumo heya* are created is evident, and, as in the family, quarrels often occur in the heya at the time of segmentation.

The terminology used in sumo is very similar to that of kinship. Distinctive suffixes, *-zeki or -seki,* are applied to the wrestlers' names instead of the suffix *-san* used for people in general. When an elder *sumo* wrestler is referred to in the context of the brotherly relationship, *-deshi* is suffixed to the kin term for elder brother, thus, the term becomes *ani-deshi.* The older wrestler addresses the younger disciple with his name followed by the suffix *-zeki,* whereas in kinship *-san* or *-chan* would be affixed. The elder disciple is addressed by the kin term *aniki* (elder brother). While the term *aniki* is occasionally used in families, *niisan, oniisan, niichan,* or *oniisama* are more usual choices. In reference, the head of the heya is called *oyakata* (boss or chief), similar to the reference term for parent, *oya.*

Neophytes enter the heya after winning three of five matches with other neophytes. Their names are then listed on the official ranking list in the lowest rank. A successful wrestler rises through a series of ranks. Once the rank of yokozuna, or grand champion has been attained, a wrestler may never be demoted. The wrestler of the next lowest rank, *ozeki,* must lose more than half his bouts in three successive tournaments before he may be demoted, but wrestlers of lower rank are promoted or demoted after each tournament.

Ranks are grouped into divisions, the highest of which is *makuuchi,* meaning "inside the curtain." Grouping the wrestlers in this fashion allows matching of opponents of more nearly equal skill, increasing the competition and thus the interest of the audience. Sumo divisions are largely based on skill, in contrast to Euroamerican boxing, in which the opponents must always be in the same weight division regardless of skill. At times, opponents in sumo matches are of markedly different physical size.

A hair-cutting ceremony marks a wrestler's retirement. Those who retire without reaching the rank of yokozuna are usually not able to find a place in the sumo institution. A grand champion may decide for himself when he will retire, while others are forced into retirement by the embarrassment of declining rank. When wrestlers grow too old to compete successfully, roughly between the ages of 30 and 40, they enter other occupations, often the restaurant business. Throughout a wrestling career a man seeks to put on as much weight as possible by eating huge amounts of food and drinking large quantities of beer in order to be immovable in the ring, and therefore the restaurant business offers him an opportunity to gratify an appetite grown gargantuan.

Connections with the Larger Society

The world of sumo is not bounded by the heya, the arena, and the Sumo Association. The Emperor himself is a sumo fan and makes his appearance at a tournament with an appropriate ceremony in his honor about once a year. However, the most frequent link between the sport and the rest of society is through sumo patrons. Patrons, usually influential men, choose a favorite wrestler, representing for them a valued character trait, such as fairness, skillfulness, dignity, or strength. With great generosity patrons give ceremonial sumo aprons, money, or gifts of the wrestler's choice to their favorites. A patron may offer prizes for winners of matches in which his favorite participates, and he may tempt his favorite out for evenings of gaiety. If such evenings become too frequent or the celebrations too immoderate, they interfere with the training of a rising wrestler and end otherwise promising careers.

From the wrestlers the patrons gain prestige. They receive autographs and large, signed palm prints of the wrestler, which they may, in turn, distribute to their favored friends. The possession of one of these palm prints is a source of pride to the household in which it hangs.

Wrestler and patron are expected to be loyal to each other; in sumo folklore the patron often pauperizes himself in patronage of his favorite. In stories, the patron conceals his pauperization, but the wrestler discovers it and makes some dramatic gesture by means of which the patron regains and even improves his fortune.

In addition to patrons, sumo has millions of fans, the grand tournament having perhaps the largest television audience in Japan.

One of the most interesting features of sumo is the adaptability of the rules in response to historical events. Conflicts inevitably arise when pressure for change occurs, and even though some effort is made to keep disagreements within the institution from the public, they usually become matters of popular interest. To illustrate this process and the association of changes in the institution with changing Japanese values as well as the flexibility of sumo rules, two rules—one recently changed and one which is under pressure to change—will be considered.

The rule regarding the length of time allowed for posturing before the opponents begin to wrestle seems to be particularly sensitive to change and has changed frequently in the past. The posturing allowed for unexpected attacks, formerly an exciting feature of wrestling. Players caught off guard by these attacks could refuse the challenge under the rules, but such a refusal, though often used, was considered a sign of inferiority. Under the older rules, small fast wrestlers were able to tire their heavier opponents with lengthy posturing. Now, with the televising of sumo matches, posturing becomes boring for the audience. Even before the matches began to appear on television, the audience was pressuring for a change in this rule. Television speeded the change, not only because the audience was bored but because television time is expensive. Many champions who had achieved their positions through use of the posturing technique resisted the change, so a compromise was reached: only champions were allowed a four-minute posturing period. As time goes on, the psychological possibilities in the technique are being ignored as more and more wrestlers simply wait until the four minutes have passed and the referee gives the signal to fight. Only infrequently, now, a wrestler tries to catch his opponent off guard, and when he does the challenge is as often as not refused by his opponent, who stands up, turns away, and walks to the side of the ring. Yet, referring to a recent champion an informant asserted, "If you asked any Japanese why Futabayama was so popular, it is that he had never said 'Wait!' So that even though he was not ready, he fought when he was challenged."

This particular rule shift is consistent with other changes in Japanese society, such as those in competitive techniques. The inability or lack of willingness to make quick decisions has long been a criticism leveled at Japanese by foreigners. Now, the Japanese themselves feel that they need to adjust their decision-making methods, especially in the business world, if they are to be successful in the highly competitive foreign trade market. Formerly, in making decisions, desirable conduct entailed remaining impassive, at least in appearance, while one studied one's opponents and planned strategic moves. Individuals who are best equipped to make fast decisions now appear to be most adapted to modern conditions. Accordingly, the shift away from the technique of sizing up the opponent and catching him off guard in sumo seems to be associated with a change in an older valued way of making decisions.

Pressure exists now for a change in the rule which prevents ritual brothers from fighting. The argument in favor of this change is that it will increase competition, for at present, if two outstanding wrestlers belong to the same or closely related heya, they are not allowed to wrestle. Wrestlers in strong heya win more often under this rule since they usually have less skillful opponents. The argument against the present rule is that it gives an unfair advantage, while the argument for it is that it is contrary to the spirit of sumo for brothers to fight. Recently, pressure from the audience has forced more and more closely related heya members to fight each other. The Sumo Association is now giving serious consideration to the change. Gate receipts are expected to increase if heya brothers are matched.

Social rules regarding the relationships between siblings in the Japanese kinship system, again, appear to be changing in a manner concordant with the changing sumo rule. Since the war, there has been a tendency in law and in social relationships toward the equality of siblings and toward the weakening of traditional family ties. Greater residential mobility and industrialization have lessened the authority of the elder brother over the younger. At present, they meet more nearly as equals, although conflicts in the old and new ideals are evident.

Discussion

The controversial issue of the relationship of expressive institutions to other institutions in a society can be partially clarified by sumo. Whether one wishes to show that an expressive activity performs the function of the working through of unresolved conflicts of the individual, as Freud and others have proposed, or to suggest that it serves as a guide for conduct in the more ambiguous situations of life by educating a group in the proper attitude to rules as Roberts and Sutton-Smith (1962:178), Erikson (1950:195), Callois (1961:65), and Piaget (1948:95) have suggested for games, sumo as a national sport would seem to offer a good example. Whatever its functions, the point which I wish to emphasize in this paper is that the continued popularity of sumo rests partially on its adaptability to changes in Japanese society. The preferred conduct, or values, as shown in the rules of sumo are extremely responsive to changes in other parts of Japanese society, and thus reflect the changing situation in which people find themselves.

Either change or lack of change in an expressive institution may result in the loss of audience or participants, or in the replacement of one set of participants by another.[1] The loss of audience and participants can be documented historically in sumo, for example, during a part of the Meiji period when a few remaining wrestlers practiced in secret heya.

However, when changes occur in any institution, they are met with resistance from individuals who have achieved success by virtue of special talents or advantages fostered by the previous rules or state of affairs. In sumo these individuals are important to the institution because they are excellent performers, and the audience enjoys watching them. When a rule changes, a compromise is usually needed between the best players, who resist a change, and the audience, which favors it. For both players and audience are dependent on each other for maximum satisfaction within the functioning institution.

A third set of people, the members of the Sumo Association, devote themselves to the best interests of the total institution, whose welfare is interpreted in terms of the biggest audience and the most skillful wrestlers. At times the Sumo Association has been unable to effect an acceptable compromise between these two groups, and sumo has either lost much of its audience because of wrestler resistance to change, or the best wrestlers have resigned in protest over a change which has occurred.

The changes in the rules considered in this paper—the limitation of posturing and the matching of more closely associated wrestlers — seem to increase the accuracy with which current values are reflected in sumo. Both of the rules examined indicate changes in the direction of Western values—the making of quick decisions and the equality of siblings. It should be noted that there is apparently very little lag in the changes of this expressive institution in relation to other changes in Japanese society.

It is well to state that there are many Japanese who do not like sumo. The chief reason given for the rather strong distaste often expressed by young people is that the sport is saturated with the traditional culture of Japan, inappropriate to the modern world. Those, the more numerous among the young people, who find a sentimental delight in visiting Kyoto and in the tradition-laden aspects of Japanese culture, almost invariably have a favorite sumo wrestler. An interesting aspect of the feelings of some university students about sumo is their disapproval of the nakedness of the wrestlers. These young people consider such a display of bare flesh both embarrassing and barbaric. The nakedness of wrestlers has been disapproved by one or another group of Japanese for a long time, at least since the period of the Meiji reforms; it is not a new objection. Here, then, is an aspect of sumo which has resisted change, despite some pressure from parts of the society, and which has resulted in a loss of part of the possible audience.

In addition to allowing for individual stylistic differences in performance, it seems evident that an expressive institution must reflect the current values in a society to remain in popular favor, and changes in rules are one means by which this is accomplished. Therefore, such rule changes are convenient markers suggesting directions which the society is taking. They occur generally after the change has occurred or been suggested elsewhere in the society but before the change has solidified into definitely prescribed conduct. Possibly changes in rules in expressive institutions hasten the solidification or acceptance of value changes and ways of behavior reflecting them.

FOOTNOTE

1. This can be seen most clearly in the changes of interest and participation in certain games as well as in changes of the rules and of the attitudes toward the rules by which they are played with changing age. Piaget (1948: 16-17) has given a thorough description of the change in the attitude toward and application of rules in four stages of moral development in childhood in connection with the game of marbles.

BIBLIOGRAPHY

Bennett, John W., and Iwao Ishino
   1963 *Paternalism in the Japanese Economy: Anthropological Studies of Oyabun-Kobun Patterns.* Minneapolis: University of Minnesota Press.
Caillois, Roger (Tr. by Meyer Barash)
   1961 *Man, Play and Games.* Glencoe: The Free Press.
Erikson, Erik H.
   1950 *Childhood and Society.* New York: W. W. Norton and Company Inc.
Ishino, Iwao
   1953 The Oyabun-Kobun: a Japanese Ritual Kinship Institution. *American Anthropologist 55:695-707.*
Piaget, Jean (tr. by Marjorie Gabain)
   1948 *The Moral Judgment of the Child.* Glencoe: The Free Press.
Roberts, John M., and Brian Sutton-Smith
   1962 Child Training and Game Involvement. *Ethnology* 1:166-185.

JAPANESE VALUES AND THE DEMOCRATIC PROCESS

F. Kenneth Berrien

Introduction

Japan has undergone one of the most dramatic political metamorphoses in modern history. For centuries prior to the end of World War II it was ruled by a succession of shoguns, military cliques, and dictators whose common underlying assumption was that the government should be obeyed—not necessarily understood. Since 1947, the country has been nominally democratic with a constitution modeled after those of the West that presupposed a fundamentally changed orientation toward political and governmental processes. The rights of individuals and local groups to protest, petition, and assemble are guaranteed. A free, privately owned press has been established. The new constitution in contrast to the old implies that governmental processes should be influenced by an informed and understanding electorate.

It is therefore a legitimate question to ask, "Have the Japanese at the grass roots reorganized their pattern of values and attitudes from one of deep deference toward and ready acceptance of authority to one characterized by a willingness to express responsible opposition and to take local initiative?" On a gigantic scale Japan represents an effort to change attitudes, albeit an effort that was not deliberately planned as such.

The case of Japan is different from the German situation with respect to the forceful suppression of dissenting minorities, which in Germany were vigorously persecuted and liquidated. Benedict (1) pointed out that the authoritarianism of Japan was based on a pervading sense of the inevitability and essential rightness of hierarchy.

The Japanese (prior to 1945) rely upon old habits of deference set up in their past experience and formalized in their ethical system and their etiquette. The State can depend upon it that, when their Excellencies function in their "proper place" their prerogatives will be respected, not because the policy is approved, but because it is wrong in Japan to override boundaries between prerogatives (1, p. 86).

It is important for our purposes to note that in the Meiji era the *tonari gumi*—small groups of 10 or 15 families loosely organized in rural and semi-rural areas to deal with their own affairs—were abolished. The central government via directives to its local bureaucrats apparently reached down even to this level.

Prior to World War II, the tonari gumi were re-established, functioning,

Berrien — *From The Journal of Social Psychology*, Vol. 168, (1966), pp. 129-138. Reprinted by permission of The Journal Press and the author.

however, largely in matters of rationing and relief under formulas handed down from higher authority. Consequently the Japanese, although experienced in dealing with local matters under guidance, have had no extended tutelage with those processes of initiating proposals at grass roots levels and drawing the attention of higher authorities to local issues, inequities, and injustices. To do so would have, in Benedict's words, "transcended the boundaries of prerogatives." Thus, respect for the wisdom of those above them stifled interest in dealing with local matters on their own initiative or focusing a public opinion on national issues. In Reisman's terms they were other directed with a vengeance: deferent to authority and willing to accept orders supinely, avoiding conflict, and taking upon themselves major responsibility for errors (exemplified in extreme cases by that nearly unique practice of harikari).

In an effort to probe Japanese values after a period of some 15 years experience under the democratic constitution, a research study was mounted having two prongs: one behavioral, the other attitudinal. First, we explored the value patterns of Japanese college students with the Edwards Personal Preference Schedule for which comparable American norms were already available. Second, we interviewed officials in 50 villages and small cities concerning the organization and duties of volunteer firemen. The latter were compared with data obtained from 58 volunteer companies located in New Jersey.

In selecting fire-fighting organizations as an example of local initiative and local responsibility we were mindful of the special fire hazards in Japanese villages where the houses are more inflammable and closely spaced as compared with conditions in American communities. However, in both cultures fire protection is by its very nature a local problem calling upon local resources. Presumably, effective fire-fighting methods in one culture are equally appropriate in another. However, were the organizational features in one culture more or less democratic than in the other? We wondered whether the Japanese, given the opportunity to organize themselves at the local level to deal with a local problem requiring little or no coordination with higher levels in the political hierarchy, would gravitate toward the traditional rigidities in organizational form and process or (on the contrary) would they "spontaneously" adopt procedures similar to those found in the United States? The purpose of this article is to present the findings of these studies and to discuss their psychological and political implications.

Edwards Personality Preference Schedule

The E.P.P.S. contains measures of 15 social needs as originally defined by Murray *et al.* (9) and consists of 225 forced-choice items. The Schedule was translated and revised for Japanese-student populations according to methods described elsewhere (3). Although the Japanese version is different from the American version in some minor respects, the intercorrelations (which were generally low) among the 15 needs were remarkably like those found in an American sample. The correlation of the social desirability of an alternative with the probability that a given alternative is actually chosen was shown to be .40 (4) for the American version and .37 for the Japanese version. By these and other means the two versions were tested statistically and found to be satisfactory for the purpose of making gross transcultural comparisons.

The Japanese college students responding to the E.P.P.S. were drawn from five colleges and universities located in Tokyo, Kyoto, and Hiroshima and were approximately equally divided between men (N=458) and women (N=504). The

American data are those presented by Edwards (5) as the normative sample.

Comparative scores on the E.P.P.S. for Japanese and American college students are given in Table I and show that the Japanese men score lower on achievement, deference, and dominance, but higher on abasement, change, and endurance. Translating these labels into descriptions based on the items making up these categories, the Japanese male students are *less* interested than American counterparts in *(a)* solving problems others have found difficult, *(b)* being recognized as an authority in some special field, *(c)* accomplishing something of great significance (achievement). They are less interested also in *(d)* accepting the leadership of people they admire, *(e)* conforming to customs, *(f)* reading about the lives and thinking of great leaders (deference). Their lower dominance shows in *not* preferring *(g)* to accept leadership positions on committees or other organizations, *(h)* to defend one's point of view when attacked, *(i)* to settle disputes, or *(j)* to persuade and influence others.

On the other hand, the Japanese male students report that they, more than Americans, *(a)* accept blame personally when things go wrong, *(b)* feel inferior to others, *(c)* feel better when they give in to avoid a fight rather than force their own way (abasement). They, more than Americans, *(d)* like to experience novelty and change, *(e)* like to meet new people, *(f)* like to move about the country and live in different places (change). They also prefer to *(g)* work hard, *(h)* complete one job before taking on another, and *(i)* avoid interruptions in their work (endurance).

TABLE I
Means of the E.P.P.S. Variables

	College men		College women	
Need	Japanese (N = 458)	American (N = 760)	Japanese (N = 504)	American (N = 749)
Achievement	12.65	15.66*	12.23	13.08*
Deference	10.08	11.21*	11.24	12.40*
Order	10.73	10.23	10.57	10.24
Exhibition	10.17	14.40	10.03	14.28
Autonomy	15.23	14.34	14.97	12.29
Affiliation	15.08	15.00	16.31	17.40*
Intraception	16.05	16.12	18.15	17.32
Succorance	15.09	10.74	15.71	12.53
Dominance	12.49	17.44*	11.56	14.18*
Abasement	16.31	12.24*	17.67	15.11
Nurturance	13.04	14.04	13.43	16.42*
Change	16.19	15.51*	17.08	17.20
Endurance	16.49	12.66*	16.63	12.63*
Heterosexuality	17.35	17.65	12.48	14.34
Aggression	13.05	12.79	11.93	10.59

* Difference significant beyond the .01 level.

The Japanese women compared to American college women show much the same pattern—lower on achievement, deference, and dominance; and higher on endurance, although their scores on abasement and change are about equal to those for Americans. In addition they score lower on affiliation and nurturance. These latter two labels refer to preference for making and maintaining strong attachments with friends (affiliation) and assisting or sympathizing with others less fortunate (nurturance).

If we confine the discussion for the moment to the data on the men, it is clear that (except for the categories of deference and change) the values appear to conform with the stereotype of the Japanese general population as revealed by their cultural and political history. The pattern of self-abasement, an unwillingness to accept leadership responsibility, a capacity for hard work, and a low level of personal aspiration appear to mesh with the structure of grass roots society that characterized Japan prior to World War II. The deference and change categories are in marked contrast.

Persons intimately acquainted with the Japanese have suggested that especially among the students (during the period of this study) there existed a faddish preoccupation with rejecting tradition and what in Japan is often called feudalistic concepts.[1] The rejection appears to be more verbal than behavioral and appears, furthermore, to be one avenue through which students can express their new-found independence and the spirit of the new Japan. To some extent, rejection of "feudalism" may be not unlike the radical liberalism that at times sweeps American collegiate populations. It has been a common observation in America that the extreme liberal students often gravitate toward more conservative views as they attain maturity in their postcollege reference groups. It is possible that the higher scores in both the change and deference categories observed among the Japanese may be accounted for by these conditions which appear to be somewhat temporary, although time may prove this judgment incorrect.

In addition to scoring as the men do on achievement, deference, and dominance, the Japanese college women score lower than their American sisters on affiliation and nurturance. These categories appear to have little direct relevance to political behavior. Both suggest that the women prefer to avoid involvement at the personal level with others. (They are also lower in heterosexual interests and higher on autonomy but not significantly so). Perhaps these scores are a reflection of a condition one can observe throughout Japan which can be best described as a steep negative gradient in concern with matters lying outside the home. The typical Japanese home is spotlessly clean and well ordered. Leaving one's shoes at the entrance is but one of the customs that emphasizes this fact. The traditional daily bath and the immaculate personal grooming of all but the very lowest laborers further accents the concern with self. However, as one looks beyond the garden wall he is struck by the contrasts as evidenced by rubble heaps, the cluttered drainage ditches, the grime of unswept public buildings, litter on trains, and dusty streets which even the rains seem unable to clean. Although these matters are not alone under the control of the female segment of the population they do suggest that the Japanese give these public problems markedly less attention than their immediate personal environment. This lack of interest in and action directed toward the common-community welfare perhaps stems psychologically from low preferences for nurturance and affiliation especially noted in the college women. (College men also score lower on nurturance but not significantly so.) These scores and unsystematic general observations bespeak a preference for personal insulation from community matters. If this is true, then one could *not* interpret these symptoms as favorable for the development of the kind of democratic processes that characterize the United States.

The Volunteer Fire Companies

Some confirmation of this inference was found in our comparison of volunteer fire companies in both Japan and the United States. The differences in organizational structure are revealing. The typical American village-fire company is one that has been organized by a few men taking the initiative to pool their personal resources and raise additional funds by solicitation. Gradually they accumulate equipment, build a fire house, and enlist new members running up to 30-50 men with token assistance from municipal budgets. To a very large extent they are autonomous organizations dedicated, however, to protecting their communities from fire damage. The members pay dues, expend their own time, soil their own clothes, use their own cars, all without direct compensation to themselves.

The fire company of a Japanese village, although manned by "volunteers" is typically an arm of the municipal services supported by tax monies that are expended partly to pay the members a small annual stipend and partly to maintain or buy equipment and provide for one or more fire stations. A national law specifies the number of firemen, pumpers, and hose nozzles that every community ought to have as a function of the population density, the nature of the building construction, and the average annual wind velocity. Formulas also exist for granting to resort communities specified amounts of national aid based on the flow of transient population. A clerk is required by the national fire law to be assigned by the municipal government to maintain records of personnel (who may number up to 500-600 men) fire calls, extent of damage, and expenditures.

These differences suggest that the Japanese villagers presumably accept a much closer guidance over their local affairs than is true in the United States. On the other hand the national government may believe that the local leaders do not possess the necessary foresight, initiative, or interest to manage their fire-protection services effectively. Since these interpretations are not mutually exclusive, it is possible that elements of both are true. In any event, it appears that less autonomy is exercised at the community level with respect to fire protection and probably in other respects than is evident in the United States.

Another contrast appeared in the comparison of American and Japanese village-fire companies. The American units contained two hierarchies: one involved in the fire-fighting activities and consisted of a chief, deputy chief, lieutenants, driver engineers, etc.; the other, a maintenance hierarchy starting with a president, vice-president, secretary, treasurer, and a roster of committee chairmen. The more effective companies (as judged by five persons acquainted with their operations and performance in a fire school) were those in which the offices of the two hierarchies were distributed more widely over the membership than was true of the least effective companies, as shown in Table II. The table shows a steady increase in the number of persons holding offices in both hierarchies as their rated effectiveness declines. Other data analyzed more completely elsewhere (2) led to the conclusion that the observations given in Table II could not be attributed to either a larger pool of leaders or larger average membership in the A-rated or B-rated companies. Men in the most effective companies who held supervisory posts in their regular occupations were *less* likely to be officers in the fire company. It appeared that the effective companies were those with greater flexibility in the roles assumed by their members. This means, for instance, that at a fire, the chief or even one of the lieutenants may direct the president to perform certain tasks. At the monthly business meeting, it is the president's prerogative to issue the orders rather than accept them. This flexibility in status and role appeared to be related to the effectiveness of the organization in the United States.

TABLE II
Average Number of Persons Holding Offices in Fire-Fighting
and Maintenance Hierarchies

Parameter	Company rating			
	A* ($N = 16$)	B ($N = 12$)	C ($N = 12$)	D** ($N = 17$)
Average per company	.73	.83	1.00	1.24

*High.
**Low.

In Japan the two hierarchies do not exist. The fire organization typically was headed by a chief, his deputy chiefs, a number of geographical division captains, and so on. The chief not only directed operations at the fire but was the presiding officer at meetings, and the point of contact with the municipal government, public, and higher levels in the Prefecture office. The chief was ordinarily elected by the other officers of the company and was invariably a person prominent in other aspects of the community life. In most cases the chiefs were prominent politicians (although we never found a mayor serving also as fire chief), professional persons, or leading business men. We were told that the chief is often selected either because he has demonstrated his ability elsewhere to organize and lead a group or because he is the best educated person in the area. Although some had served an "apprenticeship" as a lesser officer in the company, only three out of the 50 had risen "from the ranks." In other words, position in the community hierarchy had a great bearing on becoming the fire chief, almost regardless of the individual's experience in or knowledge about fire fighting.

Translated into role-flexibility terms these data suggest that the Japanese are less flexible than their American corresponding numbers both with respect to the complexities of the structure and with respect to the selection of their leaders.

Implications for Democratic Processes

It has never been established empirically that the personal values of a population have any relevance to their political behavior. However, on *a priori* grounds it appears reasonable to expect that a population's predispositions for accepting social responsibility, for personal autonomy, or for public debate would have relevance to their governmental procedures. One finds in reading between the lines of many political scientists (7) assumptions of this sort which have never been put to a cross-cultural test. It is of some historical interest to recall that deTocqueville in 1835 made the following observation:

Amongst the novel objects that attracted my attention during my stay in the United States, nothing struck me more forcibly than the general equality of conditions. I readily discovered the prodigious influence which this primary fact exercises on the whole course of society: it gives a certain direction to public opinion, and a certain character to the laws; it imparts new maxims to the governing powers, and peculiar habits to the governed. I speedily perceived that the influence of this fact extends far beyond the political character and the laws of the country, and that it has no less empire over private society than over the government: it creates opinions, engenders sentiments, suggests the ordinary practices of life and modifies whatever it does not produce *(London and Westminister Review,* October, 1835).

Although we are now in a position to make some cross-cultural comparisons of a psychological kind as this and other studies demonstrate, we have no systematic means of quantifying the governmental processes which might, for instance, place a government somewhere on a scale running from totalitarian to town-meeting democracy. The absence of such a government index prevents us from being as rigorous in drawing inferences as would otherwise be the case. With this caveat, let us proceed.

As indicated in the previous section, the evidence from the students (although different in kind from the fire-company data) nevertheless converges on a general inference that the Japanese become ego involved with community affairs less readily than do Americans. The students are less interested than Americans in assuming leadership positions, and in providing help and assistance to their friends. The volunteer fire companies have shown less initiative and autonomy than their American counterparts and appear to have been directed from the upper levels of the hierarchy to organize themselves in specific ways; this, in spite of the fact that the fire danger is one that is controllable only by local means and would seem to be a threat having direct personal consequences. If a community problem of these dimensions does not stimulate strong local initiatives, it is difficult to conceive of one that would. Nevertheless, the Japanese villages and small towns appear to have been dependent upon higher authority to give them guidance if not more direct orders.

The greater self-abasement found among the students is likewise a symptom that suggests the Japanese are less likely than Americans to question the directives that come down through a chain of command. One of the features of the democratic process is just such evaluation of policies and operations which permit those in authority to shape their actions in accord with the wishes of the governed. If the people at the base of the hierarchy fail to express themselves, an important strength of the democratic procedures is lost.

In this connection McGinnies (8) has reported that Japanese and American college students endorse the following statement with about the same frequency (77 per cent): "Any private individual should have the right to criticize any government or governmental official anywhere in the world." The inference from McGinnies' data therefore, appears to run counter to those presented herein. Perhaps the last phrase of the statement "anywhere in the world" rather than "in our country" leaves the statement sufficiently broad in scope to erase a tendency (if it exists) to avoid criticism of one's own reference group.

It is also relevant to call attention to the general conclusions of McGinnies' study comparing Japanese and Americans on a number of civil-liberty issues. In general the Japanese appear to voice greater concern over censorship, freedom of speech, fair-employment practices, and the like than their American counterparts. The Japanese are the more liberal, although the differences are not as great as those found in previous studies by Remmers and Radler (10) or Kato (6).

The apparent disagreement between McGinnies' data and the E.P.P.S. findings reported herein can be resolved if one assumes that the civil-liberties responses of the Japanese are a reflection of their lower deference toward authority. Freedom from censorship and other forms of hierarchical controls appear to be more closely related to deference than to any of the other categories in the Edwards Schedule, and it was on this category that the Japanese scored lower than American students. In the previous discussion we tended to minimize the importance of this finding for the long run as a phase through which students in both countries seem to pass toward more conservative views.

It would have been a major miracle if the Japanese had been able to overturn their traditional value system as rapidly as the governmental structure was changed. The Emperor's directive to collaborate with the Occupation Forces and the subsequent adoption of the democratic constitution were in accord with the traditional orientations toward authority. It is in this one area that the Japanese appear to have made some modification in their value system, although we have no precise data on this point at an earlier time. The major thrust of the data suggests that traditional Japanese values still persist which provide only weak psychological support for the democratic processes as they are practiced in the United States. It is therefore a mistake to believe that the Japanese political and governmental operations, although outwardly similar to our own, are basically "westernized."

FOOTNOTE

1. I am especially indebted to Dr. Shin-ichi Takezawa of Rikkyo University for this insight.

REFERENCES

1. BENEDICT, R. The Chrysanthemum and the Sword. Boston: Houghton Mifflin, 1946.
2. BERRIEN, F. K. Democracy in village Japan. Tech. Rep. 12, Contract Nonr 404-10, Rutgers University, New Brunswick, New Jersey, 1963.
3. ———. Values of Japanese and American students. Tech. Rep. 14, Contract Nonr 404-10, Rutgers University, New Brunswick, New Jersey, 1964.
4. EDWARDS, A. L. Social Desirability Variable in Personality Assessment. New York: Dryden, 1957.
5. ———. Manual, Edwards Personal Preference Schedule. New York: Psychological Corp., 1959.
6. KATO; R. Political attitudes of Japanese adolescents. *Psychologia,* 1961, 4, 198-200.
7. LASSWELL, H.D. Power and Personality. New York: Norton 1948.
8. McGINNIES, E. Attitudes Toward Civil Liberties Among Japanese and American University Students. College Park, Md.: Univ. of Maryland, Inst. for Behav. Res., 1963.
9. MURRAY, H. A., *et al.* Explorations in Personality. New York: Oxford Univ. Press, 1938.
10. REMMERS, H. H., & RADLER, D. H. The American Teenager. Indianapolis-New York: Bobbs-Merrill, 1957.

AUTHORITARIANISM IN AN AUTHORITARIAN CULTURE: THE CASE OF JAPAN

Agnes M. Niyekawa

How authoritarian are the people of an authoritarian culture? Can their authoritarianism be measured by a scale developed to discriminate authoritarian individuals in a democratic culture? Is the "authoritarian personality" a universal concept, applicable to any culture? These are the basic questions this study was interested in answering, using Japan as an example of an authoritarian culture. More specifically, this study attempted to test the applicability of the F scale[1] for cross-cultural research, and to explore in a limited fashion the factors associated with authoritarianism in Japan.

The instrument used to measure authoritarianism was Christie's version of the F scale, consisting of the ten best original items from the California F scale and ten best reversed items.[3] This scale had the advantage of giving, besides an overall authoritarianism F score (1) an F score based on responses to authoritarian items; (2) an F score based on responses to democratic items; (3) an agreement or acquiescence score; and (4) an extremity score. In addition to the 20 items from Christie's F scale, ten items from the original F scale were added for the purpose of item analysis. The scoring system is shown in Table 1.

Table 1
SCORING OF F-SCALE ITEMS

Answer Category					F Score Straight Items	F Score Reversed Items	Extremity Score
Agree strongly	...	...	...	...	7	1	9
Agree somewhat	...	...	...	...	6	2	4
Agree slightly	...	...	...	...	5	3	1
No answer	...	...	...	...	4	4	0
Disagree slightly	...	...	...	...	3	5	1
Disagree somewhat	...	...	...	...	2	6	4
Disagree strongly	...	...	...	...	1	7	9

Scores:

F+ score: mean of the ten straight items.

F− score: mean of the ten reversed items.

Overall F score: mean of the 20 (F+ and F−) items.

Extremity score: sum of the variances from the neutral point for the 20 items. Theoretical range of scores: 0 to 180.

Acquiescence score: difference between the total F score of the ten F+ items and that of the ten F− items with a constant of 50 added. Theoretical range: −10 to 110.

F+ score: mean of the ten additional items from the original F scale.

Niyekawa − *From The International Journal of Social Psychiatry,* Vol. 12, No. 4, (1966). Reprinted by permission.

The subjects were high school seniors drawn from two urban and four rural high schools in Japan. The total Japanese sample of 543 was used for comparisons with an American college sample of 814 from three geographically widely separated areas, and an American high school sample of 23. The sample size was reduced for comparisons among various subcultures within Japan.

The first hypothesis was that authoritarianism in Japan is characterized by acquiescence, and therefore, that both the acquiescence and extremity scores of Japanese would be higher than those of comparable groups of Americans.

Christie, Seidenberg and Havel[3] found the tendency to agree to be more prevalent among those with moderate attitudes than those with extreme attitudes. They suggested that it is those persons who do not have strong attitudes pro or con who should be most apt to display a response-set to agree. Such a relationship actually had been found by Brim.[2] In other words, extremity and acquiescence are not expected to go together.

The post-war change in Japan from authoritarianism to democracy has puzzled many foreigners. Stoetzel, in his book *Without the Chrysanthemum and the Sword,*[6] states "Such docility (to the Occupation Forces) is not merely suspicious after the determination shown by the people in its struggle against half the world, it is incomprehensible". The inconsistency of the Japanese seems to be explainable only by acquiescence. It was the Emperor's wish that his subjects follow the orders of the Occupation Forces. Thus, for the Japanese to switch from one extreme end of militarism to the other end of democracy was not inconsistent but consistent, not disloyal but loyal. There is no absolute right or wrong, but the word of the authority is right. On the basis of this assumption, it seemed likely that Japanese would show acquiescence and extremity at the same time.

The hypothesis was supported in that Japanese were found to be significantly more acquiescent and extreme in their manner of responses than comparable American groups. The results are shown in Table 2. Thus the findings in the United States that acquiescent individuals have moderate rather than extreme attitudes

TABLE 2
DIFFERENCES BETWEEN JAPANESE AND AMERICAN SAMPLES ON THE
ACQUIESCENCE AND EXTREMITY SCORES

Score Sample	N	Mean	S	SE_D	t	p*
Acquiescence						
Amer. Colleges	814	54.4	12.32	.61	15.05	p<.001
Jap. High Schools . . .	543	65.58	10.19	2.52	2.34	p<.01
Amer. High School . . .	23	57.7	11.90			
Extremity						
Amer. Colleges	814	97.8	25.89	1.47	4.18	p<.001
Jap. High Schools . . .	543	103.95	26.86	4.88	2.24	p<.025
Amer. High School . . .	23	93.0	22.74			

*One-tailed test.

were not substantiated in Japan. Japanese were more authoritarian than Americans on authoritarian items (F+ scale), while on democratic items (F− scale) they turned out to be more democratic than Americans. The fact that they can agree strongly with ideologically inconsistent statements suggests that they are agreeing with the source of the statements, namely the authority, rather than with the content of the statements. The implication of these findings is that Japanese have accepted democracy only superficially. They had been told that "democracy" is the right thing. Thus in being democratic, they are actually being authoritarian, acquiescence being the major component of authoritarianism in Japan.

The second hypothesis tested was that upper-class students would be more authoritarian than lower-class students. This meant that, if the first hypothesis was supported, the upper-class students would have a higher acquiescence score. Comparisons among subcultural groups, however, indicated that, in general, the lower class tended to be higher in both authoritarianism and acquiescence than the upper class when the socio-economic classification was dichotomized, the rural group higher in acquiescence than the urban group, and the females higher in authoritarianism but not in acquiescence than the males. While none of these differences were significant, they were in general agreement with findings in the United States.

Significant differences, however, were found in acquiescence when the sample was divided into five groups according to levels of cultural sophistication. The index of cultural sophistication was based on the number of family subscriptions to papers and magazines. Table 3 indicates that cultural sophistication had a curvilinear relationship with acquiescence, and therefore with the positively worded authoritarian scales F+ and F+.' It can be seen that the democratic scale F−, consisting of negatively worded items, has two forces working against each other. If one has a tendency to agree, which is an authoritarian characteristic, one gets a *low* authoritarianism score. The F− score and the resulting Overall F score, therefore, do not fall in the same pattern as the F+ or acquiescence score.

TABLE 3
MEANS ON VARIOUS F-SCALE SCORES FOR GROUPS DIFFERING
IN CULTURAL SOPHISTICATION

Score			I	II	III	IV	V	p*
					Cultural Sophistication			
F+	...	...	4.19	4.25	4.28	3.90	5.84	.001
F−	...	...	2.83	2.83	2.73	2.69	2.79	—
Overall F		...	3.51	3.54	3.51	3.30	3.34	—
F+'	...	...	4.52	4.58	4.65	4.43	4.44	.001
Acq.	...	...	63.53	64.22	65.52	62.10	60.49	.05

*Based on analysis of variance.

The group at the median level of cultural sophistication was highest in acquiescence, while those less as well as more sophisticated were lower on this score. Since one of the roles played in post-war Japan by papers and magazines, or by the mass media of communication in general, is to introduce what is "modern" and fashionable, such as Western concepts, the index of cultural sophistication may also be considered an index of Western democratic influences in the family. It was therefore interpreted that the low scores obtained by the most sophisticated group at level 5 were due to greater Westernization on their part, while the low scores of the least sophisticated group were considered to have been obtained without their having been subjected to strong democratic influences. In Fig. 1, the empirical relationship found between authoritarianism, that is acquiescence, and level of cultural sophistication is shown by the solid line. Since Western influences tend to lower authoritarianism scores, one might assume that the middle group at level 3 was even more authoritarian before it was subjected to Western influences, and that the group presently at level 5 possibly one step higher than the middle group before Westernization. The broken line in the figure expresses the hypothetical relationship between cultural sophistication and authoritarianism before the introduction of Western democratic ideology, assuming that these groups occupied the same level of cultural sophistication in the past. The relationship is expected to have been linear, with the least sophisticated group ranking the lowest, and the most sophisticated group highest in authoritarianism.

FIGURE 1

Relationship between authoritarianism and cultural sophistication
before and after Westernization

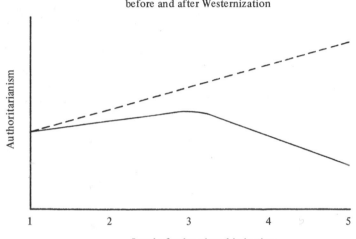

Level of cultural sophistication

– – – – – – Before Westernization (Hypothetical)

—————— After Westernization   (Empirical)

The curvilinear relationship found seemed to provide a clue to the lack of supportive data on the second hypothesis that the upper-class students would be more authoritarian than the lower-class students. Since cultural sophistication and socio-economic level are usually correlated, this curvilinear relationship should be found between authoritarianism and socio-economic class only if more than two categories are used in the socio-economic classification.

In order to find out whether such an assumption about the curvilinear relationship would be supported, the rural agricultural group was divided into three classes based on their pre-war agricultural status, namely landlords, farmers with their own land, and tenant farmers. The results are shown in Table 4. A clearly inverted V curve was found on all the authoritarianism scores. The differences between the groups were not significant for any of the scores, however.

Table 4

MEANS ON VARIOUS F-SCALE SCORES FOR SUBGROUPS IN AGRICULTURE

Score					Tenant Farmers	Farmers with Own Land	Landlords	p*
F+	...	...	...	...	3.76	4.28	4.09	–
F–	...	...	...	...	2.72	2.80	2.79	–
Overall F		...	...	...	3.24	3.53	3.44	–
F+'	...	...	...	...	4.38	4.52	4.38	–
Acq.	...	...	...	...	60.37	64.79	63.05	–

* Based on analysis of variance.

This finding on the curvilinear relationship between authoritarianism, mainly acquiescence, and cultural sophistication or socio-economic class in Japan has an important implication. It has been assumed that education tends to liberalize the individual's ideology. Supportive data have been found not only in the United States, but also in Japan by Kido and Sugi[4] when only urban samples were used. However, until the end of the last war, Japanese education emphasized traditional value systems, such as self-discipline, or the observation of hierarchical relationship among people by showing respect and obedience to one's superiors. In such a society, the individual less exposed to education was likely to be less influenced by these authoritarian values, and therefore to be less authoritarian. When there is a sudden change in the value system, the change seems to start with the upper class, and gradually spread to lower levels. The recent change to a democratic value system in Japan seemed to have resulted in a clear picture of cultural lag among the various classes—the middle class being one step behind the upper class, and the lower class one step behind the middle class.

It might be emphasized that the value orientation of the culture needs to be taken into consideration before any assumption as to class differences are made. Findings based on urban samples or college students can be misleading if these findings are generalized to the whole nation. It is suggested that the patterns found in this study of the differential impact of Western ideology on various subgroups in Japan may be generalizable to other cultures in which the values of the dominant elite had previously been highly authoritarian.

Now I would like to go back to the general questions posed at the beginning. How authoritarian are the people of an authoritarian culture? Can their authoritarianism be measured by a scale developed to discriminate authoritarian individuals in a democratic society?

As mentioned earlier, authoritarianism in Japan was found to be character-ized by acquiescence. Japanese tend to agree with authoritarian statements as well as democratic statements. Thus, ideologically consistent authoritarianism as defined by the California group does not seem to be an important part of authoritarianism in Japan. The fact that acquiescence was found to go hand in hand with extremity of responses suggests that even when their responses are ideologically inconsistent, Japanese respond with certainty. In other words, their certainty is not based on ideological conviction, but the conviction that the words of the authority are right. In this connection, Christie's version of the F scale was found to have high utility. When respondents tend to be acquiescent, results for items disagreed with can be taken more at face value than items agreed with, since agreement cannot be taken to mean endorsement of the ideological content. Thus, if the F scale in its original form consisting of only authoritarian statements had been given, it would have been difficult to separate ideologically consistent individuals from acquiescent individuals. The prevalence of response sets of various types, as well as the difficulty of obtaining exact translation equivalents of test items point to the danger of relying heavily on the *content* of responses. A test with greater emphasis on the *manner* of response rather than *content* will be a more valid tool in cross-cultural research.

The question as to whether the authoritarian personality is a universal concept applicable to any culture has already been partially answered. If it turns out that acquiescence is the major component of authoritarianism in other authoritarian cultures also, then it would *not* be quite correct to say that authoritarian cultures produce authoritarian personality of the type postulated by Adorno's group. Can we then say that authoritarian cultures produce what might be called an "acquiescent personality"? The answer to this question would also be "no" if we assume a certain personality syndrome.

In a cross-cultural comparison of racial prejudice, Pettigrew[5] found that where prejudice was the cultural norm, prejudice was not related to authoritarianism. In other words, whether a person goes against his cultural norm or stays with the norm of being prejudiced seems to make a difference in whether or not prejudice is related to personality structure. Similarly, the personality structure of two acquiescent individuals may not be the same if one is a member of a democratic society where independence is stressed and the other a member of an authoritarian society where acquiescence is the norm. The latter would be considered a well-adjusted person fitting into his authoritarian culture, while the former would not be regarded in the same manner. Rather, his tendency to agree would be interpreted to stem from feelings of insecurity and the need to be liked. Thus the personality syndrome into which "acquiescence" would fall may be quite different for the two cultures.

In conclusion, it is suggested that the use of a term like authoritarian personality or the acquiescent personality as if it were a universal personality syndrome be avoided until we have strong enough cross-cultural evidence to that effect.

REFERENCES

1. Adorno. T. W., Frenkel-Brunswik, Else, Levinson, D. J., and Sanford, R. N.: *The Authoritarian Personality*. New York: Harper, 1950.
2. Brim, O. G., Jr.: "Attitude content-intensity and probability expectations." *Amer. Sociol. Rev.,* 1955, 20, 68-76.
3. Christie, R., Havel, Joan, and Seidenberg, B.: "Is the F scale irreversible?" *J. Abnorm. Soc. Psychol.,* 1958, 56, 143-159.
4. Kido, K., and Sugi, M.: "A report of research on social stratification and mobility in Tokyo (III)—The structure of social consciousness." *Jap. Sociol. Rev.,* 1954, 13-14, 74-100. (In Japanese.)
5. Pettigrew, T. F.: "Personality and socio-cultural factors in intergroup attitudes, a cross-national comparison." *J. Conflict Resolution.* 1958, 2, 29-42.
6. Stoetzel, J.: *Without the Chrysanthemum and the Sword.* New York: Columbia Univ. Press, 1955.

SOCIAL STRESS AND CORONARY HEART DISEASE IN JAPAN: A HYPOTHESIS

Y. Scott Matsumoto

Japan has one of the lowest rates of coronary heart disease in the world; the United States, one of the highest. In 1960-1961, the white male American possessed the highest known age-adjusted death rate in the world for arteriosclerotic and degenerative heart disease—326.2 per 100,000, as compared to 67.8 for the Japanese male.[1] The standardized male mortality ratio for coronary heart disease, according to Haenszel and Kurihara,[2] was 481 white Americans for every 100 Japanese. In a 1962 symposium the ratio of the death rate from coronary heart disease to the total death rate was reported as 33.2 for U. S. whites and 8.7 for Japanese.[3] For Japanese men age 50—54, the death rate in 1953-1954 was less than a tenth of that for white American men.[4] Coronary heart disease remains the most serious health problem for the middle-aged U. S. male.

This remarkable difference between Japan and the United States in their respective tendency to coronary heart disease cannot be regarded as merely accidental, nor is it possible to foist the blame entirely on hereditary or ethnic factors. Any racial tendency toward disease of the heart or vessels is discounted by comparison of rates for Japanese residing in Japan, in Hawaii, and in the continental United States. Gordon, in his provocative article, noted that the trend for the Japanese in Hawaii, especially the men, was intermediate with respect to cardiovascular mortality between the Japanese of Japan and of the United States.[5] The Japanese who migrate to mainland United States exhibit American coronary rates.

Explanations in Etiology

In the search for possible factors involved in the etiology of coronary heart disease, the phenomenon of disease has been suggested as the possible product of the way of life of a people, where cultural and social components may well have an important bearing on health and illness. During a lifetime differences in the mode of life and social environment may exert an accumulating influence. In current studies it seems reasonable to state that the two major factors of (1) high-fat diet and (2) emotional stress, both concerning living habits, seem to be increasingly implicated in the development of coronary heart disease.

Diet. Laboratory research and epidemiologic studies support the postulate that the fat content of the daily diet, especially highly saturated animal fats, has an important effect on the frequency of coronary heart disease in a population. Keys contends that the incidence of coronary heart disease is related to the high-fat diet

Matsumoto — *From The Milbank Memorial Fund Quarterly,* Vol. 43, No. 1, (January, 1970). Reprinted by permission.

by virture of its influence on the level of serum cholesterol. Blood levels of cholesterol and of triglycerides are elevated in, and are directly related to, the development of atherosclerosis, a basic disorder in coronary disease. In his study of the Japanese in Japan, Hawaii and Los Angeles, Keys further denoted the relation of low serum cholesterol and dietary fat to the uncommon occurrence of coronary heart disease in Japan. Gore and Snapper also emphasized the importance of diet in atherosclerosis. However, these interpretations have not been completely clarified nor universally accepted. Stout and his associates report that the Italian-American community of Roseto, Pennsylvania, has a strikingly low death rate from myocardial infarction although total fat consumption is at least equal to that of the average United States citizen. Among the Navajo Indians, despite fat intake and serum cholesterol levels comparable to those of urban United States inhabitants, ischemic heart disease remains infrequent. Dietary studies by Paul, Malhotra, Thomas and Ross and others reveal no significant association of intake of dietary fat or of serum cholesterol level with the probability of developing coronary heart disease. The diet hypothesis, nevertheless, is strongly supported by the fact that the diet of Japan derives less than ten per cent of its calories from fat as compared with 40 per cent in the American diet and by the findings relative to the differences between Japanese living on different diets. Furthermore, in recent years, as the intake of dietary fat in Japan has steadily increased, a simultaneous increase in coronary heart disease has been reported.

Social Stress. The factor of social stress is also widely postulated as occupying a foremost position in the development of coronary heart disease. Regardless of how stress is operationally defined, clinical physiologic and psychologic studies have shown it to be related to factors implicated in the etiology of coronary heart disease. As is the prodigiously high-fat diet, emotional stress is associated with the elevation of serum cholesterol. This has been demonstrated in studies of cholesterol levels on medical students during examinations, accountants during tax preparation deadlines and patients undergoing surgery. Studies by Russek and Zohman, Ostfield and his colleagues, Miller and other investigators show that coronary patients tended to be under greater chronic stress, particularly occupational pressures, than a similar group of persons without heart disease. Friedman and Rosenman have been extensively studying the profile and behavior pattern of patients who are "coronary prone." Coronary heart conditions may have their onset in the setting of stressful life situations that are associated with a rise in cholesterol and other lipids, and be related to disturbances of fat metabolism. Chronic and cumulative stress without relief may reach a point of sudden cardiac illness after years of apparent toleration.

Numerous other studies have strongly indicated that the chronic stresses and strains of modern Western life may be major contributing causes to coronary heart disease. The processes of urban-industrial change are seen to create a universal style of life in modern cities where traditional behavior patterns were disrupted by an increased impersonality in interpersonal relations. Tyroler and Cassel explored the effect of urbanization and found that mortality from coronary heart disease for rural male residents of North Carolina increased with the increasing urbanization of their county of residence. Wardwell and his colleagues in a study of white males in Connecticut, found that increasing frequency of coronary heart disease was associated with "emancipation from traditional orientation." Syme and his associates studied "cultural mobility" in relation to coronary heart disease in North Dakota and in California, and found a higher rate of coronary heart disease for men of urban American background than for men of rural or urban European background. In 1966, at the National Workshop Conference on Socioenvironmental Stress and Cardiovascular Disease, a consistent finding in the comprehensive review of published works in the field indicated that higher rates of heart disease occurred in the more modern urban-industrial settings than in rural nonindustrial areas. However, the relations of modernization and urbanization to coronary heart disease cannot be accepted as sufficient explanation. The contemporary Japanese, like the Americans, are highly urbanized and industrialized. Yet, differences in coronary heart disease are major and persistent.

Hypothesis

Although the diet factor is strongly supported by studies of the Japanese on a low-fat diet, the stress interpretation appears to be contradicted in the case of Japan, the only nation outside of the West to achieve industrialization and urbanization yet possess low coronary rates. Deeper probes into the social integration of the individual within a particular social system may provide insight into sociosomatic processes that may be related to human stress and illness. Individual measures of the level of cholesterol, blood pressure or triglycerides do not necessarily assist in clarifying group differences in diseases. The differences of coronary heart disease rates between Japan and the United States might be comprehended more clearly in social terms, using the group principle.

Some behavioral scientists view the sociocultural system as a stress-inducing environmental factor, but it is well to remember that stress-reducing components are also present simultaneously. In well-integrated societies, attempts are made to contain anxieties and tensions within appropriate limits. In Arsenian's terms, the *easy* cultures prescribe techniques to engender stress-reduction for members, whereas, in *tough* cultures, tension dissipations are chronically blocked.[6] All societies have not equally evolved stress-resolving techniques to reduce in the individual those excessive strains that may aggravate physiologic reactions.[7] Thus, sociocultural factors may either facilitate or inhibit the extent of disease in a given population.

The basic hypothesis to be explored here is that stress is one of the complex and interrelated factors involved in the etiology of coronary heart disease. The hypothesis further assumes a duality in the relations of the sociocultural system to stress and hence to coronary heart disease. Aspects of the sociocultural system may induce stress, but institutions and orientations within the system may reduce or contain stress. Those factors in the society that are productive or ameliorative of stress need not be independent of other factors. Rather, they are interrelated as predisposing or minimizing factors with other aspects of environment, of diet, of health habits and of ways of living.

This broad hypothesis is not susceptible to empirical exploration without specifications. A working hypothesis specific to disease and culture may be stated as follows: The etiology of coronary heart disease is multiple and complex, but in urban-industrial Japan, the in-group work community of the individual, with its institutional stress-reducing strategies, plays an important role in decreasing the frequency of the disease. If adverse and stressful life experiences may be translated through physiologic mechanisms into bodily diseases, then the converse seems reasonable. Deleterious circumstances of life need not be expressed in malfunctioning of the physiologic or psychologic systems if a meaningful social group is available through which the individual can derive emotional support and understanding.

Japanese Society and the Individual

Although the history of Japan extends back several millennia, contemporary Japan traces primarily from the tradition of the Tokugawa oligarchy and hierarchy, beginning early in the seventeenth century. In the traditional society, the *girininjo* (moral duty versus human feelings) psychology was intermixed with Confucianism and Buddhism. During the two and a half centuries of the Tokugawa regime, the *ie* (house) and the family orientations assumed great social importance.

Studies by Japanese and Western scholars concur that the basic values and the sociocultural structure of industrialized Japan do not seem the same as those of the West. A persistent social trait, as seen by these studies, is the tendency toward group emphasis in Japan. In the West the increasing importance of individualism, focused on the relative autonomy of the person, has been emphasized as an outstanding correlative to modern industrial-urban growth. In spite of rapid social change in Japan, observers agree that Japan has not moved from group values toward individualism, but rather retains strong emphasis on collectivity orientations within the in-group.[8] Modern Japanese tend to judge one another rather less as individuals than as representatives of groups. As Japan moves from an agrarian community to an urban-industrial society, this writer believes collectivity orientations have been strongly maintained while shifting from the traditionally hierarchical basis to increasingly egalitarian principles.[9] Caudill and Scarr, in an empirical study of the Japanese value system, state the dominant value orientation as that of collaterality that stresses group welfare and group consensus rather than lineality or individualism as primary goals.[10] A recent publication indicates that the Japanese sociologists have begun to critically view their urban society in terms of the group idea of *dozoku*, the locality blood and/or fictitious kinship ties.[11] Group orientations remain a dominant part of the social environment of Japan.

Western observers also note a greater sense of dependency in the modal Japanese personality. Marked dependence, or interdependence, may be an outcome of the group emphasis in Japan. The Japanese socialization of dependency has been indicated by many writers. In comparison with the American sample in Vogels' study,[12] the Japanese children required a great deal more emotional support from their parents. The Japanese child does develop increasing independence as he matures, but his desires for dependence are much more socially approved. Goodman, in a study of occupational choices of Japanese and American children, found that the Japanese children were markedly less self-centered and egocentric than were the American children. [13] Caudill has observed the pattern of dependent relations between psychiatric patients and hospital staff in Japan.[14,15] Doi has discussed the term *amaeru* (wish to be loved, or dependency needs) as a key idea in comprehending Japanese personality structure,[16,17] although it seems dangerous to seize upon a single notion as the magic key to explain the tone of a culture. Currently Japan shows a trend toward greater independency, and as Whyte[18] and Riesman[19] contend, Americans are becoming more dependent and "other-directed." Nevertheless, expressed in extremes for the sake of contrast, it can be said that the Japanese prefers a situation in which he can be fairly dependent, whereas the American prefers conditions that permit a measure of independence.

Work Group Characteristics. In urban-industrial Japan, as in the West, the shift has been from residential collectivity to work collectivity. The immediate work group is of primary importance. The integration of the average Japanese male into the social and economic order, however, is not through his occupation *per se*, but through his firm. The individual's sense of identity originates with his employment by a particular business company or government ministry. If asked about his work, the Japanese male will most likely reply by stating the name of his firm, not by giving his occupation. An employee, once hired, generally is never dismissed unless strong evidence is found of gross negligence, disobedience or commission of a crime, all of which are extremely rare. Seniority, as much as competence, is important for advancement of wage or rank within the business enterprise. Once recruited even the inefficient employee is usually retained until his retirement age. A Japanese employee almost never leaves his company to work for another firm. In contrast the American is likely to move from one job to another fairly often. Once hired, the Japanese worker tends to have greater employment security until his retirement than does his American counterpart.

Paternalism is exhibited by Japanese enterprise by the various welfare facilities and benefits offered exclusively to its own employees. An employee and his family often may live in company housing free or at a low rental. All fairly large business companies offer medical treatment and care at the company hospital at minimal cost. At the company cooperative, household needs and general goods can be bought at cheaper prices than at the ordinary stores. The employee can eat inexpensively at the company dining room and participate in various forms of recreation subsidized by his firm. For example, the Rohto Pharmaceutical Company of Osaka, a leading producer of eye-lotion in Japan, with over 800 employees, boasts "a spacious dining room with elaborately designed tables, a workers' assembly hall of semi-domed structure being used for movies, concerts and lecture meetings, an athletic hall, a two-storied boarding house for bachelor workers, a tremendous swimming pool and a boating pond." Thus, it is often said that the Japanese firm is "not a profit-making organization but a social welfare organization."

Group structure. An important characteristic of the group structure in Japan is the tremendous feeling of in-group solidarity. The focus is on the in-group as opposed to the out-group. In contrast, the dichotomy of the individual pitted against the group is the difference frequently described in the sociologic writing in the United States. In Japan, the crucial distinction is between the closed community in-group of one's own collectivity and other out-group collectivities. Such a distinction is almost unknown among Americans under ordinary circumstances, although Stouffer documents such social solidarity in groups of fighting American soldiers under military stress in combat situations.[20]

Another Japanese characteristic appears to be the lack of any real existence or importance of the individual apart from his group. Only through the intimate group membership that absorbs his total personality does the individual find meaning to his existence. Doi, a Japanese psychiatrist, notes that in therapy many of his patients have no clear conception of self apart from the group.[21,22] When the individual has little importance outside his group, any "disharmony," as often described in American studies,[23] between the individual and the group tends to dissolve. The individual and group interests are united, which sharpens the demarcation between in- and out-groups. Motivations for achievement and mobility do exist, but within the same membership group rather than as is so often true in the United States, a desire to gain admission and acceptance into a new group.

Group membership is continuous over the years. Both the individual and the firm look upon his employment as a lifetime commitment. The commercial firm recruits the fresh graduate from school, trains him and keeps him until his retirement age. As companies usually hire new employees only once a year during the college and high school graduation season, the individual joins at the same time as a large number of other men. In the orientation programs and daily tasks he is in constant contact with his peers. Those workers who entered before him become the *senpai* (senior or superior), and anyone employed after him is a *kohai* (junior), both terms being frequently used in company conversations. Employees expect to continue together for their entire careers.

The work collectivity offers satisfying emotional support and social attachment in a group relation of human feelings and intimacy. In psychiatric terms, the affectively-involved contacts of total personalities exist with a heightened sense of interactions. Minc and his associates observe that the coronary patient in urban Australia tends to maintain an intellectual control of his behavior, but that his planned activities lack emotional backing. Among his fellow employees, the Japanese individual can relax, argue, criticize and be obstinate without endangering relations. Caudill suggests that communication and expression of tenderness and affection are handled well and adaptively in Japan, whereas such expressions of tenderness, especially between American men, are very difficult.[24,25] The Japanese can forego the privacy that screens his inner self and merge himself within the identity of his group.

Another important characteristic is that each person has his own intrinsic worth because of the contribution he makes to the group. No member of the group is considered an independent individual in the Western pattern, but his individual importance to the group is by no means minimized. At the proper place and at the proper time, each can express his personality and has a role to play. Furthermore, under certain circumstances it is possible, because of his group attachment, for the expression of strong individualism. When criticized or attacked by an outsider, the individual, right or wrong, will have the group's support and backing.

Closely related to the above characteristic, a greater sense of mutual tolerance and respect is also developed. Although a group may contain persons antagonistic to each other, the number of persons in the group is enough that an individual is able to select close comrades. Simultaneously, understanding and compassion for each of his fellow workers in the group are fostered through the years. In his study of the Japanese salary man, Vogel keenly observes: "Because most groups are relatively stable, a person usually is not judged on the basis of a single performance. The intimate association of group members over years makes it possible for them to know each other's abilities and weak points intimately."[26] Each individual is able to establish an area of competence in an activity where his talent in some manner is better than that of his co-workers.

Within the strong collectivity orientation, no distinction is made between work and leisure and between "public" and "private" life. Unlike the American view, which holds that leisure is an individual and private affair apart from work, no clear division exists for many Japanese between work and play that is performed together with his co-workers. The Japanese is not an enthusiastic joiner of formal leisure-time clubs separated from his group, even for specific recreational purposes. In both labor and leisure, the Japanese individual is involved primarily with his fellow workers. The work collectivity is almost always composed of a group of male associates. Closest friendships are formed between people of the same sex who are in constant contact. Vogel writes that in Japan the husband's friends are his fellow workers; the wife's friends are her female neighbors. Vogel further notes that "these relationships are remarkably intimate." A husband centers his social life at his place of employment; the wife on her immediate neighbors and relatives. In their separate social communities, the husband seldom meets his wife's friends, and the wife does not associate with her husband's friends. The Japanese salary man clearly differentiates his activities between his work and his family life. As stated above, work and leisure are performed together with his co-workers, but a distinction is made between the establishment versus the family. In this sense, the American man is probably much more a family man than the Japanese husband who spends much less time with his wife. The Japanese women, notably the wives, act to preserve the male's position of superiority with the traditional prerogatives. For the Western man, Simmons and Wolff have speculated that "the 'emancipation of woman' that has characterized western nations during the past half-century or more has placed a differential stress in man-woman relationships with the 'pace' of modern life adversely affecting the security of men more than that of women . . . This tide of change can be viewed as undermining the established statuses and emotional supports for man."

In Japan, also, as more women find jobs and work outside the home, the husbands of Japan may find their position being altered. In 1955, 6.3 per cent of all married women worked, and, by 1960, that figure rose to 9.3 per cent. The general situation persists, however, whereby the Japanese male is permitted much emotional support from his women. Within a social matrix of male dominance and superiority, much of his leisure-time activities are spent with his co-workers, which may involve female participation in lesser roles as waitresses or hostesses, but almost always exclude the wives.

Stress-Reducing Activities and Facilities

Sociocultural systems inculcate stress as part of the normal social processes. Japanese society is no exception. Continuous and accumulating stress of various types and varying degrees is part of the daily living pattern in the modern urban-industrial milieu. In the impersonal environment of the modern world, it is not unusual for the individual of the West to spend the major portion of his working hours among persons in whom he cannot usually confide or from whom he can expect little guidance. The Japanese individual, however, is sheltered within his personal in-group community with built-in social techniques and maneuvers for diminishing tension.

After-Work Socializing. By relaxing " on the way home" with his fellow office mates, the Japanese salary man can maintain camaraderie with his closest associates. Perhaps a case can be made that such daily or weekly socializing may be necessary to seek relief from the often excessive tensions and obligations of interpersonal relations in Japan. After-hours socializing may not seem a part of a job description, but as Plath points out, "it is so much a part of what is routinely expected of him that if he persistently fails to join in the 'fun' he risks serious sanctions."[27] Vogel, in his description of the "father and his company gang," writes:

> Various polls have shown that it takes the husband an average of two to three hours to get home. While commuting may require a long time, the transportation alone could not possibly take that long. It is rather that this is the time for recreation. After work, the men stop off someplace to sit and chat, have a drink and perhaps a bite to eat. Most company gangs have their own favorite hangouts: bars, coffee houses, small food-specialty shops, and the like. Here, by spending only a few cents, they can have long leisurely

conversations. It is here that they talk and laugh freely about sports, national and world events or the daily happenings in the company, complain about bosses and wives, and receive the consolation of their friends and of the sympathetic girls behind the counter.

Tea shops. Although called *kissaten* (tea shop), the obviously correct nomenclature would be coffee shop. From a tradition of drinking ceremonial tea in the *chasitsu* (tea room) to regain composure and serenity, the modern Japanese have evolved the coffee shop, uniquely their own *ikoi no ba* (a relaxing place). A coffee shop may be found in almost every building and business corner in every city and town in Japan. Throughout Japan, the estimate for the number of coffee houses approaches 100,000. In 1966, the telephone directory in Tokyo listed 8,600 such shops, and in Osaka, 4,600. The usual coffee shop has "mood," a romantic atmosphere created by luxurious furnishings with soft lighting effects, air conditioning and continuous music. The novelty coffee shops fit every possible taste, interest or hobby. Various coffee houses cater to enthusiasts of rock and roll, hillbilly tunes, French chanson, Japanese traditional songs or the music of Brahms or Beethoven. In Tokyo coffee shops, one can sip coffee and watch models parade past in the latest fashion in wedding gowns, bathing suits or in girdles, bras and panties. Whether for after-work socializing or a break from office routines, small bands of salary men visit their favorite coffee shop for diversion and rest. The coffee shops also serve as ideal rendezvous for young couples, for shopping wives and even as an *omiai* meeting place for the prospective bride and groom for an arranged marriage. The coffee shop is a somewhat distinctively Japanese facility for relaxation away from the tensions of modern urban life and is unlike anything in the United States. A similar phenomenon, to be sure, can be observed in many other societies, as in the Middle East, in Spain and Portugal and throughout Latin America, but in Japan it appears to be a more firmly institutionalized facility that has been incorporated into the life style of an industrialized society.

Drinking places. A further extension of relaxation and deeper involvement in group cohesion occurs in drinking *sake* (hot rice wine) or beer at drinking places, usually more elaborate than the kissaten. Such places are limitless throughout Japan. Drinking together remains for the Japanese an indispensable means of creating mutual intimacy accompanied by the greater release of emotions from everyday formalities. A man who will not partake of alcoholic drink with the group is one not to be trusted. While drinking, men can argue, shout or even cry if they feel so inclined. The important ingredient at the drinking places is the feminine companionship that is offered, often referred to as *yoru no cho* (butterfly of the night). All drinking places with hired hostesses cater almost exclusively to the male clientele. The girls, though not taken seriously, are skillful in making a man feel important and superior.

Mizushobai (water-trades) range from the lowly *shochu* (potato-spirit) night stalls in the backstreets where one can buy a drink for a few cents to the plush night clubs where a single glass of beer may cost many dollars. The expensive geisha houses or the Western-type night clubs are visited only when entertaining important business clients and always on the firm's expense account. The plushness of the cabaret and the beauty of the hostesses will diminish with receding prices, but the enjoyment and relaxation remain. Japanese visitors to the bars and cabarets do not just look at the entertainment, they participate and become part of the entertainment. Stopping off at a favorite drinking place on his way home with his office group, especially on payday or on a Saturday night, is an important aspect of life for the average Japanese husband. It can lead to an expedition of *hashigozake* (ladder-drinking) which takes the group from bar to bar far into the night.

The American male who is admired is the man "who can hold his liquor." This is not so in Japan where drinking is a permitted normal indulgence with no reprimand or guilt associated with it. Westerners are impressed at how quickly the Japanese can get drunk, and how much emotional release he gets from a small amount of sake. "Oh, he was drunk" is an acceptable excuse for some unusual behavior, as is "Why, he was ill" on the American scene. Such leniency has given Japan the reputation of a "drunkard's paradise." However, in spite of the high consumption of alcohol in Japan, little alcoholism is known, compared to that in the United States.

Bathing. Often for after-work socializing a group of men may head for the nearest public hot-bath house before venturing off to their favorite bar. The Japanese find bathing a satisfying experience for relaxation and gregariousness as well as for cleanliness. Historically this may be related to the abundance of natural hot-spring spas in Japan. Children from infancy bathe together with one of the parents either at the public bath or the family bath at home. In the status-conscious society, all men become equal, at least momentarily, while bathing together in the "public bath-house democracy." The bathrooms in a public facility are segregated for males and females, and each room is usually big enough to contain approximately 50 persons; the bath itself is large enough for 15 or 20. A *sento* (public bath house) is located in every ward in a city, and is the community center of local gossip and socializing. A recent innovation in the cities combines the bath house and the spa resort into the "health center," which also contains restaurants and recreation such as bowling and stage shows. *Toruko-buro* (Turkish baths) attended by young female masseuses are also popular. Ruth Benedict succinctly summarizes the pleasure of the hot bath by the Japanese as: "They value the daily bath for cleanliness' sake as Americans do, but they add to this value a fine art of passive indulgence which is hard to duplicate in the bathing habits of the rest of the world."[28]

Seasonal Group Activities. The distinct climatic changes in Japan accentuate the idea of group leisure as being seasonal. The institutionalized activities, in turn, make the individual aware of the delights of the four seasons.

Spring. Hanami or the viewing of the cherry blossoms in springtime after the winter months is an important seasonal event. The cherry blossoms, which suddenly burst into bloom and then fall within a short period, have often been linked to the Japanese "spirit," and have delighted the eyes and fancies of the Japanese since time immemorial. Throughout Japan during the fine April days, parks and other sites, no matter how small, that contain blossoms become packed with groups of office workers and families with children. The cherry blossoms provide the excuse for sitting and relaxing on straw mats beneath the blooming trees. Large quantities of food and drink—sake and beer for men and juices for children and women—are spread out. When the men become well-primed with drinks, they sing and dance, clap hands with much gaiety, and also often argue and fistfight, usually with men from other groups.

Summer. A day at the beach is a favorite summer outing for the salary man and his work group. Often their wives and children are included in this activity. Most large companies have their own "House by the Sea" for use by their employees. The company group can also take advantage of the firm's discount on bus fares and at special hotels. Other summer group activities are fishing trips, mountain climbing and camping.

Fall. With the briskness of autumn, the two- or three-day excursion trip to a hot-spring resort by the work collectivity is extremely popular in current Japan. The *onsen* (spa) combines the two most relaxing pleasures to the Japanese—bathing and drinking together. On the volcanic isle of Japan, the 1,335 spas are utilized by over 60 million persons yearly. The week-end or three-day vacaction tour of an office group of male co-workers, sometimes including female workers but not their spouses, going off together is commonplace in Japan, but is almost unknown in the United States. The group often charters a bus or occupies most of a train car, and the fun begins as soon as they get aboard. The plush red carpet at the resort's entrance lobby, the attentive maids, the huge 80-mat banquet room, the overflowing hot water in elaborately tiled or rock-arranged Roman-type baths looking out on a scene of natural beauty—all engender a sense of elegance and extravagance not experienced at home or work. A stronger sense of group unity seems to emerge with everyone wearing identical cotton *yukata* of uniform design and similar *tanzen* (thickly-wadded kimono for cold weather) supplied by the inn after the bath. The camaraderie reaches its height in the evening feasting, drinking and singing together. As one Japanese journalist puts it, "the onsen serves as an air pocket in the stressful atmosphere of a modern urban society."

The *undo-kai* (sports field day) is another popular autumn event, though sometimes held in the spring. It is sponsored by schools for students and their parents, and by companies for their employees. It features various sports events and usually the members' families are invited. Folk dancing and a masquerade contest may be included as part of the program. Other group activities during the fall months may be an excursion trip to a national shrine or a mushroom hunting expedition.

Winter. Group recreation during the winter season may include skiing, ice skating, and other winter sports, with Christmas Eve fast becoming an occasion for carousing in bars and cabarets. However, the most important event by far, and for the entire year, is the *bonen-kai* or "party to forget the outgoing year." This event held in December is a definite must on the list of annual activities of all work groups. It is important to the Japanese to commence the new year with a fresh start, and every effort is made at the year-end to foster a genuine feeling of rapport, high morale and close comradeship among the members of the group. Committee members work hard to arrange the program and entertainment. The cost of year-end party is usually covered by funds the employees set aside from their monthly salaries, plus donations contributed by the company president, other executives and supervisors. Large companies and government offices hold the party on a departmental basis with each department having its own binge.

The bonen-kai begins with formal speeches and gradually works up to an uninhibited release of emotions and goodwill. Individuals will exchange sake cups and drink together as a symbol of their family-like unity. For entertainment, each person is expected to perform, and such an occasion permits the full expression of the individual's personality. Some sing, dance or tell amusing stories; others perform parlor tricks, stunts or even juggling. Vogel observes:

> In contrast to the American social hour or cocktail party, where one talks personally to one or two at a time, Japanese parties or trips are oriented to the whole group . . . Although as many as 20 or 30 people may sit together listening to stories and joking, speakers are often more intimate than they are

in private conversation. On such occasions men openly air their troubles and sometimes make personal confessions or tell jokes designed to correct personal problems within the group. At other times, someone in the group with special talent will tell funny stories or perform by singing or playing a musical instrument.

When inhibitions are removed through intoxication, the men may sing risque songs and dance with suggestive motions. As a Japanese writer states: "It is an unrestrained reverie where all decorum is thrown aside, and men and women enjoy themselves to their heart's content and consign to oblivion—at least for the while—the dry, nerve-racking routines of their everyday existence." The bonen-kai party is not truly successful if it does not produce *don-chan sawagi* (boisterous merrymaking). In the midst of all this, some serious heart-to-heart talk may be going on between various individuals in a corner of the room, in the hallway or in the men's room. At the proper moment the maids begin to serve rice, which indicates that the drinking is to stop and that the party is over.

This brief description of the various activities and facilities for after-work socializing and seasonal recreation in the context of strong group interaction illustrates the provision of institutional means for dissipating tensions and stresses for the Japanese individual. Studies of Japanese society and personality have not sufficiently emphasized the psychobiologic importance of social mechanism for stress-reducing factors in a stress-inducing environment. Japan, known as a highly structured society, is also counterbalanced by the institutionalization of strategies for stress meiosis, which permits, though it never fully guarantees, periodic remittance from mounting life stress.

Research Strategies

It has been posited that the stress-reducing mechanisms in Japan tend to diminish the negative consequences of stress and presumably lead to lower coronary disease incidence. The analytic focus is on the dynamic interrelation between the individual and the group in which he seeks to satisfy his social and psychologic needs. The important task is to begin meaningful study of the role of social factors involved in etiology. This will not be easy, however, in view of the enormity and complexity of the problem.

Measurement of Social Interaction. The need remains for penetrating and rigorous statistical indicators for the degree of group interaction and relations. This could be constructed in an attitude-type scale to represent the respondent's definition or perception of his own interpersonal situation. A retrospective study designed to investigate the extent and significance of social interaction and integration could compare individuals with cardiac illness with a carefully matched control group composed of persons free of symptoms of coronary disease. A comparative study could also contrast the characteristics of social interactions of those with high serum cholesterol level to those with low cholesterol level. On a long-term basis, a cohort study could involve the prior selection of individuals with meaningful group ties and those without such attachments and view their cholesterol levels and prospective coronary heart disease rates.

A helpful tool in measurement may be what Jules Henry terms the "personal community," defined as a group of people on whom one can rely for support, acceptance and approval in intimate and satisfying ways.[29] The "personal community," be it the nuclear family, the work group, a religious order or the military unit, is the core of a man's security system. Henry presents the precise specifications of the statistical properties of the "personal community" in terms of *number,* which is determined by counting those who most frequently contribute to an individual's welfare and approve his actions; *constancy,* which is measured by the time spent by its member in direct interaction; and *involvement,* which is the obligation to give heed to and be swayed by each other's wishes. The latter dimension is the most complex to measure and most variable. Such a scheme to measure the extent and degree of group associations must be further refined and developed.

Group Studies by Diet and Stress. The relation of diet and stress to coronary heart disease remains an intriguing sociomedical problem. It seems well established that the rice diet, which is low in fat, is an effective means of lowering serum cholesterol. However, at the current stage of knowledge, it would be equally hazardous either to dismiss the stress hypothesis because its mode of bodily action is not clearly understood or to attribute a total causative role to social factors.

To weigh the relative importance of the factors of diet and psychosocial stresses, different groups with various combinations of the two components of diet and stress should be studied. It seems reasonable to suggest that societies may be classified with respect to high- or low-fat diet and to high or low social stress. In the American society, susceptible individuals may virtually invite atherogenesis caused by inordinate amounts of fat in the diet while being under excessive and continuous stresses, whereas the Japanese subsist mainly on a rice diet low in fat and live within a social system that fosters intense work group interaction, which tends to make them less vulnerable to coronary heart disease.

Research along such lines has included studies of men in the service of the Roman Catholic Church. The American and European Trappist Monks eat no meat or eggs and lead a placid life. The American and European Benedictine Monks also lead a subdued life, but do eat meat and eggs regularly. The Trappists had lower serum cholesterol than the Benedictines. Barrow and his associates also found 2.1 per cent of the 1,253 Benedictines and 0.4 per cent of the 684 Trappists showed evidence of atherosclerotic complications, but Groen and his colleagues found no differences between the Benedictines and Trappists in their sample. In a study of 39 Trappists, Calatayud and his associates found no association between serum cholesterol and low-fat diet. Further results from such epidemiologic and population field studies should prove enlightening in the etiologic understanding of coronary heart disease.

Relation between Coronary Heart Disease and Cerebral Vascular Accidents. Whatever the etiologic explanations advanced for the remarkably low mortality from coronary heart disease in Japan, such explanations must also take into account the significantly higher Japanese mortality from cerebral vascular accidents. The high rate of cerebral vascular accidents is the most notable feature of Japanese mortality, whereas it is the opposite in the Americans. The International Atherosclerosis Project has reported similar prevalence of atherosclerosis in the cerebral arteries as in the coronary arteries, but the changes in cerebral arteries begin one to two decades later and are not as severe. Gordon and Haenszel and Kurihara postulate that hypertension rather than atherosclerosis may be the differential factor in the etiology of cerebral accidents. Hypertension may be more likely involved in vascular lesions affecting the central nervous system than in heart disease where the atherosclerotic process is considered more important. Johnson and his associates, in a study of a population sample in Hiroshima City, document the "most essential role" played by hypertension in the development of cerebral vascular disease. The disparate trends in coronary heart disease and cerebral vascular accidents and the relations of atherosclerosis and hypertension to stress remain an intriguing medical puzzle.

Summary

The foregoing discussion, much of it speculative and impressionistic, constitutes at best a point of departure. This paper has not been the presentation of empirical research, but rather a discussion of a social hypothesis to be verified, amended or discarded. The primary task here has been the description of a framework indicating some of the characteristics of social structure and the dynamics of social processes in Japan that may be of potential relevance to health. The tentative hypothesis advanced needs to be refined and amended theoretically and tried out empirically by cross-cultural comparisons.

The problems involved in the epidemiology of coronary heart disease are multitudinous and complex. At this stage of knowledge, the etiology of cardiovascular disease remains an enigma. Although the diet factor remains dominant in current thinking, the stress hypothesis merits the most intensive probing as alternate or associated explanations of observed relations and differentiations.

References   REFERENCES
1. Segi, M., Kurihara, M. and Tsukahara, Y., MORTALITY FOR SELECTED CAUSES IN 30 COUNTRIES (1950-1961), Sendai, Japan, Department of Public Health, Tohoku University School of Medicine, 1966, pp. 26-27.
2. Haenszel, W. and Kurihara, M., Studies of Japanese Migrants: I. Mortality from Cancer and Other Diseases among Japanese in the United States, *Journal of the National Cancer Institute,* 40, 51, 1968.
3. Luisada, A. A., Introduction to Symposium on the Epidemiology of Heart Disease, *American Journal of Cardiology* 10, 316, 1962.
4. Keys, A., Diet and the Epidemiology of Coronary Heart Disease, *Journal of the American Medical Association,* 164, 1916, 1957.
5. Gordon, T., Mortality Experience among the Japanese in the United States, Hawaii, and Japan. *Public Health Reports,* 72, 550, 1957. *See also,* ————, Further Mortality Experience among Japanese Americans, *Public Health Reports,* 82, 973-984, 1967.
6. Arsenian, J. and Arsenian, J. M., Tough and Easy Cultures, *Psychiatry,* 11, 377-385, 1948.
7. Simmons, L. W. and Wolff, H. G., SOCIAL SCIENCE IN MEDICINE, New York, Russell Sage Foundation, 1954, p. 90.
8. *Cf* Dore, R. P., CITY LIFE IN JAPAN: A STUDY OF A TOKYO WARD, Berkeley, University of California Press, 1958; Fukutake, T., MAN AND SOCIETY IN JAPAN, Tokyo, University of Tokyo Press, 1962; Reischauer, E. O., THE UNITED STATES AND JAPAN, Revised edition, New York, Viking Press, 1957.
9. Matsumoto, Y. S., *Comtemporary Japan: The Individual and the Group,* Philadelphia, Transaction of the American Philosophical Society, New Series, Volume 50, 1960, Part 1.
10. Caudill, W. and Scarr, H. A., Japanese Value Orientations and Culture Change, *Ethnology,* 1, 53-91, January, 1962.
11. Yamane, T. and Nonoyama, H., Isolation of the Nuclear Family and Kinship Organization in Japan: A Hypothetical Approach to the Relationships between the Family and Society, *Journal of Marriage and the Family,* 29, 783-796, November, 1967.
12. Vogel, E. R. and Vogel, S. H., Family Security, Personal Immaturity, and Emotional Health in a Japanese Sample, *Marriage and Family Living,* 23, 161-166, 1961.
13. Goodman, M. E., Values, Attitudes and Social Concepts of Japanese and American Children, *American Anthropologist,* 59, 979-999, 1957.

14. Caudill, W., Similarities and Differences in Psychiatric Illness and its Treatment in the United States and Japan, *Seishin eisei (Mental Hygiene)*, No. 61-62, 15-26, 1959.

15. ———, Around the Clock Patient Care in Japanese Psychiatric Hospitals, *American Sociological Review*, 26, 204-214, 1961.

16. Doi, T., Amae: A Key Concept for Understanding Japanese Personality Structure, *in* Smith, R. J. and Beardsley, R. K. (Editors), JAPANESE CULTURE, ITS DEVELOPMENT AND CHARACTERISTICS, Viking Fund Publications in Anthropology No. 34, New York, Wenner-Gren Foundation for Anthropological Research, Inc., 1962, pp. 132-139.

17. Doi, T., Some Thoughts on Helplessness and the Desire to be Loved, *Psychiatry*, 26, 266-272, 1963.

18. Whyte, W. H., THE ORGANIZATION MAN, New York, Simon & Schuster, Inc., 1956.

19. Riesman, D., with Glazer, N. and Denney, R., THE LONELY CROWD: A STUDY OF THE CHANGING AMERICAN CHARACTER, New Haven, Yale University Press, 1950.

20. Stouffer, S. A., *et al.*, THE AMERICAN SOLDIER: COMBAT AND ITS AFTERMATH, Studies in Social Psychology in World War II, Princeton, Princeton University Press, 1949, Volume 2.

21. Doi, T. Jibun to Amae no Seishinbyori (Psychopathology of self and amae), *Seishin Shinkeigaku Zasshi (Psychiatria et Neurologia Japonica)*, 62, 149-162, 1960.

22. ———, Naruchishizumu no riron to jiko no hysho (The theory of narcissism and the representation of self), *Seishin Bunseki Kenkyu (Psychiatric Research)*, 7, 7-9, 1960; English summary, 42-43.

23. See, for example, Parsons, T. and Shils, E.A. (Editors), TOWARD A GENERAL THEORY OF ACTION, Cambridge, Harvard University Press, 1951, p. 80.

24. Caudill, W., Observations on the Cultural Context of Japanese Psychiatry, *in* Opler, M. K. (Editor), CULTURE AND MENTAL HEALTH, New York, The Macmillan Company, 1959, pp. 213-242.

25. ———, Anthropology and Psychoanalysis: Some Theoretical Issues, *in* Gladwin, T. and Sturtevant, W. C. (Editors), ANTHROPOLOGY AND HUMAN BEHAVIOR, Washington, D.C., The Anthropological Society of Washington, 1962, p. 208.

26. Vogel, E. F., JAPAN'S NEW MIDDLE CLASS: THE SALARY MAN AND HIS FAMILY IN A TOKYO SUBURB, Berkeley and Los Angeles, University of California Press, 1963, p. 157.

27. Plath, D. W., THE AFTER HOURS: MODERN JAPAN AND THE SEARCH FOR ENJOYMENT, Berkeley and Los Angeles, University of California Press, 1964, p. 39.

28. Benedict, R., THE CHRYSANTHEMUM AND THE SWORD, Boston, Houghton Mifflin Company, 1946, p. 178.

29. Henry, J., The Personal Community and its Invariant Properties, *American Anthropologist*, 60, 827-831, October, 1958.

SOCIAL CONFLICT AND COHESION IN A
JAPANESE RURAL COMMUNITY

Teigo Yoshida

This paper reports the results of an investigation of social conflict and cohesion in Moroo, a rural community or *buraku* (the small face-to-face living community) of Sado Island, Niigata Prefecture, Japan.[1] The conflict in this case involved, not a factional split of the community into segments, but a situation of class conflict initiated by subordinate tenants or lower-class farmers against superordinate landlords. Despite a series of internal disputes, the social cohesion of the community did not break down. In contrast to some neighboring communities, innovations in the traditional social structure were followed by counter-movements tending toward the restoration of the *status quo*.

Community Background

Moroo is located on the east coast of Sado Island in the Sea of Japan 4.5 miles east of Ryotsu, an urban center and the principal port of the island. In 1954, when the town *(machi)* of Ryotsu and six *mura* (villages comprised of several buraku or small communities) were amalgamated to form a city, Moroo was subsumed under the municipal administration of Ryotsu city. In 1961 Moroo had a population of 484 (277 females and 207 males) and consisted of 92 households. The number of the households had remained stable for many years; according to an old local document, written in 1784, there were 88 households at that time.

All the households, except one which has recently arrived, practice wet-rice cultivation, from which some 70 per cent of the total income of the inhabitants is derived. Since 1959 a few farmers have begun to cultivate persimmons and vegetables and to raise chickens and pigs, but these subsidiary products yield only 5 per cent of the community's income. Many of the inhabitants are poor; the average cultivated area per farming household is approximately 1.5 acres. The agrarian land reform of the late 1940s was highly effective in transferring land ownership to former tenants. The two largest landowners, who formerly held some 7.5 acres of agricultural land each, have lost about two-thirds of their holdings, but they are still the largest landholders. Thus the reform did not change the economic status order of the community. Moreover, it did not affect forest land, and the two individuals who own the most agricultural land still retain their large holdings of forest land.

Formerly many farmers engaged in fishing as a subsidiary job, but in recent years the catch has greatly declined, as has the number of individuals engaged in fishing. Only two farmers still pursue net fishing in the coastal waters, employing residents of the community as crew. Thirteen men in Moroo are occasionally employed as fishermen either by these two individuals or by other fishermen

Yoshida — *From Social Conflict and Cohesion in Japanese Rural Community*, Ethnology, Vol. 3, No. 3, (July 1964), pp. 219-231.

outside the community. In the late 1940s many of the inhabitants went to sea in small rowboats to catch squid. People in other communities then began using motor boats, but the inhabitants of Moroo did not, with the consequence that they could not compete and their catch declined.

A new source of income, however, has replaced that formerly provided by fishing. National industrial and urban developments have recently created a considerable demand for wage labor on public works projects such as building construction, the improvement of the port of Ryotsu, and the construction and repair of roads and bridges. Most of these projects are conducted in the urban center of Ryotsu, which is within cycling distance from Moroo. Some twenty local individuals, mostly heads of lower-class farming families, have received employment as day laborers in these construction works, commuting from the community.

As indicated earlier, there are 70 more women than men in Moroo, and this disparity is particularly extreme in the 20 to 34 age bracket. This reflects a growing tendency for young men to leave the community to obtain permanent city jobs on the Honshu mainland, especially in the Tokyo area. This exodus of young men is not a new phenomenon, for it goes back at least half a century, but it has greatly increased since World War II. The tendency for young men to leave the community either temporarily or permanently, coupled with the increasing participation of other men in urban wage labor, has seriously reduced the number of male agricultural workers in the community.

Certain innovations have substantially reduced the time and effort which farmers must devote to agricultural tasks. Thus the irrigation ditches were lined with concrete in 1959, chemical fertilizers and weed-killers have gradually been introduced, and upper-class farmers have recently adopted motor-driven cultivators, threshing machines, and other agricultural machinery. The process of mechanization has nevertheless been greatly limited by poverty, by the predominance of terraced fields over flat lands, and by the relative disinterest in improving agricultural production on the part of the many farmers who are seeking jobs outside the community.

The traditional pattern of labor exchange between relatives and neighbors in the planting, weeding, and harvesting of rice—locally called *ii*—is still maintained in Moroo and is even more widely practiced today than before the war. Although some of the larger landholders hire labor, the supply of agricultural laborers is far from sufficient because of the competition of outside employment. The wage for agricultural labor, which is decided at a community conference each year, is about 350 yen per day ($1 U.S. = 360 yen), whereas the wage for public construction work is approximately 450 yen per day. Moreover, agricultural labor is more seasonal than construction labor, and some of the construction companies provide the added benefit of social security privileges. For the performance of agricultural tasks, therefore, most farmers are forced to depend upon the labor of their family members or of their relatives and neighboring farmers. The perpetuation of the traditional system of co-operative work seems thus to be a result of the scarcity of agricultural wage labor.

Social Strata

Moroo has had, and to a considerable extent still has, a highly stratified social system. According to privately owned records, which date back to 1839, there were formerly five social classes. At present, three social classes are distinguishable:

(a) the *oyasan*,[2] an upper class of landowning gentry;

(b) the *churo*,[3] a middle class, mainly of independent farmers;

(c) the *komae,* a lower class, mainly of tenant farmers.

Excluding one household of newcomers, whose members have not yet been socially integrated into the community, the households of Moroo are distributed by class as follows: 12 oyasan, 24 churo, and 55 komae. The oyasan, in addition to enjoying the highest socio-economic status, are in general the largest landholders. The four householders who own the most forest land and five of the six who cultivate the largest tracts belong to this class, and the other members till areas that are larger than the average.

The class structure is complicated by another status relationship—that between patrons *(oyakata)* and clients or followers *(kokata)*—which Ariga (1959) regards as one of the most basic relationships in Japanese social structure. Though most oyasan were formerly also oyakata, and both words have the same root *(oya,* parent*)*, the terms are not synonymous.[4] Whereas oyasan refers to those who hold the highest rank in the community's class hierarchy, oyakata refers to those who stand in the relationship of patrons to kokata (from *ko,* child) or clients. Prior to 1943, nine members of the oyasan class were also oyakata, whereas three were not. In the intermediate churo class, ten were oyakata and fourteen were not. There were no oyakata in the komae class, 47 of whose 55 members were kokata or clients.

The relationship between patron and client likewise does not coincide with that between landlord and tenant. While some 20 per cent of all kokata were both clients and tenants to the same individual, the majority were clients of one oyakata and tenants of one or more other individuals. For example, Saijuro and Seizo were kokata to Sazaemon but tenants of Sakyo, and Kyuzaemon was kokata to Sakyo and a tenant of both the latter and Nojo.[5]

The patron-client relationship is a contractual one which is generally entered into by persons who are unrelated by kin ties and who assume various reciprocal obligations. It is usually regarded (cf. Shiomi *et al.* 1957; Ishino 1953) as a relationship of fictive or ritual kinship since the terms oyakata and kokata are derived, respectively, from those for "parent" and "child" and since the parties adopt terms of address and roles analogous to those of the Japanese family system. The relationship shows some regional variation. In the San'in region of northwestern Honshu, as noted by Wakamori (1951: 62), it was primarily ritual in character and did not involve the economic subordination of the kokata. In Moroo it had deep roots in the economic life of the community and revealed characteristics approximating those described by Kitano (1959); the kokata rendered labor service to his oyakata in return for protection and economic support. The relationship was essentially an economic one in which an individual subordinated himself to a patron because of his inability to make an independent living.

There seem to have been three ways by which an individual could become a kokata in Moroo. The most common was for a man who had been a servant to a wealthy farmer for many years to receive from his master a small plot of land, enabling him to settle permanently in the community. In return for the land he obligated himself to contribute a certain amount of labor to his patron. Though he received no cash wages for his labor, it was not wholly uncompensated, for he received his meals on the days when he worked and was occasionally given clothing, salt, and medicines by his patron. Moreover, he could, if necessary, borrow money or grain from him without interest.

A second way of becoming a kokata was through marriage with the daughter of the oyakata. Though class endogamy is customary in Moroo, there are occasional instances where a girl of a higher class, unable to find a husband within her own class, is married to a man of a lower class. In such cases her father gives a certain amount of land to her husband, who thereby assumes the obligation of rendering certain labor services to his father-in-law as a kokata. Third, poorer "branch families" sometimes become kokata to the "main family," although as a rule kokata and "branch families" are distinguished. When the first son inherited the land and other property of his father, and succeeded the latter as the head of the "main family," the father might give small parcels of land to the second and third sons to enable them to settle in the community as "branch families." Usually a kokata was expected to show a submissive attitude toward the branches as well as the "main family" of his oyakata (Wakamori 1951: 63).

Once a man had become a kokata, his relationship and obligations to his oyakata were inherited from father to son in succeeding generations. In Moroo, prior to 1943, there were nineteen oyakata who had more than one kokata, nine of them being of the oyasan class and ten of the churo class. The maximum number of kokata for a single oyakata was nine. At least seven kokata maintained this subordinate relationship to two or three oyakata at the same time. One individual was a kokata in one relationship and an oyakata (with kokata of his own) in three other relationships. There were 28 households, mostly of independent farmers and including three oyasan, who were involved in no relationships of this kind, either as patrons or as clients. Most of the oyakata were also landlords, but three had no tenants.

The labor service which kokata owed to their oyakata included such agricultural tasks as the planting, weeding, and harvesting of rice and such domestic work as the cleaning of the patron's house and the pounding of rice cake *(mochi)* for him at the end of the year. (In most Japanese rural communities it is customary to clean one's house and to pound rice cake as a preparation for the New Year's celebration.) The amount of labor owed was negotiated at the time an individual became a kokata and was binding upon his descendants without the right of reduction through renegotiation. In the case of one kokata, Magozaemon, for example, the traditional obligation consisted of 50 days of agricultural work during the year and of ten days of housecleaning and rice-cake preparation at the end of the year.

Besides the negotiated labor service, the kokata performed additional labor for debts incurred to their oyakata instead of making reimbursements in cash. Since most kokata were also tenants, their burden of labor service was correspondingly increased. Moreover, kokata were frequently required to provide the labor, not only of themselves, but of all the members of their families, including children old enough to work, especially at the time of rice planting. The following is the main portion of a written statement made in 1876 by a kokata named Sataro Shirai to his oyakata, Yasokichi Shirai,[6] reconfirming his obligations of labor service, presumably at the instance of his patron:

> The lands mentioned above were given by your [ancestral] family to my ancestor, Magataro, in 1703. Therefore, my ancestors and I have been working throughout the past years for your family line. I shall hand these lands down to my descendants, and we shall never forget the *ongi* [our feelings of gratitude and obligation][7] to you, sir. Thus we shall give you our labor service exactly as before.

The oyakata-kokata system was apparently reinforced by social interaction on the occasion of rites of passage, local festivals, and other celebrations (cf. Nadel 1951: 136). At the New Year's celebration the kokata, after attending the buraku shrine and calling upon the headman, paid a formal visit to their oyakata, who then gave them rice cakes as a New Year's gift. Oyakata acted as go-betweens for their kokata in arranging marriages. When a patron's son was to be married, his kokata visited his house to assist in the wedding preparations, and when his daughter was married the wife of his kokata accompanied her in the wedding procession and attended the marriage ceremony. When a funeral was held at the home of a kokata his oyakata assumed leadership in conducting the ceremony.

Class Conflicts

During the present century, the community of Moroo has been torn by a series of serious internal conflicts, each involving a cleavage along the lines of its social stratification. The first of these involved the question of eligibility to participate in the political affairs of the community. Until the 1920s the upper class, the oyasan or gentry, had exercised autocratic political control. The position of headman *(sodai)* of the community had rotated among the family heads of this class, and the members of the churo and komae classes had been excluded from this office. Moreover, all buraku conferences were held in the house of a member of the oyasan class, and all the family heads of this class sat in the best room *(zashiki)* of the house, whereas those of the churo class sat in the adjoining room and those of the komae class on a wooden floor with very limited rights to participate in the discussions (Wakamori 1951:60-61).

In the late 1920s the underprivileged classes raised a protest and demanded that their members likewise be made eligible to hold the office of buraku headman. The men of the upper class resisted this proposal, but they were unsuccessful and eventually were reluctantly compelled to accept it. Within a few years headmen began to be selected occasionally from the lower classes. Today the buraku assemblies are held in a public hall erected after World War II, and household heads are seated according to age rather than family rank. The effect of this victory, though considerable, should not be overestimated. More headmen have been selected from the oyasan, even since then, than from the other two classes, and the upper class still maintains its political power to a substantial extent.

The second conflict, which occurrred in 1943, was on a larger scale, involved many more poeple, and had more far-reaching consequences. It was started by the kokata or clients with the aim of terminating their subordination to their oyakata or patrons. In 1943 the kokata were suffering from a severe labor shortage caused by the military draft, and they complained bitterly about the excessive burden of their traditional labor service. Their oyakata, however, who were confronted with the same labor shortage, refused to reduce the amount of the traditional services. One man, who had attended a junior college and thus had a higher education than most of the inhabitants, encouraged the kokata to initiate resistance against the oyakata. He was, incidentally, not a kokata himself but a member of the independent churo class. Eventually 36 kokata united and submitted the following proposals to the oyakata:

(1) that the *oyakata* abrogate all required labor services;

(2) that they give to the *kokata* all lands registered in the names of kokata but actually held by oyakata;

(3) that the *kokata* return all rented lands to the oyakata.

The oyakata were taken by surprise and were extremely angry. They felt betrayed because they believed they had a sort of moral justification for requiring labor service from their kokata. At the time the total number of kokata households had been reduced from the previous 47 to 42, five kokata having already dissolved their subordination to the oyakata prior to the dispute. Six of the 42 kokata did not join the rebellious group since, according to their own statements, the amount of labor service for which they were obligated was less than that required of the rest.

The oyakata did not at first accept the proposals of the kokata, and repeated meetings were held. The community was in a state of chaos. Agricultural labor and co-operative activities practically ceased for several days. Some oyakata initiated legal action, and the police began to investiage the situation. The kokata, suspected of being Communists, burned the contract they had jointly signed. No one, however, was arrested. Eventually the kokata group won; at the fourteenth meeting the oyakata finally accepted the proposals completely. The dispute was thus settled, and, as a consequence, most of the oyakata-kokata relationships in the community were dissolved.

The third and last conflict was initiated by tenants just prior to the postwar agrarian land reform. Two of its three leaders had also been leaders in the previous dispute. Farm rents had been traditionally paid in kind, i.e., in rice, for irrigated land and in labor—two days per year per *se* (*ca.* 60 square yards)—for dry land. The tenants proposed that rents for irrigated land be paid in cash rather than in kind and that the amount of labor given as rent for dry land be reduced. The landlords did not like this, and conflict was generated. In the end, however, the landowners acceded to the demands of their tenants.

Conflicts of the above types are by no means unique to Moroo. Tenant disputes have also occurred in other villages, even in pre-war Japan prior to the democratization of the national government (see Fujita 1925; Uchiyama 1955; Noseichosakai 1959).

Socio-Cultural Change and Continuity

Three socio-cultural innovations, as we have seen, have resulted in Moroo from disputes initiated by lower-status groups. The first opened the position of buraku headman, previously monopolized by the privileged oyasan class, to members of the lower strata. The second abolished, in large measure, the traditional socio-economic relations between partons and clients. The third improved the conditions of tenant farmers. The social status of former kokata and tenants has been enhanced still further by the postwar land reform carried out by the national government. In addition, the standard of living has been raised by the provision of wage labor on public works projects. As the inhabitants themselves point out, the differences between rich and poor are much less today than formerly.

These innovations have brought about changes in the attitudes toward the traditional system of stratification. The terms of address used between members of different social strata, for example, have been considerably simplified. Household heads of the upper class, to be sure, are still called *totsan,* an honorific term for father, by the other inhabitants of the community, but tosan, the term of address formerly used for household heads of the churo class by their social inferiors, and *ishi,* that once used for *komae,* tenants, and kokata by their social superiors, have almost disappeared. The special honorific terms of address formerly used for an oyasan's wife *(kakayan),* son *(kankan),* and daughter *(biko-yan)* are practically obsolete today. Moreover, the traditional value once attached to the oyakata-kokata system has been modified. Many inhabitants, including oyasan people, no longer speak of this institution as a "good custom," although some moral resentment still persists in the older men and women of the oyasan class against their former kokata who initiated resistance.

It should be emphasized at this point that the disputes of the past never brought about the complete disorganization of the community. Following each conflict the community regained its previous cohesion, which stressed the social unity of the buraku. Even though psychological tension persisted, it was suppressed in interpersonal relations sufficiently to maintain social cohesion. Despite the profound socio-cultural changes, the traditional social hierarchy of the community and its buraku-centered norms have been largely preserved. The oyasan have by no means entirely lost their superior socio-economic status and prestige. Some of the former kokata, indeed, commented that the community has not changed very much despite their former efforts. At the time of a social gathering and feast called *dake-ko,* held once a year on the 24th of November following the harvest, it is still customary for the oyakata to celebrate separately from the kokata and tenant groups, despite the dissolution of most patron-client relationships.

The local inhabitants, now condemning the oyakata-kokata system as "feudalistic," tried to convince the author that it had completely broken down. It was discovered, however, that it has actually shown a revivalistic trend. Thus eight (or some 20 per cent) of the 36 kokata who had participated in the dispute that had dissolved their subordination have returned to their former relationships and perform labor service for their oyakata, and one man who did not join the disputants has never severed his relationships with his two patrons. In all nine cases the revived or continued relationships are traditional ones; no new ones have been established. The individuals involved are, on the one hand, blamed as "betrayers" by the former disputants and, on the other hand, praised for "having a strict sense of *giri* [duty]," not only by the former oyakata but also by many of the former kokata. This ambivalent attitude seems to indicate psychological conflict over the values associated with the patron-client relationship. Those who have revived or maintained such relationships give as their reasons their personal loyalty to their oyakata, their kinship ties with them, and/or the economic difficulty of getting along independently from them.

There has also been a recent movement to revitalize the traditional buraku controls as a response to external pressures threatening the disorganization of the community. Co-operative enterprises such as repairing roads and bridges and cleaning the irrigation ditches have traditionally been performed on a buraku basis, each household donating labor as a public service. Since many farmers now leave the community to earn money as day laborers in construction work, the number of households contributing no labor to such enterprises has increased, and it has become difficult to perform them adequately. To solve this problem the buraku in 1960 established a penalty system, levying fines against the households which do not contribute labor to the co-operative enterprises. The number of farmers who do not attend the buraku assemblies has likewise been increasing for the same reason, and in 1961 the buraku initiated another penalty system to increase the attendance. External pressures, in short, have threatened the traditional norm whereby the head of every household was expected to attend the assemblies and one male member of each household was expected to contribute labor to community enterprises. The initiation of penalty systems can be interpreted as a socio-cultural response to counteract the resulting tendency toward community disorganization. At the same time it is clearly a reflection of the continuity of the values attached to buraku integrity.

Discussion and Conclusions

A direct incentive for the conflict between the kokata and the oyakata was provided by the increasing frustration of the former over their sufferings caused by the wartime shortage of labor and by their suppressed hostility toward the latter for their refusal to reduce the traditional labor obligations. A great many other communities, however, also suffered a shortage of labor during the war without becoming involved in class conflicts. The precipitation of the dispute must therefore have depended upon other variables as well.

Over the past 60 years, as we have seen, many young men from the lower class families have left the community to obtain jobs, first in Hokkaido and since the 1920s in the Tokyo area. This tendency has undoubtedly increased in accordance with the national development of industrialization and urbanization. As jobs outside the community became increasingly available, the economic dependence of the kokata upon the oyakata decreased. As the former became relatively independent, they were able to give concrete expression to their pre-existing tension by initiating an organized protest. Had their economic dependence upon their oyakata been absolute, this would have been impossible (Ouchi 1955). Moreover, new ideas and values had entered the community in consequence of increasing contacts and relations with the outside world, especially with the industrial and urban subculture of the larger society. Thus the conflict over community leadership in the 1920s and those initiated by the kokata and tenant classes in the 1940s seem to have been facilitated by the two new factors of the decreasing economic dependence of the lower class farmers on the elite class and the introduction of new values and behavior patterns.

An additional factor is discernible in a particular strain at the cognitive and emotional levels which the kokata had experienced prior to the conflict of 1943. The people of Moroo were aware that in the preceding years the patron-client system had practically disappeared in the neighboring community of Shiidomari and that in another neighboring community, Haniu, the oyakata had reduced the amount of labor owed to them by their kokata, whereas neither had happened in Moroo. Recognition of these differences must have intensified the strain to organize a movement to terminate the local system of subordination.

Finally, account should be taken of the role of leadership in the dispute assumed by one educated man with new ideas and values presumably derived from his superior education in a junior college. Though a member of the intermediate churo class, he sympathized with the underprivileged kokata and exercised leadership behind the scenes throughout the dispute. Without his encouragement and support the protest might well have been unsuccessful. It is worth noting that he is currently a member of the Ryotsu city assembly.

In brief, the factors possibly responsible for the disputes appear to have included the relative independence achieved by lower-class farmers, the introduction of new values and behavior patterns, the model of similar social changes achieved earlier in neighboring communities, and the leadership role of one man of superior education. All of these, of course, are related to the impact of modernization and industrialization from the outer world. As the phenomenon of "pervasive factionalism," the origin of the disputes, and of the process of socio-cultural change which they express, can be attributed to the various external pressures to which the community has been subjected, and the forms which they took appear to have reflected the pre-existing potential strains among the various social strata of the community (Siegel and Beals 1960; Collins 1952).

We may next consider the possible factors contributing to the maintenance of community cohesion. The conflicts never developed to the point of shattering this cohesion. The disputes were invariably settled very soon, and the community returned to its previous state of peace. To explain the continuity of cohesion within the community it seems to me necessary to consider a variety of other social relationships. If the community had been organized exclusively along class lines, it is likely that it would have been split asunder by the disputes. Actually, however, its organization was complex, and its class components were bound together by intersecting relationships of various kinds.

First, as we have already noted, stratification along the lines of social class, patron and client relationships, and landlord-tenant relationships did not coincide but was characterized by considerable intermixture.

Second, the community of Moroo is also divided into four *kumi* or neighborhoods, and the houses of oyasan and oyakata are dispersed among all of them, except that one kumi has no oyasan households. The office of kumi chief *(kumi-cho)* who mediates communications between kumi members and the buraku headman, rotates every two years among the households of each kumi. The traditional labor exchange in weeding is performed in groups of five to eight neighboring households within each kumi.

Third the community is further divided into seventeen "five-men's associations" *(gonin-gumi)*, which date back to the feudal period. Membership is hereditary and is usually composed of neighbors, though occasionally members live in other kumi. Each association has five or six members, all of them household heads, and a head who is an oyasan or oyakata. The principal function of these associations is to provide mutual assistance at funerals and in house construction.

Fourth, there is considerable social interaction among kinsmen across class lines. The patrilineal relationship between "main" *(honke)* and "branch" *(bunke)* families,[8] though weaker than patron-client relationships in Moroo as in other Japanese rural communities where the oyakata-kokata system has developed (Shiomi *et al.* 1957: 122-123; Ogyu and Tashiro 1957), still involves a degree of social interaction. Relations with affinal relatives are promoted by buraku endogamy. Though this traditional norm has been weakened in recent years, some 70 per cent of the married women in Moroo were born in the community. Class endogamy was also a traditional norm, but the number of marriages between social strata has been increasing, with a corresponding increase in affinal relationships which cross class lines.

Fifth, the community is divided into five irrigation areas, each with its own irrigation ditch and its own co-operative organization for its maintenance. Since membership in these groups is determined by the location of farm lands, farmers of different social statuses co-operate in the same organization.

Sixth, the buraku of Moroo owns collectively a forest area of some 120 acres and holds certain public moneys as common property. The common land is utilized for obtaining firewood and charcoal, for planting cedar trees, and formerly also as a source of grass compost. The community funds, derived mainly from the sale of timber from the forest land, are used for various public expenses of the buraku, e.g., for road repairs, for support of the local primary school, and for loans to inhabitants. With the exception of three households—two "branch families" established since the 1920s and one recently arrived nonfarming household—all the households of the community have equal rights of access to the common forest land and the communal fund. Unquestionably the existence of these forms of common property has contributed strongly to the traditional feeling of loyalty to the buraku.

Seventh, certain religious associations *(ko)* comprise individuals of different social strata. Among them are eight *Ise-ko* (associations for pilgrimage to the Ise shrine in Honshu) and four *Zenkoji-ko* (associations for pilgrimage to the Zenko temple).

The complex interweaving of these various social relationships within the community is largely responsible for the continuity of buraku cohesion in spite of the series of class conflicts recounted above. In the performance of labor exchange and irrigation activities, in the conduct of communal enterprises, in the joint access to the community's common property, and in participation in neighborhood, kinship, and religious groups and associations, the people are involved in a wide variety of interpersonal relationships which intersect and crosscut the community's status hierarchy. The social system of the buraku is, of course, not a complete system but a part-system within the larger society, and the characteristics which it shares with the latter have also been markedly increasing. The complexity of social relations within the buraku appears to have operated over the years as a dynamic support of community cohesion and as a preventive of disintegration at times of conflict.

Another factor in the maintenance of buraku cohesion is the loyalty of the inhabitants to the community and the value they assign to its unity, which, even though not universally accepted, are related to their continued dependence upon mutual aid in farming and upon the common property of the buraku.

The partial revival of the oyakata-kokata system, the attempts to revitalize the traditional buraku controls, and the continuity of the traditional system of co-operative labor, which are probably structurally interrelated, are doubtless also functionally related to both the perpetuation of community-oriented values and the complexity of social relations within the buraku. This complexity, in conjunction with the value placed on the integrity of the buraku, appears to operate as a check upon, and a means of absorbing, radical change and conflict within the community.

FOOTNOTES

1. The field work for this paper was conducted in the summer of 1961 with financial support from the Japanese Ministry of Education as a part of the Japanese Sado Research Project of the League for the Study of Human Affairs. I am indebted to Kenzo Tsukishima and Morio Ono, with whom the field work was jointly undertaken, for collecting information and offering suggestions. Grateful acknowledgment is made to John L. Fischer for reading the manuscript, suggesting stylistic revisions, and supplying valuable comments, and to the Department of Anthropology, Stanford University, which provided the undistracted circumstances in which this paper was prepared in 1962.

2. The term *oyasan* is compounded from *oya,* meaning "parent," and *san,* an honorific suffix. The *oyasan* are sometimes referred to in the plural as *oyasan-gata,* or alternatively as *totsan,* a modified dialectic form of *tosan,* meaning "father."

3. The term *churo* literally means "middle age" or "middle-aged man" and sometimes refers to an age group in other Japanese rural communities (Yoshida 1963), but in Moroo usage it has nothing to do with age, referring exclusively to an intermediate social class.

4. The terms *oyakata* and *kokata,* more frequently used in Moroo than the synonymous terms *oyabun* and *kobun,* are also widely current in Japan and are therefore used in this paper. The suffixes *-kata* and *-bun* are translatable as "manner of–," "part of–," "status of–," or "role of–."

5. These names are *yago* or household names, which are still widely used by the inhabitants to identify a household head or a household. All households (except the newly arrived one)

have these *yago,* which have been transmitted without change from generation to generation. The *yago* are more familiar than family names to the older inhabitants, though family names are now increasingly used.

6. This *oyakata* and his *kokata* are unrelated by kin ties. It is common for a client to take his patron's family name.

7. The term *ongi* is nearly synonymous with *on,* which connotes an important norm governing the traditional behavior among the Japanese (cf. Benedict 1946: 99-117; Sakurai 1961).

8. The custom of granting plots to second or third sons, to establish them in the community as "branch families," has, however, greatly declined in Moroo, as in other parts of Japan (Takeuchi 1962), because of the increasing shortage of land.

BIBLIOGRAPHY

Ariga, Kizaemon. 1959. Oyabun Kobun (Patron and Client). Nihon no Minzoku Bunka (Race and Culture in Japan), ed. S. Iwamura, pp. 226-246. Tokyo.

Benedict, R. 1946. The Chrysanthemum and the Sword. Boston.

Collins, J. McC. 1952. An Interpretation of Skagit Intergroup Conflict during Acculturation. American Anthropologist 54: 347-355.

Fujita, Gunta. 1925. Kosaku-sogi no Kenkyu (A study of Tenant Disputes). Tokyo.

Ishino, I. 1953. The Oyabun-kobun: A Japanese Ritual Kinship Institution. American Anthropologist 55: 695-707.

Kitano, Seiichi. 1940. Koshu Sanson no Dozoku-soshiki to Oyakata-kokata Kanko (The *Dozoku* System and the *Oyakata-kokata* Custom in a Mountain Village in Koshu). Minzoku-gaku Nenpo (Annual Report of Ethnology) 2: 41-95. Tokyo.

—1959. Oyakata Kokata (Patron and Client). Nihon Minzoku-gaku Taikei (Outline of Japanese Folklore), ed. A. Omachi, M. Oka, M. Sakurada, K. Seki, and T. Mogami, 4: 35-62. Tokyo.

Nadel, S. F. 1951. The Foundations of Social Anthropology. London.

Noseichosa-kai (Agricultural Survey Association). 1959. Kosaku Sodo ni kansuru Shiryo-shu (Historical Materials of Tenant Disputes). Tokyo.

Ogyu, Chikasato, and A. Tashiro. 1957. Sadogashima Ichi-sonraku ni okeru Kon'in to Shinzoku Soshiki (Kinship Structure and Marriage in a Rural Community of Sado Island). Jinrui-gaku Shuho (Anthropological Report) 18: 73-108.

Ouchi, Chikara. 1955. Buraku-kozo to Nomin Undo (*Buraku* Structure and Farmers' Movements). Nochi-kaikaku to Nomin Undo (Agricultural Land Reform and Farmers' Movements), ed. Sonraku Shakai Kenkyu-kai (Research Committee on Village Community), pp. 1-27. Tokyo.

Sakurai, Shotaro. 1961. On to Giri: Shakai-gaku-teki Kenkyu (*On* and *Giri:* A Sociological Study). Tokyo.

Siegel, B. and A. Beals. 1960. Pervasive Factionalism. American Anthropologist 62: 394-417.

Shiomi, T., Y. Watanabe, Y. Ishimura, T. Oshima, and H. Nakao. 1957. Nihon no Noson (Japanese Agricultural Village). Tokyo.

Takeuchi, Toshimi. 1962. Dozoku to Sono Henka: Noson no Baai (*Dozoku* and Its Change in Agricultural Villages). Shakai-gaku Hyoron (Japanese Sociological Review) 12: 8-22.

Uchiyama, M. 1955. Nomin Undo ni kansuru Shuyona Bunken to Shiryo (Main Literature and Material on Farmers' Movements). Nochi-kaikaku to Nomin Undo (Agricultural Land Reform and Farmers' Movements), ed. Sonraku Shakai Kenkyu-kai (Research Committee on Village Community), pp. 198-217. Tokyo.

Wakamori, Taro. 1951. Rekishi to Minzoku-gaku (History and Folklore). Tokyo.

Yanagida, Kunio. 1937. Oyakata Kokata (Patron and Client). Kazoku Seido Zenshu (Series on the Family Institution) 3: 89-124. Tokyo.

Yoshida, Teigo. 1963. Cultural Integration and Change in Japanese Villages. American Anthropologist 65: 105-116.

AN ETA COMMUNITY IN JAPAN:
THE SOCIAL PERSISTENCE OF OUTCASTE GROUPS

John D. Donoghue

Introduction

This paper describes and analyzes an Eta community in northern Japan in order to draw attention to the social persistence of this Japanese pariah group. At present, the Eta comprise a significant proportion of the Japanese population; between 1.5 and 3 million reside in some 6,000 "special communities" *(tokushu-buraku)* throughout Japan. Prior to their liberation in 1871, they were required to live in designated quarters and to observe special regulations with reference to dress and behavior. Since then although legally "emancipated," they have remained a socially subordinated and despised minority, considered inherently different and inferior. Not only are the Eta overtly discriminated against in schools, occupations, and marriage, but they are regarded by the non-Eta with disgust and apprehension.

This paper is directed to the questions: Why do the Eta remain a distinct subgroup of the Japanese society? Why do members of the tokushu-buraku remain in overpopulated, substandard communities, rather than migrate to large cities where the Eta stigma may be lost? The Eta are not racially distinct nor do they possess any overt cultural characteristics which might differentiate them from the majority society. They are not required to live is segregated villages, and the hierarchical social structure of the feudal period no longer exists. Moreover, Buddhist religious taboos against the taking of life and Shinto conceptions of pollution associated with blood, dirt, and death, both of which contributed to the early formation and development of the Eta, have undergone essential modifications. Most Japanese people now eat meat, and "legitimate" butchers, tanners, and shoemakers, occupations formerly held only by Eta, are found throughout the nation. The primary distinguishing feature of the Eta is residence in a socially segregated and isolated community. This paper focuses specifically upon the dynamics of intergroup and interpersonal relations, and the socioeconomic organization which influences the social persistence of this community.

Historical Background

The formation of the Eta class was effected largely by the conjunction of a hierarchical social system, combined with handicraft industries, and the popularization of Buddhism. Evidence indicates that a stratified social system existed in the earliest known period of Japanese history; each of the numerous clans was internally ranked, with an hereditary nobility at the top, and peasants, artisans, and slaves at the bottom (Sansom 1943:36). The Imperial House formalized the hierarchy by edict during the Taikwa Reform in 645 A.D. and two major categories

Donoghue — *Reproduced by permission of the American Anthropological Association from The American Anthropologist, Vol. 59, No. 6, Yr. 1957.

were created, the free and the "base." The latter consisted of the peasantry, members of certain artisan guilds, and the slaves. Gradually the elaborate and formalized class distinctions among the majority of the population became meaningless. Social differences between the free and the unfree were no longer observable, and most of the "base" guilds were legally freed by the beginning of the tenth century (Ninomiya 1933:70).

During this period of social upheaval, Buddhism, which had previously been the religion of only the court nobility, became popularized and accepted throughout the country. (The beliefs of Buddhism, especially the concept of the essential unity of all sentient existence, fused with native Shinto beliefs about the avoidance of impurity.) The syncretic religious concepts that evolved associated the taking of life with ritual impurity, and the guilds whose livelihood depended upon animal slaughtering were physically and morally isolated from the "legitimate" society. The outcastes became known as Eta.

The Eta, legally freed from governmental service, formed small enclaves on the periphery of towns and villages and continued their occupations. They were joined in the "special communities" by other occupational and social groups that existed on the margins of society—beggars, criminals, vagabonds, and entertainers *(hinin)*. In short, unattached groups, people with no "proper" communities or social status, found refuge in Eta localities.

Although the Eta were religiously tabooed and considered immoral, they continued to serve useful economic functions, especially during the period of continuous internecine strife immediately prior to the Tokugawa (1615–1868) era. Leather goods essential for warfare could only be supplied by the Eta. Thus, each feudal lord sought the services of leather workers, who were as necessary as the farmer and the samurai for the survival of the fief. In the era of power struggles for absolute control of the land, interspersed with occasional attacks from without, the Eta became an economically prosperous class.

However, when Tokugawa Ieyasu (1615) emerged victorious and succeeded in unifying the land, a three-hundred-year period of peace set in. The Eta's position of importance diminished, as did their economic circumstances. The merchants and artisans who had experienced prosperity during the war years were relegated the lowest position in the social hierarchy and stripped of all symbols of prestige. The Eta were particularly despised, not only because of lowly occupational practices but also because they were called upon to act as executioners.

In an attempt to stabilize the social and economic system, oppressive measures were instituted by the feudal lords. Spatial mobility and communication were minimized; no man could leave the station in life into which he had been born. The Eta were thus firmly established in a subordinate social position from which they have yet to emerge.

The social degradation, increased population, and serious economic decline experienced by the Eta in the Tokugawa era clearly differentiated them from the majority society. These distinctions persisted even after the Eta were legally emancipated during the Meiji reform (1871), in part because of the indifference of both Eta and non-Eta. In short, legal freedom failed to effect substantial changes in the relationships of the Eta with the larger society.

Not until after Japan had emerged from two major wars as a world power were there any large-scale, organized attempts by the Eta to gain social and economic equality. In 1923, the *Suiheisha,* a national movement "for the liberation of Eta," was formed, but the organization's goals were never realized. On the contrary, the early aggressiveness of the Suiheisha movement brought open conflict and increased the hostility of the "ordinary people."

At present, the special communities, traditionally located on river banks and other marginal lands, maintain a perceptible distinctness because of sub-standard, slum-like dwellings and serious overpopulation. Although many of the *buraku-min* (people of the special community) are employed in the customary Eta occupations of butchering, leather and fur processing, begging, and other menial tasks, the largest percentage are farmers, fishermen, and unskilled laborers. They are further differentiated from non-Eta because of an income far below the national average, and because of their tendency toward local and "caste" endogamy.

In summary, the Eta may best be understood as a corporate group, the members of which are ascribed inferior status by virtue of such membership. Outcaste identification has been determined variously through history: first by affiliation with specific clan and kinship groups, later by association with certain occupational guilds, and finally by membership in Eta communities. In addition to these constantly fluctuating societal definitions of the outcaste categories, there has been a continual movement of individuals both into and away from these groupings. After the popularization of Buddhism in the middle of the Heian Period (794-1185), animal slaughterers and tanners were permanently classified as Eta, but even the members of these occupations enjoyed relatively high status in subsequent periods of Japanese history. Thus, the Eta are not to be conceived of as an inferior alien enclave or a degenerate segment of the native population, since both assume a static and intransitory population, and a definite, unchanging racial or ethnic group.

The remainder of this report is a summary of field research in northern Japan in which the major objectives were to determine some of the factors contributing to the social persistence of Shin-machi, an Eta community located on the outskirts of Toyoda City in Northeast Japan (Tohoku District). [1]

Attitudes and Beliefs of the Non-Eta in Toyoda

A great deal of misunderstanding and misconception exists in Toyoda concerning the Eta. Most citizens prefer to avoid the subject of the Eta people even in conversation. Most informants, although unaware of the location of Shin-machi, know the term *Shin-machi-nin* (people of Shin-machi), which is applied to the Eta of Toyoda. Few city residents have ever been to Shin-machi and most never knowingly met an Eta. Briefly, the Eta do not affect the lives of the Toyoda people, and do not constitute a recognized social problem.

However, this lack of concern with the Eta in no way diminishes the attitudes of prejudice and hostility; rather, it propagates ignorance, obscurity, and even mystery. Four of the most general attitudes held by Toyoda informants toward the Eta are offered.

Disgust is the most widely held and commonly verbalized attitude. Individuals who are unwilling even to discuss the Eta distort their faces and exclaim, *"kitanai"* (dirty). These feelings are sometimes manifested more directly. For example, after one of the customers in a small wine shop noticed blood on the hands and shirt sleeves of a young Eta, he shouted disparagingly at him. Several other guests joined in the mockery: "You are dirty, you animal killer! Look at the blood all over you! You are a filthy *yaban!* (barbarian, savage)."

Fear is an attitude of the Toyoda people. The Eta are considered dangerous and capable of inflicting bodily injury on non-Eta. This conception is supported by exaggerated stories of their physical prowess and fighting skill; they are likened to the gangsters and hoodlums portrayed in American movies. There is also the fear that surrounds the unknown. The Eta are believed by some to be sinister characters with evil powers, and mothers sometimes frighten their children with gruesome tales of the Eta similar to our bogey-man stories. It is said, too, that the Eta are afflicted with such contagious diseases as syphilis, gonorrhea, tuberculosis, and leprosy.

Because the Eta and their village are forbidden, the attitude of curiosity prompts such questions as: "Do the Eta look different? Are the women really beautiful? Are they rough, like gangsters? Do they actually speak a different language? What kind of food do they eat?" Many non-Eta wonder if Eta girls are "better" than ordinary women, some young males have erotic desires for Eta women, and restaurant hostesses often joke about an imputed distortion of the Eta male sexual organs.

The final attitude, which might be termed objectivity, seems to be increasing steadily among the younger generation, but it has the fewest adherents in Toyoda. This attitude is not widespread because it depends primarily on some knowledge of objective conditions. Such viewpoints exist, as Merton (1949:182) states in another context, not as prejudice or prejudgment, "but as the irresistible product of observation. The facts of the case permit no other conclusion." Thus:

> Look at the Eta and their houses—they *are* dirty. The Eta always marry each other, so their strain is weak. They are an exclusive, intimate group that reject outsiders and any form of aid; they have dirty occupations and they are diseased. I feel sorry for the Eta because of their lowly position, but I will have nothing to do with them until they learn to live like other Japanese, that is, give up their occupations, marry outside their small community, clean up their village, homes, and selves, and drop their hostile "clannish" attitudes.

This attitude is based less on legend than the others but, as with dominant Negro-white relations in the United States, it operates as a self-fulfilling prophecy in maintaining the Eta status (Merton 1949; Myrdal 1944; MacIver 1948).

The beliefs and myths of the Toyoda citizenry function to preserve majority group exclusiveness by associating the Eta with violations of some of the most fundamental and sacred Japanese values—those centering around purity, lineage, and health. The following are two of many popular legends.

> One time a young man met a beautiful girl in a restaurant. After a short courtship they were married against the wishes of the boy's parents. They lived happily for awhile, but when their children were born idiots with spotted complexions, it was discovered that the girl was an Eta.

> It was customary prior to the turn of the century for Eta to wash the bodies of deceased "commoners" in return for an offering of sake. After the Eta began to realize their emancipation, however, they frequently requested money from clients in payment for the washing services. Sometimes the demands were exorbitant. When the sum was refused, the Eta would threaten the family by vowing to drink the water used in bathing the body of the family ancestor. The people were usually frightened into relenting to the Eta demands.

The general theme of the first story is the unhappiness of anyone who marries an Eta, and the physical and mental distortion of the offspring. This is probably the most widespread myth, as it is employed by parents to discourage children from affairs that might result in a "love marriage." Even the most informed Japanese would balk at the thought of marriage to an Eta because of the popular notion of their "weak strain" from long intermarriage. The second legend is supposed to illustrate the barbaric quality of the Eta; not only were they mercenary, but they profaned the sacred, defiled the dead, and even drank the impure and dirty.

Shin-Machi

Shin-machi's 347 inhabitants are housed in forty-three dwellings, some including as many as ten households, located on a narrow dead-end road on the southeast edge of Toyoda City. Several relatively new houses dot the village, but the majority are old and dilapidated. Windows are covered with newspapers, and holes in the roofs are patched haphazardly with cardboard and paper held in place by large stones.

Family genealogies indicate only eighteen surnames in Shin-machi, and seven of these account for the majority of the seventy-eight households. The *buraku-min* tend toward local and "caste" endogamy; sixty-two percent of the marriages were between residents of the community, and seventy-nine percent between individuals with Eta occupations and status. Thus, almost every individual is either consanguineally or affinally related to every other individual. Adoptions are frequent, especially between families of siblings, and illegitimacy is common; few families have no illegitimate births recorded in the city registration book *(koseki)*.

The traditional Eta occupations of shoemaker, leather worker, furrier, and butcher, support thirty percent of the households. Another thirty-five percent are day laborers or claim no occupation. The remainder are dependent upon menial, low-income occupations such as begging, rag collecting, knife-grinding, peddling small confectioneries at festivals, and collecting food and clothing left at graves after certain religious festivals. Only four residents hold jobs that might be construed as non-Eta occupations.

Analysis of the social and economic structure of Shin-machi reveals two clearly defined status groupings, with marked differences in prestige, power, attitudes toward Eta status, and systems of interpersonal relations. The members of each generally identify themselves with the group to which they objectively belong (in terms of occupation, wealth, education, house type, and kinship orientation), and they are rated by others as belonging to one or the other of the groups. The terms upper class and lower class are used here to differentiate them. (The Eta themselves make the distinction between "the people down there" and "the people up there," which are not altogether accurate references to the geographical location of lower and upper class dwellings.)

The upper class is composed of thirteen households with a total of seventy-five members, forty-six female and twenty-nine male. The residences, many of which are clustered in one section of the village, are typical modern Japanese houses, each owned by its occupant. The heads of the households are usually literate, and several have reached high school. Upper class children have attended school regularly since the end of the war, and most will probably finish high school. Constituted authority in Shin-machi is vested in the upper class, with the headman and his assistants being members of this group.

There is a high degree of occupational stability in this class. All of the trades have been practiced in the households for at least three generations and, typically, a household has only a single occupation such as drum-maker or shoemaker. In some instances, however, secondary income may be supplied by the employment of unmarried sons and daughters in wine factories and in offices outside the community.

The lower class has a total of 272 persons, 137 males and 135 females, residing in sixty-five households. The makeshift lower class dwellings, none of which are owned by the occupants, are overcrowded and poorly heated and lighted, thus sharply differentiating them from the upper class houses. Only two lower class individuals have completed the third grade. While recent educational reforms have tended to increase school attendance by lower class children, it remains sporadic due primarily to the lack of adequate clothing, irregular diet, and prolonged illnesses. Also, ridicule by both teachers and students in the public schools reduces incentives for education; post-war hostility against the Eta in school is apparently directed at lower class students, who are distinguished by shabby clothing and dirty appearance.

In contrast to the upper class, the low-income occupations of the lower class are marked by diversity and irregularity. Forty-three of the families receive the major part of their incomes from fur-processing (12), day labor (17), begging (4), peddling (7), and relief (3); ten families claim no employment. Since these jobs are seasonal and part-time, lower class families are generally supported by more than one occupation.

The class division is a fairly recent phenomenon in Shin-machi. Prior to the depression of the 1930's, the people of the buraku had been a rather homogeneous and economically prosperous group. Although overt discrimination had been severe, the monopoly in the fur and leather crafts assured them an adequate income. During the depression, however, many of the Eta, especially the animal slaughterers and fur workers, experienced a marked decline in income. The demand for leather goods declined, the prices of Eta handicraft were depressed, and opportunities for outside employment were virtually eliminated. Few Eta starved during this crisis, partly because of their reliance upon the meat from slaughtered animals, but many were reduced to begging for the additional income necessary for survival. Some sold all personal belongings including houses, household equipment, and clothing.

The demand for fur goods never again reached a predepression level, so the majority of those engaged in the fur business have not been able to regain their former living standard. However, all Eta were not equally affected by the depression, and many have since become prosperous. As a result, there are now two sharply differentiated groups, the relatively wealthy and the poor.

Community Persistence

At the outset of the research in Shin-machi, it was believed that the Eta were forced to remain in the outcaste community because of the discrimination and prejudice of the larger society. The intense feelings of the "ordinary people" conjured up the image of an almost impenetrable barrier through which the Eta must pass in order to lose the social stigma. As the research progressed, however, it became increasingly apparent that the problem was not simply the relationship of the Eta group to the larger society, but also relationships within the Eta community. Although the Eta are despised and discriminated against, the attitudes, beliefs, and fears of the outsiders are insufficient explanation for community persistence. In response to these external forces and Eta subordination, Shin-machi has developed a distinct socioreligious identity and unity, and a strong set of social, economic, and psychological restraints upon individual mobility.

Community Organization and Social Solidarity. Shin-machi is a subdivision of Toyoda City, but it is unique in that it is the only district within the framework of the city administration which elects its own headman, holds town meetings for the discussion of local affairs, and maintains a liaison officer between itself and the municipal government. It a sense these are extra-legal functions, since they are not provided for in the post-war city charter. However, they indicate the realization by both the city officials and the buraku people of the "special" *(tokushu)* character of Shin-machi. They also tend to stimulate community identity and cohesiveness by directly involving community members in local Eta problems.

The village headman *(soncho)* and his assistants (secretary, treasurer, fire and health commissioners, and Shrine attendant) handle disciplinary matters within the community, cases of discrimination by outsiders, and such general issues as the raising of money for special purposes, collecting taxes, and arranging details of religious festivals. General meetings, held in the village shrine and attended by at least one member of each household, are called by the headman to discuss village problems and, if possible, to reach decisions by agreement among the villagers.

In addition to sounding out opinion and disseminating information, the town meetings reinforce community solidarity. Few issues are settled at any meeting, but individuals become aware of their involvement in the problems of the whole community. The town meetings generate feelings of belongingness primarily because the problems are unique to the community and, in most instances, directly related to Eta status. Except for religious celebrations, these meetings are the only occasions when all members of the community assemble for business and entertainment. Large quantities of sake are consumed, and status differences and special interests are subordinated to the greater general interest.

The pattern of social control that has developed in Shin-machi is related to its system of self-government. The Eta, particularly those at the apex of the power structure (the upper class), are intent upon concealing from outsiders every aspect of their life-ways, especially those believed to violate or differ from normative Japanese standards. Stringent controls are therefore exerted upon community members to restrict relationships with non-Eta. Public disturbances, law-breaking, or any behavior which might bring disrepute to the whole Eta class, are discouraged by ostracism, ridicule, and criticism, and even by threats or acts of violence. The kind of information about the village which may be divulged to a non-Eta is similarly controlled, and a person who discusses community affairs with an outsider is treated as a "stool pigeon" with pressures comparable to those employed by criminal groups and juvenile gangs in America. These measures obviously stimulate in-group exclusiveness and set the Eta off as a closed subgroup.

Religious affairs also function to integrate the community. These observances, like all public community activities, are held at the Shinto Shrine in the center of the Shin-machi graveyard, and are presided over by the headman. Religious festivals are of two kinds: the Buddhist festivals which commemorate the dead, and the Shinto or Shrine festivals in honor of the local tutelary deities. While their thematic emphases differ, the rites are identical and the overall unifying symbols are those of common ancestry, common territory, and common problems—those of the underprivileged minority.

On Buddhist holidays the close kinship ties between the members of the community are made explicit by the homage rendered to common ancestors. These bonds are reinforced by community decoration of the graves, and the prayers and speeches at the Shrine make constant reference to the relationships between the behavior of the living and the expectations of the dead. Perhaps the most dramatic suggestion of kinship unity occurs during the spiritual interaction between the old men of the village and their common ancestors through a medium at the celebration of *Higan* (a Buddhist holiday commemorating the dead).

At the Shinto festivals, the major emphasis is on cooperation and community welfare. The headman reviews the past accomplishments and failures of the community, suggests ways to bring about greater realization of community goals in the future, and asks the gods for their protection and good will in the attainment of these goals. The principal concern is with the continued well-being of the community; *Inari-sama* (fox-god), the local deity and god of abundance, symbolizes this hope.

In every speech and in every prayer there is mention of the community in its relation to the world outside. Some are pleas for greater cleanliness in the village, or on the advisability of curtailing dog killing; others center on the Eta's lowly position in Japanese society, or on the cruelty of the world as signified by some particular instance of discrimination. Some orations invoke the intercession of the gods for the attainment of economic success, for the marriage of daughters, and for less discrimination by non-Eta.

Clearly, the shrine and its gods are the locus of community and territorial identification; the religious rites express a system of relationships which differentiate this territorial grouping from those surrounding it, and which give it a distinct socioreligious identity and unity.

During the drinking sprees which accompany the festivals, conversation invariably focuses on the common enemy, the outsider. Occupations and poverty, family difficulties and poor living quarters, all are discussed in the context of relationships with non-Eta. All the fears and hopes expressed in the ceremonials are reiterated in conversation at the sake parties. Songs are often sung in a secret Eta vocabulary (a kind of Japanese pig-Latin used frequently when outsiders are present), and they are joined with an enthusiasm which reflects the intensity of the individual's identification with the community. The subordinate relationship of the community to the larger society, then, is an essential aspect of the social and religious life of Shin-machi, and it is an important mechanism for maintaining social solidarity.

Social Organization and Patterns of Stability and Mobility. As a result of the Eta's minority status, individual members of Shin-machi are torn between the desire to emigrate and in so doing lose Eta identity, and to remain in the community, thereby assuring a degree of social and economic security. Since the Eta emancipation in 1871, and probably before, individuals have "passed" into the larger society. However, the opportunity for leaving the tokushu-buraku has become greater since World War II, and this has intensified the ambivalence toward remaining in the community, despite the difficulties emigration makes for securing a livelihood in a competitive and job-scarce economy. Remaining in the community has been the stronger sentiment, since the community not only continues to exist but has increased in population from 310 in 1920 to 347 in 1954. A brief analysis of the socioeconomic organization of the two classes may reveal some of the factors underlying this situation.

Upper Class. The household is the basic social and economic unit of the upper class. Each household is ideally composed of a man and wife, and their eldest son and his wife and unmarried children. By the rule of primogeniture, the eldest son inherits the family property, debts, obligations, and occupation. This system of transference, which maintains continuity, is supported by complex patterns of obligations. One of these, *ko* (filial piety), obligates and subordinates the individual to his parents and ancestors. Benedict (1946:115) describes this as a never-ending indebtedness which is a compulsory part of man's "universal lot." Support of aged parents and maintenance of the lineage are the duties which befall the eldest son. At the death of the household head, the eldest son incurs even more concrete obligations along with title to the family property and occupation—he is bound indefinitely to the residence and trade of his father.

Junior sons in the upper class are encouraged to migrate and seek employment in one of the larger cities. All obligations between the migrant and his family are terminated by mutual consent, and he is free to seek his fortune independent of family considerations. When such emigration occurs, Eta identity presumably is lost and the individual may be assimilated into the general population. Although the position of the younger sons appears advantageous insofar as it enables them to escape the Eta stigma, considerable anxiety results from the situations into which they are thrust. Outside the community, Eta migrants live in constant fear of discovery, and the consequences for those detected in their attempts to pass are usually disastrous. Several disillusioned persons have returned to Shin-machi after such failures; breakup of marriage, loss of family and job, and sometimes suicide, result from detection in an attempt to pass.

However, one of the greatest sources of frustration for the emigre stems from the still undeveloped wage-earning economy, combined with the pressure of overpopulation. Employment opportunity in Japan is still largely regulated by kinship affiliation and its extension—"The society is no more than an organization of families" (Stoetzel 1954:57). The migrant Eta has no family connections; he has no sponsor and no reference in the society outside his community. Furthermore, in order to lose the Eta stigma it is almost essential that he move to the urban centers, the major underemployment areas of the country into which a vast number of persons from rural areas flow daily. (It is estimated that more than 1,000 job seekers per day arrive in Tokyo alone.) Migrants from tokushu-buraku have only limited employment possibilities. The social and economic factors that arouse anxiety in the migrant junior sons also tend to reduce any mobility aspirations of the eldest sons, whose duty is to remain in the community. The eldest sons of upper class families are highly skilled craftsmen, as a result of years of apprenticeship in the family trade. If they remain in the community, as they must in order to practice the inherited occupation, they are assured a degree of economic security which otherwise is virtually unattainable.

The choice therefore lies between abandoning a means of livelihood in order to erase the degradation of "caste," and remaining in the lowly status with an assured means of subsistence. The psychological dilemma is never solved. Those who stay constantly ask themselves, "Would I be better off here or on the outside? Am I doing the right thing?"

The precarious economic balance in the upper class depends upon the regular out-migration of junior sons. The household economy is unable to support an additional individual or family, and the overcrowded housing conditions in Shin-machi make it impossible to shelter new members. Moreover, the Eta occupational monopolies are so marginal that the addition of a single competitor would seriously depress individual incomes. Although mass production in the leather industries has reduced the market for handicrafts, the Shin-machi tradesmen still have a steady but limited outlet for their goods. If these conditions remain unaltered, the upper class Eta are assured a regular and relatively high income. The system of out-migration may therefore be viewed as a conscious attempt by the craftsmen to limit competition from junior sons, who are potentially new members of the guild. Consequently, both the guild and the separate families have a vested interest in maintaining the continual flow of individuals from the community.

The upper class attitude toward the elevation of Eta status also bears upon the emigration pattern. Upper class Eta generally claim that they remain in the community because of family obligations; they are destined by birth order to remain Eta. As a consequence, their interest and effort is focused upon raising the collective status of the community. Members of this class believe that the Eta stereotype held by the majority society will be modified by changes in the condition of the community. As the deplorable physical environment of Shin-machi results in part from large population and low income, Eta leaders feel that a stable population is a major factor in the status enhancement of the whole community.

The intensity of upper class desires to erase all "caste" barriers cannot be overemphasized. Members of this class believe that they have acquired the material symbols and social skills necessary for recognition as members of the Japanese middle class; but because of Eta or community identification, this privilege is denied them.

The fervor with which the upper class now seeks social and economic equality is probably a recent development, and has coincided in general with the rising educational standard and the decrease in direct discrimination. Prior to World War II, the motives, values, and aspirations of the community leaders with reference to the Eta place in Japanese society were predominantly those of acceptance; the roles the Eta were destined to play in the society were conceived as immutable. Thus, instances of discrimination were treated either with passive acceptance or with flagrant and rash behavior.

With the return of the war veterans, the character of the upper class and the pattern of community leadership underwent significant changes. In contrast to the older generation, the young returnees were literate, optimistic, and experienced in the outside world. They were unable to accept the inferior Eta status based upon tradition, ignorance, and prejudice; they did not believe the Eta were destined to eternal subordination, but felt that the majority society must eventually accept them as equals.

The recent decrease in the incidence of overt and direct hostility toward the Eta has tended to reinforce the new upper class beliefs, since it appears that non-Eta attitudes are now shifting toward greater tolerance. This apparent trend has impressed upper class members with the proximity of their goal of equality, but psychological anxiety has been magnified because the actual status of the Eta has not changed significantly, and there are still sporadic cases of discrimination and out-group hostility.

In order to facilitate changes in non-Eta attitudes, upper class leaders have instituted an improvement program designed to eliminate conditions within Shin-machi believed to be at variance with the normative standards of the larger society.

Specific improvement is sought in the dirty physical appearance of the community, and in the "barbarian" behavior of certain Shin-machi residents. The former is difficult to eradicate because it is largely a consequence of inadequate housing and overpopulation. However, periodic inspections are made by the health and sanitation officers, and suggestions offered for improved utilization of existing facilities.Community-wide cleanup days are held several times a year; such practices as killing animals within the community and littering the area with garbage are discouraged.

Behavior is an area in which improvement may be more feasible. The upper class Eta are at least partially aware of the outsiders' conception of them as immoral, criminal, irresponsible, and alcoholic, and they are also aware that such accusations are sometimes justified. A campaign is therefore being conducted to promulgate such upper class virtues as maintaining family obligations, honesty in business dealings, moderate drinking, and interest in child welfare. In short, middle class Japanese norms are stressed. Failure to conform evokes gossip, ridicule, and condemnation.

The specific improvements desired by the upper class necessitate alterations in the living conditions and behavior of the lower class. By and large, the lower class does not act in accordance with the new rules and it thereby evokes hatred and disgust from the upper class, attitudes which are similar to those expressed by outsiders toward the Eta. In fact, upper class Eta often refer to members of the lower class as "those barbarians," "those dirty people," "beggars," and "*hinin*" (not people, or not like other people).

The upper class social mobility pattern is complex. Because members feel they are obliged for economic and moral reasons to remain in Shin-machi, they make every effort to raise the collective status of the "caste." The notion of "caste mobility" does not spring from a deep-rooted sympathy with the Eta people and their problems, but has developed because the leaders feel that they will be able to enhance their own status only by elevation of the entire "caste."

The Lower Class. The social and economic life of the lower class is dominated by the fur and leather processing industry and regulated by a system of fictive kinship relationships. Thirty-seven of the lower class households, or nearly two-thirds of the total, receive a substantial proportion of their income from the production and distribution of fur and leather goods. One wealthy and powerful individual, himself an Eta, has an absolute monopoly of the industry, including the allocation of employment and the ownership of all lower class houses—the homes of his employees. Between this man and his employee-tenants there has developed a system of relationships characterized by a set of diffuse reciprocal obligations and duties, collectively known as the *oyabun-kobun* system. These relationships are essential features of the socioeconomic life of the lower class, and are crucial to the understanding of community persistence.

Ishino (1953:696), who has treated the oyabun-kobun (literally, father status-child status) most extensively, describes it as a system "in which persons not usually related by close kin ties enter into a compact to assume obligations of a diffuse nature similar to those ascribed to members of one's immediate family." It is a ritual kinship generally established by a special rite of passage. Members address one another by kin terms. Although it satisfies many of its members' expressive needs, its primary function is the ordering of economic relationships. It operates in many spheres and on various levels in Japanese society, and there are a number of variations in its form, duration, and specific functions.

In Shin-machi the oyabun-kobun institution regulates two interrelated aspects of economic organization: landlord-tenant and employer-employee relationships. During the depression a representative of a large Tokyo fur company loaned money to a number of Shin-machi inhabitants, as well as to the Toyoda butcher shop proprietors. In time the borrowers became hopelessly indebted and were forced to sell their homes and businesses to their creditor, and a group of Eta thus became dependents of the new landlord, who required his tenants to work for him to pay the high rents he exacted. Through his financial control over the local butchers he demanded that they pledge him the hides of all animals slaughtered in the Toyoda area. In addition, he owns the large leather and fur stores in Toyoda as retail outlets. His enterprise has flourished.

The system of relations which developed between this man and his retainers typifies many organizations throughout Japan. By incurring obligations *(on)* from the oyabun, the followers are pledged to his service; in return, the oyabun assumes responsibility for their support. Because of his control over the supply of hides, his readily available labor force, and his system of distribution, the oyabun gradually forces the smaller independent furriers into the organization. At present, all but one of the furriers in the community are his employees, and he allocates the amount and kind of work done by each.

Informants state that "the oyabun controls all of the fur goods and most of the leather products handled in Shin-machi. All the people, except a few of the wealthy, are financially dependent upon him; in fact, the people could not live without him." The oyabun is the most revered man in the community. There are innumerable stories of his kindness and generosity, and each lower class Eta is able to recount his own family's gratitude for the oyabun's benevolence. He continues to aid the poor with favors and loans, and thereby reinforces his dominant position by constantly increasing the bonds of obligation between himself and the rest of the community. (The oyabun is outside the community class structure because he does not participate in community affairs, and because he is not considered a member of Shin-machi by other members of the community. However, he lives on the periphery of Shin-machi, and is regarded by Eta and non-Eta alike as an Eta.)

While the oyabun demands favors and a disproportionate share of the proceeds from the fur and leather industry, it must be stressed that he gives something in return, as the favorable attitudes of his followers attest. In fact, the oyabun-kobun system is characterized by a pattern of reciprocal obligations, duties, and loyalties. In this case, the patron is committed to aid impoverished families, to assign jobs to clients in proportion to need, and to assure a certain minimum income to the families under his protection. Because of his wealth and record of generosity, the oyabun has created a kind of economic security which would otherwise not be available to the lower class.

The obligations that characterize the oyabun-kobun relationship are a powerful deterrent to mobility, especially when reinforced by financial indebtedness. These dual obligations ordinarily obtain between the oyabun and an entire family, because favors or loans are usually granted to relieve economic pressure on a household. Individuals are not usually recipients of the obligation, and, in fact, it is referred to as a family debt. Indebtedness to the patron is therefore not the obstacle to a junior son or a daughter that it is to the family as a whole. However, most of the members of the families realize the impossiblity of repaying the obligation to the oyabun in kind, and they continue to work for him in the fur and leather crafts.

The obligation of the patron to assure his followers a subsistence is an incentive for individuals to remain in the community. Although several lower class families must resort to begging, and others may occasionally go hungry, it is believed that no one will starve in Shin-machi as long as the oyabun-kobun system exists. The people have faith that any crisis can be met by resort to the patron's benevolence. There is also the possibility that some may gain more than a mere subsistence from their relationship with the oyabun. In addition to the opportunity for at least limited mobility within the occupational hierarchy, there are other possible advantages such as loans for house repair, clothes, tools, and in one case, the initial investment in a confectionery and wine shop.

Economic considerations are thus the major factors inhibiting lower class movement from Shin-machi, but certain cultural and psychological conditions are also notable, although they may be indirect consequences of economic pressures. A large percentage of lower class Eta would be unable to pass into the larger society, regardless of the economic situation, because they lack the ability to handle social relationships and speech forms properly outside the community—two rather rigorously defined areas of Japanese culture.

The Japanese language is more than a mode of communication and expression; it is a highly respected art and an index of social class. The Japanese are most conscious of the variations in their language and of kinds of people who use them. Upper class urban dwellers, for example, use standard forms, while rural folk speak local dialects. This immediately marks them as rustics disdained by the urbanites. The lower class Eta have a distinctive dialect which is similar to that spoken in isolated communities in the mountains nearby. They are also distinctive because they are illiterate in a society in which literacy and learning are valued skills.

Members of the lower class are also conspicuous because of their insufficient knowledge of correct Japanese behavior. The way in which interpersonal relations are conducted indicates an individual's social class background, and deviations from the rigidly prescribed behavior constitute a breach of etiquette. Lower class Eta have not learned these norms, and they are branded as "curious," "different," or "barbarian."

The Eta are conscious of differences in background between themselves and outsiders: they tend to withdraw from situations that might demand social interaction with non-Eta, as these are threatening and embarrassing. An example is afforded by the following experience:

A young man left the community to look for employment in Hokkaido, where there is little discrimination against Eta. Upon his arrival, he became lonesome because he had no place to go and had no acquaintances in the city. In an attempt to ward off solitude he stepped into a cabaret, but as he pushed open the doors, the hostesses began to laugh. Embarrassed, he immediately returned to Shin-machi. The young man claimed that "the girls laughed at me because they knew where I came from." (Obviously, however, the girls would be unable to distinguish him from any other stranger.)

Lower class Eta frequently make unsuccessful attempts to migrate, but, as in the incident described above, failure is only in part a result of the actions and attitudes of non-Eta. One significant factor is the Eta definition of self and of situation. In contrast to the upper class self-conception, members of the lower class generally regard themselves as truly inferior. Furthermore, they believe their position in Japanese society to be predetermined and immutable. Their circuitous argument is, "We are animal slaughterers because we are base; we are degraded because we kill animals. But we must do this because we are Eta, who make a living from fur and leather working." The following excerpts from an interview with a lower class Eta conveys this self-image even more clearly:

Q. Are you the same as common people (heimin)?
A. No. We kill animals. We are dirty, and some people think we are not human.
Q. Do you think you are not human?
A. (long pause, and then) I don't know.
Q. Are the common people better than you?
A. Oh, yes!
Q. Why?
A. They do not kill animals. They don't live here (Eta quarters). They are good people.
Q. Do you think you or your children will ever leave this district or change occupations?
A. No, we are new common people *(shinheimin)*.
Q. Do you think outsiders will ever come to this village and treat you as friends?
A. No, people on the outside don't like us. Things haven't changed for a hundred years.
Q. Do you believe this right or fair?
A. (long pause) I don't know; we are bad people, and we are dirty.

Eta status is a matter of indifference and acceptance, except when specific questions are asked about it. In general, members of the lower class are willing to discuss Eta problems, and are even flattered that outsiders will deign to speak to them. They do not feel threatened, and usually accept their status. However, similar questions about the Eta could not be asked of upper class members. They vigorously deny that there is any difference between themselves and non-Eta, and insinuations that such distinctions exist would evoke antagonism and a resounding refutation.

Intragroup Relations. In part as a result of the differences in Eta attitudes toward their status, hostility has developed between the classes; and the net effect of this has been to increase community solidarity by intensifying intragroup interaction. It has been suggested that members of both groups are constrained to remain in Shin-machi. However, the upper class is mobility-oriented while the lower class is characterized by status-acceptance and indifference. The upper class is committed to improving conditions in Shin-machi in order to raise the collective status of the Eta, a program which can only be effected by total community participation. Since they are not mobile, persons of the lower class either do not comprehend or are unable to respond to the upper class innovations. This refusal or inability to conform to the standards dictated by the community leaders has alienated the two groups. Members of the upper class feel disgust, hatred, and embarrassment because of lower class indifference, while lower class members believe that upper class policies are unnecessarily restrictive and unwarranted. If this situation were to exist in a society where both groups were readily mobile, these differing orientations might stimulate serious conflict or else be eliminated altogether. But since both segments of this community are predisposed toward spatial immobility, the latent conflict is partially channelized into solidarity behavior.

The mechanisms described earlier for maintaining Eta secrets have been designed and implemented by the upper class, and are directed specifically at the lower class. Clean-up days, sanitary inspections, town meetings, and religious ceremonials are also intended at least in part to educate the lower class to upper class conventions. These events, sanctions, and regulations require a high degree of interest and participation by the upper class. Therefore, leadership which might otherwise be directed away from the community and toward tasks more directly relevant to individual or class mobility is oriented toward the internal affairs of the community. Although the motivations of the dominant group spring from a desire for individual status enhancement, the consequence of these drives is to solidify the community by focusing social action on problems of an intracommunity nature. The integration thus achieved is functional in maintaining the Eta as a distinct and unified subgroup of the larger Japanese society.

Conclusion

We may now summarize our analysis by means of a list of conditions which have been influenced by the relationships of the Eta with the larger society, and which bear directly upon the social persistence of Shin-machi.

1. A system of sanctions has emerged in Shin-machi which is intended to conceal from non-Eta many of the physical and social characteristics of the community. These controls engender exclusiveness and prohibit intercourse with the non-Eta.
2. The socioreligious organization, which is oriented toward the social problems of the underprivileged minority, stimulates ingroup unity and identity.
3. The normative system of Japanese social relations, with its emphasis on obligation, loyalty, and duty, discourages migration.
4. Mobility aspirations have been inhibited by the traditional Eta occupational monopoly, coupled with the job-scarce Japanese economy.
5. Tensions have developed between the two classes within the community, and these increase the intensity of social interaction between community members. Although hostile, these relationships are functional in creating community solidarity.
6. Because of vested economic interests in Shin-machi, the community leaders are oriented toward "caste" mobility, and are predisposed to remain in the community. Consequently, leadership emphasizes community stability and unity.

This study indicates that the persistence of the Eta in contemporary Japan cannot be explained simply by the discriminatory attitudes and prejudices of the non-Eta. Although these are necessary conditions, the Japanese scarcity-economy, the traditional system of Japanese social and economic relations, and the internal structure and organization of the tokushu-buraku, are also essential in maintaining the continuity of the Eta community.

Economically marginal groups in Japan, such as the Eta of Shin-machi, are often bound internally by close-knit systems of social and economic relationships and characterized by the prevalence of protective, hierarchical, kinship-oriented institutions such as the oyabun-kobun system and the extended family. These traditional Japanese tendencies, which may develop as adjustments to precarious social and economic conditions, foster in-group solidarity, dependency, and socioeconomic rigidity. However, Ishino and Bennett (1953), in their analysis of Japanese rural communities, note a decline in the importance of "feudal" socioeconomic institutions under more favorable and prosperous economic conditions. It is therefore tentatively suggested that if the employment capacity of the Japanese economy is expanded, the Eta may disappear as a distinctive subgroup of the society. Conversely, if the Eta continue to be an economically underprivileged group, they may remain socially and economically dependent upon "feudal," protective institutions and continue to reside in tokushu-buraku, despite possible changes for the better in the majority society's attitude toward them.

FOOTNOTE

1. All place names in this paper are pseudonyms. The nature of the community and its relationship to the majority society makes this necessary.

REFERENCES

Benedict, Ruth
    1946 The chrysanthemum and the sword. Boston, Houghton-Mifflin Company.
Ishino, Iwao
    1953 The oyabun-kobun: a Japanese ritual kinship institution. American Anthropologist 55: 695–707.
Ishino, Iwao and John W. Bennett
    1953 Types of the Japanese rural community. Interim Technical Report No. 6, Research in Japanese Social Relations, Ohio State University.
MacIver, R. M.
    1948 The more perfect union. New York, Macmillan Company.
Merton, Robert
    1949 Social theory and social structure. Glencoe, The Free Press.
Myrdal, Gunnar
    1944 An American dilemma. New York, Harper and Bros.
Ninomiya, S.
    1933 The origin and development of the Eta class. Transactions of the Asiatic Society of Japan No. 10 (second Series).
Sansom, George B.
    1943 Japan: a short cultural history. New York, Appleton-Century Company.
Stoetzel, Jean
    1955 Without the chrysanthemum and the sword. New York, Columbia University Press.

THE STRUCTURE OF URBAN SOCIETY

Susumu Kurasawa

The large cities of the modern world, especially those of Western Europe, did not come into being until the industrial revolution. Among those cities, London was the earliest and most typical. In contrast, Japan already had fairly large cities even under the feudal system. Edo, Japan's largest castle town, with an estimated population of 1,400,000, was the world's largest city during the early part of the eighteenth century. The population of London during the same period was only about 700,000.

When the industrial revolution came to Japan after the Meiji Restoration, modern techniques and the capitalistic mode of production were introduced into Japan's fedual cities. Because of the peculiar way in which Japanese capitalism has been formulated, two factors should be taken into account when analyzing the social structure of modern Japanese cities. These factors are, one, the historical backgrounds of the particular cities in question and, two, the impact which industrialization has had on those cities. The former may be called the premodern factor and the latter, the modern factor. In this paper, I will first categorize modern Japanese cities on the basis of these premodern and modern factors. I will then proceed to observe how these two factors have been projected into the social structure of modern Japanese cities. To say this in another way, I will attempt to make a sociological analysis of Japanese cities in terms of how they reflect what our economists refer to as the dual structure of the Japanese economy.

From the point of view of social structure, Japan's modern cities have developed principally from three types of feudal settlements: castle towns, including way stations and towns that grew up around temples and shrines; farm villages in which the inhabitants engaged in manufacturing as well as farming; and pure farm villages. The great majority of Japan's modern cities had their beginnings in the first type, the castle town. The social structure of the castle town consisted of three strata, the feudal lord and his retainers, the artisans, and the merchants. The feudal lord and his retainers functioned as the administrative bureaucrats and armed forces of their day, but the high taxes they extracted from the surrounding farming villages also made them the major consumer class. The artisan and merchant classes were completely dependent upon this consumer class, supplying it with weapons and essential commodities. The social structures of the towns that grew up at way stations and around temples and shrines were virtually identical to that of the castle town. These towns at way stations and temples also had their artisan and merchant classes which supplied goods and services to a major consumer class. The only difference lay in the nature of that class. The major consumer class

Kurasawa — *From The Journal of Social and Political Ideas in Japan,* Vol. 3, No. 3, (December, 1965), pp. 21-31. Reprinted by permission.

in the towns which grew up at way stations was made up of passing travelers, while that of the temple and shrine towns was composed of the priests with their prerogatives and special privileges.

When, following the Meiji Restoration in 1868, the feudal class system was officially abolished and people were granted the freedom to move from one part of the country to another, the establishment of the prefectural system of local government and the introduction of modern industry gave rise to new kinds of cities. One of these, the prefectural capital, developed directly from the castle town. Most of the castle towns which did not become prefectural capitals evolved into small commercial cities. The manufacturing-farming villages that lost their status as manufacturing centers because they were unable to compete with modern manufacturing techniques also evolved into small commercial cities. The manufacturing centers that were not adversely affected by the introduction of modern techniques were those whose industries were either of such a nature as to make it unnecessary for them to compete with modern industrial techniques or those whose industries were such that they could be managed profitably on a very small scale. Examples of such places are the city of Seto, which produces chinaware, and the city of Kawaguchi, which produces metal castings. The earliest industrial modernization following the Meiji Restoration was effected in government-operated factories, many of which, with the exception of those producing military supplies, were later sold off to various zaibatsu. The giant-government-operated factories which were built in such places as Kawasaki and Yahata, where there had been nothing more than small farming communities, led to the growth of new, large industrial cities. The last classification of modern Japanese city is the metropolis, of which Tokyo is the only really clear example. As mentioned earlier, Tokyo (i.e., Edo) was already a giant castle town during the Edo, or Tokugawa, period (1600–1868). After the central government was moved there from Kyoto following the Meiji Restoration, Tokyo quickly took on the character of a mammoth prefectural capital. Over the years, it has also taken on the characteristics of all the other kinds of modern cities mentioned above. The chart on the following page shows the origin of several kinds of modern Japanese cities and the principal social classes within each.

Modern Japanese cities, according to the social relationships found within each, can be divided into two broad types: the traditional consumer-type and the industrial-type. On the chart, the first type includes consumers cities A and B and small industrial city C; the second type includes industrial cities D and E. An example of the traditional consumer-type city is the city of Tokushima on the island of Shikoku. Tokushima was originally a castle town, the center of a fairly large fief. By the end of the Tokugawa period, Tokushima, at that time Japan's sole merchandising center of indigo, had developed into a large commercial town. Although Tokushima became a prefectural capital following the Meiji Restoration, it has never had any large-scale industry. Thus, we see that, more narrowly defined, Tokushima is a classic example of consumer city A on the chart. The largest and most important social class in consumer city A is made up of white-collar workers, who are employed in locally-owned firms, prefectural and city government offices, educational institutions, and branch offices of banks, commercial firms and ministries of the central government. The white-collar workers in consumer city A can be divided into two groups: the lower-to-middle class white-collar workers who have been locally educated and recruited and the upper class white-collar workers who have been sent there either by the ministries of the central government or the companies for which they work and, as such are candidates for executive positions in their home offices. There is a gulf between these two groups of white-collar

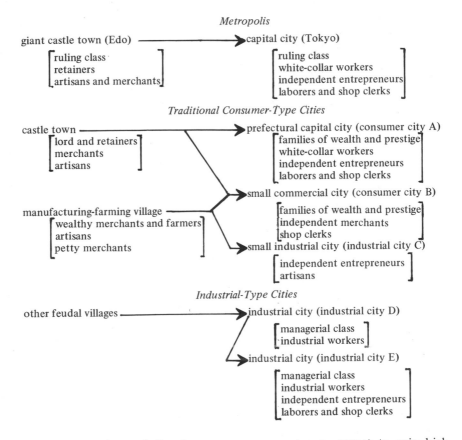

workers; the members of the former group cannot ever expect to gain high positions in the local branch offices of the central government or big business. Even though they can look forward to higher positions in locally-owned firms, the highest positions in such firms usually go only to the members of local families of wealth and prestige. Local families of wealth and prestige in this type of city always dominate the local small-to-medium enterprises, especially the financial and commercial enterprises. Although most of the small-to-medium enterprises owned by these local families have taken on a modern appearance, the social relations within them remain premodern. This, plus the fact that the local families of wealth and prestige monopolize the best occupational positions by maintaining close contact with one another, prevents free and rational opportunity for employment and reinforces the traditional social structure.

In many of the smaller enterprises, including retail and wholesale shops and small factories with only a few employees, no distinction is made between the owner's residence and the work site, both of which are usually located in the same building. In many cases the employees live in the same quarters with the proprietor and his family. The relationship between the owner and his employees is not that which exists between modern capital and wage labor: it is the traditional master-apprentice relationship. Noteworthy here is the fact that the owners of these small enterprises, rather than training their younger sons to work in the family business, look to nearby farming villages for their labor supply. The eldest sons, of course, are groomed to succeed to their fathers' positions, but the younger sons are either sent to the metropolis to work or are educated to become local white-collar workers.

To summarize the structure of this type of society from the point of view of social mobility and aspiration, upper-class white-collar workers in consumer city A always have their attention turned toward the home office in the metropolis of Tokyo. As temporary residents, they follow the living patterns of the metropolis and do not take active part in the affairs of the local community. Middle-to-lower class white-collar workers, most of whom have gained their positions through personal connections at the local level, do not develop a sense of social fellowship with their metropolis-oriented colleagues. Although middle-to-lower class white-collar workers do not have very bright prospects for promotion, they are satisfied with their working conditions, which are much better than those of the small-enterprise families or upper-to-middle class farming families from which they came. They therefore identify themselves with the community, being grateful to it for having provided them with their present positions. They also know that by sending their sons to college in the metropolis, they can give their sons a chance to become upper-class white-collar workers, thereby raising the family another rung on the socioeconomic ladder. The owners of small enterprises accept the traditional value system of the society because they are satisfied to continue operating their own small places of business along premodern, paternalistic lines. Only a few such entrepreneurs have their sights set on someday becoming accepted as a part of the circle of local prestigious families. Those few who have such aspirations strive to increase their wealth and influence by expanding their businesses and becoming active as officials in various community and trade organizations.

The lowest stratum of society in consumer city A is made up of the workers and shop clerks in smaller enterprises. For the most part, these people are the younger sons from farming families. Although their life in the city is confining and ill-paid, it is much freer and better than the life they knew in the farming villages where they grew up. They easily come to identify themselves with the value system which the cramped, narrow world of the premodern and paternalistic family-management system represents, because even that world offers them more than they ever had before, and because they know no other ways of life. In a word, the traditional value system continues to survive in consumer city A because of social stability, but this statement is not meant to imply that there is no social mobility in such a city. To the contrary, a high degree of social mobility is to be found among both upper-class white-collar workers and employees of smaller enterprises. But the members of both these groups are only temporary residents, and, as such, they exert no influence on the structure of the local society. The remainder of the people, that is, the local white-collar workers and entrepreneurs, are bound to the community because they receive certain benefits from it through personal connections and territorial relationships. They identify themselves with and support the traditional value system that is upheld by the local families of wealth and prestige.

Consumer city B and industrial city C also fall in the category of the traditional consumer-type city, but they differ from consumer city A in that they are not the sites of prefectural government offices, institutions of higher education, and branch offices of big business and central-government ministries. Consequently, consumer city B and industrial city C lack that segment of the population represented by the upper-class white-collar workers in consumer city A. In both consumer city B and industrial city C, local families of wealth and prestige are in firm control of their communities. The local families of wealth and prestige in consumer city B are usually engaged in small business, largely in the areas of commerce and service, whereas the same families in industrial city C are engaged in manufacturing goods of a traditional nature. Some of the well-to-do retailers in cities B and C are now gaining influence in local politics through their positions in neighborhood associations and other community organizations. These retailers, however, seldom attempt to challenge the established leadership of the prestigious families. To the contrary, they conform to the norms and traditional value system upheld by those families; their aspirations are usually limited to attaining the same standard of living and adopting the same patterns of life as the local prestigious families.

As pointed out earlier, the second broad type of modern Japanese city, that is, the industrial-type city, is represented on the above chart as industrial cities D and E. Industrial city D, a good example of which is Kamaishi in Iwate Prefecture, contains only one large enterprise. Kamaishi had a population of less than 4,000 when, in 1874, a government-operated iron foundry was established there. The construction of the foundry, which at one time before World War II produced forty percent of the nation's pig iron, brought about the rapid urbanization of the surrounding area and swelled the population to its present level of approximately 100,000. Although management of the foundry has changed hands several times since 1874, the foundry has always been controlled by big capital in the metropolis of Tokyo. Furthermore, the foundry has always been the only large enterprise in the community, and, as such, the sole support of the local economy.

The foundry's home office in Tokyo naturally expects its top executives at Kamaishi to operate the foundry efficiently. In order to do so, the top foundry executives have to manipulate local politics in Kamaishi through their lower-echelon counterparts and representatives of the local small-to-medium entrepreneurs, whose businesses largely depend on contracts with the iron foundry. The foundry executives resemble the upper-class white-collar workers of consumer city A in that they are only temporary residents of the local community who look forward to the time they can return to the metropolis. They differ, however, in that the necessity of manipulating local politics for the sake of their company does force them to participate to a degree in the affairs of local society.

In order to maintain effective control over local politics, the foundry utilizes a paternalistic system of management aimed at keeping its employees happy and avoiding any conflict of class interests between its employees and management. Most workers in Kamaishi are foundry employees, the majority of which are drawn from farm villages in the Tohoku region, where Kamaishi is located. The foundry's employees live in company housing, completely set apart from the other residents of Kamaishi, and they are provided with various fringe benefits. They therefore develop a deep sense of loyalty toward the company and a strong feeling of superiority toward the other residents of the community. They particularly tend to hold themselves aloof from the workers and shop clerks in smaller enterprises.

The owners of the smaller enterprises in industrial city D differ from those in the traditional consumer-type city in that they are not native to the area; they enter the community to set up businesses only after the large enterprise has been established. They have neither wealth nor prestige, and their businesses are not established on solid foundations; their existence as subcontractors and independent shopkeepers depends entirely upon the one large enterprise and its employees. This situation often prompts them to engage in injurious price wars, the effect of which is to undermine their solidarity and further weaken their collective independence. Their constant vying with one another for a share of a limited market renders them easy prey to the manipulations of the large enterprise. The workers and shop clerks in these small, independent businesses make up the lowest class in this kind of city. There are widespread feelings of discontent among these workers because, although they come from the same areas as the employees of the large enterprise, the conditions under which they must work are far inferior. Thus, we see that the social structure of industrial city D reflects the dual structure of Japanese capitalism. While this duality may potentially foster dissatisfaction with, and deviation from, the established pattern of social relationships, it serves at present as the key by which the large enterprise controls society in this type of city.

In industrial city E, where two or more large enterprises are in operation, workers tend to have a greater degree of freedom in seeking employment, and the small and medium enterprises, unlike their counterparts in industrial city D, are not necessarily dependent on a single large enterprise for their existence. In reality, however, these differences between industrial cities D and E are minimal; the system of life-time employment persistently maintained by large enterprises prevents any significant degree of mobility among workers, and subcontractors tend to be kept under the firm control of a single, parent company. An additional feature of industrial city E is the presence of large numbers of unemployed people and temporary employees of the large enterprises. The very presence of these people produces stratification of the laboring class, because full-fledged employees of the large enterprises tend to look down upon their unemployed and temporarily employed counterparts as comprising an inferior social class.

Standing above the various consumer cities and industrial cities is the metropolis of Tokyo. The politicians who represent the interests of the traditional consumer-type cities, and the big-business interests who control the industrial-type cities, for their mutual benefit join forces in the central government in Tokyo. It might well be said that the major function of the metropolis of Tokyo is to produce political and economic policies for the entire country. The people of all classes in Tokyo owe their livelihood either directly or indirectly to the fact that all the political and economic policies implemented in the other two types of cities and throughout the nation are formulated in the metropolis. The largest class in the metropolis is the white-collar class, for the simple reason that the ministries of the government and home offices of large companies, the places where policies are formulated, employ a tremendous number of white-collar workers. By reason of the taxes collected by the government and the profits made by big business, a vast amount of money is concentrated in the metropolis. Aside from the portion that is reinvested, all of this money is spent in the metropolis. The ever-growing consumer market made up of government and company executives and white-collar workers, the largest consumer group in the metropolis, constantly spawns the small-to-medium enterprises which produce consumer goods as well as the wholesale and retail businesses which distribute the goods. The development of business opportunities in Tokyo leads to an ever-increasing number of independent entrepreneurs and an ever-growing army of laborers and clerks who work for them. The everyday demands of this vast group of white-collar workers employed in government and business offices produce still another group of white-collar workers: those involved in such fields as publishing, entertainment, and news gathering and distribution. Needless to say, the presence of these additional white-collar workers, by further expanding the metropolitan consumer market, causes the number of small-to-medium businesses to increase even more. Thus we see that the fact that the policy decisions of both government and big business are made in Tokyo has created a vicious circle of supply and demand which causes the population of the metropolis to spiral ever upward.

Although most metropolitan white-collar workers perform their duties in modern office buildings, they work in an atmosphere dominated by pre-modern social relationships similar to those found in the traditional consumer-type city. The promotion system, though supposedly based on objective considerations of ability and performance, gives priority to educational background, seniority and personal connections. The small-to-medium entrepreneurs, which make up the second largest stratum in the metropolis of Tokyo, differ from those in the traditional consumer-type in that they have no long-standing territorial relationships or local personal ties to support and protect them in time of crisis. The resultant instability of small-to-medium enterprises spells a life of insecurity for the workers in such enterprises, a life that stands in sharp contrast to that of workers in big businesses, who enjoy secure, lifetime employment. Although there is a notable amount of social mobility within each of these two groups, that is, the white-collar workers and the workers and owners of small-to-medium enterprises, there is almost no mobility between the two groups. What little there is consists of some members of the latter group becoming lower-echelon white-collar workers.

Since the beginning of World War II, considerable transformation has taken place in Japan's cities. This transformation has been produced principally by five factors: one, the war and the consequent relocation of population and industry; two, modification of the system of local government; three, the advance of technology; four, changes in farm-village life; five, the decline in prestige of the nation's traditional value system. The evacuation of the populations of large cities to rural areas during the war brought city residents, particularly those of the metropolis of Tokyo and the industrial cities, into close social contact with the people of farming communities and traditional consumer-type cities. The contact prompted numerous changes in the living patterns of large segments of the rural population. In addition, the large-scale incendiary bombing raids near the end of the war reduced to ashes a large number of Japan's cities, including many cities of the traditional consumer type. Although these cities were rebuilt after the war, a tremendous blow had been dealt to traditional social relationships, relationships that are particularly important in the traditional consumer-type city, where the community tie depends so heavily upon constant personal, face-to-face contact. Another important aspect is that most of the factories which were evacuated from large cities to escape the bombing raids were moved to smaller cities in rural areas which theretofore had had no large industries. Following the war, many of the evacuated factories continued or resumed production on the sites to which they had been removed. This fact, plus the fact that the criteria governing the selection of favorable industrial sites were changing, brought about nationwide alterations in the industrial map of Japan.

The second factor, modification of the system of local government, was generated by the Allied Occupation's democratization policies, particularly by the reforms instituted in the systems of local government and taxation. Although the reforms in the system of local government, such as the new law which designated that the heads of local governing bodies be chosen by popular vote, were aimed at establishing a high degree of local autonomy, local autonomy was not forthcoming because the tax reforms deprived local governments of sufficient income. The principal tax categories were taken over completely by the central government and local governments had to satisfy themselves with getting what income they could from business taxes, property taxes, and other miscellaneous categories. The fact that local governments increasingly have had to seek subsidies from the central government in Tokyo to cover their perennial deficits has given the metropolis increased control over rural areas.

The third factor, the advance of technology, includes both technological innovation, that is, the mechanization and automation of factories and offices, and the development of transportation and mass-communication media. As a general rule, these advances in technology tend to inhibit or destroy local autonomy and to promote geographical integration, with the result that the metropolis strengthens its control over other areas of the country.

The fourth factor, changes in farm-village life, has been brought about for the most part by the development of diversified commercial farming. This development has directly influenced city life and the structure of urban society by reducing the prewar practice of city laborers' maintaining their own small farming plots and by bringing about an expansion of the marketing areas of provincial cities to include the surrounding hinterlands.

The fifth and final factor which has contributed to the transformation of postwar Japanese cities, the decline in prestige of the traditional value system, has been brought about by Japan's defeat in the war and the subsequent democratization policies instituted by the Allied Occupation.

All of the above factors have combined to bring about vast modifications within the various types of Japanese cities and their respective social structures. In the first place, factories owned by big business, which before the war were found principally in the industrial-type city, began to appear in increasing number in the traditional consumer-type city. In order to enhance revenues from property and other taxes, local government authorities in traditional consumer-type cities began to act in concert with their national Diet representatives for the purpose of having factories located in their areas. When a large factory is built in a consumer-type city, local prestigious families can continue to maintain control over the city only by cooperating with big business. Even in such cities where no large enterprise has been located, prestigious families can no longer depend solely on their wealth and local prestige; whether or not they are able to maintain their authority in the community depends upon their ability to influence the policies of big business to a degree sufficient, for example, to ensure a factory's being located in their area. In order to maneuver into such a position, they must establish direct connections with influential people in the metropolis. Conversely, the management of a newly-erected factory in the traditional consumer-type city does not exert influence on the local government by participating directly in local politics as does factory management in the industrial-type city. Instead, the home office of the factory maintains indirect control over local politics by exerting pressure from the metropolis on the wealthy families at the top of the local social pyramid.

The injection of big business into the traditional consumer-type city has also served to strengthen the control of the metropolis over local small-to-medium enterprises. The mass production methods used by large industrial enterprises, and the mass-media advertising techniques used by those enterprises to build solid markets for famous name brands, have made it decreasingly profitable to market the types of little-known brands that are generally manufactured by small, independent firms. Thus, rather than attempting to market their own products, more and more small-to-medium industrial enterprises are tying in with large industries by subcontracting to handle that part of the production process which requires cheap manual labor. Only by so doing can the smaller manufacturers protect themselves financially. There is a developing tendency for retailers also to become allied with large manufacturers. By selling franchises and other special contracts, the large manufacturers attempt to skip as much as possible the middlemen in the wholesaling process and sell directly to the retailer. The trend toward smaller enterprises allying themselves with larger, parent companies has had two principal results: it has encouraged the modernization of management in the smaller enterprises, and it has hastened the demise of independent entrepreneurs. The small-to-medium entrepreneurs who ally themselves with larger companies tend to become more prosperous, while the business of independent entrepreneurs tends to decline. Thus we find in the traditional consumer-type city the same instability that threatens small-to-medium enterprises in the metropolis.

The changes that Tokyo has undergone since the war have been even more drastic than those that have occurred in the traditional consumer-type cities. These changes have served to concentrate more and more of the nation's power in the metropolis. In the first place, Japan's big business before the war was characterized by the close ties it had developed with the nation's political world. This 'traditional' character of Japanese capital became even more pronounced following the war because the Allied Occupation had absolute control of both the political and economic life of the nation. In order to survive and expand, Japanese capital directed a great deal of energy toward winning the favor of the Occupation authorities in Tokyo. In the second place, in Japan, as in all advanced capitalist countries, the central government has tended to assume an increasingly greater role in the nation's economic life since the war. This tendency, plus the traditional character of Japanese capital mentioned immediately above, has contributed to the further concentration of capital in the metropolis. In the third place, postwar streamlining and standardization of production techniques, coupled with improvements in transportation and communications, have led the home offices of large companies to play a much more direct role in administering their local offices and factories. This has meant increased concentration of administrative power in home offices, most of which are located in the metropolis. The constantly expanding functions of the metropolis cause ever-greater portions of the surrounding area to become involved in the economic and social structure of the metropolis itself. For example, when the area between Tokyo and Yokohama had reached a point where it could accommodate no additional industries, the metropolis began to plan a new industrial complex to be built on reclaimed land between Tokyo and the city of Chiba. As Tokyo thus continues to grow, the surrounding prefectures, which now constitute fairly independent marketing areas, will inevitably become an integral part of the metropolis.

Before concluding this article, I feel that mention should be made of the recent mushrooming of public housing areas in the suburbs of the metropolis. Tokyo's housing areas began to expand toward the western suburbs of the city around the middle of the 1920's. Following World War II, Tokyo housing areas began to expand away from the center of the city with such speed that they soon invaded the smaller cities surrounding the metropolis. The National Public Housing Corporation and the metropolitan government have been particularly active in marking off large areas of farm land and converting them into giant public housing projects. The central portions of nighttime Tokyo are becoming increasingly uninhabited; many of the uptown stations at which commuters change trains are becoming the new entertainment and shopping centers of the city, replacing the older centers in the downtown area.

JAPANESE AND AMERICAN PERCEPTIONS OF OCCUPATIONS

Charles E. Ramsey and Robert J. Smith

This paper reports a study of the ideas of occupational prestige, social importance, and income in the minds of high-school seniors in Japan and the United States.

Studies of occupational prestige have revealed striking similarities between one culture and another, between one subculture and another, and at different times within the same culture. Except for minor variations, the following regularities in ideas of occupational ranking are found: *(a)* white-collar jobs are accorded higher prestige than blue-collar and agricultural work; *(b)* occupations requiring no training rank lower than those requiring manual skill and apprenticeship, while both of these are accorded lower prestige than occupations for which a high formal educational attainment is required; and *(c)* the few differences observed in the cultural comparisons make sense in cultural terms. These uniformities are all the more impressive when it is realized that a diversity of techniques have been used to arrive at the rankings of prestige. In the present paper ratings of prestige are studied among comparable samples of Japanese and American high-school seniors, using, as nearly as possible, identical research procedures in each. The literature suggested that few cultural differences in ratings of prestige could be expected. The important problem is, then, the relating of the ratings to other variables.

A reward associated with occupations, in addition to prestige, is income. The perception of the income rank of occupations may, of course, differ from the actual income received. Since the problem of the interrelation of variable perceptions requires that the judgmental dimension be measured, the present study includes only the perceived rating of occupations on income.

A third basis for rating occupations, is social importance, a term which does not mean inherent importance to social structure in general. Rather it refers to the fact, that within a culture, some tasks are deemed essential, some important but not essential, still others of no importance, while some occupations may be perceived as harmful to society. The cultural or perceptual nature of this phenomenon corresponds to the theoretical treatment[1] although the theory does not prescribe the operational procedures.

The population of interest consists of high-school seniors in Japan and the United States. As in previous studies, no attempt was made to draw a systematic sample from this population. Rather, high schools are selected on the basis of certain supposedly known and relevant characteristics and on the basis of willingness to co-operate. While this procedure does not yield a probability sample, it has rendered findings in various types of studies in which, where a check can be

Ramsey/Smith — *From The American Journal of Sociology*, Vol. 65, No. 5, (March, 1960), pp. 475-479. Coypright 1960 by the University of Chicago Press. Reprinted by permission.

made against other data, no systematic bias has been discovered.

The present report is based upon responses given by high-school seniors from rural and urban schools in Japan and the United States (Table 1). The data were gathered in the spring of 1958 by means of questionnaires administered in the schools. The questionnaire included items on the position of the student's family in the social structure, the aspirations and plans of the students, value orientations (familism, individualism, creativity, altruism, and life-goals), and the occupational variables used in the present analysis.

TABLE 1
RESPONSES OF HIGH-SCHOOL SENIORS, RURAL AND URBAN SCHOOLS,
JAPAN AND THE UNITED STATES

	Boys	Girls	Total
Japan	*248*	*288*	*536*
Tokyo (all seniors in two high schools)	91	87	178
Centralized school in center of approximately 20,000 population (all seniors in two schools) .	157	201	358
United States	*174*	*219*	*393*
New York City (all seniors in one school)	83	111	194
Centralized school in center of approximately 20,000 population (all seniors in one school) .	91	108	199
Total	422	507	929

The intention of the researchers was to make the questionnaires identical. The questionnaire was first constructed in English and then translated into Japanese. The translation revealed several inadequacies: some questions were meaningful in one culture but not in another, and distinctions in the categories of answers were impossible to translate. These findings resulted in several fundamental revisions in the final questionnaire as administered in both cultures.

The methods of analysis assume that one person's response is equally as important as another's and that individual responses, if added together, will reveal some cultural characteristics. It is recognized that there are other concepts which would require weighting, although no satisfactory procedure has been developed to do so. The concept and method used in the present analysis are essentially the same as those employed by other research workers, although there is some variation in technique from one study to another; they appear to render results similar to those found by direct observation and selected informants, but with considerably more precision. In the present report a few findings are at variance with those derived by other methods, but many are the same.

In the measurement of prestige and income the respondents were asked to rate each occupation in one of five categories from "very high" to "very low." The rank is therefore not a response but an inference from the mean of the ratings. In the measurements of social importance the procedure and assumptions were the same, except that the answers were more categorical: "essential," two degrees of "important," "not important at all," and "better if it did not exist."

The list of occupations rated on prestige and income were identical, but this list differed somewhat from the list for rating social importance. However, there were thirteen occupations common to the two lists. Functional necessity was rated for twenty occupations, and the other factors for twenty-three.

A simple comparison in prestige ranking by Japanese and American high-school seniors reveals striking similarities (Table 2). The comparison of twenty-three occupations gave a rank order correlation of + .80 between the two cultures. The ranking of the occupations also bears out the generalizations stated earlier as a summary of previous studies of occupational prestige. At the top of both were professions and at the bottom were occupations either agricultural, blue-collar work, or clerical jobs requiring little formal training.

TABLE 2
PRESTIGE RANK OF TWENTY-THREE OCCUPATIONS BY
JAPANESE AND AMERICAN HIGH-SCHOOL SENIORS

Japanese Rank	Occupation	Japanese Mean Rating	American Mean Rating	American Rank
1	College Professor	1.51	1.59	4
2	Doctor	1.69	1.22	1
3	Lawyer	1.81	1.37	2
4	Corporation executive	1.86	1.64	5
5	Author	2.23	2.02	6
6	Union leader	2.48	2.20	8
7	Primary-school teacher	2.61	2.40	10
8	Policeman	2.63	2.63	12
9	Small factory owner	2.65	2.82	15
10	Private secretary	2.72	2.53	11
11	Government clerk	2.79	2.74	14
12	Nurse	2.81	2.25	9
13	Priest (or minister)	2.97	1.46	3
14	Office worker	3.04	3.11	18
15	Beautician	3.15	3.19	19
16	Movie performer	3.19	2.19	7
17	Department-store clerk	3.23	3.55	21
18	Small shopkeeper	3.24	3.34	20
19	Soldier	3.37	2.71	13
20	Carpenter	3.48	3.07	17
21	Farmowner	3.49	3.06	16
22	Small shop salesclerk	3.67	3.78	22
23	Farm laborer	3.99	3.81	23

Within any given subsystem, a farm, a factory, or a hospital, there is usually a fairly clear ranking. In the examples given, farmowner is ranked above farm laborer, corporation executive above skilled worker, and doctor above nurse. These differences are maintained when two or more systems are combined; that is, farmer was still above farm laborer and so on. It was apparent, however, that systems themselves are ranked, so that a high position in one system may not assure a high position in total.

In a few occupations cross-cultural differences of some magnitude were observed. Of great interest is the difference in prestige assigned the solider: American students ranked the soldier thirteenth, which is below the median rank but still in the middle third; Japanese students ranked the soldier nineteenth, or fifth from the bottom of the list, a striking reflection of the wave of post-war pacifism which has swept the country. The soldier was accorded higher prestige by rural respondents than by urban, and higher by girls than by boys in both cultures.

Also of interest is the ranking of the clergy, which was third in the American sample but thirteenth among the Japanese, a difference which corresponds to other findings in the present study—that religion seems to have considerably more importance in the verbalized value system of American than Japanese seniors. This is but another reflection of the strong secular trend in Japan: the Buddhist clergy is thought of as closer to a character in a medieval Italian farce than to Barry Fitzgerald or Bing Crosby.

If the prestige rating of college professor reflects a general value of intellectualism, then the anti-intellectualism often attributed to American youth is not evident in the present study. Many other cultures accord higher prestige to professors than does American, although other rewards are often much lower. The rank of college professor was first among the Japanese and fourth among Americans. However, approximately half of each sample rated the college professor "very high" and the other half "high," with the mean approximately halfway between the top and second highest items in both cultures. Extremely few American seniors ranked this occupation in the middle or lower two categories of prestige. The difference in rank, given the nearly equally high rating in both cultures, is accounted for by the fact that American seniors generally accorded even higher prestige to three other occupations while the Japanese did not.

The movie performer was ranked sixteenth by Japanese students but seventh among American students. The low prestige which Japanese youth assign to him is at first surprising, since teen-agers flock to the theater, collect stars' autographs and photographs, and, within limits, imitate the behavior of actors and actresses. But the entertainer has traditionally been accorded an ambiguous status in Japan, and presumably admiration and envy are not lessened by their lack of respectability.

Rural-urban and sex differences were small. The rank-order correlations between rural and urban seniors and between boys and girls were above + .80. Similar correlations were found in comparing Japanese urban respondents with American urban (and the same holds for rural) as well as in comparing each sex cross-culturally.

In sum, the prestige rankings reveal little in the way of cross-cultural differences generally, although differences in the rank of particular occupations are theoretically interesting. The relationship between the prestige rankings in the present study are compared with those in previous studies (Table 3). Again, the general relationships are high and positive.

The roles in occupations are assessed differentially within a culture: some are considered essential, others important but not essential, and some are judged to be harmful. This variation in cultural assessment we will call "social importance."

The similarities between the Japanese and American ratings of occupations on social importance were nearly as great as those previously reported for similarities in prestige rankings (see Table 4). The rank-order correlation between the two cultures was + .74.

The rankings in both cultures suggest that the judgment of social importance is determined not only in terms of the role itself but also by the subsystem of which the occupation is a part. In both cultures at least one occupation from each of four institutions was in the top five, namely, physician, policeman, farmer, and college professor. It was also observed that, in both cultures, the mean rating of all four of the occupations named was closer to the value of the category "essential" than to the second category, "important." Actually 79 per cent of the American seniors and nearly as high a proportion of Japanese rated college professor as "essential"; extremely few rated him in the bottom three categories of social importance.

TABLE 3
RANK-ORDER CORRELATIONS BETWEEN THE RESULTS OF THE PRESENT STUDY
AND THOSE OF PREVIOUS STUDIES OF RANKINGS OF PRESTIGE

Study	No. of Common Occupations	Rank-Order Correlation with Japanese Rankings	Rank-Order Correlation with American Rankings
Smith* (345 American students)	14	.70	.84
Deeg and Paterson† (475 American students) . .	6	.77	.83
North and Hatt (nation-wide sample)	9	.50	.78
Odaka (2,000 adult Japanese males)	10	.89	.86
Counts (372 American students)	6	.77	.83
Tiryakian (641 Filipino adults [556 males, 85 females])	12	.86	.94

*Mapheus Smith, "An Empirical Scale of Prestige Status of Occupations," *American Sociological Review,* VIII (April, 1943), 185–92.

†Maethel E. Deeg and Donald G. Paterson, "Changes in Social Status of Occupations," *Occupations,* XXV (January, 1947), 205–8.

Cecil C. North and Paul K. Hatt, "Jobs and Occupations. A Popular Evaluation," in Logan Wilson and William Kolb (eds.), *Sociological Analysis: An Introductory Text and Case Book,* (New York: Harcourt, Brace & Co., 1949), pp. 464–74.

Cited in Nobutaka Ike, *Japanese Politics: An Introductory Survey* (New York: A. A. Knopf, 1957), pp. 11–16. (From an article by Kunio Odaka, "The Class Structure of Japanese Scoiety" [in Japanese], which appeared in *Asahi Shinbun* [Tokyo], February 10, 1953.)

G. S. Counts, "Social Status of Occupations," *School Review,* XXXIII (1925), 16–27.

Edward A. Tiryakian, "The Prestige Evaluation of Occupations in an Underdeveloped Country: The Philippines," *American Journal of Sociology,* (January, 1958), 390-99.

TABLE 4
SOCIAL IMPORTANCE OF TWENTY OCCUPATIONS RATED BY
JAPANESE AND AMERICAN HIGH-SCHOOL SENIORS

Japanese Rank	Occupation	Japanese Mean Rating	American Mean Rating	American Rank
1	Doctor	1.10	1.05	 1
2	Policeman	1.34	1.40	 4
3	Farmer	1.37	1.47	 5
4	College professor	1.47	1.27	 2
5	Journalist	1.59	2.02	 10
6	Nurse	1.77	1.31	 3
7	Carpenter	1.88	1.99	 9
8	Author	2.03	2.04	 11
9	Union leader	2.35	2.50	 14
10	Corporation executive	2.37	1.87	 8
11	Streetcleaner	2.41	2.47	 13
12	Undertaker	2.73	2.19	 12
13	Beautician	2.77	2.93	 17
14	Priest (or minister)	2.79	1.49	 6
15	Janitor	3.01	2.71	 16
16	Movie performer	3.25	3.04	 19
17	Professional baseball player	3.31	3.24	 20
18	Insurance salesman	3.59	2.66	 15
19	Soldier	3.61	1.57	 7
20	Political boss	4.82	2.98	 18

The cultural assessment of soldier was varied more as to social importance than as to prestige. American students considered the occupation of soldier as seventh in importance, with the mean rating between "essential" and "very important." However, the Japanese ranked it lower than any occupation (other than political boss, which was considered harmful). The mean rating of soldier places it in the category "of no importance at all."

The social importance of the minister corresponded to the prestige ratings previously discussed. The American sample ranked it sixth in importance, between "essential" and "important," while the Japanese sample ranked it fourteenth, or "of little importance."

Movie performer, which ranked high in prestige among American youth, and baseball professional (not included in the list of occupations for prestige rankings) were both assessed as of little importance. This may indicate an attitude of austerity of both cultures toward occupations essentially recreational. It may be that recreation, to be recreational, must be viewed as not essential, even though people actually use it in an "essential" way.

Political boss was viewed as of no importance by American seniors and received the lowest ranking in importance. However, more than half of the seniors in Japan felt it would be better if this status and role did not exist at all.

Union leader and coporation executive were deemed equally important by Japanese youth, but the corporation executive ranked considerably higher in importance among the Americans.

The very high rank-order correlations between the sexes and between rural and urban ratings in each of the two cultures again corresponded to the uniformity found previously for prestige rankings.

The income ratings were an estimate of the actual income received by persons in the occupations. The ranks, based on the ratings, appeared to correspond to the actual case very closely, with large variation in the ratings of any one occupation, and with greatest variation in the occupations with the middle range of income.

The cross-cultural comparisons on estimated income revealed much greater differences than were observed in ratings of prestige and social importance. The previous cross-cultural comparisons have given a picture of similarity, while the Japanese-American comparisons of estimated income render a low positive rank-order correlation (+ .26). This low correlation doubtless reflects the differences in actual income, and the total difference reflected in the low correlation may be attributed to greater differences in five occupations. The Japanese ranked policeman, primary-school teacher, and soldier much higher in relative terms than the Americans; the Americans ranked carpenter and farmowner much higher than did the Japanese.

In the interrelation of the three variables here studied, it was necessary to reduce the list to those occupations which were assessed on all criteria. The resulting thirteen occupations included most of those on which cross-cultural differences were observed. The net effect was to reduce the rank-order correlations between variables, although it did not change the direction of these relationships. The absolute rank of any occupation may be changed, but the relative rank is as before (Table 5).

Stated in summary: (1) the highest relationship between assessments was found between perceived income and prestige (rank-order correlations was + .65 in Japan and + .52 in the United States); (2) the relationship between social importance and prestige was low to moderate but in a positive direction (rank-order correlation was + .35 in Japan and + .37 in the United States); and (3) the relationship between social importance and estimated income was negative and low (rank-order correlation was − .24 in Japan and − .09 in the United States).

TABLE 5
RANKING OF THIRTEEN OCCUPATIONS ON VARIOUS DIMENSIONS
BY JAPANESE AND AMERICAN HIGH-SCHOOL SENIORS

| Occupation | JAPANESE | | | AMERICAN | | |
	Prestige	Social Importance	Income	Prestige	Social Importance	Income
Author	4	7	4	5	10	6
Beautician	9	10	7	13	12	10
Carpenter	12	6	12	12	9	7
College professor . .	1	4	5	3	2	5
Corporation executive	3	9	1	4	8	3
Doctor.	2	1	3	1	1	1
Farmer	13	3	13	11	5	8
Movie performer	10	12	2	6	13	2
Nurse	7	5	11	8	3	9
Policeman	6	2	10	9	4	12
Priest (or minister) . .	8	11	8	2	6	11
Soldier	11	13	9	10	7	13
Union leader	5	8	6	7	11	4

In the light of this and other studies it appears that similarities in prestige ratings are characteristic of Asian as well as Western societies. The findings of the present study indicate that these similarities will be found to extend to the perception of social importance.

Generalizations about the prestige system strongly suggested by this and previous studies are: higher occupational prestige is associated with higher educational requirements for the occupational role; white-collar work, especially the professions; higher status rewards in income; more authority within the subsystem of which the occupations is a part; the prestige of the subsystem itself; and, to a lesser extent, the social importance of the occupation.

Social importance did not differ greatly between the two cultures, but less evidence can be given for this as a generalization because of the lack of evidence from other studies. Functional necessity appears to have a low positive correlation with prestige. Part of this low correlation is accounted for by the assessment of farmers, policemen, and some types of skilled work as essential or important. The assessment of occupations in these terms appears strongly influenced by the assessment of the general function of the subsystem of which the particular occupation is a part. However, the differential assessment of social importance within the system is maintained in the general rank of occupations, for example, the comparison of doctor with nurse.

The negative correlation between income and social importance suggests the need for further research on social importance as a basic condition producing stratification. Of course, a single study is inadequate for testing a theory. However, more specifically, there appears to be contradictory evidence on the theory. Insofar as "social importance" is similar to the concepts of "functional necessity," the negative correlation between social importance, and income contradicts the hypothesis derived from the Davis-Moore theory of stratification. However, the low positive correlation between social importance and prestige corroborates the theory, except that a higher correlation would be expected. Other features of the same theory also are borne out, particularly the idea that scarcity of talent is a condition necessitating status rewards. The higher prestige given to occupations requiring a prolonged formal education would support this idea, assuming that such a prerequisite limits the number of qualified persons.

The similarities in ratings accorded the occupations by boys and girls and by rural and urban students suggest that these statistical categories do not represent clear-cut subcultures insofar as occupational values are concerned. This contributes to the mounting evidence that rural-urban differences are disappearing generally in industrialized societies.

Although striking differences are found between Japan and the United States in particular comparisons, the crucial findings of this study are the similarities in general comparisons of occupational prestige and social importance. These similarities obtain for cross-cultural comparisons as well as the interrelations of these variables with each other and with estimates of income.

FOOTNOTE

1. Kingsley Davis and Wilbert E. Moore, "Some Principles of Stratification," *American Sociological Review,* X (April, 1945), 242−49. See also Melvin Tumin, "Some Principles of Stratification: A Critical Analysis," *American Sociological Review,* XVIII (August, 1953), 387−94; Melvin Tumin, "Rewards and Task-Orientations," *American Sociologial Review,* XX (August, 1955), 419−23; Richard D. Schwartz, "Functional Alternatives to Inequality," *American Sociological Review,* XX (1955), 424−30; Richard L. Simpson, "A Modification of the Functional Theory of Social Stratification," *Social Forces,* XXXV (December, 1956), 132−37; Walter Buckley, "Social Stratification and the Functional Theory of Social Differentiation," *American Sociological Review,* XXIII (August 1958), 369−75; and Anderson, *op. cit.*

THE FUNCTION AND SOCIAL STRUCTURE OF EDUCATION: SCHOOLS AND JAPANESE SOCIETY

Mikio Sumiya

Education and Class Mobility

From well before World War II and through the early postwar years, scholars have made two dissimilar analyses of the character of Japan's social system.[a] The first views Japan's industrialized society in terms of the continuity of a traditional, feudalistic status hierarchy *(mibunsei)* in which social stratification is relatively fixed and allows little internal mobility. Those who emphasize the remnants of tradition and feudal values in Japan naturally tend to support this interpretation. An eminent scholar describes the "structure of status hierarchy" that "exists everywhere in Japanese society" as follows:

At the top of the status hierarchy in a typical Japanese village are the Houses *(ie)* whose ancestors were the first settlers and served at one time or another as village headmen *(shoya)*. In succession are the *ie* of group heads *(kumigashira)*, other landowners who cannot qualify as any of the above, and then farmers who till their own land. Finally come tenant farmers and, at the very bottom, day laborers.[1]

Certain foreign specialists take a similar viewpoint. In *The Chrysanthemum and the Sword,* a book which made a powerful impression on postwar Japanese intellectuals, Ruth Benedict says the key to understanding Japan is to realize the meaning of "take one's proper station." She writes:

Japan's confidence in hierarchy is basic in her whole notion of man's relation to his fellow man and of man's relation to the State . . . .

. . . .

The hierarchical arrangements of Japanese life have been as drastic in relations between classes as they have been in the family. In all her national history Japan has been a strong class and caste society . . . .[2]

The second analysis, diametrically opposed to the idea of continuity, views Japanese industrialized society from the standpoint of change. According to this view, there has been tremendous class mobility in Japan ever since the last few decades of the nineteenth century (and to a certain extent even during the Tokugawa period, 1600–1868). Indeed, some believe Japanese society allowed much more social mobility than many contemporary Western European societies. For example, in 1912 the agronomist Yokoi Tokiyoshi lamented the consequences of extreme mobility in his country:

Sumiya- *From The Journal of Social and Political Ideas in Japan,* Vol. 5, No. 2-3, (December, 1967), pp. 117-138. Reprinted by permission.

Why is it that nowadays so many young men go off to the city to get an education? They claim they go to make their mark in the world. As long as they are motivated by the desire to succeed, they will doubtlessly be hounded by the possibility of failure. But once they are educated, what sort of enterprise do these country youths undertake? From the time children enter elementary school they hear the teacher telling them religiously day in and day out, "Be a somebody! Be a somebody!" By "a somebody" is meant a teacher or bureaucrat, the professions to which most pupils aspire. If their teachers told them to go into business, these children would have a different ideal: a shyster with a pile of money.

The great aspirations of young men affected with what we might call "urban fever" have produced many unfortunate results; ambition has brought to many the notoriety of a prison record. This is proof of the "efficacy" of an education which emphasizes personal advancement and worldly success.[3]

What should concern us here is not whether the results of education are positive or negative, but Yokoi's anxiety over the unlimited social mobility of his day. Of course even those who stress the continuity of a premodern status hierarchy recognize the horizontal movement from villages to cities. But the issue here is whether or not vertical mobility between social strata accompanied horizontal movement.

Results of recent surveys in Japan have forced social scientists to note the tremendous degree of vertical mobility and the numbers of people involved in such movements. It is true that in prewar days any who "stuck out" or got "out of order" were brought back into line; taking "one's proper station" was worldly wisdom. Nevertheless, young people were greatly encouraged to make their mark in life, to work hard and study diligently so as to "be a somebody." Many struggled through school at great personal and family cost, throwing their entire energies into the effort to be successful.

It is unrealistic to debate whether Japanese society is most accurately characterized by continuity *or* change, whether the primary issue is frozen status hierarchy *or* free social mobility. The truth lies somewhere between. On the one hand, we must recognize that Japanese society has never displayed the openness and competitiveness characteristic of American society, nor has it allowed people to contend freely under equal conditions or to be successful on their own merits. The reality in Japan, as countless observers frequently remind us, is a rigid class structure characterized by premodern interpersonal relations. Those who emphasize these characteristics point out the continuity of class distinctions and the system of ascribed personal status in Japan. They say that Japanese interpersonal relations can be described most accurately in terms of a "vertical society"[4] which puts a fundamental stress on affiliations between superior and inferior. None can deny the persistence of such vertical relations in our society. In fact, not even the aristocratic British society can match the extent to which Japan has preserved them. On the other hand, we must recognize that it has always been somewhat easy to scale the social ladder in Japan. At least it has never been as difficult as in England, for the Japanese social ladder is there *to be climbed.* The greater opportunity one has to ascend the ladder, the greater the danger of slipping and falling off. Or, as Yokoi says above, people with ambition must face up to the "possibility of failure," never certain of ultimate success, and always plagued by the fact that social mobility could be downward as well as upward.

The difference between social ladders in Japan and Great Britain is instructive. For example, the British made a clear-cut class distinction between blue-collar and white-collar workers. They even go so far as to differentiate blue-collar workers into sub-classes on the basis of skills. Depending on their social ladders, different groups even speak differently. There are also language barriers between the two classes.[5] Ferdinand Zweig, a student of the British working classes, says:

> A workingman speaks a language of his own, while the middle class man generally speaks the King's English. This language barrier is very difficult to break and more than anything else keeps men in different classes. As soon as a man opens his mouth everybody knows to which class he belongs. In England this is the primary criterion of class membership.[6]

Such rigid distinctions among classes in England make class mobility rather exceptional. Zweig further points out that "To climb is to break away from the group, to look down on it, and to reject its values and standards; so the group discourages social climbers."[7]

Quite to the contrary, Japanese can be classified as skilled workers after they gain a certain amount of experience. Furthermore, when such a worker has served his company for a long time, say twenty years, he increases his chances of being promoted to a supervisory position such as foreman (shokucho). Until World War II it was even possible for Japanese blue-collar workers (koin) to acquire the status of white-collar staff members (shokuin).[8] And there were innumerable stories of sons of small farmers who had risen to positions of eminence in the bureaucracy or military service. The reason for the flexible attitude toward class boundaries in Japan is partly historical. Because of the tremendously accelerated process of modernization experienced since about 1870, no distinct patterns of class culture, no established, stratified modes of life, developed in our society. In fact, the rapid changes in Japan during the last century have allowed the ambitious and the gifted to climb the social ladder with relative ease.[9] Because of the lack of specific life styles, such people have had little trouble adjusting to life on the rung to which they have climbed.

In Japan, education has been one method providing people from lower classes with the broadest opportunity to climb the social ladder. By contrast, school systems in Great Britain and throughout Europe generally reflect the social class structure. Indeed, there is an intimate relationship between social classes in Europe and the schools to which people send their children. A son is expected to enter the same stratum as his parents after graduating from a school comparable to his father's. He is unlikely either to aspire to a "higher" school or, consequently, to rise above his father's class status. Since World War I there has been a gradual erosion of this relationship. Nevertheless, it is perhaps safe to say that European schools continue to function as preservers of class status. This is notably different from Japanese educational institutions which serve to promote and regulate class mobility. The Japanese school has functioned as a mechanism by which the leading group controls the specific direction of social mobility. The historical needs of the time made this control urgent and possible.

Following the 1868 Meiji Restoration and the rapid development of Japanese industrialism, extraordinary demands were made for trained and educated people. Men were needed to fill posts in the bureaucracy and the educational system, and industry demanded engineering and managerial personnel in industry.[10] Meiji leaders had no choice but to fill these posts with available manpower. To do so, they had to reach lower and lower into the Japanese class· structure. They established the school system as an instrument by which to select and train the able from among the largest possible segment of the population. In other words, the heavy demand for qualified personnel helped consolidate the schools and forced them to determine and train "men of talent" in an organized manner. Those whose ability recommended them to higher levels of education qualified at the same time to scale an appropriate rung of the ladder. Their education entitled them to a higher social stratum.[b] This meant that no matter how humble one's social origins, if he graduated from a high-ranking school he was eligible for a social class appropriate to the level of his alma mater.[c] Herein lies one of the secrets of Japan's high rate of social mobility.

Postwar Society and the School

There is no need to go into great detail regarding educational reforms instituted after World War II. But though we know they were carried out under the direction of Occupation authorities on orders from SCAP, we often forget the background of these reforms. We should not overlook these two points: even before the war there was (a) an increasing demand by indigenous industrialization for an extension of compulsory education and for a better educated labor force; and (b) a tendency toward increased standardization and improvement of the nation's educational level.[11] By 1940, education had acquired such an important status among the people that forty-six percent of those who graduated from elementary schools continued their studies, either in higher primary school *(koto shogakko,* two years) or in various kinds of middle schools (four or five years).[12] At the same time large enterprises gave preference to employees with at least eight years of formal education, although only six were required by law. Recognizing the gap between the law and practice, the Ministry of Education resolved *before the end of the war* to extend compulsory education to the secondary level. In short, pressures to expand the scope and improve the level of national education originated from within Japanese society itself. By the time the system became single-track,[13] the possibility that students might continue their schooling beyond the secondary level had increased.

That possibility became a probability with postwar social reforms and economic growth. Two aspects of social change contributed especially to the extension of formal schooling: collapse of the premodern status hierarchy and the subsequent disappearance and reduction of class differentiation. Not only did the Emperor system and the aristocracy which supported it disintegrate, but distinctions between white-collar and blue-collar practically disappeared. Conspicuous discrepancies in salary which separated the two groups in prewar days vanished after 1945, and it became more and more difficult to distinguish between white-collar and blue-collar by outward appearance alone. The postwar labor union movement, moreover, organized and launched in great haste, did not discriminate between the two; unions became "mixed" organizations composed of both "classes." And during the unprecedented postwar housing shortage, people from both classes were forced to live side by side in similar areas, thus breaking the prewar pattern of segregation and erasing significant differences in consumption patterns.

A combination of these factors speedily increased the ratio of students who went on to high school. Moreover, Japan's rapid economic growth after 1955 raised worker and farmer incomes and further stimulated the common people to give their children a high school or even college education. As a result, an ever larger percentage has been continuing school beyond the lower limits set by the government. This increase can be seen in the following table:

PRECENTAGE OF THOSE CONTINUING THEIR EDUCATION
AFTER COMPULSORY EDUCATION

year	male	female	average	year	male	female	average
1920	19.7	11.5	15.8	1960	59.6	55.9	57.7
1930	21.1	15.5	18.3	1961	63.6	60.3	62.0
1940	28.0	22.0	25.0	1962	65.5	62.5	64.0
1945	46.9	43.6	45.3	1963	68.4	65.1	66.8
1950	55.0	38.0	46.7	1964	70.6	67.9	69.3
1955	55.5	47.4	51.5	1965	71.7	69.6	70.6

NB, the figures through 1945 include among primary school graduates those who went on to prewar middle schools and Class A vocational schools. Percentages after 1950 include only those who went on to postwar senior high schools (in a 6-3-3 system).

The industrial reorganization which accompanied the dissolution of the zaibatsu, together with the collapse of the premodern system of status hierarchy, brought Japanese society a good deal closer to the competitive model provided by America. Class differences were considerably reduced and the proportion of those, including workers, stratified into "middle" areas of the society increased markedly. Accordingly, compared to prewar days, competition also increased dramatically, and as a result it is now far more intense than before 1945. With fewer barriers between social classes there is also less to inhibit interclass and intraclass rivalry, and thus the expansion and intensification of struggle for higher positions on the social ladder is inevitable. Again, the more intense the social rivalry the greater the tendency to allow everyone the same opportunity to compete. The demand to give every child a high school education, pressed by parents and educators alike, is a typical manifestation of this tendency.

If, however, Japanese society were truly competitive at every level—or at least among those striving for leadership— the expansion of educational opportunity in our society would not have raised such profound problems. Under such a situation, the problems generated by competitive education and its institutionalization do not spring from the way society and its educational system are related. They are rather problems which spring from competition itself. But in Japan the situation is somewhat different. Throughout the nation we have achieved an equalization of educational opportunity, at least to the high school level. Moreover, university entrance is competitive and anyone with a high school diploma can sit for the entrance examinations. By contrast, universities in prewar days were considered organs to educate the elite and were open only to a restricted number of students, namely, those who had diplomas from the old style higher schools.

In spite of these changes, we must realize that postwar Japanese society is still not truly "competitive." That is, competition is restricted or circumscribed in business, in the bureaucracy, and in the university. Of course, I do not mean to suggest that contemporary people refrain from competing with one another. To the contrary, as I have stated, competition is considerably more intense now than it was before the war. But we must call such competition limited. It does not occur, for example, within "non-competing groups." The chief factor differentiating non-competing from competing groups is schooling; those who have graduated from a "good" college, one recognized as having high status, do not compete with each other. They "compete" with graduates of a college having inferior status. Thus, for all practical purposes, competition ends the moment one enters the freshman class because passing the entrance exam in most cases means that in due time the student will receive a bachelor's degree. His future status is, in a word, granted well before graduation. The somewhat automatic nature of the student's academic progress accounts for the fact that competition with one's peers is unimportant at the university level.

Many observers point out that it is easy to be accepted by an American college but hard to stay in, for daily life is dominated by grades and credit points—by competition. In order to receive a bachelor's degree, especially at better known colleges, a student must have a good deal of ability and invest a considerable amount of effort. The American system presents quite a contrast with the English system and its Japanese-like lack of scholastic competitiveness on the university level. In the United Kingdom it is reputedly not too difficult to graduate from college. The problem is getting in. The sociologist Ralph H. Turner writes:

> The [American] university itself is run like the true contest, standards being set competitively, students being forced to pass a series of trials each semester, and only a minority of the entrants achieving the prize of graduation. Such a pattern contrasts sharply with the English system in which selection is supposed to have been relatively complete before entry into university, and students may be subject to no testing whatsoever for the first year or more of university study. Although university completion rates have not been estimated in either country, some figures are indicative. The ratio of bachelor's and first-professional degrees in American institutions of higher learning, in 1957—58, to the number of first-time degree-credit enrollments in the fall, four years earlier, was reported to be .610 for men and .488 for women.[14]

A much higher percentage of those who enter Japanese colleges ultimately graduates.

In educational systems characterized by a plurality of "tracks," such as in Great Britain, those who desire a college education must plan ahead. Parents must decide to groom their child for college sometime in primary school because, unless he enters one of the "classical" schools, the so-called grammar schools, by at least the seventh grade, he will not receive adequate preparation for college. The fact that an English student cannot graduate from a university and gain membership into the elite without a specific preparatory education somewhat resembles the situation in prewar Japan.[d] Commenting on this point, Turner says:

> In England, a study following up the careers of individual students, found that in University College, London, 81.9 percent of entering students, between 1948 and 1951, eventually graduated with a degree. A similar study a few years earlier at the University of Liverpool revealed a figure of 86.9 percent.

. . . [S]ystems of mobility precipitate different emphases regarding educational content. Induction into elite culture under sponsored mobility makes for emphasis on school *esprit de corps*, which can be employed to cultivate norms of intraclass loyalty and elite tastes and manners. Likewise, formal schooling built about highly specalized study in fields with entirely intellectual or aesthetic concern and no "practical" value serves the purpose of elite culture. Under contest mobility in the United States, in spite of faculty endorsement of "liberal education," schooling tends to be measured for its practical benefits and to become, beyond the elementary school, chiefly vocational. Education does not so much provide what is good in itself as it provides skills necessary to compete for the real prizes of life, and of these vocational skills are the most important.

In postwar Japan, on the other hand, competitiveness has not been completely realized throughout society. In the educational field, it exists only to the college level. Once a person enters the university, free competition is avoided and a graduate acquires social status and "vies" with other college graduates on the basis of ascriptive rather than competitive criteria. That is, in Japanese society a man is selected for a job on the status of his alma mater rather than on his personal merit. Therefore postwar Japanese education no longer resembles the British method of training an elite. Rather, the entire system of primary and secondary education in Japan is markedly competitive up to the university level. Beyond that, little weight is given to merit and the system can no longer discharge its prewar function of controlling the distribution of the labor force. Consequently, our society acknowledges only one sort of quality differentiation, the kind which makes distinctions among universities. And so the question of distributing manpower is not dealt with till the last moment before one enters society. It is at best an incomplete solution to the problem.

Thus postwar Japan has become a battleground where the ideal of a truly competitive educational system based on actual accomplishment stands pitted against a social reality which ascribes high status to graduates of a limited number of prestigious colleges. Caught between the ideal and the reality, students and their families must chaff under the tension—and prepare for entrance examinations from the moment formal schooling begins, if not before.

Inconsistencies in Postwar Education

The contradictions between a competitive educational system and ascriptive social convention disturbed the function which formal education in Japan had discharged a distributor of social status. In the prewar system, those graduating from grade schools, middle schools, professional schools *(senmon gakko)*, and universities were sorted out into different social classes which roughly corresponded to levels of education. For most, this allotting was "prearranged," and everyone knew which class and which job corresponded to which level. But at the same time rapid social change provided opportunities to transcend this pattern. Accompanying the development of capitalist society was a rising demand for white-collar workers, and since there was an increase also in the number of those entering managerial ranks, it became possible for a few to climb the social ladder with no reference to educational background. Such an ascent was, moreover, applauded by social values as "making one's mark in the world" *(risshin shusse)*.

Nevertheless, in prewar days the relationship between levels of education and social class was strong. Laborers and farmers were generally identified with an elementary, lower level white-collar workers with a middle school, and the social elite with a university education. That is why special considerations were made for one who, despite his ability, had been prevented for economic reasons from going on to a higher level of education (see Note b above). In a word, prewar schools discharged the basic function of determining one's position in society.

Postwar educational and social reforms eradicated this arrangement and established in its place a more democratic system and more democratic educational ideals. During this time, many people began to think that secondary and higher education should not be the special province of a specific social stratum and that education at all levels should be liberated from class privilege and made available to every member of society. The spread of the labor union movement and other postwar reforms also contributed to the rapid disintegration of feudalistic social relations and other premodern features of Japanese society, elements which had tenaciously persisted since the nineteenth century. The people rejected not only the notion that white-collar are superior in status to blue-collar employees—and that both in turn are inferior to employers and managers—but the idea that the way a blue-collar worker "advances" or "ascends" the status hierarchy is by attaining white-collar status.

After the war, Japanese began to consider blue-collar and white-collar, employer and employee, labor force categories differentiated only according to function; they were no longer regarded as distinct status levels.

However, the functional as opposed to the hierarchical view of occupations and positions does not deeply affect social action, nor has it taken root in Japanese society. Blue-collar workers themselves continue to be divided into two distinct "statuses," temporary laborers *(rinjiko)* and permanent employees *(honko).*[15] The honko are accorded higher status, given greater security, and have more privileges, yet they persist in their envy, and constantly aspire to what they regard as the "higher" status, of white-collar workers.

Theoretically, social mobility occurs in two directions, horizontal and vertical. In a society where guilds or unions strictly regulate the labor market, mobility is horizontal, that is, craftsmen generally move across enterprise and regional lines within their trade. But when industrial societies arrive at the stage of maturity, the apprentice system begins to collapse and mobility becomes vertical rather than horizontal. This universal tendency can also be applied to modern Japan. In the case of Japan, however, an even more important factor contributes to the predominance of vertical mobility: survival of a feudalistic status hierarchy involving inferior-superior relations. Near the beginning of the twentieth century these factors combined to produce a system which stressed lifelong employment with the same company and gave promotions and wage increases on the basis of seniority, i.e. number of years of service. This system has proven quite persistent and—despite the fact that the Japanese people emphatically denied the hierarchical status system after World War II, thus striking a telling blow against the aristocracy, zaibatsu, and other especially conspicuous elements supporting the premodern social structure—has successfully resisted change. Indeed, the social relations in every pipe of Japan's "vertical society" are so deeply entrenched that they are not easily budged. That is to say, functional social groups in Japanese society are composed not of individuals who, despite differences in roles, form horizontal relationships with one another, but of persons who are both socially and often economically stratified into a status hierarchy and who accordingly relate to each other vertically in terms of who is superior and who is inferior.

In a society of this nature, the educational system constitutes the means by which people achieve status. The higher one goes in the scale of formal education, the higher the social status he can acquire. Parents respond to the pressure of status by making every effort to get their children into college. There is little concern for the child's ability or desires. What is important to parents is the child's *future* social status. Efforts are especially conspicuous at either end of the social scale. The upper classes are forced to maintain their family ranking in a society where status per se is not ascriptive. Hence every generation must recreate its social and economic status by having its children acquire the requisite "academic background." A lower class parent, in turn, attempts to liberate his offspring from the social and economic handicaps he has experienced by giving them a better education than he received.

Schools in Japan are compelled to function as determiners of social class because no other appropriate mechanism exists to distribute manpower. This means, however, that competition is based not on ability but on the amount and quality of education acquired. It is inevitable then that parents become uncommonly concerned with the end, a college education, and with the means to that end, the entrance examination. We cannot deal adequately with the problem of "test hell" *(juken jigoku)* if we imagine it is rooted only in parental egoism or in misconceptions regarding the purpose of higher education. Nor will it do to load the blame for making children into status-seekers on the frustrated "educational mama" *(kyoiku mama)* who, thanks to the readily available electric washing machine, the automatic rice-cooker, etc., finds time to spur her children on. We must rather see these contradictions as symptoms of the tension between the expansion of *equal opportunity* to obtain a higher education on the one hand, and, on the other, the continuing social reality which recognizes status distinctions based on a *hierarchy* of educational institutions.[e]

Excessive desire for a higher education produces numerous social problems, the greatest of which hampers the secondary school's ideal function of determining the type of job a graduate gets on the basis of how high a rung he has achieved on the educational ladder. This is attested by the fact that there is a serious shortage of junior high graduates on the labor market. In order to improve one's competitive situation, almost everyone aspires to at least a senior high diploma. But though seventy per cent of all junior high graduates went on to senior high in 1965, many industrial firms continued to advertise on a massive scale for employees who had just finished the ninth grade. This was true whether business was brisk or in a slump. During periods of prosperity, firms need an increased labor force; during periods of recession, firms try to minimize labor costs by hiring younger workers who begin work at a low point on the pay scale.

Part of the tension arising between the desires for higher education and the needs of the labor market is caused by the profit motive which affects the policies of big business employers: it is cheaper to hire a worker with less education. Thus, if a prospective employee wishes to enter and enjoy the superior working conditions offered by a large enterprise, he is well-advised to leave school at the junior high level. If he waits until he graduates from senior high, he will find it difficult to enter one of the mammoth firms. The beginning wage for those with twelve years of schooling is somewhat higher than for those who have finished only the ninth grade, and yet there is an infinitesimal difference in productivity between the two. Under these circumstances, industry naturally prefers the worker who can be hired at the cheaper wage.

At the same time we must keep another factor in mind: the nature of the labor force makes a junior high graduate more desirable because of the time necessary to train a skilled worker. It is best to begin one's apprenticeship in the low teens rather than after senior high school, especially (as is the rule in Japan) if the school has not provided the student with experience in industrial arts. There is a tremendous gap between formal classroom education and the kind of skilled labor industries require.[f]

The situation is completely different for the college graduate. Before the war, only three per cent of the eligible age group had graduated from institutions of higher learning, including professional schools. They made up the social elite. After the war, however, the number rose to twenty per cent. College graduates in the 1950's constituted a no more significant element in the society than middle school graduates in the 1930's. This was a natural consequence of the liberalization of educational opportunity which occurred after World War II. Japanese society now allows anyone to apply to the school of his choice. He can enter as long as he passes the entrance examination. Ideally, this should lead to a situation wherein many college graduates compete for posts on the basis of their ability and diligence. But, as noted above, this expectation is frustrated by an ascriptive factor. Society has chosen to confer status according to preconceived notions as to the quality or rank of the various *schools*.[16]

Ascriptive criteria have produced a system which designates a few "famous" colleges,[17] particularly the former imperial universities and a few of the older private schools, as suppliers of candidates for large firm management personnel and upper-level bureaucrats. The remaining colleges become instruments to train personnel for smaller firms and for middle-ranking positions in the bureaucracy. Graduation from a prestigious university is not the whole story, but it has become one necessary condition for entering the elite. Contradictions inherent in the sort of society which confuses ascription and ability appear in the college entrance exam system. On the one hand, preparation for these tests dominates education in both senior and junior high schools. On the other, so much effort is expended on getting *into* the university that education on that level becomes an after-thought. If these contradictions are pushed to their extremity, the college will turn into nothing more than a degree mill which graduates people largely on the basis of their successful performance on the entrance examination. Education will then take a back seat to college entry.[g] Already schools are under enormous social pressure to refrain from expelling those who have been successful in passing entrance exams. Faculties therefore tend to graduate those who have "put in" their four years.

Education and the Value System

After 1947 Japanese education was rapidly converted from the prewar multitrack to the postwar one-track system. There are no longer any options. Everyone travels the same route. And since upward social mobility continues to require graduating from a school of higher rank than one's parents, fewer and fewer desire to be side-tracked to a lower job and lower social status. With almost every secondary school trying to get its students into the limited number of first-rate universities, there is understandably a severe "traffic problem" on Japan's single-track educational railroad.[18] The problem is that enthusiasm for "education" in this country focuses on the *end* of the line. When parents investigate the quality of a school they do not seem primarily concerned with what kind of human being it tries to train. They become absorbed in helping their child get into a "famous" university. Education, if that is the proper term, is thus totally ruled by the entrance examination syndrome.

People attach such high value to gaining entrance to a prestigious college that the Japanese family has been relegated to the post of an educational assistant charged with the task of preparing its children for examinations. Educators nevertheless continue to emphasize the important role that the family and other institutions and agencies play in the child's character development. One text on education comments on this role as follows:

> When we hear the word *education,* the first thing that comes to our mind is the school: we see a picture of systematic instruction in the classroom under the direction of a teacher. In contemporary society, however, education certainly extends well beyond the younger generation's formal schooling. Nor are schools the only institutions concerned with education in the broader sense of the term. Despite the importance of personality formation—that is, the way children acquire definite attitudes, beliefs and values, and the way they master knowledge and techniques—these other agencies are nowhere near as well organized as the schools. Nevertheless, it seems to us that they play a vital role in personality formation.[19]

Such "agencies" are the family, the occupation, and the peer group.

In the case of South Asia and the West, a list of organizations concerned with character development would definitely include religious institutions, e.g., temples or churches. But in Japan, the educative function of these organizations is extremely limited, notwithstanding a terrific passion for education among the people. This limitation forces us to take a serious look at the inconsistency of families deeply committed to the best possible "education" for their children and yet unwilling to provide them with proper discipline and training in morals. Regarding the educational role of the home, the above quoted textbook says:

> The process whereby children absorb social values and standards does not rely entirely on the child's unintentional spontaneity. Parents actively contribute to the process of socialization by the way they discipline and train their children . . . . The parent, for example, responds to the child's behavior, this time with a reward, another with punishment. By example and informal means, parents teach their children the pattern of behavior expected of them and thus contribute to the child's internalization of values.

The theory this textbook preaches is one thing. The reality of the Japanese home, which no longer plays such a complementary role in the child's education, is another.

Complaints that the family is losing its traditional functions are also heard from educators in Europe and America. In early modern times the Western family was the focus of production as well as consumption; in Europe it was the basic unit of a society that focused on the community church. As the home became the location where workers slept and ate, the family gradually lost its organic connection with the community. In the ensuing process of secularization, it also lost its religious functions. Some even maintain that, as an institution, the Western family is in the process of dissolution. The Japanese family appears headed for a similar crisis.

In Western Europe, however, the task of socializing the child and providing "psychological security" continues to be carried out by the family, at least in the opinion of Talcott Parsons.[20] Security remains one of its important functions in the West, for though values may be in flux and the social system unsteady, the family continues to be the gyroscope of social relations. The family plays a somewhat different role in contemporary Japan where it has abandoned its responsibility to socialize the child or stabilize social values. To oversimplify, one might say that the Japanese family has completely surrendered its educative functions to the school. The home has become committed to a single-minded value: getting children the best possible formal education so that they can enter social life with the best possible academic background. This is the sense in which I stated above that "the Japanese family has been relegated to the post of an educational assistant charged with the task of preparing its children for examinations."[h]

What then has assumed the central socioeconomic role in educating the child? To say that the home is no more than the locale where people eat and sleep is tantamount to limiting it to a place where workers recuperate after a day's work and raise a new generation to enter the labor force. After the war, a series of debates among Japanese educators was prompted by this concept of the family's function. These debates centered on "education of productive labor," an idea which assumes that the function of education is the "production of productive power." Aside from touching on the political and ideological implications of the proposed concept, these debates described schools as vital links in the formation of society's "productive power." It seems to me that there is a general concurrence between the way Japanese educators and Friedrich List (1789-1846) define the meaning of productive power.[21] That is, educators regard it not simply in material terms but more essentially as something human and subjective.

These debates are interesting primarily because they deal with personality formation and other subjective elements, areas which Japanese society has consistently disregarded. We might remember, as an appropriate illustration of this lack of concern, that although after the war there was a violent reaction against the ideology of the Emperor system and the militaristic values which dominated Japanese thinking until 1945, we failed to develop a satisfactory substitute. "Social development" became the dominant value in postwar Japan but the problem of man's character formation—his *ethos* and spirit—was virtually ignored. The schools were accordingly burdened with the added responsibility of building character as they assumed responsibilities for "psychological security" usually borne by other agencies in society. Thus, educators were reduced to conducting their programs without the complementary support from the home expected in Western countries. Moreover, Japanese educators have been obliged to resist political pressures which, emanating from above, would use education as a means of reinforcing the Establishment. Schoolmen consequently feel antagonistic to politicians, and debates on educational problems become markedly political.

Tensions between educators and authorities did not help meet the postwar challenge of providing alternatives to pre-1945 values, especially those concerned with character formation. The greatest educational problem in contemporary Japan is the vacuum in this area, for the confusion of the value system has resulted in the family's gradual surrender of all responsibility for giving children character training. Family interest in education has degenerated into a single-minded concern to get children into schools which serve as feeders to the best universities. Various social problems have inevitably resulted. As one countermeasure against the conspicuous lack of moral training in the home, the government repeatedly has stressed the need for a supplementary course in the curriculum. After a good deal of debate, the Ministry of Education in 1958 introduced ethical education into the elementary and junior high school levels.[22] It is now an important item on the curriculum in a country where neither religion nor the family has customarily played a genuine educative role.

The "ethical education" instituted in Japanese schools, however, tends to be little more than the preaching of abstract virtues. Fundamentally, it is impossible to conduct ethical education apart from person-to-person relations. If appeal to the student's inner life is lacking, principles learned during the ethics period will be no more than meaningless maxims on theoretical behavior, much as traditional prewar ideals had little genuine connection with practical behavior.[i] Unfortunately, the more schools stress ethical education as a part of the regular curriculum, the more danger there is that morality will become a hollow affair of repeated formulae and superficial injunctions.

Thus education in contemporary Japan bears a double burden. On the one hand, because equal opportunity is the standard, schools must somehow function as distributors of man power. On the other, because they bear the entire burden of education, schools are also required to assume responsibility for character formation and personality development. It is no easy task to deal with both of these functions at the same time. This analysis of the issues will, I hope, at least make the reader aware that the serious problems affecting Japanese education cannot be solved merely by improving techniques and systems.

FOOTNOTES

a. These two views reflect, at least partially, the *Kozaha* and *Ronoha* interpretations of Japanese capitalism.[23] The views I am going to discuss, however, are more oriented to sociological than economic factors.

b. In order for the State to absorb the energies of people in the lower classes, the government completely subsidized students who attended normal schools and military academies.

c. I stated earlier that "no distinct patterns of class culture . . . developed" in Japan since the Meiji period. The circumstances which gave rise to this situation enlarged the role of the schools in providing for social mobility and, as a result, filled Japanese families with a passion for education *(kyoiku nesshin).* Thus, education became a matter of classroom training or, to put it bluntly, it was distorted into a process of acquiring an academic record. Japan never developed anything corresponding to the formal religious education, the stress on discipline in the community, etc., found in the West. Schools in Japan even took charge of ethical instruction.

d. Before establishment of the postwar educational system, higher schools in Japan functioned much the same as public schools in England: they were places for cultivating and training people to enter the elite. Only graduates of these old-style higher schools were eligible to enter the imperial universities.

e. The Ministry of Education has been dealing with this situation by gradual realization of a scheme of pluralized high school education not "loaded" in favor of college preparatory work. There has been considerable criticism of this scheme on egalitarian grounds, though the educators who disapprove of the plan have so far neglected to touch on the basic nature of the problem. Their criticisms are accordingly not completely convincing.

f. At the moment, the Law Regulating Vocational Training[24] is aimed at the junior high school graduate; it has become somewhat dysfunctional, however, because of the overwhelming popular desire for at least a senior high education. Authorities concerned are therefore in the process of probing ways to reorganize training programs to fit the high school graduate.

g. While this statement is true for courses in one's specialty or major, it is especially valid as a judgment of the general education curriculum which has been thoroughly emasculated by the stress on entrance examinations.

h. In contrast to the Japanese family's apparent abdication from an active educational role, note the part Western churches have played in personality and character development. Those concerned with the problem should give special consideration to the fact that in Japan, at least in modern times, religion has rarely played an active role in training children, either within or without the home.

i. Another rival problem, frequently debated on the topic of teaching abstract ideals in the classroom, relates not so much to the content of the courses or to the ideals themselves as to the fact that the value system taught in the schools is provided by the authority of the State. This is, after all, similar to the way the Japanese government has dealt with ethics since the 1890 Imperial Rescript on Education. What is lacking in this approach to morality is an appreciation of the internalization of ethical principles and how to achieve it.

TRANSLATOR'S NOTES

1. Kawashima Takeyoshi, *Nihon shakai to seikatsu ishiki* [Japanese society and attitudes] (Tokyo: Gakuseisha, 1955), p. 58.

2. Ruth Benedict, *The Chrysanthemum and the Sword* (Boston: Houghton Mifflin, 1949), pp. 43 and 57.

3. Yokoi Tokiyoshi [or Tokitaka], *Tokai to inaka* [City and Country] (Tokyo: Seibido Shoten, 1913), pp. 17–18. This work was based on a comparative study made by the Yomiuri Shimbun in 1906 and aimed at a mass audience. A more recent printing of the same work appears in Dai Nippon Nokai, ed., *Yokoi Tokiyoshi zenshu* [The works of Yokoi Tokiyoshi] (Tokyo: Zenshu Hakkokai, 1925) in X volumes; the quote in question is found in IV, 546–547.

4. For an analysis of Japan's vertical society, see Nakane Chie, *Tate shakai no ningen kankei: tan'itsu shakai no riron* [Human Relations in a Vertical Society: a Theory on a Unitary Society] (Tokyo: Kodansha, 1967), 189 pp. An English summary of the *Chuo Koron* article on which Professor Nakane based her book can be found in *The Japan Missionary Bulletin,* Vol. XXI, No. 6 (July 1967), 373–378, 386; and Vol. XXI, No. 8 (September 1967), 496–502. Certain effects exerted by a vertical society on political forces are examined in Ito Mitsuharu, "A Structural Analysis of the Conservative and Progressive Forces in Japan," *JSPIJ,* Vol. IV, No. 2 (August 1966), 85–93.

5. George Bernard Shaw noted this language discrepancy in *Pygmalion.* In their musical adaptation of Shaw's play, Alan Jay Lerner and Frederick Loewe describe England's linguistic hierarchy as follows:

> Why can't the English teach their children how to speak?
> This verbal class distinction by now should be antique.
>
> ·
>
> An Englishman's way of speaking absolutely classifies him;
> The moment he talks he makes some other Englishman despise him.

From *My Fair Lady* (New York: The New American Library, 1958), p. 22.

6. Ferdinand Zweig, *The British Worker* (London: Pelican Books, 1952), p. 204. A Japanese version of Zweig's book appeared as *Rodosha: seikatsu to shinri* [Workers: their life and psychology], trans. by Ouchi Tateo, Fujimoto Kihachi, and Ando Mizuo (Tokyo: Daiyamondosha, 1957), 258 pp.

7. Zweig, *The British Worker,* p. 93.

8. In prewar Japan, one method used to control labor was a hierarchical system of personal status. White-collar workers *(shokuin)* were engaged in management or related activies; they included clerks and technicians. Blue-collar workers *(koin)* were laborers engaged in production. Conspicuous status differences existed between these two classes. *Shokuin,* for example, enjoyed better working conditions, higher pay, superior opportunities for advancement, etc. Even among *shokuin* there were a number of hierarchical distinctions, and *koin* were divided into two general groupings (see Note 15 below).

In postwar Japan, however, sharp distinctions between the two have partially disappeared, largely as a result of the union movement. About 60 percent of all unions are composed of *shokuin* and *koin*, and union contracts apply equally to either category. These two statuses have been drawn together in recent years because each needs the other's "support to assure their continued attachment to the enterprise. Both groups equally felt the ravages of the rampant inflation and dire shortages—their economic interest in sheer subsistence became identical"; Solomon B. Levine, "Postwar Trade Unionism, Collective Bargaining, and Japanese Social Structure," in R. P. Dore, ed., *Aspects of Social Change in Modern Japan* (Princeton: Princeton University Press, 1967), p. 259; see also pp. 258–262 and 276.

9. For appropriate background information on status mobility in postwar Japan, see Ujihara Shojiro, "Japan's Laboring Class: Changes in the Postwar Period," *JSPIJ*, Vol. III, No. 3 (December 1965), 60–67.

10. The Meiji period (1868–1912) produced many successful entrepreneurs who by dint of effort and ability managed to transcend their original class status. Two of the most famous of these are Iwasaki Yataro (1834–1885) and Shibusawa Eiichi (1840–1931). Iwasaki was the eldest son of a samurai who had become a landlord in Tosa (an area in Shĭkoku). Following restoration of Imperial rule in 1868, Yataro turned to commerce. In 1871 he established a shipping line which later became the Japan Mail Line; and he founded the Mitsubishi (literally, "Three Diamonds") Company. His premature death at fifty-four occurred before the establishment of European-style ranks of nobility and doubtlessly prevented his being elevated to one of these ranks. Shibusawa was the second son of a wealthy farmer who, as a pawnbroker, financed small local projects among peasants in Saitama, just north of Tokyo. Eiichi moved from handling the money of former feudal lords *(daimyo)* into banking, textiles, and shipping; almost everything he touched seemed to turn to gold. He was made viscount for his contributions to the nation.

11. Compulsory education in Japan has had an interesting history. The first attempt to compel citizens to attend school was made in 1872 by the Fundamental Code of Education, a code based on the French educational system. But attempts to enforce it met vociferous opposition, especially from the agricultural population. The primary reason for opposition was the burden education placed on the family. In the early years, local communities had to finance these efforts and education was by no means free of charge (in fact, though compulsory, *free* education was not provided until after 1900). In 1878, for example, tuition was between 25–50 sen a month at a time when incomes averaged less than 20 yen (1 yen = 100 sen) per month. Thus, if a farmer's income was "average," sending one child to school would consume approximately one-eighth of his income. Other estimates place the cost at nearer 10 percent of total family income. The 1872 law prescribed four years of compulsory attendance at school. Violent farmer uprisings against the law compelled the government in 1879 to reduce the requirement to sixteen months, but opposition within the government, in turn, forced an 1880 revision in which three years were required. In 1886 this was increased to four years, in 1907 to six, and after World War II to nine.

Estimated percentages of children in school at various times during the Meiji period are as follows:

1873: 29%	1883: 50%	1899: 73%	1904: 94%
1877: 40%	1897: 66%	1901: 91%	1910: 98%

During the 1870's, however, 60–80 percent of those in school were in the first grade only. Information and statistics are based primarily on Kaigo Tokiomi, "Primary education after [sic] the Meiji era," *Education in Japan,* Vol. II (1967), 33; Herbert Passin, *Society and Education in Japan,* pp. 69, 73, 78; and Mombusho [The Ministry of Education] , ed., *Gakusei 80nen shiryohen* [Historical materials: eighty years of the school system] (Tokyo: Okurasho, 1952), pp. 1182.

12. The easiest way to understand the different kinds of "middle schools" in Japan's prewar educational system is to study a schematic representation of the system; see Appendix I.

13. Japan's change from a multitrack to a singletrack system can best be appreciated by inspecting Appendix III; n.b. also Kazuo Kawai, *Japan's American Interlude* (Chicago:

University of Chicago Press, 1960), pp. 191–192.

14. Ralph H. Turner, "Models of Social Ascent Through Education: Sponsored and Contest Mobility," in A. H. Halsey, Jean Floud, and C. Arnold Anderson, eds., *Education, Economy, and Society: A Reader in the Sociology of Education* (Glencoe, Ill.: The Free Press, 1961), p. 131. Turner's figures are taken from the U. S. Department of Health, Education, and Welfare, Office of Education publication, *Earned Degrees Conferred by Higher Education Institutions* (Washington, D.C.: Government Printing Office, 1959), p. 3.

15. *Rinijiko* and honko are blue-collar categories *(koin)*; see Note 3 above for details and comparisons with *shokuin* (white collar). The distinction between temporary and permanent blue-collar workers is, however, a good deal more rigid than the one between *koin* and *shokuin*. Even though the postwar labor movement has considerably tempered status differences between blue collar and white collar, there has not been a parallel amelioration of differentiation between temporary and permanent employees. Perhaps it is easiest to understand why this is so by sketching briefly the histroy of the *rinjiko*.

During the Meiji period (1868–1912), there was great mobility among workers of all categories. Skilled workers, especially, were in heavy demand as Japan's industrialization program built up momentum. In order to secure the services of workers with special abilities for specific periods of time, these workers were usually given good conditions of employment. Those hired in this way were called *rinjiko,* temporary workers. Near the end of the Taisho period (1912–1926), however, mobility decreased considerably in response to the growing stability and development of the industrialized modern sector of the society. In this period, temporary workers were often hired at times of special demand, or in periods of prosperity, to supplement the work of permanent employees. These part-time workers were also called *rinjiko,* but they were unskilled manual laborers who generally performed menial tasks considered beneath the dignity of the *honko.* When business was brisk, *rinjiko* were likely to be employed; when business was bad, they were out of work. Thus they functioned to take up the slack in the labor market, allowing companies to effect considerable savings. Moreover, *rinjiko* received no fringe benefits and the company assumed no responsibility for their welfare. They were no more than day laborers whose continued employment under whatever conditions was extremely tenuous. During the Pacific War, when sources of labor virtually dried up, they finally disappeared.

After World War II, reforms abolished the labor supply system *(romu kyokyu jigyo)* which negotiated directly with labor bosses in industries for the hiring of *rinjiko.* But the advent of the Korean war—and the sudden and mammoth demands placed on Japanese industry, and hence on the domestic labor market—brought about the reorganization of the prewar labor supply system and the reappearance of the *rinjiko.* Although they enjoyed practically no improvement in working conditions, some *rinjiko* were hired to work on assembly lines or assigned to other jobs in production (rather than as coolies who did various odd jobs around the plant, the prewar pattern). They were given this completely new function in order to save companies money. Remember that a *honko* is considered a permanent employee (permanent, that is, until retirement age or death, whichever occurs first), and that he must be given wage increases in accordance with the seniority rule. In times of temporary expansion or sudden demand, hiring a large number of new *honko* means a firm must assume permanent responsibilities for an increased labor force. Firms naturally want to avoid putting such a millstone around their necks, and so they hire *rinjiko* whom they are not bound to provide security or welfare benefits. Thus, though *rinjiko* supply a necessary service to management, especially in times of peak demand, they are extremely vulnerable and constantly exposed to the possibility of being laid off.

Since the end of the Korean war, the technological revolution in Japan has produced a situation where *rinjiko* continue to be in demand. Rationalization of production and other technological advances have systematized and simplified many tasks which young workers with a minimum of education can perform adequately. Hence there is a strong demand in Japanese industry for *rinjiko* who have finished school (compulsory education at 9th grade) and who can carry out tasks supplementary to the more skilled *honko.* Wage differentials between the two categories remain vast in spite of the fact that their productivity appears to be on a par. The rinjiko, for example, get on the average only sixty percent of the wages received by *honko* and none of the latter's security. In other words, *rinjiko* continue to serve as a kind of cushion on the labor market and as a shield to the security enjoyed by *honko,* for the savings effected by hiring temporary workers help management live up to its paternalistic obligations to permanent employees. John W. Bennett and Iwao Ishino, *Paternalism in the Japanese Economy: Anthropological Studies of Oyabun-Kobun Patterns* (Minneapolis: University of Minnesota Press, 1963), pp. 43–54, discuss the system for hiring *rinjiko,* etc.

16. This is precisely what one would expect in a "vertical society" dominated by hierarchical concerns; cf. Note 4 above for appropriate references dealing with the nature of a vertical society. It would not do to forget either that intellectuals themselves are intensely aware of college rankings or that they feel no compunction in using their graduation from a "superior" university as a kind of "one upmanship."

17. Among the best-known "famous colleges" are the so-called big three: Tokyo University, Kyoto University, and Hitotsubashi University (formerly the Tokyo University of Commerce), all national universities. Each of the former imperial universities is also included in the "famous" category. The two leading private universities are Kejo and Waseda.

18. Note Appendix I for a schematic outline of the school systems before and after the war. One of the distortions of the single track educational "railroad" in Japan is the increased competition for college entrance it has generated. This competition has led parents to resort to bribery or "donations" to get their offspring into a university, usually a private one. Often called "back door entrance," entering college by either of these methods demonstrates that the *moment of entry* is of utmost importance; once in, the student is generally moved along automatically until he graduates (see the Orihara article in this issue). Direct cash donations become an option when the applicant's score on the entrance examination is above or below the borderline and an "objective" criterion is necessary to determine acceptance. Families who · can afford to pay appropriate donations are allowed to register their son or daughter in the freshman class.

Bribes are another matter. In this case, "gifts" might be given to an influential professor, department head, member of the board of directors, or a powerful political figure in the community, whether he is associated with the university or not. The recipient is then expected to exert pressure to get an unqualified student—i.e., one who has not passed the entrance exam—accepted. Very frequently the "gifts" are in the form of cash, and more often than not the money involved is considerable. As far as parents who can afford the luxury are concerned, such payments constitute a good investment in the child's future, for the college graduate's chances of promotion to a managerial position are far superior to those of a high school graduate. As a rule, under-the-table gifts are in inverse proportion to the student's test scores: the lower the result, the higher the ante. As far as officials at private colleges are concerned, the donation method of backdoor entrance is necessitated by financial pressures, rising operating expenses, and niggardly government aid (around three percent of the total school budget.

A concrete example of a recent *cause celebre* concerns a professor in the science department of a large private university in Tokyo who was arrested in January 1968 for tax evasion. The professor was charged with failing to report over a three year period extra income amounting to 51,000,000 yen (US $141,666). About 30,000,000 yen ($83,333) came as "gifts" for helping students get accepted into the university despite their having failed the entrance examination (to see these sums in perspective, note that the average monthly salary of full professors in private colleges amounts to less that $240. The professor in question allegedly received 500,000 yen ($1,390) for each student he helped get into the university. References to normal student tuition and fees, and knowledge that the annual income of the average Japanese is well under $2,500, puts the size of these gifts in perspective. Aside from public scandals, it is understandably next to impossible to obtain information on this clandestine practice.

The poor financial situation of private universities encourages officials to admit a percentage of students whose families can afford a cash donation, and the low salary of professors in private colleges tempts them to accept bribes. But it cannot be said that illegal or irregular entrance procedures never occur at *public* schools, as two well-known scandals attest. In one incident, the Nara Prefectural Medical College admitted ten students after receiving payment of entrance procedures never occur at *public* schools, as two well-known scandals attest. In one incident, the Nara Prefectural Medical College admitted ten students after receiving payment of "gifts [*kifu*]" amounting to 500,000 yen each. In another, fifty-one parents were indicted for offering inducements to get their children accepted into the elementary school attached to a national university in Kyushu. In early August 1968, as a matter of fact, "nine parents . . . were charged with bribery and fined 100,000−500,000 each for having given between 150,000 yen and 550,000 yen to various teachers of the Fukuoka Elementary School attached to Fukuoka Kyoiku Daigaku (Education University). These "gifts" were given "go that the applications for admission of their children might receive favorable consideration in disregard of results of competitive examinations"; The Japan Times, August 8, 1968, p. 3. Seven teachers charged with receiving the money are now on trail. Other data was culled from reports appearing in the *Asahi Janaru,* February 11, and May 26, 1968.

19. Shimizu Yoshihiro and Amano Ikuo, "Shudan‾ to ningen keisei [Peer groups and character development]," Part III of Katsuta Shuichi, ed., *Gendai kyoikugaku nyumon* [Introduction to contemporary pedagogy] (Tokyo: Yuhikaku, 1966), p. 67.

20. Talcott Parsons, *Essays in Sociological Theory* (Glencoe, Ill.: The Free Press, 1954), p. 192. Parsons is not by any means the only Western observer holding this opinion. Note the following statements which seem to represent an identical view: "The burden of education and socialization everywhere falls primarily upon the nuclear family . . . "; George Murdock, "The Universality of the Nuclear Family," in Norman W. Bell and Ezra F. Vogel, eds., *A Modern Introduction to the Family,* p. 43; Bell and Vogel in their introductory essay, "Toward a Framework for Functional Analysis of Family Behavior," state that "in modern industrial societies, the nuclear family . . . is becoming almost exclusively responsible for primary socialization . . . but it does not provide . . . formal education . . . " p. 7.

21. List saw the *nation* as the "most important link between the individual and mankind" and "emphasized the close interrelation of economic theory and political factors"; Edgar Salin and Rene L. Frey, "Friedrich List," in David L. Sills, ed., *International Encyclopedia of the Social Sciences* (New York: Macmillan Company and the Free Press, 1968), IX, 410.

An especially penetrating complaint that the modern university seems concerned primarily with "labour power" is made by a teacher who states: "The colleges and universities have gone beyond their traditional task of socialization and acculturation. They are deeply involved *in the production of a crucial and marketable commodity–labour power* [italics added] . . . The production of an increase in socially useful and necessary labour power is the new historic function of our educational institutions that enables us to name them, quite accurately, *knowledge factories.* In this process of historical change, liberal education has been transformed into its opposite, and what we are witnessing is the advent of training and indoctrination. The core of the university, with its frills removed, has become the crucible for the production, formation, and socialization of the new working class"; Carl Davidson, "The New Radicals and the Multiversity," *Our Generation,* Vol. 5, No. 3 (November-December 1967), 71−72.

22. The issue of ethical education in Japanese schools has been dealt with by Osada Arata, "Problems in Providing Ethical Education," *JSPIJ,* Vol. I, No. 3 (December 1963), 67−70; and, in the same source, Oshima Yasumasa, "Japan's Defeat and Ethical Education," pp. 70−72. Note also a 1958 report by Lawrence Olson, "Ethics, Yes, But Which Ethics?" in *Dimensions of Japan* (New York: American Universities Field Staff, Inc., 1963), pp. 123−137. The Ministry of Education required Japanese elementary and junior high schools to introduce a one hour weekly course on ethics starting in September 1958. Naturally, schools have always been expected to teach ethical principles, especially through the nine years of compulsory education, but the new ruling placed a special focus on these classes and stimulated a spirited debate among scholars. The bibliography in *JSPIJ,* Vol. I, No. 3 (December 1963) includes a number of essays related to the debate. Note also the Introduction to that special issue for a summary of the debate.

In 1963, Japanese high school curricula were revised and a new course titled *Rinri shakai* (Ethics and society) was introduced. One 1968 version of this course, offered by correspondence on educational radio and television stations, features lectures and discussions (thirty minutes on television, twenty minutes on radio) which include the following titles: Socrates, the Thought of the Gospels, Bacon, Kant, Buddha, Confucius, Shinran, Fukuzawa

Yukichi, Socialism (focus on Marx), Pragmatism (focus on William James), Existentialism (focus on Sartre), and The Ethics of a Democratic Society. The stated aim of this course is to "nourish *[shishitsu o yashinau]* students as peaceful and democratic members of the society." The ethics hour is used to teach democratic procedures and morality as well as a modern rational view of the world and of man.

Several years ago a Catholic educator evaluated the materials used for these courses: "The textbooks thus far available contain little more than an historical outline of moral ideas and systems, cultural trends, etc. They do not give a solid philosophical foundation for moral obligation and behavior. However urgently the idea of *'hitotsukuri'* *[sic]* (formation of man) may be advocated at the present time, the efforts being made are not likely to bear the desired fruit, since the schools cannot offer a religious background nor a solid philosophy of man and life." Quoted in Joseph Spae, "Japan's Youth in Transition," *The Japan Missionary Bulletin*, Vol. XVIII, No. 10 (December 1964), 659.

23. The debate between the *Ronoha* and the *Kozaha* raged between the mid 1920's and early1930's (under Communications in this issue, note Professor H. D. Harootunian's comments and Professor Matsumoto Sannosuke's reply for a discussion of aspects of this debate that relate to the modernization of Japan). The primary issue was the nature of Japanese capitalism and the interpretation of the 1868 Meiji Restoration. Members of the *Ronoha* interpreted the Restoration as a bourgeois revolution which effected modest democractic reforms; they held that Japan's immediate *need* was a socialist revolution—this was essentially the view of leftwing social democrats. Members of the *Kozaha* disagreed with the *Ronoha* interpretation and regarded the system established after 1868 as a mere transfer of power from feudal lords to the Emperor; they held that Japan's immediate *need* was a bourgeois revolution—this was essentially the view of the Japan Communist Party; n.b., *JSPIJ*, Vol. II, No. 1 (April 1964), 38–39.

24. This law *(shokugyo kunren ho)* was enforced in 1958 with the intention of rectifying the critical shortage of technicians which occurred in the wake of Japan's economic growth and technological revolution. See Note 15 above and mark especially the way industry has used part-time help *(rinjiko)* since the Korean war, and the boom that followed, as a stopgap measure to meet this shortage.

APPENDIX I
SCHEMATIC CONTRAST: JAPANESE SCHOOL SYSTEMS*

The Japanese School System, 1937

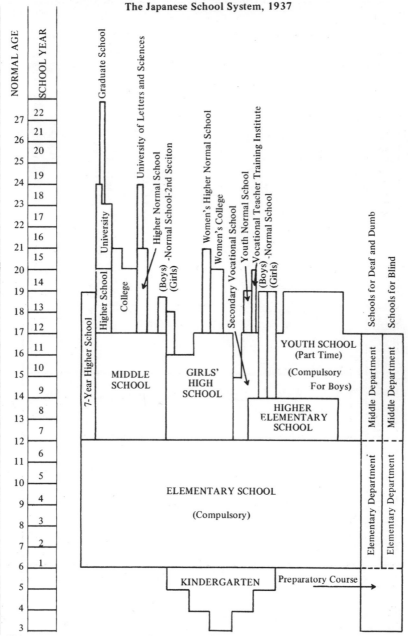

*Reprinted with the permission of the publisher from Herbert Passin, *Society and Education in Japan* (New York: Bureau of Publications, Teachers College Columbia University, 1965), pp. 308-309.

The Japanese School System, 1963

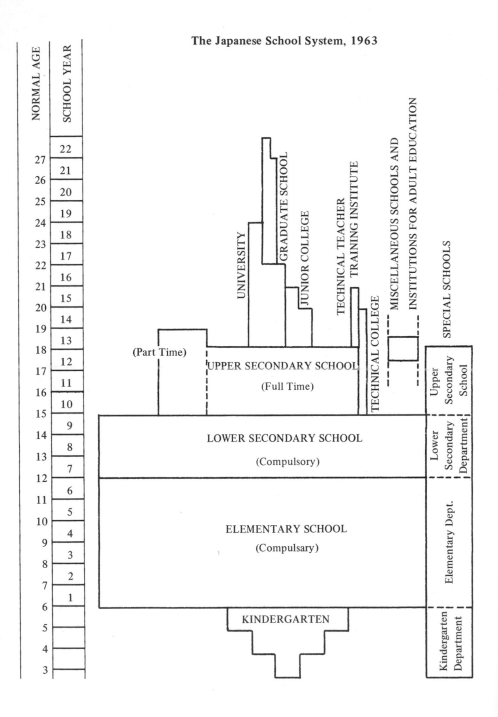

COMPARISON BETWEEN PRE- AND POST-WAR
STUDENT MOVEMENTS IN JAPAN

Michiya Shimbori

History of Zengakuren

Since June, 1960, the word *"Zengakuren"* has been added to the vocabulary of other languages than Japanese, from which it originated.

Zengakuren is an abridgement of *Zen*-Nihon-*Gakusei*-Jichikai-So-*Rengo,* which means literally "All Japan Federation of College Student Governments." Although the association was formally organized on September 18, 1948, political movements among Japanese college students can be traced back to much earlier times. While most writers recognize that the student political movement began hand in hand with the spreading labor movement after the first World War, a few contemporary writers say that this movement is as old as Japanese higher institutions, starting its history in 1876. Anyway, it is certain that Japanese students did not begin their movement against the political regime all of a sudden, but that they had a fairly long tradition along the same lines.

Although the students had a political movement prior to the formal organization of Zengakuren, it is proper for us to pay attention first to the *post-war* development of student movements. In the first few years after the Second World War, when there was scarcely an elite of substantial power except the occupying forces, there was no student political movement. This period is characterized by the uprooting of the war leaders, the anarchy of the political and ideological orders, and by the disastrous destruction of the economy. The main concern of the people was to survive each day. The evacuated, the jobless, and the returned soldiers crowded into the destroyed cities. The whole value system and the class which had ruled the country were regarded with disgust. Nevertheless this economic, political, and ideological anarchy did not necessarily lead to utter despair in the people's minds. It may be said that, in a sense, there had been no period when the Japanese were more idealistic or more oriented to their future than this. The pre-war value system was dominated by an authoritarian, semi-feudalistic, ultra-nationalistic ideology, and this fact was favorable to keeping the Japanese from desperate pessimism at the defeat, since they had been accustomed to following and internalizing the value system given from above. The occupying forces imposed a thorough reform in the name of "democrary." This newly-introduced value system was easily accepted and appreciated because of its universal applicability. The people were convinced that it could be realized in a country which had lost everything and which, therefore, was like virgin soil. "Government of the people, by the people, for the people," "Switzerland in Asia," "equality of human rights," "abolition of all armed forces" were phrases given by the occupying Americans and

Shimbori — *From Sociology of Education,* Vol. 37, No. 1, (Fall, 1963). Reprinted by permission of The American Sociological Association and the author.

accepted by the Japanese people.

Thus, in this period, when the only power elite was the occupying forces which could not be criticized or attacked, and when the people consumed their whole energy in maintaining a mere existence, there could not be a student movement of a political kind. In the educational world, democratic reform—including the introduction of a one-track system and of coeducation; the abolition of nationally unified textbooks; the purge of militaristic curricula and teachers; and the callback of previously-fired democratic, liberal, or communist professors—was imposed by General Headquarters and enforced by the Japanese government. The survivals of the pre-war order were easily removed. The occupying forces, the government, and the students implemented the democratic reform in education.

Student movements in this period focused on "democratization" of the campus. Their efforts were devoted to purging the militaristic professors; just distribution of rations or of the products of the school farm; reorganization of the student government; and more voice for the students in school administration. We define this kind of student movement as an "in-campus movement," because it is confined to the students of a particular institution and its activities take place on a particular campus. The years which immediately followed the war saw frequent "in-campus" movements. For instance, two months after the end of the war, in the Ueno Girls' Middle School, Tokyo, students won a victory over the school authorities in their claim for democratization of the administration by going on a strike.

These in-campus movements developed spontaneously and fought separately. There were no common targets for attack among students in various schools, but there was a general slogan of "democratization of the campus." Gradually, however, the movements came to be organized beyond the limits of each individual campus. This happened mainly because of three political events: the governmental policies of 1) increased fees (1947); 2) decentralization of national universities (1948); and 3) the "red-purge" (1949). These policies were ordered by General Headquarters and were to be enforced by the Japanese government. They were taken to be real and vital threats to their welfare by the academic world of Japan.

In October 1947, the Ministry of Education showed its intention to raise the fees of the national university students by 300%. Historically, the leading higher institutions of Japan were established and given various privileges by the government. One of the privileges is low fees, which attract a great many bright students of humble origin. The students, who were suffering from miserable economic conditions after the war, were indignant at the news, thinking it a challenge to equality of educational opportunities. In December, 1947, CIE[1] published a plan which recommended reorganization of national universities into local ones, supported by prefectural governments instead of the central government, after the model of the American state universities. This plan met ardent opposition on the part of academic men. Many felt that the financially and academically poor local authorities could not ensure a high standard for universities; that the nationally-founded universities had enjoyed a precious freedom from lay control or from control by narrow local interests; and that the higher institutions were distributed—as they should be—according to nationwide considerations and not local ones. Not only the so-called progressive professors and students, but also the governmental Committee on Education Reform, and the Association of Accredited Universities showed strong opposition to this plan.

Facing this opposition, the CIE and the Ministry of Education, in March

1948, substituted a plan to establish boards of trustees, again after the model of American state universities. The idea of lay control of higher institutions along with the proposed strengthening of the supervising power of the Ministry, was again seen as a threat to academic freedom. The National Association of University Professors, the Committee on Educational Reform, the Japan Academy of Higher Learning, and some university presidents expressed opposition to this plan, and at last the government withdrew this "University Bill" in May 1949.

These conditions stimulated a different kind of student movement from the previous ones, since the problems were national in nature and could not be effectively attacked by the students of a particular college. The students resisted the governmental plans. The raising of fees and the proposed bill on university administration, as distinct from "democratization" of a particular campus, were issues common to all campuses. Faced with these new problems, the students united. The government plans to raise fees and to reorganize university administration mobilized the students' energy easily, and the leaders of various organizations made quick use of the fact.

Thus, the Zengakuren was organized on September 8, 1948, with 168 national, 31 municipal, and 61 private universities as its members. The membership of Zengakuren consists of student *governments* on various campuses, *not* of individual students. And student governments, as a rule, have all the students as their members automatically.[2] It is reported that student governments in 76.5% of the national universities held membership in the Zengakuren in 1959, so that more than half of the students in the national universities have at least nominally a relation with the Zengakuren.

However, student governments differ in their aims.[3] While it is commonly held by neutral researchers that the Communists took a decisive role in organizing the Zengakuren, and while it may be argued that its movements have been always the outcome of agitation by Communist leaders—the majority being always indifferent—the crucial point is that the Zengakuren has developed along a line different from the intention of its originators. It has really mobilized the majority of the students throughout the country *under certain circumstances.*

Following the struggle against the proposed University Bill, the so-called "Red-purge *Toso*" (struggle against the Red-purge) stirred the students into action. On July 19, 1950, Dr. Eels, consultant for the CIE, publicized the intention of the occupying forces to dismiss "Red" professors. This announcement had a most profound impact upon academic circles. The following two years saw a great many resistance movements by the students. Eels was scheduled to give speeches on "Academic Freedom," "Academic Freedom and Communism," and the like on several university campuses to propagate the policy. He met a strong protest on the part of the students and he stood helplessly on the stage. The struggle against the Red purge culminated in the general strikes on June 3 and October 5, 1950, as well as in the fight between students and policemen in the Students' Assembly at the Waseda University on October 19, and at the Kyoto University on November 25, 1950. Faced with this violent resistance, the government and the administration authorities could not implement their initial intention, except in a few private universities. These are examples of the second stage of the student movements.

Thus, gradually, the student movements passed from the first stage with spasmodic demonstrations, isolated organizations, and "campus" concerns through the second stage with nationwide, permanent, co-campus organizations but still with concerns related to academic life, to the third stage with the same organizations as in the second stage but with "extra-campus," political concerns not directly related to education.

In the third stage, purely national political matters stimulated the student movements. Some of the issues were: whether Japan should conclude a peace treaty with the western nations as early as possible or with all nations, including the Communist camps, even if this could come only later; whether or not Japan should protect her safety by means of a U.S.-Japan Security Pact; whether or not Japan should revise the Constitution for rearmament; whether or not Japan should agree to a universal nuclear test ban. All of these were controversies in which students were involved as citizens rather than as students. Their movements were characterized at this stage by cooperation with non-student organizations. Therefore, they can be named "extra-campus" movements in contrast to the second stage when the movements were still run mainly by students themselves. Roughly speaking, the first stage covers the period from 1945—47, the second 1948—50, and the third 1951 to date. (Nineteen fifty-one is the year of conclusion of the Peace Treaty at San Francisco.)[4]

Pre-War Student Movements

As said before, student movements can be traced back to much earlier times; they are not exclusively phenomena of the post-war period. The pre-war period had two cycles. The first ran roughly from 1874 to 1917, from the period of the *Jiyu-minken Undo* (a movement which struggled for civil liberties) to the period of the Russian Revolution. The second proceeded from 1918 to 1944; from the period of *Taisho* Democracy, a democratic movement during and after the First World War which struggled for universal suffrage, to the end of the Second World War.

The ideology in both cycles began with democracy and developed into socialism, syndicalism, anarchism or communism. However, the pre-war student movements were concerned from the beginning with non-academic, policital matters as well as issues affecting the campus.

In-campus movements in the pre-war period, apart from various kinds of school revolts, were usually in defense of academic freedom. The pre-war movements were a result of governmental efforts to purge progressive and critical professors. Another important pre-war movement was against introducing military training into the college curriculum. After the First World War, the government tried to employ surplus army officers in the schools, and the military authorities propagated the necessity of military training in school. In 1923, a dramatic event occurred at Waseda University where a pro-military student organization called The Study Group on Military Matters was to be founded. The opening assembly was attended by leading generals as well as the President and some professors. They were barracked and could not complete their address. In the student assembly after a couple of days, some five thousand students, half of all the enrollment, participated in attacking militarism in education and the Study Group, as a result, could not be formed. Starting with this episode, both in- and extra-campus movements against military training were seen elsewhere and mobilized a great many students. A co-campus organization, named the National Student Union against Military Training, was organized, sponsored by the Student Federation of Social Science, which was an offspring of the Federation of Students.

Distinct from the in-campus movements, co- and extra-campus ones did not occur spontaneously, but were organized deliberately by leaders. They were not stimulated by a particular affair as were the in-campus movements, but affected by a more or less general atmosphere of the time. The difference between the pre-war and post-war movements consists in the fact that in the pre-war period a sharp line could not be drawn between co- and extra-campus movements. Co-campus, federated organizations were, from the beginning, political and non-campus orientea. In the post-war movements, as seen before, co-campus organizations developed from in-campus into extra-campus ones by an evolutionary process.

Another important difference lies in the fact that the pre-war co-campus organizations afforded membership to individual persons, not to the whole body of students in an institution, as in the post-war ones. This means that the pre-war organizations were more or less closed, "underground societies" in time of oppression, while in the post-war period any student is a potential member of the organization and thus can participate in any action he considers urgent. Thus the pre-war, co-campus organizations were formed and led by non-students, participated in by a minority of member-students, and fused with non-campus organizations.

Many influential organizations were born in 1918, the year of the end of the First World War when the ideology of democracy and socialism poured into Japan, the Russian and the German Revolutions had a strong impact upon intellectuals and laborers, and the class conflict grew keener owing to the rapid development of capitalism, industrialism, and urbanism during the War. *Rogaku-kai* (Association of Laborers and Students) around Tokyo and Kyoto Universities, *Shinjin-kai* (Society of New Men) in Tokyo University, *Minjin-domei* (Union of Common Men) in Waseda University, *Gyomin-kai* (Society of Pioneers) around Waseda University, *Kensetsusha-domei* (Union of Builders) around Waseda, *Fushin-kai* (Society of Common Faith) in Hosei University, *Shakai-shiso-kenkyu-kai* (Society for the Study of Social Thoughts) in the First High School were founded mostly in that year. Although most of them were organized within the campus, they cannot properly be called "in-campus" organizations because membership was not restricted to students of a single university. Cooperation was sought with the students of other universities, with laborers, and with intellectuals. Progressive professors and alumni helped in organizing and acted as consultants. For example, *Shinjin-kai,* the most famous and influential organization of the time, was formed in 1918 by a group of progressive students who had gathered around Professor Sakuzo Yoshino, the intellectual leader of *Taisho* democracy. They published a journal entitled *Democracy* and ran lectures by sympathizing intellectuals. Laborers joined the Society. Thus the Society was from the beginning an extra-campus as well as in-campus organization, and so also with other associations.

In 1922, *Gakusei-Rengo-kai* (Federation of Students) was formed to unify those who had already cooperated in the "campaign to rescue hungry Russians" in the preceding two years. Likewise in 1923, *Koto-gakko-Remmei* (High School League) was founded by representatives of several high schools in order to propagate Communism among students. These are typical co-campus organizations. Since all forms of socialism, to say nothing of communism, were tabooed legally, and organizations with the slightest inclination toward socialism were at once suppressed, many of them were underground organizations with a few militant devotees. For instance, the High School League, in spite of its grand name, was founded in secret by some ten members who had been endeavoring to establish a society for the study of ideological matters, and it did not last long.

As the action movements with a revolutionary orientation were suppressed, the students who had been concerned with non-campus matters moved in safer and more socially acceptable directions. One was the formation of study groups, and the other, formation of *non-militant* action organizations. The *Shakai Kagaku Kenkyu-kai* (Society for the Study of Social Science) and *Gakusei* Settlement (Students' Settlement Working) movements were initiated and spread in 1924.

The students' efforts to find a safer channel for their movements in the form of study groups can be traced in the following way. The movement for universal suffrage in 1923 and 1924 had not won substantial victory, but on the contrary, the legal basis for suppressing social movements was laid in 1925 under the name of the notorious *Chian Iji Ho* (Law to Maintain Order). Terrorism at the hands of militarists and chauvinists became a common experience for progressives. The disorder following the Great Earthquake in Tokyo in 1923 gave the government an excuse for forceful suppression of radicals. Moreover, the Communist Party of the time was thrown into confusion by the opinion that it should be liberalized and enter into "the mass" before undertaking a communist revolution.

All this had a profound effect upon student movements around 1924. Formerly the members were urged to take an active part in revolutionary movements but now this emphasis on "practice" was replaced by "theory." It was claimed that a theoretical study of revolutionary doctrine had to precede practical activity.

In 1924, the assembly of *Gakusei Rengo-kai* discussed whether theoretical study or practical movements should come first, and a conclusion was reached in favor of the former. The organization changed its name to *Gakusei Shakai Kagaku Rengo-kai* (Student Federation of Social Science). The Federation, although it resumed the initial practical orientation now and then, and met with continuous suppression, attracted a relatively larger number of students, and lasted until 1929; then it was reorganized into the Student Group of Communist Youth. Already on March 15, 1928, the government arrested Communist leaders, including students, and shortly after, the administrative authorities of all schools forbade student organizations with a political orientation. Thus the Federation became an underground organization.

The Student Settlement movement, on the contrary, had a much more fortunate fate, because its activities were humanitarian and peaceful. Professors and students built a settlement in a slum area which served as a university extension for laborers, a nursery school for their children, and a medical clinic for them. The students entered into the proletariat and helped them with their knowledge and skills. This moderate type of student movement, although it became a refuge for revolutionary students, survived until the outbreak of the Second World War. This was also the case with the student cooperative movement. This movement, which was initatied by the members of the Society for the Study of Social Problems at the Waseda University in 1926, ran a cooperative store at many universities.

Similarities

Reviewing the history of student movements in pre- and post-war Japan, we can generalize their similarities in the following way:

1) Student movements were likely to appear first in times of social emancipation. If we begin the history of pre-war student movements with 1874, the time was known as *Jiyu Minken Undo* (Movement for Civil Liberties and Human Rights), or if we begin with 1918, it was the time of *Taisho* democracy and the Russian Revolution. In both periods, the demand for democracy was quite popular, and the government itself was inclined to inaugurate a new regime along this line. The post-war movement began in 1945, when the old regime was overthrown, and

the people were emancipated under the occupation policy. In short, the emergence of student movements in an overt form is possible in a more or less democratic social climate or when the oppressive power of a reactionary political elite is weakening.

2) In-campus movements appeared naturally and spasmodically. They were concerned with matters related directly to student life on the campus of their own institution, for instance, raising the fee, firing a favorite professor, imposing military training, appointing an autocratic principal. They were stimulated by particular events. They could usually mobilize many students and succeed in realizing their initial aim, but the organization was usually loose and short-lived. Academic freedom was the commonest ideology of movements of this kind.

3) Extra-campus movements tended to develop stimulated by more general social movements, e.g., the campaigns for universal suffrage and trade unionism before the war; and movements against *Hakai Katsudo Boshi Ho* (The Law Prohibiting Destructive Actions), *Anzenhosho Jyoyaku* (The U.S.-Japan Security Pact), United States military bases and nuclear testing after the war. These were all nationwide controversies of the period. Movements of this kind cooperated closely with outside organizations, and had a more or less solid and continuing organization of their own. They usually met with attempts at suppression on the part of the elite in power, and the probability of success was lower than for in-campus movements.

4) Some of the in-campus movements were necessarily organized into co-campus ones. For example, introducing military training, purging Red professors, or raising the fees in governmental universities were proposed or enforced by the government, so that they could not be fought solely within a single campus. Intercollegiate cooperation became necessary. Since Japanese higher education has been built and controlled by the government, and the most active leaders of the student movements have been in the national universities, not the private ones, the transformation from in-campus into co-campus movements was natural. When this transformation occurred, the organization of the movement grew clearer.

It is also common to the pre- and post-war movements that most of the co-campus as well as the extra-campus movements took form in metropolitan areas, where most of the students gather and where most of the leading universities are located; where the target of attack—the government—is also located; where organizations such as labor unions are powerful; and where social problems are highly visible.

5) The ideology and tactics of the movements were likely to become more radical as time passed and as movements went from in-campus through co-campus to extra-campus form. The moderate claim for democracy or liberalism developed into a demand for socialism and still further to communism. Tactics, too, proceeded from the moderate and peaceful type, such as lectures and student assemblies, to more violent types, such as general strikes and mass demonstrations.

The reasons for this last are several. The more organized the movement, the more necessary are radical professional leaders. The more suppression there is, the more violent the counteractions. The more political the movement, the more influential are non-student revolutionary organizations. The more idealistic the students, the more thoroughgoing and clear-cut is their ideology. A circular process can be noticed. The more radical the movement, the greater the suppression and the less the possibility of success, thus the still more radical the movement. The result is professionalization of leadership and greater distance between leaders and followers. Also, professors who had been consultants or sympathetic guides of student organizations could not continue to be associated with the radical students.

Differences

1) While before the Second World War political movements could mobilize only relatively few students and non-political movements mobilized more, the post-war political movements mobilized a general majority of the students. The political organizations of the pre-war period were mostly underground and had a radical revolutionary ideology, while those after the war were open. The former were composed of members who were keenly class-conscious and revolutionary, and recruited only those who had been converted to a definite ideology. Their members had a high degree of solidarity, loyalty, sense of mission, and heroism. Between the members and the rest of the students there was a strong barrier, psychological as well as organizational. After the war, all students were potential members of all student organizations, and they could participate in any action if they wished.

Thus the post-war student organizations were less cohesive, and less continuous, and the number of mobilized members was in flux. The psychology of the participants in the post-war movements was also characterized by less loyalty to the organization, more diverse attitudes toward the ideology, less feeling of grandeur or mission, and less sense of guilt. The movements themselves lost the dark complexion of underground, unlawful associations, and were taken-for-granted. They grew from monopolization by half-professional leaders, to a phenomenon of the masses of ordinary students.

2) The more diverse attitudes toward ideology, the greater number of participants; the heterogeneity of the members; the ease of being either active or passive in organizations—all these contributed to a growing autonomy of the students in post-war extra-campus movements. In the pre-war extra-campus movements, the students were eager to assimilate themselves to non-student members, especially laborers. To accomplish this, for example, they put off their college uniform and cap, which symbolized the status of a student. The movements were often led by organizations other than those of the students.

On the other hand, in the post-war extra-campus movements, the students gained more hegemony and autonomy. Sometimes they became far more radical than the former sponsoring agency, so that they were dismissed from membership in the extra-campus organization.

3) It follows that the post-war organizations were more likely to be split into many opposing factions.[5]

4) Co-campus organizations or federations became more popular after the war. Before the war, such federation, if any, was nominal and regional. After the war, federation was built on a nationwide scale. Thus the student movements could no longer be monopolized by the active students in the metropolitan areas. This was partly due to the rapid development of mass communication and transportation facilities, and also to the decentralization of higher education.

5) There were fewer *counter*-movements, i.e., movements *defending* the elite in power after the war than before. The pre-war period saw a great many conservative student organizations which were against progressive students. Ultra-nationalistic, chauvinistic, militaristic, Emperorcentric, or shintoistic ideologies which opposed all kinds of civil state regimes whether democratic, socialistic, or communistic, were their leading principles. The students with these ideologies, led by conservative professors, were organized as soon as the progressive movements began. When the

leftist organizations were forced underground, these rightist organizations became the only lawful ones. But their members were limited in number and could not get much sympathy among the majority of the students. After the war, this kind of counter-movement scarcely existed. All the members of the progressive student movement enjoyed freedom of expression, without any forceful or legal opposition on the part of the government or rightist organizations.

FOOTNOTES

1. CIE means the section of Civil Information and Education of the General Headquarters of the United States occupying forces.

2. According to a survey by the Ministry of Education, the system of involuntary membership, namely, the system whereby all students shall be members of the student government of the university they attend, is adopted by 79.7% of all the departments in national universities, while 12.7% have voluntary membership systems. Cf. "The Current Situations of Student Government in National Universities," [mimeo], Ministry of Education [June, 1960], p. 8.

3. *Ibid.*, p. 14. 21.8% are aimed at academic freedom, peace, and democracy, while 14.2% have the aim of in-campus friendship, and 62% have both aims combined.

4. With the growing tendency toward politicalization in student movements, especially of the third stage, there are two seemingly contradictory situations: their liability to be affected by the political parties and at the same time their effort to be independent and autonomous in ideology. The students tend to split into many factions parallel with their counterparts in the political parties.

Thus the leading ideology of *Zengakuren* changed quickly and the organization had a great many factions. For instance, in 1958, when the Communist Party revised its principle of ultra-leftist, violent "adventurism" to "peaceful coexistence" and cooperation with all democratic organizations, the leaders of *Zengakuren* attacked this change of tactics, and being dismissed from the Party, they formed the *Kyosando* (*Kyosan-shugi-sha-Domei*, Communist Organization). The faction in *Zengakuren* under this influence is named *Shagakudo* (*Shakai-shugi Gakusei Domei*, Socialist Student Association); it held the hegemony until 1961.

In 1961, when the *Kyosando* fell into disorder owing to conflicting appraisals of the struggle against the United States-Japan Security Pact, the so-called *Ampo-toso, Marugakudo* (*Marx-shugi Gakusei Domei*, Marxist Student Association) took the leadership, representing the ideology of *Kakukyodo* (Revolutionary Communist Union).

There are many other factions in *Zengakuren*, such as: *Shaseido* (*Nihon Shakaishugi Seinen Domei*, Japan Socialist Youth Association), which was founded in 1960, under the influence of the Japan Socialist Party; *Minsei* (*Nihon Minshu Seinen Domei*, Japan Democratic Youth Association), which was founded in 1960, under the influence of the Japan Communist Party; *Kokaiha* (*Kozo Kaikaku Ha*, Structural Reform Faction), which was founded in 1961, influenced by anti-Stalinism in the U.S.S.R.; and *Heimin Gakuren* (*Heiwa to Minshushugi o Mamoru Gakusei Renraku Kaigi*, Student Federation to Preserve Peace and Democracy), which was founded in 1962, with a moderate ideology.

5. The hegemony of *Zengakuren* has been struggled for by two factions since about 1950. *Shuryu-ha* maintains the principle of both anti-Americanism and anti-Stalinism, i.e., against all kinds of "imperialism," whether American or Russian. The ideology is so radical and thoroughgoing that the *Shuryu-ha* faction was dismissed from the Communist Party. The centers of these ideologies are in Tokyo and Waseda Universities. *Han Shuryu-ha* held the theory of "two-step revolution," i.e., that revolution should proceed from moderate parliamentaristic socialism to communism. Tokyo University of Education is the center of this group.

POLITICAL ROLE ATTRIBUTIONS AND DYNAMICS IN A JAPANESE COMMUNITY

Yasumasa Kuroda

Political resources, as well as political influence, are unevenly distributed everywhere.[1] The study of political influence can be approached from the point of view of role analysis. By examining the kinds of political roles citizens play at the local level, we might be able to contribute to the understanding of the power structure. The major questions this study raises are: What are the attributes of the various political roles at the community level? What are the dynamics of political participation of each of these roles in community decision making?

The present analysis is based upon a study conducted in a small community of 16,500 people located near Tokyo. Our sample for the general population was secured from the list of 9,345 registered voters in this community at the time of the election on April 30, 1963. Every thirtieth voter was selected as one of our respondents. This gave us 321 systematically selected respondents. Out of the 321 we were able to interview 287, about 90 per cent of the sample.

Political Roles

A role is defined by Sarbin as "a patterned sequence of learned actions or deeds performed by a person in an interaction situation."[2] A political role is defined here as a patterned sequence of political behavior performed by a citizen in the communication network of decision making. By political behavior we mean any behavior affecting others that determines the activities of government.

There are those who give advice and those who seek advice, those who discuss, those who attend political meetings, and those who take an active part in political issues. These categories are obviously not mutually exclusive. Many of those who give advice are likely to attend meetings, take an active part on issues, and discuss these issues with others. All these roles constitute the power structure in a community.

Following the theoretical model underlying the present analysis of the community power structure, political roles are functionally defined in terms of the kinds of communication activity that characterize community politics. Questions used in constructing the operational definition of political roles include not only the formally structured political mechanisms but also what Katz and Piret refer to as "circuitous" participation.[3] Active advisors, passive advisors, talkers, listeners, workers, and nonparticipants are defined as shown in Table 1.

This study is designed to build on the pioneering effort of Agger and Ostrom in their study of "Political Participation in a Small Community."[4] An equivalent set of questions and the same mechanical procedures are used in this study to make

Kuroda — *From Public Opinion Quarterly,* Vol. 29, No. 4, (Winter, 1965-66), pp. 602-613. Reprinted by permission of the publisher and the author.

a cross-cultural comparative analysis of political roles at the community level. In addition to Agger and Ostrom's six role types, a set of leaders selected through a variant of Hunter's reputational technique[5] is included in the analysis to compare the top leaders with the active advisors and other active role types.

TABLE 1
POLITICAL ROLES AND COMPONENT ACTIVITY PATTERNS

Role Types	Number of Respondents	Advise	Discuss	Active on Issues	Attend Meetings
Active Advisors	5	+	+	+	+
(N = 11)	1	+	+	+	−
	4	+	+	−	+
	1	+	+	−	−
Passive Advisors	5	+	−	−	+
(N = 21)	12	+	−	−	−
	3	+	−	+	+
	1	+	−	+	−
Talkers	3	−	+	+	+
(N = 13)	2	−	+	+	−
	2	−	+	−	+
	6	−	+	−	−
Workers	4	−	−	+	+
(N = 17)	13	−	−	+	−
Listeners	23	−	−	−	+
(N = 23)					
Nonparticipants	181	−	−	−	−
(N = 181)					

Not ascertainable
(N = 21)

Note: This procedure is adopted from Robert E. Agger and Vincent Ostrom, "Political Participation in a Small Community," in Heintz Eulau, Samuel J. Eldersveld, and Morris Janowitz, eds., *Political Behavior,* Glencoe, Ill., The Free Press, 1956, pp. 138-148.

Scoring Procedure: + = Participated   − = Did not participate

Questions used for the construction of this scaling are the same questions used by Agger and Ostrom:

1. Has anyone come to you within the past year for advice on political party or election matters? Yes (+), No (−)

2. How often have you seriously discussed local government or community matters during the past year with your friends? Often (+), Once in awhile (−), Not at all (−)

3. Have you taken an active part on any local government or community issue since the annexation in 1955? Yes (+), No (−)

4. I have a list of some of the things people do that help a party or a candidate to win election. Could you tell me whether you did any of these things during the last election campaign [House of Counselor] last year [1962]? Did you attend any political meetings? Yes (+), No (−)

The Findings

Roles Isolated. The six roles are isolated as follows: 11 Active Advisors (4 per cent), 21 Passive Advisors (7 per cent), 13 Talkers (5 per cent), 17 Workers (6 per cent), 23 Listeners (8 per cent), and 181 Nonparticipants (63 per cent). Twenty-one respondents failed to answer one or more questions used in the construction of the role types.

The proportion of Nonparticipants is considerably higher in this Japanese community than in the American community studied by Agger and Ostrom.[6] A little over one-fifth of the adult citizens of this Japanese community were engaged in political activities beyond the voting level. This may be due to differences in size of the community, political culture, and many other factors. Since there are no comparable Japanese data on such figures, one is compelled to refer to speculative theories rather than to empirical data.

1. *The Top Leaders.* The distribution of characteristics among the political roles is presented in Table 2. All Top (Reputational) Leaders are men, most of whom are between forty-five and sixty-four years of age. They are married, highly educated, and in general people of high income and status. All of them read newspapers regularly. They have lived in the community all their lives or have lived there a minimum of thirty-one years. They have no disposition to move away even if there is an opportunity to do so. Most of them belong to more than three organizations. Their parents were more involved in community affairs than those of Nonparticipants. They are predominantly Liberal Democrats, indicating their conservative ideological orientation.[7]

It is rather important to note here that all Top Leaders associate with city officials as well as with other community leaders. This may be considered an indicator of the validity of the reputational technique in ascertaining the community power structure even outside the United States. So far, all these findings about the Top Leaders roughly correspond with the findings of the community power structure studies in the United States. These findings also fit with the qualifications for local community leadership described by Beardsley *et al.*[8]

2. *The Active Advisors.* The Active Advisors resemble the Top Leaders in many ways. They are highly educated men who keep abreast of the news. Nearly all of them belong to two or more organizations, while less than half the Nonparticipants belong to two or more organizations. They associate with city officials and community leaders more often then any other group except the Top Leadership. Their parents were just as highly involved in community affairs as the Top Leaders while they were growing up.

However, there are some interesting differences between the Top Leaders and the Active Advisors. The Active Advisors include some young men. They were born and raised in the community, but they would be willing to move out if there were a good opportunity to do so. This differs from Agger and Ostrom's findings that most of the Active Advisors preferred to remain in the community. This might be due to the fact that there are more farmers among the Active Advisors than among the Top Leaders. Some of these farmers might be thinking of changing their occupation. The proportion of farmers in the Japanese labor force has been decreasing at the rate of almost 2 per cent annually in the past several years. The larger number of farmers among the Active Advisors may also account for the fact that the Active Advisors' income is about the same as that of the rest of the population. Farmers are not paid well in comparison with other jobs in Japan.[9] With the exception of the Top Leaders, income appears to have no significant bearing on the political role types.

The Socialist Party is most popular among the Active Advisors, who are more liberal than the Nonparticipants. All of them feel politically potent. Their sense of civic duty or political obligation is high. They are, however, politically more cynical

TABLE 2
DISTRIBUTION OF CHARACTERISTICS AMONG THE
POLITICAL ROLE AGGREGATES
(In per cent)

Characteristics	Political Role Aggregates*						
	(1) N=22	(2) N=11	(3) N=21	(4) N=13	(5) N=17	(6) N=23	(7) N=181
Sex:							
Male	100	73	71	62	59	70	45
Female	0	27	29	38	41	30	55
Age:							
20-29	0	27	24	31	18	30	28
30-44	4	36	43	46	18	30	29
45-64	82	36	28	23	58	26	29
65 and over	14	0	5	0	6	13	14
Marital status:							
Single	0	18	14	23	6	26	19
Widowed	5	9	5	0	6	4	13
Married	95	73	81	77	88	70	68
Education:							
Beyond compulsory education	91	91	67	69	35	44	43
Compulsory education only	9	9	33	31	59	52	53
Did not complete compulsory education	0	0	0	0	6	4	4
Income:							
70,000 yen or more	73	27	5	23	29	22	16
50,000–69,999 yen	9	27	24	31	35	13	19
49,999 yen or less	18	37	57	31	7	43	35
N.A.	0	9	14	15	29	22	30
Occupation:							
Professional and proprietors	55	9	29	0	18	4	9
Clerical and skilled laborer	9	27	14	15	0	13	8
Unskilled and farmers	32	64	52	62	71	70	60
Housewife, retired or not classified elsewhere	4	0	5	8	11	9	19
N.A.	0	0	0	15	0	4	4
Newspaper:							
Read regularly	100	91	86	54	53	70	67
Do not read regularly	0	9	14	46	47	30	33
Length of residence:							
31 years or more or all my life	91	91	67	69	35	44	43
30 years or less	9	9	33	31	59	52	53
N.A.	0	0	0	0	6	4	4
Disposition to move away:							
No	95	64	76	46	76	78	84
Yes	5	36	15	54	12	22	12
N.A.	0	0	11	0	12	0	4
Organizational affiliation:							
Belong to no organization	0	0	24	8	6	13	27
Belong to one organization	14	9	14	15	29	17	33
Belong to two organizations	14	45	33	23	24	22	23
Belong to three or more	72	45	29	54	41	48	17

TABLE 2 (*continued*)

	Political Role Aggregates*						
Characteristics	(1) N=22	(2) N=11	(3) N=21	(4) N=13	(5) N=17	(6) N=23	(7) N=181
Association with city officials:							
Frequently	100	55	48	31	53	35	15
Very seldom or not at all	0	45	52	69	47	65	85
Association with community leaders:							
Frequently	100	73	52	46	47	35	17
Very seldom or not at all	0	27	48	54	53	65	83
Parents' community affairs involvement while respondents were growing up:							
Very interested	36	45	24	8	24	17	16
Somewhat interested	50	45	52	69	41	44	44
Not at all interested	9	10	14	8	11	26	16
N.A.	5	0	10	15	24	13	24
Party preference:							
Liberal Democrat	91	27	33	46	59	65	42
Socialist†	4	55	24	23	0	9	13
Independent	0	18	43	31	41	17	38
N.A.	4	0	0	0	0	9	7
Ideological orientation:							
Conservative		36	24	23	47	48	46
Liberal		64	71	77	53	52	38
N.A.		0	5	0	0	0	15
Political efficacy:							
High		100	76	77	76	52	36
Low		0	19	23	24	39	45
N.A.		0	5	0	0	9	19
Political obligation:							
High		73	57	69	59	48	35
Low		27	38	31	41	43	53
N.A.		0	5	0	0	9	12
Political cynicism:							
High		64	62	62	35	35	42
Low		37	33	38	65	52	29
N.A.		0	5	0	0	13	29
Nationalism:							
Nationalistic		54	52	69	47	70	34
Internationalistic		46	38	31	41	22	34
N.A.		0	10	0	12	8	32
Manipulativeness:							
High		18	14	38	65	9	41
Medium		55	62	38	18	52	37
Low		27	24	23	18	39	13
N.A.		0	0	0	0	0	9
Sociability:							
High		82	57	92	76	48	30
Low		18	38	8	24	43	59
N.A.		0	5	0	0	9	11

*Political role aggregates: 1 = Reputational Leaders, 2 = Active Advisors, 3 = Passive Advisors, 4 = Talkers, 5 = Listeners, 6 = Workers, 7 = Nonparticipants.
†Includes 1 Social Democrat and 2 Communists.

than the Nonparticipants. This may be because more socialists are included in the Active Advisors. The Active Advisors are much more sociable than the Nonpartici-pants.[10]

Their political values suggest dissatisfaction with the existing political order of the community. Since half of them have frequent contacts with city officials and community leaders, the Top Leaders must be aware of their existence and their political values.

3. *The Passive Advisors.* The Passive Advisors are not too different from the Active Advisors in terms of sex ratio, age, and marital status. They are better educated than the Nonparticipants, but not so well educated as the Active Advisors. Their income, too, is slightly lower than that of the Active Advisors, but there are more professionals and proprietors among them than among the Active Advisors. They read the papers less regularly than the Active Advisors but more often than the other four role types. While they have not lived in the community as long as the Active Advisors, they have less disposition to move away. They belong to about the same number of organizations as the Nonparticipants. They interact more often with city officials and community leaders than the remaining four role types, with one exception: listeners react more with city officials. The parents of the Passive Advisors were not much more involved in community affairs than the Nonpartici-pants' parents.

In terms of political party preference, nearly half the Passive Advisors are independents, while half the Active Advisors are Socialists. These independents, however, appear to be quite liberal in their ideological orientation.[11] Their political efficacy and political obligation scores are not so high as the Active Advisors, but they scored significantly higher than the Nonparticipants. They are about as cynical as the Active Advisors, while their sociability scores show that they are significantly less sociable than the Active Advisors, although they are still more sociable than the Nonparticipants.

4. *The Talkers.* There are more women among the Talkers than among the Advisors. The Talkers are as highly educated as the Passive Advisors. They are mostly farmers who do not read the newspapers as regularly as the Nonparticipants. They have lived in the community as long as the Passive Advisors, but they are more interested in moving out of the community than any of the other role types. Over half of them indicated that they would move out if there were an opportunity. Again this may be due to the high proportion of farmers who comprise the Talkers. Talkers belong to more organizations than the Advisors, which probably gives them an opportunity to satisfy their personality needs, but they do not interact as often with city officials and community leaders. Their parents were not involved in community affairs as much as the Advisors' parents were.

Nearly half the Talkers are Liberal Democrats (the ruling conservative party), but they are as liberal as the Advisors in their ideological orientation. They are considerably more liberal than the Nonparticipants. They resemble the Passive Advisors in their scores of political efficacy and political obligation. They are, however, more nationalistic than the Advisors or the Nonparticipants.

As can be imagined, since they are the Talkers, they are the most sociable group of all role types. Their interest in politics may derive mainly from their personality characteristics.

5. *The Listeners.* The Listeners are less educated and read newspapers less frequently than many other role types, including the Nonparticipants. Most of

them are in the forty-five to sixty-four age group. Most of them are married. In these two respects they are much like the Top Leaders. Their disposition to move away is about the same as the Advisors. They have about the same amount of contacts with city officials and community leaders as the Passive Advisors. As listeners, they belong to more organizations than the Nonparticipants or even the Passive Advisors. They are more sociable than the Passive Advisors. They are the most manipulative of all groups. They are the least cynical about politics and politicians.

They are Liberal Democrats in their party choice. None of them identifies with the Socialist Party. They are more conservative than the Advisors and the Talkers in their ideological orientation. Their political efficacy scale scores are about the same as those of the Passive Advisors and the Talkers. Their sense of civic duty is higher than that of the Nonparticipants, but not so high as that of the Advisors and the Talkers.

6.   *The Workers.* The workers are more often men than women. Their education, age distribution, marital status, income, occupation, newspaper-reading habits, length of residence, disposition to move away, and parents' community involvement cannot be distinguished from those of the Nonparticipants. Their contacts with city officials and community leaders are appreciably more frequent than those of the Nonparticipants. Of all the groups, they are least manipulative.

Politically speaking, they are the most conservative and the most nationalistic, and they are the strongest supporters of the Liberal Democratic party after the Top Leaders. They are less cynical about politics than the Nonparticipants. Their political efficacy and political obligation scores show that their sense of efficacy and of civic duty is lower than the Advisors, the Talkers, and the Listeners, although they scored higher than the Nonparticipants on these two scales.

7.   *The Nonparticipants.* The Nonparticipants have social backgrounds similar to those of some of the particpants, particularly the Listeners and the Workers. They read the newspapers more often than the Talkers and Listeners.

They are less inclined to join groups than any of the role types. They may be not only political apathetics but also alienated in other areas of community activities. Their contacts with city officials and community leaders are far less frequent than for the other roles. They are predominantly conservative in party choice and ideological orientation. They feel significantly less efficacious and less obligated in the political arena of community activities. It is interesting to note that they are not very nationalistic. A surprising proportion of them scored high on the manipulativeness scale. They do not trust politicians as much as the Listeners and Workers.

On the whole, they are more anomic than the participants, but often their social background corresponds closely to some groups of the participants, particularly the Listeners and Workers. Why is this so? Since they are the least sociable of the groups, sociability may be acting as a crucial variable in inducing some of the potential Nonparticipants to become Listeners and Workers.

The Discussion: Dynamic Analysis

As can be expected, the top power structure is filled with persons of high social status. However, directly beneath this top stratum lies a group of the Advisors and the Talkers who are dissatisfied with the existing power structure of the community. Many of them are Socialists who are liberal in ideological orientation, sociable in personality, and cynical in viewing politics. They are younger, poorer, and less educated than the Top Leaders. Then come the Listeners and Workers, who are from essentially the same social backgrounds as the Nonparticipants. Their political orientation is closer to the Top Leaders than to the Advisors and Talkers. They are more satisfied with the existing political order than the Advisors and Talkers, and are much less anomic.

Under these participants lie the Nonparticipants, who are not really integrated into the polity. They will go with whatever is the general trend of the community. Hence, we have here a political system that is stable and conservative. Frustrated Advisors and other active participants can do very little in terms of bringing any significant political change. On the one hand, they have the Top Leaders whose political values they do not share, and, on the other hand, they face apathetic masses who have a traditionally conservative political orientation. The only opportunity for the reform-minded Advisors and other active participants appears to be to take advantage of the decreasing proportion in the community of farmers, who are often apathetic and conservative. With their change in occuaption, farmers might also change their political orientation. One alternative is to bring about a basic change in the process of political socialization at the public school level, but this will be very difficult, since the Education Committee is in the hands of the Top Leaders.

The Japanese people have never experienced any political revolution in the sense that Americans, French, Chinese, and Russians have, and it would appear unlikely that they will have one unless outside forces intervene. This community, then, may continue to have a stable and conservative political system for years to come. The nationwide urbanization may provide an opportunity for the Advisors and other active participants to play a more significant role in the network of political communication, but this, too, is unlikely as long as the Japanese economy continues to enjoy its prosperity.

My informal conversations with some of the Top Leaders led me to conclude that a few share the political values of the reform-minded active participants, but, because of the mores of the top leadership, they are unable to make their political views explicit.

As Agger and Ostrom warn, the Nonparticipants are not without political values, although these may appear to be irrelevant to the study of politics. They do not trust politicians as much as the Listeners and Workers. They constitute the greatest proportion of voters and nonvoters in the community. In a sense, they decide the outcome of any election. The voting turnout in the recent elections has ranged from 75 to over 90 per cent.

The findings reported here show some differences from, as well as similarities with, the Agger-Ostrom findings:

1. Japanese Active Advisors do not share the political orientation of the Top Leadership, while their American counterparts do.

2. Japanese women are politically inactive.

3. Japanese Passive Advisors, who are mostly men, are highly educated, while their American counterparts consist mostly of women as poorly educated as the Nonparticipants. Moreover, the American Passive Advisors have as little contact with the city officials as the Nonparticipants, while the opposite is the case in the Japanese community.

4. Newspaper reading appears to be less important to Japanese active participants than to American active participants.

5. With the exception of the Active Advisors and the Talkers, the Japanese respondents are not disposed to move away from the community, while the Active Advisors, the Listeners, and the Workers are the ones who are not inclined to move away in the American community.

6. In both communities, somewhat less than half the adult population participates in politics beyond voting.

7. In both communities, "joiners" take on active political roles.

8. In both communities, political participation increases with formal schooling.

The differences we find may be caused by several factors, such as translation and cultural and socio-economic factors. For instance, the Japanese woman's inactive political role may be the result of cultural factors, while the fact that the Japanese Active Advisors do not share their political orientation with the Top Leadership may be caused by socio-economic factors, since a similar political stratification might be found also in the United States.[12]

It is encouraging to find that some of the basic hypotheses we have made about politics are borne out in this analysis. For instance, political role seems to be a function of social position, and the nature of politics is such that political activities are carried out within some group context. "Joiners" in both communities play active political roles. More comparable studies everywhere are needed in order to make possible a meaningful comparative analysis of politics.

FOOTNOTES

1. Robert A. Dahl, *Modern Political Analysis,* Englewood Cliffs, N. J., Prentice-Hall, 1963, pp. 32-35.

2. Theodore R. Sarbin, "Role Theory," in Gardner Lindzey, ed., *Social Psychology,* Vol. 1, Cambridge, Mass., Addison-Wesley, 1954, p. 224.

3. Fred E. Katz and Fern V. Piret, "Circuitous Participation in Politics," *American Journal of Sociology,* Vol. 69, No. 4, 1964, pp. 367-373.

4. Robert E. Agger and Vincent Ostrom, "Political Participation in a Small Community," in Heinz Eulau, Samuel J. Eldersveld, and Morris Janowitz, eds., *Political Behavior,* Glencoe, Ill., The Free Press, 1956, pp. 138-148.

5. Floyd Hunter, *Community Power Structure,* Chapel Hill, University of North Carolina Press, 1953.

6. *Ibid.,* p. 140. They found that 51 per cent of their respondents were nonparticipants.

7. The Liberal Democratic Party, conservative in its ideological orientation, has been in power since 1948. The Socialist Party has been the major opposition party, with a little over one-third of the seats in Parliament.

8. Richard K. Beardsley, John W. Hall, and Robert E. Ward, *Village Japan,* Chicago, University of Chicago Press, 1959, pp. 404-409.

9. Farmers included in our sample also had slightly less income than nonfarmers.

10. Cf. Lester W. Milbrath, "Predisposition toward Political Contention," *The Western Political Quarterly,* Vol. 13, No. 1, 1960, pp. 5-18; Elihu Katz and Paul F. Lazarsfeld, *Personal Influence,* Glencoe, Ill., The Free Press, 1955, pp. 223-233 and pp. 287-289; Lester W. Milbrath and Walter W. Klein, "Personality Correlates of Political Participation," *Acta Sociologica,* Vol. 6, Fasc. 1-2, 1962, pp. 53-65; Yasumasa Kuroda, "Political Socialization: Personal Political Orientation of Law Students in Japan," University of Oregon, 1962, pp. 88-97, unpublished Ph.D. dissertation (Microfilm Order No. 62-2065, *Dissertation Abstracts,* Vol. XXII, No. 12, Part 1, June, 1962, p. 4397); Yasumasa Kuroda, "Sociability and Political Involvement," *The Midwest Journal of Political Science,* Vol. 9, No. 2, 1965, pp. 133-147.

11. I found that Socialists and Communists are liberal, while Liberal Democrats are conservative. The degree of political liberalism is determined by the extent to which one believes the government should be used as a vehicle for social progress. "Political and Psychological Correlates of Japanese Political Party Preference," *Western Political Quarterly*, Vol. 17, No. 1, 1964, pp. 47-54.

12. One of the techniques that might be used to estimate the effects of political culture in comparative politics is multiple-regression analysis. The multiple-regression equation can link together the sociological variables of the Japanese community and those of the American community, giving an estimate of how much the political orientation of each community would be alike if its sociological variables were the sole causal factors. This, of course, assumes that men basically follow the same behavioral laws everywhere. For the use of multiple-regression analysis in estimating the strength of political parties in voting behavior, see the pioneering effort of Phillips Cutright and Peter H. Rossi, "Grass Roots Politicians and the Vote," *American Sociological Review*, Vol. 23, No. 2, 1958, pp. 171-179.

RELIGIOUS AND CULTURAL ETHOS OF MODERN JAPAN

Joseph M. Kitagawa

The modern period of Japanese history had its beginning in the middle of the nineteenth century through the combined pressures of internal and external factors in an intricate combination. The decline of the power and authority of the Tokugawa feudal regime that had ruled Japan from the beginning of the seventeenth century, the power struggle among the influential *daimyo* (feudal lords), the contradictory features of the socio-economic framework of the feudal system, the general apathy among the populace, the infiltration of Western knowledge, the emotional appeal of the so-called "National Learning" (*koku-gaku*), and the advance of Western powers in the Far East are but a few obvious examples of the many forces that together brought forth a new era in the history of Japan. It was no longer possible or desirable for Japan to maintain her policy of national seclusion which had been enforced by the Tokugawa regime; she was destined to chart a new course in the stormy seas of the modern world.

Before we go into the discussion of modern Japan, however, a few words must be said about the Tokugawa regime. It is well known that Japan, under Tokugawa rule, was divided into over 250 fiefs of different sizes and values, and each fief was ruled by a feudal lord (daimyo). The Tokugawa ruler was both the *shogun* (military dictator) and the most important daimyo; as such he controlled nearly one fourth of Japan directly, and ruled the rest of the nation indirectly through other daimyo. The Tokugawa regime also enforced the division of the populace into four main social classes, namely, the warrior (*shi*), the farmer (*no*), the artisan (*ko*), and the merchant (*sho*), and restricted the upward mobility of the people within the framework of their prescribed classes. In addition to the above-mentioned four social classes, the Tokugawa system recognized the imperial and courtier families and ecclesiastics as special categories.[1] The backbone of society was undoubtedly the warrior class, which was expected to play the role of preserver and transmitter of culture.[2] Next only to the warrior, the farmer enjoyed prestige, because agriculture was considered to be the basis of the national economy.[3] The political stability, established by the Tokugawa regime, encouraged the growth of industry and commerce, which meant that the living standards of artisans and merchants rose correspondingly. In the course of time, successful merchants became increasingly influential, overshadowing the lower warriors. In all classes of society, the importance of the family tie was emphasized. The regime also imposed the system of neighborhood units called *gonin-gumi* ("the five-man unit"). All the families of each of these units were responsible for the welfare and behavior of every member of the households involved.

Kitagawa — *From Asian Studies,* Vol. II, No. 3, (December, 1964), pp. 334-352. Based on *Religion In Japanese History,* Columbia University Press, 1966.

The foregoing makes it clear that Japanese society under the Tokugawa rule had two main foci, namely, the nation (society) and the family (house-hold), both of which were regarded as sacred entities. As such, the nation demanded absolute loyalty, while the family demanded absolute filial piety. It was taken for granted in this connection that the nation was embodied in the figure of shogun, and the family in the figures of the parents; but should a father oppose the shogun, the children were expected to demonstrate their loyalty by deserting their father. Thus as Bellah has rightly pointed out, the "religion of filial piety" did not compete with the "religion of loyalty." The former reinforced the latter.[4] Normally, however, nation and family were considered to be in a state of harmony, and the relations of these two foci were defined by Neo-Confucianism, which was the official "theology" of the Tokugawa regime. In this respect, many scholars hold that the architects of the Tokugawa regime depended heavily on Chinese political norms, for "the Confucian concept of a human order established in harmony with immutable natural principles seemed to justify the rigid social cleavages and political absolutism of the Tokugawa system."[5] There is every indication that the Tokugawa rulers were attracted by the Chinese model for society, and thus depended heavily on Neo-Confucianism as the source of guiding principles in the socio-political realms. And yet, what the Tokugawa regime acquired from the Neo-Confucian tradition was ironically not a social model as such, but a semi-religious affirmation of an "immanental theocracy," implying that "the order of heaven is not transcendental substance but is inherent in the conditions of human existence. This is the regulative principle to be recognized and realized."[6] This regulative principle, be it noted, was not law in the Western sense. In the framework of immanental theocracy, "there are only duties and mutual compromises governed by the ideas of order, responsibility, hierarchy, and harmony."[7] These insights were appropriated by the Tokugawa regime as the principles of its social engineering. Thus, consciously or unconsciously, Neo-Confucianism was reinterpreted and transformed so as to fit into the social structure and political institutions of Japan. A leading Japanese Neo-Confucian scholar, for instance, found no contradiction between the native cult of Shinto and the *li* (reason or principle) taught by Chu Hsi (1130-1200).[8] While Japanese Neo-Confucian scholars thus reformulated the teachings of the Chinese masters and worked out philosophical ideals, it was the warrior-administrators who translated philosophical ideals into practical measures for governing the nation. The result was, as Hall points out, that the basic political institutions of the Tokugawa regime actually "owe little or nothing to Chinese models,"[9] except the underlying semi-religious affirmation of an "immanental theocracy."

It is an irony of history that the very success of the Tokugawa regime in preserving domestic peace over the years destroyed the foundation of the feudal regime itself, and that the Tokugawa rulers failed to cope with the social and economic dislocations that inevitably developed. By the middle of the nineteenth century, the once powerful Tokugawa Shogunate having lost its grip, many daimyo sensed a need to reform the political structure of the nation. Some tried to strengthen the Shogunate in Edo (present day Tokyo), while others looked toward the imperial court in Kyoto for leadership. The political climate in mid-nineteenth century was further aggravated by external factors, namely, the demand of the Western powers to open Japan's ports to foreign trade. Reluctantly, the Shogunate concluded a treaty with the United States in 1854 and similar treaties with other Western powers in 1858. Meanwhile, caught in a network of impossible internal and external problems, the last Tokugawa shogun surrendered his power to the throne in 1867. Thus ended the feudal regime; monarchical rule was resumed by the Emperor Meiji as of January 25, 1868. The city of Edo was renamed Tokyo ("Eastern Capital"), and the imperial government was established there.

The Meiji Era

With the restoration of imperial rule, at least in principle, sweeping changes were introduced by the new regime. The real policy makers of the regime were less than one hundred relatively young royalists who, motivated by different purposes, agreed on the importance of developing a modern nation-state with a strong defense system and an industrial economy. The government adopted in 1868 the so-called "Charter Oath," which promised that deliberative assemblies should be established, evil customs of the past should be discarded, and knowledge should be sought throughout the world.[10]   In 1870, the government issued the Regulations for Dispatching Students Abroad, whereby able Japanese students were sent to Europe and America to acquire up-to-date knowledge of medicine, science, law, business, and national defense. Also, the government established at home Westernized educational institutions, a postal system, a census, telegraphic service, railroads, banks, courts of justice, the patent bureau, income tax, electricity, a constitution, and parliament. The new regime attempted to do away with outmoded practices of the past, such as the system of tolls, discrimination against the *eta* ("untouch-ables"), and the tradition of wearing swords. Even Christianity, the "forbidden religion" during the Tokugawa period, was now tolerated.

Notwithstanding these modern and Westernized features and the new system of administration, the Meiji government inherited one significant characteristic of the Tokugawa feudal regime, namely, its "immanental theocracy." This in spite of the fact that the architects of the Meiji government were passionately anti-Shogun-ate in principle and outlook. In a real sense, they were not conscious of their own inner contradictions, because while they envisaged the establishment of a modern nation-state, their instincts longed for a semi-divine nation, a paternalistic and authoritarian state, that could, however, utilize the fruits of the modern civilization of the West.

The paradoxical character of the Meiji regime may be illustrated by the examples of military conscription and compulsory education. As early as 1873, a Universal Military Conscription Ordinance was put into practice. It is to be noted that military conscription was offered as a "gift" of the throne, welcoming all able-bodied males of twenty years of age, not only the sons of warrior families but also those of farmers, artisans and merchants. While military service was not popular at first, it became in the course of time an important channel for upward social mobility, so that until World War II the peasantry in times of crises often supported the military rather than civilian leaders. Equally significant was compulsory education which made Japan the first nation in Asia to have a literate populace. The educational system was designed to meet the needs of the growing nation, that is, the training of a small number of government officials and a large number of technicians. It also aimed at providing minimum training in reading and writing for the general populace. From the standpoint of the government, education was a matter of great necessity for the training of faithful and obedient subjects of the empire rather than for the development of individual personalities for participation in a full life. It was taken for granted that the fundamental educational goal was the orientation of students toward the "Imperial Way" (*ko-do*), which was set forth in the Imperial Rescript on Education. Ultimately, education was regarded as a tool of the government, teaching its subjects "what to think" rather than "how to think."

Nevertheless, during the first two decades of the Meiji era, Japan was receptive to the influence of Western thought and civilization, particularly in the government and private universities, and in educational institutions established by various Christian missionary societies. While the government was interested only in the technological and material aspects of Western civilization, the new elite, consisting of young intellectuals in urban areas, could not help but imbibe the spirit of "modernity" that was the driving force of Western civilization. Conspicuous among them were such famous modernists as Fukuzawa Yukichi, Mori Arinori, Nishi Amane, and Kato Hiroyuki who advocated the slogan of *bummeikaika* ("civilization and enlightenment"). What the new elite of Japan sensed in "civilization and enlightenment" was the modern European conception of civilization as secularized salvation, signifying "a liberation from the fetters of barbarism just as religion aims at deliverance from the powers of evil." Thus, much as modern Europeans rejected the medieval notion of the state as subservient to the church, Japanese intellectuals during the early Meiji era reacted emotionally against traditional values and ideologies. They rejoiced in being emancipated from the "immanental theocracy" of the Tokugawa feudal period, and envisaged the creation of a new social and political order along the lines of Western models. In the new Japan, so it was believed, anybody—regardless of his status and class—could attain to a high position, based solely on his ability and merit. Indeed, the motif of *risshinshusse* ("success and advancement in life") was a real gospel for the youth of Japan where social classes had been frozen for so long under the feudal regime.

The Meiji government was also motivated by the motif of risshin-shusse, in this case, however, implying "advancing Japan in the family of nations." Thus, the government was preoccupied with advancement and progress along the lines of national prosperity and defense (*fukoku-kyohei*)—"more facts, more wealth, more strength, more manufacturers, more men, ships, and guns." Realizing how much more advanced the Western nations were than Japan in global competition, Japanese leaders made feverish attempts to catch up with others in the art of international power politics. Internally, the last two decades of the Meiji era witnessed the growth of conservatism and ethnocentric nationalism. The government, which became increasingly bureaucratic, controlled the press and often interfered with activities of political parties. The arms of the government also suppressed socialist and labor movements. Nevertheless, government leaders congratulated themselves on Japan's victory over China (1894—95) and Russia (1904—05), as well as her annexation of Korea (1910). The apparent success of Japan in the arena of international politics strengthened the Meiji regime's affirmation of the principle of "immanental theocracy," which in turn helped to create a new myth, namely, Japan's divine mission to extend her "Imperial Way" abroad.

The Eras of Taisho and Showa

The Emperor Meiji, who witnessed in his lifetime the growth of Japan from her feudal past to a powerful empire, died in 1912 and was succeeded by his son, Yoshihito (the Emperor Taisho) whose reign, 1912—1926, is referred to as the Taisho era. The Emperor Taisho's sickness, however, necessitated that his son, Hirohito (1901—   ), assume control of the affairs of state as Prince Regent in 1921. In 1926, Hirohito ascended the throne, and the Showa era began.

The year 1912 was a crucial turning point in the history of Japan as well as in the history of the world. Across the Pacific Ocean, Woodrow Wilson took over the presidency of the United States which now became a new world power, surpassing many of the old nations in Europe. Also in 1912, the People's Revolution overthrew the yoke of the Manchu Dynasty in China. Ironically, the Japanese leaders failed to understand the depth of the nationalistic aspirations of the Chinese people during the twentieth century, and continued to follow their expansionist policies in Asia. When World War I started in 1914, Japan eagerly sided with the Allies, and received most of what she demanded at the Versailles Conference. Also, during World War I, Japan presented to the Chinese government the infamous Twenty-One Demands, which aimed at economic and political domination of China by Japan. After World War I, Japan was engaged in the ill-fated Siberian Expedition, at first with the Allied Powers but later all alone, due to the insistence of the military clique at home. The enormous expenditures for keeping troops in Siberia between 1918 and 1922 ended with no gain for Japan, however.

During World War I, the financial clique (*zaibatsu*) enjoyed unprecedented prosperity, and their political influence increased accordingly. As far as the masses were concerned, the slow rise in wages could hardly keep up with the rocketing prices. The government had to face a series of difficult problems, notably the "rice riots" in 1918, the labor strikes in 1919, the financial panic in 1920, the steep fall of the stock market in 1922, the great earthquake that almost disrupted the national economy in 1923, and the monetary crisis in 1927. In spite of these difficulties or because of them, during the first half of the 1920's the general populace had a taste of a liberal democratic atmosphere. Japan assented to the Five Power Naval Treaty (1921) and disbanded four divisions of the army (1925). It was but natural that young idealists had high hopes for the League of Nations. On the other hand, events during the 1920's also gave impetus to the growth of ethnocentric and fanatic nationalism. In 1922, the League for the Prevention of Communism (*Sekka Boshi-dan*) was formed, anticipating the emergence of the Communist Party in Japan during the same year. Not content with the mass hunt and arrest of the Communists by the government in 1923, the so-called patriots carried on their own zealous campaign against Communism and other foreign ideologies. With the formation in 1924 of the National Foundation Society *(Kokuhon-sha)* through the initiative of Hiranuma Kiichiro, then vice president of the Privy Council, nationalists gained prestige, and thereby increased their influence among the conservating masses.

Events in the 1930's and early 1940's are familiar stories. By this time, nationalism had become increasingly fascistic and jingoistic. It was, in the words of Yanaga, "authoritarian, anti-parliamentarian, anti-democratic, opposed to disarmament, and suspicious of the League of Nations. It was also a Pan-Asiatic movement, unafraid and unhesitant regarding the use of force."[11] In this situation, even if the militarists were aware of the seriousness of the war in Manchuria, which they had started and which they insisted on calling the "Manchurian Incident" and not a war, the general public was unaware that it was only the beginning of a chain of ominous events. Following it came the wholesale assassination of parliamentarians and financiers (1932), Japan's withdrawal from the League of Nations (1933), an attempted coup d'etat by a group of fanatic young army officers (1936), the Marco Polo Bridge Incident (1937) that precipitated a full-scale China War, Soviet-Japanese border clashes (1938 and 1939), and Japan's participation in the

Tripartite Pact (1940). In 1941, Japan took the fatal step of entering World War II.

From the middle of the 1930's, all liberal thinking and expression—be it religion, philosophy, art or culture—were condemned under suspicion of being a threat to the Japanese way of life. Freedom of the press, thought and assembly, as well as freedom of conscience and belief, were violated. Gradually, a sense of "fear" developed among the people, who no longer dared to speak their minds openly, even to close friends. Newspapers, magazines and radios repeated the same nationalistic slogans. Peoples' thoughts, values, patterns of behavior and even the meaning of life were prescribed and interpreted by militarists and jingoists. To the ultranationalists and militarists, individuals were nothing more than cogs in the huge machine of the nation. Japan became a great fortress from which war emanated relentlessly until VJ Day, 1945.

Culture and Religion

In discussing the cultural and religious development of modern Japan, we have to remind ourselves that the establishment of the Meiji regime was not only a "renovation" (*ishin*) that implied a rejection of the past. It also was a "restoration of monarchial rule" (*osei-fukko*) implying a reversion to the policy of eighth-century Japan. The effort of the Meiji government to maintain a precarious balance between these two contradictory objectives had disastrous consequences in the spheres of culture and religion, to say nothing about the domain of politics.

Following the ancient Japanese model of "unity of religion and government" (*saisei-itchi*), the Meiji regime in 1868 established the Department of Shinto and issued the Separation Edict, separating Buddhism from Shinto (*shinbutsu hanzen-rei*) on the ground that Buddhism-Shinto coexistence, practised for nearly ten centuries, was contrary to the indigenous Japanese way of life. Thus, all Buddhist priests who had been connected with Shinto shrines were returned to secular life unless they were willing to be reordained as Shinto priests. In 1871, all temple lands were confiscated by government order, and all Buddhist ceremonies that had been performed in the imperial household were abolished. In such a situation, a popular anti-Buddhist (*haibutsu-kishaku*) movement erupted. For example, in the Toyama district, the 1,730 Buddhist temples that had existed in 1870, were reduced to seven overnight. While it was not the explicit intention of the government to exterminate Buddhism, some government officials and zealous Shinto priests aroused anti-Buddhist sentiments among the masses. Meanwhile, the government adopted the policy of promoting the emperor cult as the most important ingredient of Shinto. For example, the government erected a Shinto shrine inside the imperial palace in honor of the imperial ancestors and the *kami* of the Shinto pantheon. Later, a special shrine was established inside the palace for the worship of the Sun Goddess, Amaterasu Omikami, the tutelary kami of the imperial clan. Besides, the cult of the Emperor Jimmu, the alleged founder of the nation, was created, and the custom of celebrating the current emperor's birthday as a semi-religious national holiday was instituted. The emperor was no longer just a person who held the *charisma* of the imperial office. He was elevated to the exalted status of a "living kami" — an eminence which had been claimed but never achieved by ancient Japanese monarchs.

The "back to the pristine past" movement greatly encouraged the growth of Shinto, but failed to provide the necessary impetus for the establishment of the modern nation-state, which was the second of the twin objectives of the Meiji regime. Outrageous attempts on the part of the Shinto leaders to turn the clock backward were resisted by the modernists, for the mood of the time was not altogether in favor of returning to the past, however important the past might be. The complex development in education, legislation, culture and religion during the Meiji era grew out of the tension between the "immanental theocracy" and "modernity." It goes without saying that these two elements were essentially irreconcilable. The advocates of the pristine Japanese tradition were motivated by the desire to find the model of society and culture in the past—the way of the kami (*kannagara*). "Back to the Emperor Jimmu!" they cried. The advocates of modernity, on the other hand, placed their faith in the present and future, in the new and the novel. To them, the Meiji era was the beginning of a permanent revolution along the path of enlightenment and civilization. The advocates of both principles, however, shared the same two qualities, namely patriotism and utilitarianism, and thus a compromise was achieved between them by means of pragmatic, nationalistic principles. How such a compromise was achieved may become evident when we follow the checkered development of education during the early Meiji era.

When the new regime came into being in 1868, one of its urgent tasks was the formulation of an educational philosophy and system. Prior to the Meiji era, it was taken for granted that the Confucian system provided the foundation and framework of education. This assumption was challenged in 1868 by the royalists who were determined to instill the "Imperial Way" in the minds of youth, so that there arose a conflict between the Confucian teachers (*kangaku-sha*) and the national scholars (*kokugaku-sha*). Around 1870, however, the advocates of Westernized education (*yogaku-sha*) began to play a dominant role in educational affairs. It was through their initiative that the government inaugurated in 1872 a system of universal education, based partly on the French and partly on the American educational systems. The cause of Westernized education experienced a set-back around 1881 when the conservative clan oligarchy maneuvered to squeeze out the pro-modernists from the positions of influence. Immediately, Westernized text books were censured, the Confucian classics were made required reading, and the curriculum came under the rigid control of the government. Furthermore, moral teaching (*shushin*) was stressed as the most important subject in primary education. In 1886, the government tried to control the entire educational system by issuing the Primary School Ordinance, the Middle School Ordinance, the Imperial University Ordinance, and the Normal School Ordinance. Through these ordinances, the government asserted the supremacy of the state, while welcoming only those elements of Western knowledge and technology that were useful to Japan. The logical consequences of the compromise, commonly referred to as *wakon-yosai* ("Japanese spirit and Western knowledge"), was the promulgation of the Imperial Rescript on Education in 1890. In this famous document, traditional Confucian and Japanese virtues were uplifted as the foundation of education. And, "should emergency arise," so states the Rescript, "offer yourselves courageously to the State; and thus guard and maintain the prosperity of Our Imperial Throne coeval with heaven and earth."

Even such a brief survey of educational development during the early Meiji era demonstrates how the tension between the two contradictory objectives of the new regime—"renovation" that implied rejection of the past and "restoration" that implied the preservation of and return to the past— was gradually solved by nationalistic, utilitarian principles. Even then, the National scholars, Shinto leaders, Confucian teachers and other conservatives were alarmed by the popularity of

Western civilization and the rapid growth of trade and industry. It was understandable, therefore, that they were more than willing to rally behind the bureaucrats who attempted to utilize every means in order to solidify the nation around the throne. Indeed, the religious policy of the Meiji regime was forged under the combined efforts of the conservative leaders of society and of the bureaucratic oligarchy in their attempt to make legitimate the principle of "immanental theocracy" by elevating Shinto as the national religion.[12]

The policy of making Shinto the national religion, however, came under attack by the leaders of other religions as well as by secular intellectuals who felt the necessity for freedom in religious beliefs. Also, the Iwakura Mission, which was sent abroad in 1871 in an effort to revise the treaties with Western Powers, recommended that the Meiji government adopt a policy of religious freedom in order to impress foreign governments. In this situation, the government conceded that it would alter its religious policy, as far as its terminology was concerned, while preserving its substance. Concretely, the government interpreted Shinto, especially the practice of emperor worship, as a patriotic cult and not a religion. Article 28 of the Consitution, promulgated in 1889, stated explicitly that "Japanese subjects shall, within limits not prejudicial to peace and order and not antagonistic to their duties as subjects, enjoy freedom of religious belief." At the same time, the government banished religious instruction of any kind from all schools, public and private, although "moral teaching if applicable to all religions, could be given," in accordance with Ordinance 12.

The intention of the Meiji regime was clearly twofold. On the one hand, it attempted to satisfy the popular demand for religious freedom by offering a nominal guarantee for it in the Constitution. On the other hand, the government continued to allow special privileges to Shinto by creating an artificial term, "State Shinto," and calling it a cult of national morality and patriotism, applicable to all religions. This strange religious policy was nothing but an ingenious (and dangerous) attempt at superimposing "immanental theocracy" on the constitutional guarantee of religious freedom. What is often forgotten is the simple fact that, despite the "orthodox" interpretations by Shinto and government apologists to the contrary, "State Shinto" was essentially a new concocted religion of ethnocentric nationalism. To be sure, it was based on the historic tradition and framework of Shinto, but in this new development—or distortion—of Shinto, the religious autonomy of Shinto was denied. It was the political authority, rather than the religious elite, which determined the policies and activities of State Shinto. In sharp contrast to historic Shinto, which never developed doctrinal orthodoxy and thus remained tolerant of various types of beliefs and practices, State Shinto allowed no deviation from its norms.[13] The government was determined to propagate its gospel of ethnocentric nationalism through various channels, including the army, navy, and educational institutions. In the course of time, the clever manipulation of the emperor cult by the bureaucrats, with the wholehearted support of extreme nationalists, exalted the throne in the eyes of the people, while in reality the throne was deprived of its political authority and became nothing but a convenient umbrella for the despotic oligarchy in power.

"Immanental Theocracy" vs. Religions

The architects of modern Japan who imposed "immanental theocracy" in the form of State Shinto had to take into account, however, the religious aspirations of the people. While it is well nigh impossible to discuss fully the development of non-Shinto religions in the modern period of Japan, we might perhaps sketch briefly how these religious groups have encountered the problems of "immanental theocracy" and "modernity."

(a) *Sect Shinto–* It is interesting to note that the Meiji regime, recognizing the existence of religious elements within the Shinto tradition, divided Shinto into two categories, namely, "State Shinto," which was not considered a religion, and "Sect Shinto denominations which were classified as "churches" or "sects" (*kyokai* or *kyoha*). While State Shinto enjoyed the support of the government, the Sect Shinto denominations had to depend on private initiative for organization, propaganda, and support. There were thirteen such denominations that were recognized by the government during the period between 1882 and 1908. Many of these denominations developed out of the tradition of popular confraternities established by laymen during the latter part of the Tokugawa period for the purpose of worshipping certain kami in the Shinto pantheon or some aspects of nature that were considered sacred. The three most important denominations–the Kurozumi-kyo, Konko-kyo, and Tenri-kyo–had been founded by charismatic personalities. In sharp contrast to the State Shinto that was destined to be manipulated by the temporal authority, these Sect Shinto denominations, superstitious and shamanistic though they were, have continued to meet the religious needs of the masses to this day.[14]

(b) *Buddhism.–* The complex development of Japanese Buddhism in the modern period cannot be understood without taking into account a series of events and problems that threatened as well as stimulated the Buddhist tradition. Nevertheless, it is safe to state that the first phase of the Meiji era was a shocking experience for Buddhists. It is to be noted that Buddhism in Japan had always enjoyed the favor and support of the ruling class. During the Tokugawa period, Buddhism enjoyed the prerogatives of a *de facto* state religion, collaborating with the Shogunate in its civil administration and thought control. Now, suddenly, the Meiji regime rejected Buddhism in favor of Shinto, and the popular anti-Buddhist movement arose in various parts of Japan. Confronted by hitherto unknown hardships, Buddhist leaders reacted in three different ways through (i) internal, spiritual awakening, (ii) philosophical and philological endeavors, and (iii) by catering to the wishes of the ruling regime.

(i) It is noteworthy that at a time when many were lamenting the loss of the external power and prestige of Buddhism, there were Buddhist leaders who were more disquieted by the loss of Buddhism's inner spirit and religious influence. Some of the enlightened Buddhist leaders also argued in favor of the separation of religion and state and the principle of religious liberty. The influence of the spiritual awakening was also felt in the movements of lay Buddhists that developed subsequently. (ii) Side by side with the spiritual awakening, Japanese Buddhists became concerned with the need for scholarly endeavors, both in the philological and philosophical domains. Indeed, Japanese Buddhism in the modern period was greatly stimulated by its encounter with Western civilization directly or indirectly. Prior to the Meiji era, Japanese Buddhists depended solely on the Chinese edition of the Buddhist scriptures. Some modern Japanese Buddhists began to consider the importance of learning Sanskrit, Pali and Tibetan, and able Japanese students were sent to European universities for linguistic and philosophical studies. (iii) On the other hand, a great many Buddhists wanted to restore the prestige of Buddhism by wooing the ruling oligarchy, which depended on Confucian, Shinto, and other conservative leaders, that might uphold the principle of "immanental theocracy" in order to defend the nation from the "dangerous" elements of "modernity."[15] Many Buddhists took an active part in the anti-Christian movements, and advocated emperor worship. To be sure, there were some Buddhists, especially laymen, who tried to face squarely the problems of "modernity." But, in the main, Buddhists from the Meiji era to the end of World War II tended to uphold the *status quo,* and collaborated very closely with ethnocentric nationalism.[16]

Space does not permit us to discuss educational, social, and philanthropic works sponsored by Buddhists, as well as many novel movements that emerged within the Buddhist fold. Unfortunately, while Japanese Buddhism in the modern period had many able and dedicated priests and scholars, they were removed from practical ecclesiastical affairs, so that they made little impact on the total life of Buddhists.

(c) *Christianity.*—Turning to Christianity, one can readily understand that Christianity entered the modern Japanese scene as a part of Western civilization. When the edict against Christianity was lifted in 1873 by the Meiji regime, European and American missionaries, representing Greek (Russian) Orthodox, Roman Catholic, and various Protestant denominations, started vigorous evangelistic activities. There were also ardent Christians among Westerners employed by the Japanese government as teachers in government schools. Inevitably, people in Japan experienced mixed feelings of fear and fascination toward Christianity—a forbidden faith under the Tokugawa regime—which now presented itself along with Western thought and civilization. Christianity faced a series of difficult problems. Christianity was uncritically equated with Western civilization by the people in Japan as much as by many missionaries. The prestige of Christianity was undercut by other Western ideas that were also introduced to Japan, such as Darwinism, socialism, and atheism. Japanese converts to Christianity were persecuted overtly or covertly by Buddhists, Shintoists, Confucianists and others. For these and other reasons, Christianity in modern Japan did not spread very quickly, but it attracted a small group of intellectuals and "through them the ethics and ideals of Christianity had a much more profound influence on Japanese thought and life than one might assume from the fact that less than one per cent of the population became professing Christians."[17] Christian churches also initiated many kinds of social, medical, philanthropic and educational works, and contributed much to the betterment of women's status in society.[18]

The promulgation of the Imperial Rescript on Education (1890) provided anti-Christians with a convenient weapon with which to attack Christianity. In all schools, both the faculty and students were expected to pay obeisance to the Imperial Rescript. It so happened that Uchimura Kanzo, the leader of the so-called Non-Church Movement and then Lecturer at the First Junior College, refused to participate in this cult, and was dismissed from the college. This incident solidified the anti-Christian camp, which accused Christians of being unpatriotic. But the violent anti-Christian campaigns subsided after a decade or so. In the twentieth century, the real question in Japan was not "Christianity versus Buddhism," or any other religious system for that matter, but rather "religion versus non-religion." For the most part, Japanese Christians managed to adjust to the social and political climate of the nation even though their faith never completely lost its "foreignness."[19]

With the opening of the Manchurian War in 1931, the situation became tense again. In October, 1931, students of St. Sophia University, Tokyo, refused to pay homage at a Shinto shrine. Combined pressures from the ultra nationalists once again raised the issue of obeisance at the State Shinto shrine as the non-religious, patriotic duty of all Japanese. In 1936, the Congregatio de Propaganda Fide in the Vatican instructed the Papal Delegate in Japan to the effect that such an obeisance was not to be considered a religious act. In the same year, the National Christian Council of the Protestant Bodies also publicly accepted the government's interpretation of State Shinto as non-religious. In the 1930's all religious bodies were asked to send their representatives to the front to pray for Japan's victory. In 1939, the Religious Bodies Law was enforced, by which the government obtained control over all aspects of religious organizations. Buddhism and Christianity were urged to unite their respective denominations and sects. Furthermore, through the initiative of the militarist government, a Religious League, composed of Christian, Buddhist, and Sect Shinto denominations, was organized in 1941 to provide a spiritual bulwark for the nation. This unhappy situation lasted until the end of World War II.

(d) *Confucianism.* – Lastly, we must not fail to mention the important role played by Confucianism in the religious development of modern Japan, in spite of the fact that it never claimed to be a religious system. It is significant to note that Confucianism served as an intellectual bridge between the feudal and modern periods. Many of the young warriors who shaped the course of modern Japan had been grounded in Confucian learning. For example, Sakuma Shozan advocated the famous dictum: "Eastern Ethics and Western Science." He was convinced that the *li* (reason or principle) taught by Neo-Confucianism and the principle of Western science were one and the same. It was this Confucian-inspired rationale that enabled the leaders of the Meiji era to appropriate wisdom and knowledge from abroad.[20]

Meanwhile, the Meiji regime sensed the necessity of resorting to Confucian ethics as the basis of moral education, as exemplified by strong Confucian elements in the Imperial Rescript on Education. In it, the five Confucian virtues were taught as the basic moral principles of Japan, bequeathed to the people from the Imperial ancestors. Conversely, Confucian ethical principles had to be subordinated to the claims of "immanental theocracy" of the Meiji regime. Once Japanese Confucianism accepted this premise, it was easy for the Japanese Confucianists to be champions of the ethnocentric pseudo-religion based on loyalty and filial piety, justifying authoritarianism at home and expansionism abroad. Despite the lofty ethical principles of the Chinese sages, transmitted by the long tradition of Japanese Confucianism, its highest affirmation was now addressed to the throne and to the unique national polity (*kokutai*) of Japan. The historic Confucian doctrine of *wang-tao* (or *O-do* in Japanese: "way of True Kingship") was reinterpreted in terms of *ko-do* ("The Imperial Way"), and its ethical universalism was transformed into *Nihon-shugi* ("Japanese-ism").[21] Thus, Japanese Confucianists in the modern period were not concerned with the ethical issues that confronted modern Japan; they were preoccupied with the preservation of the *status quo* against the encroachment of Western influence, and more basically of the spirit of "modernity." The anti-Western theme of the Japanese Confucianists became more accentuated in the 1930's, especially after the formation of the Japanese Society for the Promotion of Confucianism (*Nihon Jukyo Senyo-kai*) in 1934. The Confucianists asserted that Japan was a unique nation that had preserved moral virtues, and that she had as her mission the extension of her moral influence to the rest of the world.[22]

In Retrospect

In a sense, the modern development of Japanese Confucianism was closely related to the development of modern Japan with all her promise and problems. The smooth transition of Japan from her feudal past to the status of a modern state would have been impossible without the guidance of the warrior intelligentsia who had learned from Confucianism that *li* (reason or principle) is universal. At the same time, it was the same Confucian-inspired rationale that gave encouragement to the strengthening of the particularity and uniqueness of the Japanese heritage. Thus modern Japan was destined to be caught in the grip of two diametrically opposed objectives envisaged by the architects of modern Japan. One of them, the re-establishment or restoration (*fukko*) of the ancient system of unity of religion and government (*saisei-itchi*) drove Japan to assert the centrality of State Shinto as the new super-religion, ironically declared to be "non-religious," over all other religious and cultural traditions. However, the second objective, namely, renovation (*ishin*), brought about the introduction, not only of technological and scientific advances, envisaged by the Meiji government, but of philosophical and religious as well as political influences of the modern West.

Caught between these two objectives, the scholars of Confucianism, as much as the leaders of Shinto and Buddhism, sided with the conservative reaction against Western influences, against novelty, and against "modernity." They provided the moral and religious fervor for the voice of the past that cried for the preservation of the particular historic experience of the Japanese without any reference to the universal historical experience of mankind. What was taken for granted by conservative Japanese leaders in the nineteenth and twentieth century was their ethnocentric belief in the sacred super-individual which was the Japanese nation itself. It was this national affirmation of the underlying religion of "immanental theocracy" that drove Japan down the dreadful and fateful path toward World War II.

FOOTNOTES

1. The Tokugawa regime controlled the activities of the court and courtiers through the so-called Ordinances for the Imperial and Courtier Families (*Kinchu narabini Kugeshu Shohatto*). The regime also regulated the activities of religious groups and institutions by means of the Ordinances for Temples (*Jiin Hatto*).

2. As early as 1615, the Shogunate issued its Ordinances for the Military Houses (*Buke Shohatto*), the thirteen general principles governing the life and activities of the *daimyo* and the warrior class.

3. While there were many poor peasants during the Tokugawa period, "the upper strata of peasants were in many respects, not least in respect to standard of life, much nearer to the middle ranks of the warrior class than to the majority of peasants." Thomas C. Smith, "The Land Tax in the Tokugawa Period," *Journal of Asian Studies,* XVIII, No. 1 (November, 1958), p. 14.

4. Robert N. Bellah, *Tokugawa Religion* (Glencoe, Ill., 1957), pp. 81-82.

5. Edwin O. Reischauer and John K. Fairbank, *East Asia: The Great Tradition* (Boston, 1958) p. 616

6. William S. Haas, *The Destiny of the Mind—East and West* (London, 1956), p. 140

7. Jean Escarra, *Le droit chinois* (Paris and Peiping, 1936), p. 17.

8. Hayashi Razan, a leading Japanese Neo-Confucian scholar and adviser to the Tokugawa Shogunate, went so far as to state: "The Way of the Gods [Shinto] is nothing but Reason (li). Nothing exists outside of Reason." See Hajime Nakamura, *The Ways of Thinking of Eastern Peoples* (Tokyo, 1960), p. 581.

9. John Whitney Hall, "The Confucion Teacher in Tokugawa Japan," *Confucianism in Action,* ed. David S. Nivison and Arthur F. Wright (Stanford, 1959), p. 292.

10. For the Charter Oath, see George B. Sansom, *The Western World and Japan* (New York, 1962), pp. 317-20.

11. Chitoshi Yanaga, *Japan Since Perry* (New York, 1949), p. 495.

12. As early as 1872, the Meiji regime divided the cultic and religious aspects of Shinto by assigning the former to the Board of Ceremonies and the latter to the Department of Religion and Education. In 1877, the Home Ministry, replacing the Department of Religion and Education, was assigned to administer religious affairs. In 1900 the Home Ministry established within itself the Bureau of Shrines and the Bureau of Religions. Three years later, the Bureau of Religions was transferred to the Department of Education, while the Bureau of Shrines remained in the Home Ministry. These offices were abolished after World War II, however.

13. For example, a learned historian, Kume Kunitake, was expelled in 1892 from the Tokyo Imperial University because of his published article to the effect that Shinto was a survival of a primitive cult.

14. For fuller account of Sect Shinto denominations, see D. C. Holton, *The National Faith of Japan* (New York, 1938), and William K. Bunce, *Religions in Japan* (Rutland, Vt. and Tokyo, 1955).

15. The most concise and reliable description of Buddhism in the Meiji era is found in Hideo Kishimoto (comp.), *Japanese Religion in the Meiji Era,* trans. John F. Howes (Tokyo, 1956), Part II, "Buddhism," pp. 101-69.

16. There were some notable exceptions. For example, in 1899, the *Shinbukkyo-doshi-kai* ("Fellowship of New Buddhists") was organized mostly by able young lay Buddhists. This group advocated such aims as the elimination of superstition, anti-clericalism, rejection of government interference in religious matters, and the promotion of learning and morality. There were even a few Buddhists in the active socialist and anarchist movements, and some who at least worked closely with members of such movements. Some outstanding Buddhist laymen were also openly critical of the government's policies during the Russo-Japanese War.

17. Edwin O. Reischauer, *Japan: Past and Present* (New York, 1946), p. 143.

18. While the general ethos of Japanese Christianity in the modern period has been "urban" and "bourgeois," many of the early socialist leaders at the turn of the century were Christians. The Christian socialists staged the anti-war movement prior to and during the Russo-Japanese War, planted the seed for the trade union movement, and organized the agrarian movement, too.

19. From time to time, when the so-called "Christian nations" in the West did something contrary to the interests of Japan, such as the passing of the Oriental Exclusion Act by the American Congress, anti-Christian sentiment flared up in Japan. By and large, however, the situation was quiet in the 1920's.

20. It is interesting to note that some Japanese Confucianists embraced Christianity through the conviction that truth must be universal.

21. Even the monogamy advocated by Christians was criticized by a noted Japanese Confucianist as incompatible with the preservation of the imperial line, for the practice of such a principle might cause the extinction of the Imperial House. Cf. Warren W. Smith, Jr., *Confucianism in Modern Japan: A Study of Conservatism in Japanese Intellectual History* (Tokyo, 1959), p. 95.

22. See *ibid.,* pp. 166-84, for Japanese policy regarding Confucianism in Korea; *ibid.,* pp. 184-99, for Japanese use of Confucianism in Manchukuo; and *ibid.,* pp. 199-223, for a similar policy in China. The use of the Confucian heritage as an ideological weapon, however, failed to rally the majority of the Chinese people around the Japanese cause.

THE "PROTESTANT ETHIC" IN JAPAN

James Allen Dator

What are the preconditions of a nation's economic development? It seems that they must include as a minimum the possession of certain levels of natural resources of material and men, the existence of institutions and technology enabling these resources to be advantageously employed and the wit, will, and chance to use them.[1] In this paper, we shall be concerned primarily with the problem of "will." That is, what values seem to support successful economic development? In considering this, we shall focus principally on Japan.

Definition and Measurement of the "Protestant Ethic"

The prototype for modernization is Western Europe and the United States, and the value system which is most frequently alleged to have provided the required human motivations and restraints is known as the "Protestant Ethic."[2] This ethic includes, among other things, the beliefs that it is a positive good for men to work, and that it is better that they do work than that they do not, that science and technology are also good things to be used for the benefit of man; that man, through the application of reason, can in significant measure control his environment; and that while a religious consciousness is important, religious or superstitious beliefs should not discourage or prevent men from doing well economically and materially in the world, but rather that religion supports—indeed, requires—such endeavors.

Many attempts have been made, following Weber, to show that it was such beliefs in the teachings of Calvin, Luther, and their successors, in contrast to the opposite beliefs in medieval and post-Reformation Catholicism, that provided the ethical support for the economic development of the West.[3] Needless to say, such a thesis could hardly be accepted without challenge, and there have been attempts at refutation.[4]

We are not here concerned with which exegesis of Protestant and Catholic thought is correct, but rather with the problem of demonstrating the existence of links between the statements of religious leaders and the values of ordinary eighteenth and nineteenth century Westerners—a problem endemic to all historical analysis attempting to describe popular values.[5] While meaningful correlations may be shown between predominantly Catholic and Protestant areas and their respective levels of economic development, or while the proportionate number of successful Protestant and Catholic businessmen may be shown to differ significantly,[6] without knowing the people's attitudes towards work, how can we be reasonably assured

Dator — *From The Journal of Developing Areas, Vol. I, (October, 1966), pp. 23-40. Reprinted by permission.

that the observed differences were due to the "Protestant Ethic" and not to some intervening variable?

One method would be to test for differences in values and performance between Protestants and Catholics at the present time. If the hypothesized differences between these groups are evident after controlling for other factors, then there is some reason to assume that the variations existed earlier, and that the observed performance differential is in significant measure due to the dissimilar value structures. Gerhard Lenski performed just such a test on a sample of Detroit residents in 1958 and concluded that the predicted variation did exist, although there was a marked disparity among Protestants themselves on the basis of race, and within both Protestants and Catholics according to social class.[7] Nonetheless, there was a "religious factor" which could not be eliminated.

Lenski's report evoked considerable protest, both because he did not find the significant and consistent value differences between Protestant denominations which many people thought existed, and because the data did show the differences in values between Protestants and Catholics which some observers would prefer to think nonexistent. But even if these disparities between Catholics and Protestants can be shown to exist, how can we be sure that this is an essentially Protestant and Catholic divergency, and not one based upon other variables? One approach would be to determine whether an analogue to the "Protestant Ethic" exists.

An impressive amount of material has been produced which seems to show that there is an important relationship between the values of the pre-industrial and transitional period of a country on the one hand and its successful and relatively smooth economic development on the other. Conversely, studies have shown that certain types of ethical and/or religious beliefs seem to hinder economic development and political modernization. Generally, these studies indicate that values similar to those of the "Protestant Ethic"—the positive value of hard work, science, and technology, coupled with a this-worldly, nonsuperstitious eschatology—coincide with and apparently are conducive to economic development, while antimaterialistic, otherworldly, and superstitious traditions and religious beliefs hinder economic development.

The non-Western country where the "Protestant Ethic" theory has been most successfully applied, and where economic development is most spectacular, is Japan. Robert Bellah, in his study of Tokugawa society, asked, "Was there a functional analogue to the 'Protestant Ethic' in Japanese religion?"[8] He concluded that there was—as manifested in the prevailing Confucianist teachings of the Tokugawa period. Other scholars have come to similar conclusions.

But the late Tokugawa period and the Meiji Restoration took place more than a hundred years ago, and while a "Protestant Ethic" analogue may have existed then in the form of neo-Confucianism, what is the situation now? Confucian-based morals were stricken from Japanese public school texts by the Occupation, and there has been no moral education in the public schools at all until an allegedly liberal-democratic ethical curriculum was introduced a few years ago. Yet the Japanese economy is continuing to expand, save for occasional fluctuations, at an exceedingly high rate. Are, then, the critics of the "Protestant Ethic Analogy" correct? Can the initiative and persistence of economic development in Japan (and elsewhere) be explained by purely institutional arrangements, without special reference to the Japanese value structure? Or do these or similar values remain in Japanese society, even if they are not consciously taught as such?

Evidence of a "Protestant Ethic" in
Contemporary Japan

To help determine the answer to this last question, we included items similar to those of Lenski's Detroit study in a survey conducted on a random sample of nearly 1,000 (980 completed interviews) citizens of the twenty-three wards of Tokyo in 1965. The analysis of the replies, in conjunction with other survey data, should enable us to answer this question with more precision.

We first needed to know something about the religious affiliations and beliefs of our respondents (actually, one major purpose of our survey was to learn more about the religious beliefs and activities of Tokyo citizens). A more complete report of this survey is in preparation, but to mention briefly a few points relevant to this paper, as shown in Table 1: Eighty-two per cent of the Tokyo respondents had no religion; of the nearly 18 per cent who did, most were either members of the Soka Gakkai (5 per cent of the sample and 26 per cent of those who had a religion)[9] or Christians (3 per cent of the sample and 19 per cent of those with a religion). No other single religious sect accounted for more than 10 per cent of the total Tokyo sample. Shinto were only 0.6 per cent of the total, or 3.5 per cent of those with some religion. All Buddhist sects accounted for 6 per cent of the population or 33 per cent of those with religious affiliation. Three per cent of the population and 19 per cent of the religious were members of one of the new religions, such as Rissho Kosei Kai or Tenrikyo.

TABLE 1
RELIGIOUS AFFILIATION OF TOKYO CITIZENS, 1965
AND JAPANESE CITIZENS, 1958

Percentage Distribution

Religion	Toyko* Total sample	Toyko* Those with a religion	Kanto Area Total sample	Kanto Area Those with a religion	Nation Total sample	Nation Those with a religion
None	82.0	. . . .	77.0	. . . .	65.0	. . . .
Shinto	0.6	3.5	3.0	13.0	. 3.0	9.0
Buddhist	6.0	33.0	12.0	53.0	24.0	68.0
Soka Gakkai . . .	5.0	26.0	. . . .	. . . .	. . . .	. . . .
Christian	3.0	19.0	1.0	4.0	1.0	3.0
Other	3.0	19.0	7.0	30.0	7.0	20.0
N	(980)	(172)	(230)	(53)	(920)	(320)

*Variation from 100 per cent due to rounding of figures

Source of Tokyo percentages is this survey; source of Kanto area and national percentages is Joichi Suetsuna, *et al., Nibonjin no kokuminsei* (Tokyo: Shiseido, 1961), p. 181.

As can be seen in Table 2, concerning belief in God, 16 per cent of the total Tokyo sample were not sure, 50 per cent said "no," while only 34 per cent said they did believe in the existence of God (Kami, Hotoke, Law of the Universe, or the like). Of the 34 per cent who said they did believe in God, only 35 per cent indicated that they believed in life after death, while 51 per cent said they did not. Thus, apparently 88 per cent of our total respondents did not believe in life after death.

TABLE 2
BELIEF IN GOD AND BELIEF IN LIFE AFTER DEATH
TOKYO CITIZENS, 1965, AND JAPANESE CITIZENS, 1958

Percentage Distribution

		Tokyo	Nation
Belief	Total sample	Those with belief in God	Total sample
Belief in God	34	. . . .	. . . .
Belief in life after death	(12)	35	20
No belief in life after death . . .	(17)	51	59
Uncertain about life after death . .	(5)	14	21
No belief in God	50	. . . .	. . . .
Uncertain belief in God	16	. . . .	. . . .
N	(980)	(329)	(920)

Source for Tokyo percentages is this survey; source for national percentages is Suetsuna, *op. cit.*, English resume, p. 10.

The Research Committee of Japanese National Character of the Institute of Statistical Mathematics in a national survey in 1958 (see Table 1) found that 65 per cent of the Japanese population said they had no religious affiliation. Of the 35 per cent who did, 9 per cent were Shinto, 68 per cent Buddhist, 3 per cent Christian, 7 per cent other, and 13 per cent no established sect. In the Kanto area of Japan (which includes Tokyo), only 23 per cent had religious affiliations. Fifty-three per cent of these were Buddhist, 13 per cent Shinto, 4 per cent Christian, and 30 per cent other. Presumably, many in the "other" category were members of the Soka Gakkai. The survey also found that 59 per cent of the National respondents did not believe in life after death.

Of considerable significance to our study were the answers to a National Character survey question asked of persons who had no religion: "Without reference to any of the established religions, would you say that a 'religious spirit' is important, or not?" Seventy-two per cent said that it was important. Finally, 65 per cent of the total sample agreed that, "on the whole, people don't take religion seriously enough."[10] Thus, while most Japanese are not members of any religious group, they are not opposed to religion, and indeed think it is of considerable importance—as we shall see, equally as important as science.

Turning now to the specifically "Protestant Ethic" questions, we first asked our Tokyo respondents, "If you were free to choose, which one of the following sorts of persons would best describe the type you would like to be?" We then showed them a card on which were written five choices. The replies are shown in Table 3.

TABLE 3
"WHAT TYPE OF PERSON WOULD YOU LIKE TO BE?"
TOKYO CITIZENS, 1965

Per Cent

A hard worker 34
A person who has no worries 24
A person who is friendly 20
A person who does things better than others do 11
A person who is very lucky 9
Other 2
N . . . . (980)

The most frequent choice, chosen by 34 per cent, was "a hard worker," while 24 per cent chose "a person who has no worries." Twenty per cent wanted to be "friendly," and 11 per cent wanted to be able to "do things better than other persons." Only 9 per cent said that they wanted to be "a person who is very lucky."

These answers are generally in keeping with the "Protestant Ethic" hypothesis inasmuch as more people chose "hard worker" and fewer chose "lucky" (the "superstitious" response).[11] However, it is of some significance to the hypothesis—and to the nature of Japanese society—that no more than 11 per cent wanted to be able to do things better than others, while about 20 percent of the respondents wanted either to have no worries or to be friendly. The replies suggest that while the citizens of Tokyo wish to be considered hard workers, they do not wish to be so at the expense of others, or of good human relations.[12]

The introduction of controls, through cross-tabulation with other demographic characteristics, reveals interesting differences within Japanese society, which however, tend to strengthen rather than weaken the "Protestant Ethic" hypothesis.[13] "Hard worker" preferences, though the most frequent choice of almost all groups, were found to be strongest among both the highest and lowest educational groups; among persons in professional, managerial, and artisan occupations; among the higher income and older age brackets; for widows; and for members of the Social Democratic political party (a small, moderate, socialist party). It was least chosen by younger persons, by Soka Gakkai and Komei-to members, and by supporters of the Japan Communist Party.

"Do better" was preferred more often by persons with higher education, by Christians, and by Soka Gakkai and Komei-to members. It was least preferred by the less well-educated, by persons with no political party preference, persons in agricultural occupations, and by persons of any religious affiliation (in comparison with persons of no religion), except for the noted exceptions of Christians and Soka Gakkai members.

Persons who wanted to be "friendly" were younger, and of lower education, income, and occupation; persons of higher education, income, and occupation, as well as older persons, Christians, Komei-to supporters, and Social Democrats chose that answer less frequently.

Young persons, members of the Nichiren Sect, and of the Soka Gakkai and Komei-to, and those of no political party affiliation chose "lucky" more frequently, while Social Democrats and Communists chose it less frequently.

Roughly 25 per cent of all groups chose "no worries," although those in agricultural occupations, and both Social Democrats and Communists chose it least.

Thus we see that while the citizens of Tokyo generally are inclined to desire to be "friendly hard workers with no worries,"[14] and to be little concerned with doing things better than others, groups in the higher socio-economic status categories tend to combine "hard work" with "doing things better," while those of the lower socio-economic status couple "hard work" with being "friendly" and "having no worries."

Every five years since 1953 the Japanese National Character survey has asked a national sample a fixed-response question concerning what types of persons they would like to be. The alternatives which they presented to their respondents are sufficiently different from ours to prevent comparisons without a greater elaboration than is deemed appropriate for this paper, but essentialiy, the responses to the National Character survey indicate that an overwhelming and increasing number of Japanese prefer to live ordinary lives, on a day-by-day basis (50 per cent chose this) without concern for either money or fame (25 per cent said they *were* so concerned) or for the welfare of society (chosen by 25 per cent). This seems in accord with our interpretation that for most groups of Tokyo citizens, "work hard" is coupled with friendliness and "no worries" while only for the upper socio-economic strata is it combined with "doing better than others."

If this interpretation is correct, it might be suggested that one reason for Japanese economic development, then, is that most groups, while desiring to work hard, do not wish to do so at the expense of friendly human relations. Thus, the pattern-maintenance sector of the Japanese social system is not disturbed by changes in the goal-attainment or adaptive sectors. Moreover, the existence of an "entrepreneurial spirit," as expressed in the desire to work hard *and* do better than others, is appropriately found in that element of the population—especially those of higher education—which would be best equipped to do so.[15]

But what do our repondents think about work? Specifically, what characteristics do they prefer in jobs? We asked our respondents to choose whether they would prefer high income, no danger of being fired, short working days with plenty of free time, chances for advancement, or important work that gives a feeling of accomplishment.

The replies indicated in Table 4 are another strong indication of the existence of a "Protestant Ethic" analogue. Forty-five per cent of our respondents wanted "important work" and 28 per cent desired "high income." Lenski designed the "important work" response to tap the "Protestant Ethic" preference in Weber's original meaning of the term, while "high income" was meant to reflect the current popular understanding of it. "Lots of free time," intended to be the opposite of the "Protestant Ethic" response, was the least frequently chosen of all—by only 7 per cent of our Tokyo respondents—while the other two choices were made only slightly more frequently at 9 per cent each. In short, "Protestant Ethic" responses accounted for 73 per cent of the total.[16]

TABLE 4
"WHAT CHARACTERISTIC WOULD YOU PREFER IN A JOB?"
TOKYO CITIZENS, 1965

	Per Cent
Important work	45
High income	28
Chance for advancement	9
No danger of being fired	8
Lots of free time	7
Other	3
N	(980)

Cross tabulation reveals a pattern which is an even more striking confirmation of the "Protestant Ethic" hypothesis. First of all, "important work" was chosen more frequently by men, older people, the better educated and persons in higher income brackets, by persons in professional and managerial occupations, by persons who believed in God, and by Christians, Social Democrats, and Communists. It was less frequently chosen by women, younger people, the less educated, laborers, persons who did not believe in God and/or who had no religious affiliations, and by members of the Soka Gakkai.

"High income" was the more frequent choice of younger respondents and persons of lower income, by laborers and artisans, by persons who did not believe in God, and by members of the Soka Gakkai. It was chosen less frequently by older persons, people in professional and managerial occupations, by people who believe in God, and by Christians.

Persons of lower income and education, females, and laborers more frequently indicated that they preferred "no danger of being fired," while persons of higher education, professional persons and managers, and Soka Gakkai-Komei-to members chose it less frequently. "Chance for advancement" was highest for office workers and lowest for laborers, while "free time" was highest for laborers and lowest for artisans.

By adding together the "Protestant Ethic" responses, "important work" and "high income," and comparing the result with the unit composed of "advancement," "no danger of being fired," and "free time," we discovered that the "Protestant Ethic" is more frequently found among males than females; the higher educated than the lower educated; persons in professional, managerial, and artisan occupations than among office, small shop, or skilled or unskilled labor occupations; and among Liberal Democrats, Democratic Socialists, and Komei-to members than among Socialists. There was no consistent religious difference. These findings are consistent both with the earlier replies concerning "type of person" (Table 3) and with the "Protestant Ethic" as it is said to apply in Western countries.

The third and final question directly concerning the "Protestant Ethic" (also derived from Lenski's questionnaire, though applied somewhat differently) asked respondents whether, if they had a choice, they would prefer to work, or, if they could live well otherwise, they would prefer not working. We asked them to choose from among four degrees of intensity; definitely feel happier working; probably feel happier working; probably feel happier not working; definitely feel happier not working.

The replies, as summarized in Table 5, are truly revealing. Sixty-five per cent said they would definitely prefer to work, and 27 per cent said they would probably prefer to work, while the "non-working" alternatives received only 4 per cent each. In short, 92 per cent of the respondents preferred to work, and only 8 per cent preferred not working even if they could live in ease.

Since more than 80 per cent of all groups preferred working to not working, perhaps cross tabulations are not especially meaningful. But because the pattern of those groups which do differ significantly (chi square $>.05$) is generally in keeping with our other findings, it is worthwhile to note that groups especially high in the "definitely prefer to work" category were older, less well educated, believed in God, were married or widowed, and in managerial, shop, laboring, or artisan occupations. Younger, better educated persons, those who did not believe in God, who were single or divorced, and in professional or white collar occupations were significantly lower in the "definitely prefer to work" category.

TABLE 5
"WOULD YOU PREFER WORKING, OR NOT?"
TOKYO CITIZENS, 1965

Per Cent

Definitely prefer working	65
Probably prefer working	27
Probably prefer not working	4
Definitely prefer not working	4
N	(980)

David W. Plath cites a University of Tokyo study of the twenty-three wards of Tokyo in 1959 which sought preferences to six statements about work.[17] Thirty-nine per cent of the respondents agreed that, "Work is work and play is play. Work diligently during set working hours, and when released from work, forget it and play." Twenty-one per cent chose, "I like to work, but I need to have enough time for the rest and relaxation essential to build up my energy for working." Nineteen per cent said, "Since doing work is a human duty, I must work to the limit of my time," and 12 per cent agreed that, "Work is a form of enjoyment. I haven't especially thought about wanting to be emancipated from work in order to play."

Such a small number of people agreed with the other two alternatives ("Work is a means of subsistence. I try to do a suitable amount of it, then as much as possible enjoy myself playing," and "There is no point in making drudgery of human life. I think it is good to do what you yourself want to do.") that they were lumped together with the "Don't know" category to equal only 9 per cent. This pattern of response corresponds to that of our data. Cross tabulations by age and occupation were also similar to ours: "Work is a fulltime duty," and "work is a form of enjoyment" (positive "Protestant Ethic" responses) were far more frequent among older persons and "independent operators," while the mixed "Protestant Ethic" response of "work is work, and play is play" and "rest in order to work" were more frequent among younger persons, white collar workers, and laborers. The distribution of the few negative "Protestant Ethic" responses was obscured by their inclusion with the "Don't know" category.

Possible Sources of the "Protestant Ethic"
in Contemporary Japan

What then is our conclusion? Is there a Japanese analogue to the "Protestant Ethic" which would help account for Japan's successful economic development?[18] Then answer would plainly seem to be "yes." Then what is the source of the analogue? This is a much more difficult question to answer by the measures available to us. Because of the pattern of responses in the cross tabulations, it is certain that the answer does not lie in any of the organized forms of religious expression.[19]

Then could the explanation lie in the content of pre-war formal education? This very well may be the case. The respondents to our survey were all twenty years of age or older. Thus, many of them should have finished their primary school education before the end of the Second World War.

The pre-war curriculum, especially that of the specifically ethical classes, and the Imperial Rescript on Education, which was reverentially read each day, were strongly duty-achievement oriented, stressing the values of diligence, hard work, and self-sacrifice for the welfare of the nation. While many of these appeals in the texts became increasingly chauvinistic in the period immediately before the war, one reviewer of an annotated translation of the basic elementary school ethics textbook,[20] although condemning the nationalistic tone of the texts, noted that the stories were

far from bloodthirsty. Much of their content is wholesome in American eyes, and most of us would like to have our children put some of these lessons into practice .... To American ears, most of the lessons are "corny," the repetitious moralizing that specifies the exact lessons that children should take to heart .... [21]

As noted above, ethics classes and texts were abolished after the war, and only recently has a "democratic" ethical curriculum been introduced. But the government is plainly interested in stressing moral education even more. Consider the late Prime Minister Ikeda's proposals concerning *"bitotsukuri"* (literally, "people-making"), and the report, "Kitai Sareru Ningenzo" ("The Image of Man"), of the government's *Chuo Kyoiku Shingikai no Dai 19 Tokubetsu linkai,* December 1964.

It is problematic how different the pattern of "Protestant Ethic" values is now in comparison to what it was before the war. The National Character survey item cited above, concerning the types of persons respondents would like to be, has shown that since the war there have been significant shifts away from such "Protestant Ethic" responses as "resist evil and live a pure and just life" (per cent of agreement: 1953–29 per cent; 1958–23 per cent; 1963–18 per cent), "work for society" (1953–10 per cent; 1958–6 per cent; 1963–6 per cent), and "study hard and make a name for yourself" (1953–6 per cent, 1958–3 per cent; 1963–4 per cent), while preference for "don't think of money or fame, but just live the life that suits your own tastes" has steadily increased (1953–21 per cent; 1958–27 per cent; 1963–30 per cent).

Two not strictly comparable surveys conducted by the Ministry of Education for conscription purposes showed that 24 per cent of the twenty-year-olds in 1931 and 30 per cent in 1940 wanted to work for society, while 32 per cent in 1931 and 41 per cent in 1940 wanted to live pure and just lives and resist evil. Only 12 per cent in 1931 and 5 per cent in 1940 said that they simply wanted to live any life that suited them. Although the sampling method and wording of the items render the pre-war surveys somewhat suspect, nonetheless, there does seem to be a striking change.

Moreover, analysis of the National Character responses for 1963 for people who were twenty years old in 1931 and 1940 respectively, shows a sharp regression in their preferences from those held before the war and towards those of the majority in 1963. Still, these older people were, by this measure, more "Protestant Ethic" oriented in 1963 than was the sample as a whole. This is in keeping with findings of our survey, and suggests not only that the values of young Japanese are different from those of their elders, but also that there has been some shift of values among the older generation as well.[22]

It is suggested then, that the most satisfactory explanation for the persistence of these attitudes is that "Protestant Ethic" values are a central part of the traditional childhood and peer group socialization process. Available evidence indicates that the values of diligence, hard work, perseverance, and mutual responsibility have long been stressed by these socializing agencies.

Moreover, the Japanese themselves quite clearly perceive these as essential values. The National Character survey asked its two most recent samples to choose from a list the characteristics which they thought best described the strong points of the Japanese people. The most popular was *kinben* ("diligent" or "hard working"), followed closely by "tenacious," and by "courteous" and "kindly." At the bottom of the list, with less than 10 per cent each, were "rational" and "original." The 1963 sample was asked what they thought were the weak points of the Japanese. "Short-tempered" was mentioned by 52 per cent of the respondents, followed by "changeable" (49 per cent), and "insular" (42 per cent). Few Japanese agreed that "miserly," "rude," or "cruel" were national characteristics.

Thus, in addition to indicating that the "Protestant Ethic" is probably not a uniquely "Protestant" ethic, our data also suggest that the strong cultural values of diligence, hard work, and the rest need not derive from anxiety or a sense of sin in the face of a transcendental referent. Both the Japanese evidence and that of small group theory in the West indicate that family and peers are quite sufficient to this end.

Some Implications for Developing Areas

What then can the Japanese experience suggest to the currently developing countries? It has frequently been pointed out that the Western model of economic development is not the only one, and that the Soviet, Red Chinese, or Japanese model might be even more appropriate.

We do not intend to go into all of the factors in these non-Western models which seem conducive to economic development. But two comments do seem to be appropriate. First, as Niles Hansen has recently suggested, there was probably a "Protestant Ethic" analogue in all of these advanced non-Western countries. We would agree with him that "religious or ideological motivation is one of the fundamental prerequisites for economic development within a given system."[23]

Second, also as Hansen and others suggest, and as the Japanese experience makes especially clear, it is not necessary for economic development to overturn traditional values. Rather, economic development seems to have been most successful precisely where the existing values have been consciously appealed to and utilized. Thus it should not be assumed that Western (especially American) personality types, human relations, or social institutions are the only proper measure by which to gauge or guide the developing countries. Economic development and modernization can occur independently of the adoption of these Western "superstructures." Perhaps many of the strains which do occur in developing countries (and which occurred both in the USSR and Japan, though in different forms) are in part due to Western technical advisors or Westernized natives who attempt to introduce social values and institutions which are extraneous and indeed positively harmful to the process of stable economic development.[24] Japan, from the Meiji Restoration has been in favor of "Western techniques and Eastern morals."[25] Its utilization of Western technical advisors, while considerable in the initial stages, has always been (and still is) highly selective and protective of Japanese core values, Western tendencies to overstate the Western contribution notwithstanding.

Still, it does seem that we must distinguish between values which appear conducive to economic development and those which do not. Is this not the whole point of discussing the "Protestant Ethic"?

There is considerable force behind the contention that some measure of economic advancement can be achieved simply by skillfully utilizing whatever values exist. For example, it has been shown that is some Asian countries, sacred acacia trees and blessed plantings do better than those which are not because, being sanctified, they are better cared for. Hence, "superstitions" can be harnessed in the interest of "rational" economic goals. Moreover, it has frequently been pointed out that the "acquisitive urge" exists in all societies, even the most primitive.

Without question, then, *something* can be done towards economic development by selective manipulation of existing values and institutions. Hopefully, this will eventually snowball into full-scale social support of economic development without tearing the fabric of society in the process. But this is by no means certain.

The forces underlying the "flow" of societies from traditional through transitional to modern (if, indeed, there is such a movement) are still only dimly perceived. But one very helpful analysis, utilizing Talcott Parsons' familiar paradigm of a social system, suggests that primitive or traditional societies are centered in the pattern-maintenance and integrative sectors, modern societies in the goal-attainment and adaptive sectors, while transitional societies are between the two layers.[26] We would like to adopt this suggestion, and by connecting it to Bellah's implication that Japan in the late Tokugawa period was already in the goal-attainment and adaptive stage,[27] suggest that this might be why Japan was able to modernize so rapidly and successfully.

To put it tersely, Japan had a "modernized" society before the Meiji Restoration. That it was technologically and industrially backward is obvious. But the point is that it possessed a total social system which was not only highly developed in its basic pattern-maintenance and integrative sectors, but was also—except for the lack of Western technology—even advanced in institutions and attitudes appropriate for "modern" goal-attainment and adaptive sectors. For this reason, Western technology was instantly comprehended when it was introduced, and Japanese technicians were able to replace Western advisors in a remarkably short time. Through all of this, the basic values and institutions of Japanese society (in the sense of normative behavior, not formal structures) were not and did not need to be drastically altered (although they did undergo change) because, though *patterned* differently from those of the West, traditional Japanese values and institutions were essentially quite compatible with Western technology.

This analysis is extremely brief and superficial, but if it is correct in its basic premise, it does suggest that the modernization of other Asian and African societies is not, as much of our writing on development seems to indicate, merely a linear function of the introduction either of Western technology and institutions or of Western values—or even of both. Finally, while perhaps change in the basic societal processes can be speeded up by the judicious utilization of whatever institutions and values persist, economic development is going to be far more difficult and delayed for many societies then we may care to admit. That is, if the total social system is not already at an appropriately high level, peaceful development may very well be impossible for the present.

FOOTNOTES

1. On the identification of prerequisites for, and definition of, economic development and political modernization, see Alexander Gerschenkron, *Economic Backwardness in Historical Perspective* (Cambridge: Harvard University Press, 1962); the Princeton University Press series on political development; and Karl von Vorys (ed.), *New Nations: The Problem of Political Development* in *The Annals of the American Academy of Political and Social Science* (hereafter *The Annals*), CCCLVIII (March, 1965).

2. The "Protestant Ethic" concept, of course, derives mainly from Max Weber, *The Protestant Ethic and the Spirit of Capitalism* (New York: Scribner, 1958).

3. The list of books is long, but R. H. Tawney, *Religion and the Rise of Capitalism* (New York: Harcourt, 1926), probably remains the most influential.

4. See, e.g., Kurt Samuelsson, *Religion and Economic Action* (New York: Basic Books, 1961), and Hubert Luethy, "Once Again: Capitalism and Calvinism," *Encounter*, XXII (January, 1964), 26-38.

5. There is some ambiguity here. Does the "Protestant Ethic" assume that these values are held only by the successful entrepreneurs, or is it a popularly-held cultural ethic? We shall use the term as applying to a value pattern widely held by the population as a whole, although

perhaps found more intensely in certain groups.

6. See, for example, chap. xiii on England in Everett E. Hagen, *On the Theory of Social Change* (Homewood, Ill.: Dorsey Press, 1962).

7. Gerhard Lenski, *The Religious Factor* (New York: Doubleday Anchor Books, 1963). See also Albert J. Mayer and Harry Sharp, "Religious Preference and Worldly Success," *American Sociological Review,* XXVII (April, 1962), 218-27.

8. Robert Bellah, *Tokugawa Religion, The Values of Pre-Industrial Japan* (Glencoe, Ill.: Free Press, 1957), pp. 2-3. Bellah has expressed second thoughts about some of his earlier views in "Reflections on the Protestant Ethic Analogy in Asia," *Journal of Social Issues,* XIX (January, 1963) 52-60, cited previously.

9. The Soka Gakkai is a lay organization of the Nichiren Sho Shu sect of Japanese Buddhism. It is the largest religious group in Japan and is active in many fields. The Komei-to, mentioned later in this paper, is essentially the political wing of the Soka Gakkai. It is becoming increasingly important in Japanese politics.

10. For the National Character data concerning religion, see Joichi Suetsuna *et al., Nihonjin no Kokuminsei* ["Japanese National Character"] (Tokyo: Shiseido, 1961), pp. 181-93 and the English resume, pp. 9-10. Robert Dore found similar patterns in his study of a ward of Tokyo in 1951; see Robert P. Dore, *City Life in Japan* (London: Routledge and Kegan Paul, 1958), Part V.

11. The National Character study included in its nationwide survey a question about the relation between religion and science. Ten per cent of the respondents agreed with the statement, "Religion cannot save man. The only thing that can save man is the progress of science." However, 63 per cent said, "In order to save man, it is necessary for the progress of science and the power of religion always to go hand in hand." Nine per cent thought that only religion could save man, and 8 per cent said that man could be saved neither by science nor by religion (Suetsuna, *op. cit.,* English resume, p. 10). This response is in keeping with our previous summary of the "Protestant Ethic": the belief that religion and science are not incompatible; especially that religion is not superior to science.

12. Similar conclusions were reached about workers in some large Japanese industries. See Arthur M. Whitehill and Shin-ichi Takezawa, *Cultural Values in Management-Worker Relations* (Chapel Hill, N.C.: School of Business Administration, University of North Carolina Press, 1961), and Arthur M. Whitehill, "Cultural Values and Employee Attitudes," *Journal of Applied Psychology,* XLVIII (February, 1964), 69-72. See also James G. Abegglen, *The Japanese Factory* (Glencoe, Ill.: Free Press, 1958), and James G. Abegglen, "Subordination and Autonomy Attitudes of Japanese Workers," *American Journal of Sociology,* LXIII (September, 1957), 181-89.

13. All differences were statistically significant at the .05 level or above by the chi-square test.

14. In 1954, 48 per cent of a sample of Tokyo citizens replied that "hard work," rather than talent, academic record, skill at making money, or family connections, respectively, was necessary in order to become famous *(erai).* Hirotatsu Fujiwara, *Gendai Nihon no Seiji Ishiki* ["Contemporary Japanese Political Consciousness"] (Tokyo: Sobunsha, 1958), Appendix, p. 29, q. 46.

15. We will not try to determine here whether it is those with motivation to do better who receive a higher education or whether higher education encourages or produces the desire to get ahead, but it should be noted that education was the most uniform and consistent single measure of "Protestant Ethic" orientation.

16. It should be pointed out that "Don't know" and refusals on all the questions discussed in this report amounted to only about two per cent. This is extemely low, especially in view of the reported tendency of Japanese to have very high "Don't know" responses on surveys. We generally found that "Don't know's" were high only on the more difficult "public policy" and information questions, and on certain "embarrassing" personality scale items.

17. David W. Plath, *The After Hours* (Berkeley: University of California Press, 1964) pp. 92 ff.

18. Jerome B. Cohen, *Japan's Postwar Economy* (Bloomington, Ind.: Indiana University

Press, 1958), p. 23, says: "Finally, perhaps the most basic factor in Japan's recovery was the attitude and knowhow of the Japanese people. Hardworking, industrious, firm in their determination to overcome poverty and devastation, they were familiar with industrial processes and with the techniques of foreign trade. Japan is not an underdeveloped country. The Japanese know well how to produce goods and penetrate foreign markets. They did not need to learn these basic concepts from the ground up, as was true in much of the rest of Asia in the postwar decade."

19. Not only did 82 per cent of our respondents have no religion, but one-third were unable to identify what the traditional religions of their families *(ie)* were, 77 per cent said their fathers had no religions, 71 per cent said their mothers had no religions, and 88 per cent of those married or widowed said their spouses had no religious affiliations. Indeed, this very non-religious nature in so many Japanese may be a motivation behind their hard work; especially since 88 per cent of our respondents did not believe in life after death and thus can hope neither for a heavenly reward (or punishment) nor for a second earthly chance.

20. Robert K. Hall (ed.), *Shushin: The Ethics of a Defeated Nation* (New York: Columbia University Press, 1949).

21. Douglas Haring's review of Hall, *op. cit.,* in *Far Eastern Quarterly,* X (November, 1950), 106.

22. Many observers, both Japanese and Western, feel that Japanese social institutions and values generally have altered sharply since the war, mainly as a result of Occupation policies. It is extremely difficult to measure such change precisely, but it would seem that while there have been changes, they are far outnumbered by the continuities. More accurately, most basic values and behavior patterns seem to have persisted or changed endogenously in spite of extensive exogenous alterations of formal structures.

The doubts and self-criticisms expressed by many Japanese during the post-war period, based upon the fact of defeat and an idealized understanding of Western pragmatism ("rationality" and "logic"), have nearly ended–or are confined to the "Uncle Tanaka's" of the immediate post-war generation. These doubts have been replaced by a self-confident pride in Japanese traditions, which, though often not really traditional ways of doing things, are "Japanese" and different from those of the rest of Asia and the West.

23. Hansen, *op. cit.,* p. 474.

24. Ayal, *op. cit., passim,* points out that we are so captivated by our "individualistic" ideology that we assume that individualism and privatization are normative for economic development. The existence of an even more "rugged individualism" in Thailand, however is suggested as being a major factor in that country's relative economic backwardness, while the "group-centeredness" of the Japanese is said to contribute to that country's economic advance. Apter, Gould, Hansen, cited above, and Robert Bellah, "Religious Aspects of Modernization in Turkey and Japan," *American Journal of Sociology,* LXIV (July, 1958), 1-5, and Thomas C. Smith, "Old Values and New Techniques in the Modernization of Japan," *Far Eastern Quarterly,* XIV (May, 1955), 355-63, indicate that in some cases existing values and institutions, even though quite different from those of the West, may more successfully be used to further economic development.

25. But see John Bennett and Robert McKnight, "Approaches of the Japanese Innovator to Cultural and Technological Change" in *The Annals,* CCCV (May, 1956), 101-13.

26. Bert F. Hoselitz, "Levels of Economic Performance and Bureaucratic Structures," *Bureaucracy and Political Development,* ed. Joseph La Palombara (Princeton, N.J.: Princeton University Press, 1963).

27. Bellah, *Tokugawa Religion,* chaps. I and II.

A CASE STUDY IN CULTURAL
AND EDUCATIONAL MOBILITY:
JAPAN AND THE PROTESTANT ETHIC

Reinhard Bendix

"Cultural-educational mobility and development"—the topic assigned to me in this Conference—suggests that education and mobility are positively related to economic development. This positive relationship exists only, I believe, where the value of economic development is already accepted as a *sine qua non* of individual and national advance. It is true that this ideology is widespread in the many countries which since World War II have been transformed by a turn of phrase (and often by little else), from "underdeveloped" into "developing" nations. But in what general sense is it meaningful to link culture with mobility and economic development? To speak of development is to imply that at one time a given society was not developing or was "underdeveloped." With regard to that contrast culture typically maintains the established social structure; education helps to transmit and uphold the received tradition. Accordingly, the extensive literature on development contrasts—at least implicitly—tradition and modernity, and much of it is focused on the problem of how a non-industrial society can give rise to an industrial society. Each type has cultural and educational attributes of its own. It is, therefore, necessary to distinguish between the cultural *preconditions* of development and the cultural and educational *changes* that occur once development is under way, difficult as it may be to pinpoint this distinction. In the present case the question will be how cultural patterns supporting tradition can give rise to cultural patterns supporting modernity. I am concerned with the cultural preconditions of development.

Japan, in contrast with England and France, experienced rapid economic growth, especially in the industrial sector, only after 1868. She borrowed heavily from abroad in a conscious effort to benefit from the advanced technology and the political institutions of other countries. Today, she is among the most industrialized nations of the world. My principal emphasis will not be on economic development itself, but on its "cultural-educational" preconditions. Since the classic study in this field is still Max Weber's famous essay on *The Protestant Ethic and the Spirit of Capitalism,* I shall begin with a brief, critical discussion of that essay. A comparative consideration of that essay and the Japanese development yields a perspective that illuminates "cultural-educational mobility" as a condition of development in both cases.

Max Weber's study of this problem in his *Protestant Ethic and the Spirit of Capitalism* begins with the observation that societies develop differentially and that

Bendix — *Reprinted from Neil J. Smelser and Seymour Martin Lipset, editors, *Social Structure and Mobility in Economic Development* (Chicago: Aldine Publishing Company, 1966); copyright 1966 by Neil J. Smelser and Seymour Martin Lipset.

"capitalism" originated in certain areas of Western Europe. Within these areas the traditional Catholic approach to economic pursuits tended in practice to condone what it could not prevent. Continuing a moral and religious posture that condemned usury, monopolistic practices, and generally the dance around the golden calf, the Church allowed erring men to obtain, through indulgences and the confessional, sanctioned release from whatever pangs of conscience or religious tribulations their worldly activities induced in them. In their explicit teachings the great Reformers opposed the money-changers and all their works as clearly as had Catholic doctrine. Here no change is discernible, unless it be the greater ethical rigor that reformist zeal imparted to pastoral practice. But the religious doctrines of the Reformers—above all the Calvinist doctrine of predestination—introduced a basic anxiety into the believer's relation to his God, and this anxiety, so Weber's argument runs, introduced a decisive change.[1] In lieu of the permissive pastoral practice by which Catholicism softened the psychological impact of its doctrine, the Protestant believer had to face the Divinely ordained uncertainty of his salvation without aid or comfort from anyone. Only his actions could allay that uncertainty, whether through inward contrition and an abiding faith as in Lutheranism, or through self-discipline and an active life in the service of God as in Calvinism.

Weber points out that for analytical purposes he presents the ideas of the Reformers "in their most consistent and logical forms." In this way he hopes to bring out the drift of these ideas, the direction in which a sincere believer would move. The gist of the argument is to posit an intensified motivation. All men of that time were concerned with their salvation, but the pastoral practice of Catholicism had diminished that concern. It had been greatly heightened, on the other hand, by the religious zeal of the great Reformers and by the unintended implications of their theological doctrines as these were revealed in the sermons of Puritan Divines. The economic actions consistent with the "Spirit of Capitalism," were in significant measure efforts to relieve religious anxiety—at any rate during the 16th and 17th centuries.

It is difficult, however, to infer the intensification of a motive (the quest for salvation) from the logical implications of a theological doctrine (the believer's uncertainty concerning his salvation, as a corollary of the doctrine of predestination). For all its subtlety and learning, Weber's text contains evidence that he himself remained uncertain concerning the relation between doctrine and conduct.[2] In this case analysis of the text can help us understand the difference between cultural and behavioral analysis.

Weber writes:

> We are naturally not concerned with the question of what was theoretically and officially taught in the ethical compendia of the time, however much practical significance this may have had through the influence of the Church discipline, pastoral work, and preaching. We are interested rather in something entirely different: the influence of those *psychological sanctions* which, originating in religious belief and the practice of religion, gave a direction to practical conduct and held the individual to it.[3]

Since this passage states the specific focus of attention, it is all the more significant that the key word "sanction" is ambiguous. If discipline, pastoral work and preaching are *not* relevant for understanding the impact of doctrine on conduct, then what of the "psychological sanctions" that are? In the original, Weber uses the German word *Antrieb* or impulse; he thus posits psychological impulses originating in the religious beliefs evoked by a theological doctrine. His use of the term "impulse" suggests that a propensity to act in accord with the implications of the doctrine of predestination has already been internalized. But this begs the question, since he is investigating and not presupposing the impact of doctrine on belief and conduct. (The translation unfortunately obscures the passage further, since the word "sanction," which corresponds to German words like *Bestatigung, Genehmigung* or *Zwangsmassnahme,* refers to external controls. "Psychological sanction" is a contradiction in terms—in addition to being a wrong translation of *Antrieb.*) To be clear on this point, Weber would have had to use the word *Anreiz* or incentive. Thus he would have stated what indeed he shows in brilliant fashion, that the religious beliefs of the Puritans contained incentives encouraging a personal conduct of "innerworldly asceticism" *to the extent that these beliefs were internalized—* clearly a conditional assertion. Yet his whole analysis rests on the thesis that Puritan believers differed from Catholics by their *greater internalization* of religious precepts, their anxious concern with the uncertainty of salvation unrelieved by indulgences or the confessional, each man facing the stern and inscrutable majesty of God alone and unaided. In his responses to critics Weber declared that this intensified motivation had been a causal factor of great, but uncertain magnitude, because men of that day were more deeply affected by abstract religious dogmas than a more secular age can readily understand.

This reply, it seems to me, does not resolve the issue I have raised, nor does it do justice to the profundity of Weber's analysis. That profundity consists in Weber's paradoxical assertion that the Reformers continued to adhere to the traditional, Christian devaluation of mundane pursuits, that Christian believers of this period continued to be concerned with their fate in the hereafter (though in a more intense fashion than hitherto)—but that Western civilization shifted from a predominantly otherworldly to a predominantly innerworldly orientation nonetheless. In other words, the "Spirit of Capitalism" represents a direct outgrowth of the earlier, anti-materialistic tradition of Christianity and, as Weber shows, was all the more powerful for that reason. Was this due in part to the intensified motivation that Weber analyzes?

Questions of this kind have given rise to a large, controversial literature which seems to have resolved very little. One reason for this failure is probably that both critics and defenders have discussed Weber's thesis entirely in the context in which he first formulated it. It may be worthwhile, therefore, to pursue this unresolved problem in Weber's analysis in the different context of the cultural-educational preconditions of Japanese development.[4]

To do this, I must enumerate some background factors concerning Tokugawa Japan. That background, I shall suggest, militated *against* the self-disciplined vigor in action that the samurai displayed in the decades following the Restoration of 1868. There is evidence that under the Tokugawa the education of samurai and of commoners continued to inculcate the traditional ethic of the samurai, but there is evidence also that such education was at best partially successful. If one distinguishes clearly between cultural incentive and internalized, psychological impulse (as I believe one should), then the evidence of the Tokugawa regime appears to point to a partial decline (rather than the increased vigor) of the samurai ethic.[5] The post-Restoration experience suggests, on the other hand, that the Western challenge arrested that decline by providing an opportunity for the leading groups of samurai and of commoners to live up to their ideals in modified form, and thus to overcome the discrepancies between ideal and conduct in the pre-Restoration period.

Following a long succession of internecine wars lasting until the end of the 16th century, Japan underwent a massive, political and administrative consolidation, at the local as well as the national level. By 1560 Japanese fiefs had been amalgamated into large territorial units, and seignorial rights were usurped by the locally dominant daimyo families. In this process smaller lords (samurai) were deprived of their seignorial rights and forced to reside, as retainers and officials of the daimyos, in castle-towns, whose construction in the period from 1580 to 1610—together with the destruction of all other fortified places—outwardly symbolized the new dispensation. This transformation of the samurai from rural landholders into urban retainers under the authority of the daimyos occurred when the Tokugawa Shogunate was consolidating its own position at the national level by a determined policy of isolation, the expulsion or extermination of Christians, and the imposition of the alternate-residence system (*sankin-kotai*) which made all daimyo families personally and politically dependent on the Shogunate in Edo. Within this general context the samurai were transformed from an estate of independent, landed, and self-equipped warriors into one of urbanized, aristocratic retainers, whose privileged social and economic position was universally acknowledged. They remained attached to their tradition of ceremonious conduct, intense pride of rank and the cultivation of physical prowess. The problem to be explained is how this demilitarized aristocracy could retain, for some two centuries, its individualized military stance and its cult of disciplined action in a thoroughly pacified society in which differences of hereditary rank were strongly emphasized but all forms of military aggression suppressed. For at the time of the Meiji Restoration it was against this improbable background that the samurai not only provided the active political and intellectual leadership of the nation, but pioneered in modern entrepreneurial activities as well.[6]

Why is this background improbable? The demilitarization of the samurai, the employment of some of their number as daimyo officials, the opportunities, at least among the better-off samurai families, for corruption in an urbanized, retainer existence, the emphasis on rank and the discouragement of competition, and among many lower samurai families, the sheer necessity to supplement rice stipends by some employment, often menial: these were so many reasons why the samurai could be expected to lose their militancy and self-discipline. No doubt some of them did, especially among the highest-ranking samurai and daimyo, for whom the Shogunal court at Edo provided additional opportunities for corruption. But this weakening of "moral fiber" was intensely resented among many samurai, especially during the last decades of the Tokugawa regime, and so the puzzle remains. Dore's analysis of education provides an answer to these questions and enables us to pinpoint the "functional equivalents" of Puritanism in Japan.[7]

With private tutors and, since the end of the 18th century, in an increasing number of fief-schools, the samurai families who could afford it, appear to have educated their sons.[8] In addition, a significant proportion of townsmen and well-to-do farmers sent their sons to temple-schools or private tutors, where they learned the rudiments of reading, writing and arithmetic. The private schools for commoners were in large part responsible for the fact that at the time of the Restoration some 40 per cent of Japanese boys and about 10 per cent of the girls were receiving formal education; the sons and daughters of aristocratic families probably did not constitute more than 6 per cent of the school-age population.[9]

What were the aims of samurai education? In 1786 Hayashi Shihei formulated these aims in a manner that Dore considers representative:

> With the eight virtues as your basis [his list is filial piety, respect for elders, loyalty, trust, courage, justice, straightforwardness, and a sense of honor] cultivate a boldness of spirit without losing self-discipline; acquire wisdom and wide learning without despising other people. Do not become weak and feeble; do not lose your dignity; do not sink stagnantly into mere logic-chopping, nor allow yourself to be carried away by prose and poetry. Do not lose your courage; do not become introverted. Do not become an admirer of China who sees no good in Japan. Do not fall in love with novelty or with pleasures of the eye. Practice your military skills with devotion and at the same time learn something of astronomy and geography, of the tea ceremony and of No drama.[10]

Avoidance of book-learning as such, of novelty and pleasure, behavior appropriate to the samurai's rank with proper dignity of bearing and respect for elders, above all self-discipline, wisdom and an active way of life: these appear to be the principal themes in this orientation. The literary arts are of secondary significance; their importance lies primarily in providing a medium of instruction through which the pupil can acquire the proper frame of mind, conscious of his duties and earnest in his practice of military skills.

Apparently, the same ideals of conduct were instilled in pupils of commoner origin. To be sure, military skills were the exclusive prerogative of the aristocracy, while the high rank, strutting arrogance and rentier-existence of the samurai were in turn objects of emulation, envy and ridicule among the commoners. But temple-schools and private tutors taught the sons of commoners the art of writing with a single-minded emphasis on proper manners and the right frame of mind. Dore has translated a set of Terakoya (temple-school) precepts from which I quote two paragraphs, to illustrate the link between literacy, social structure and the ideology of self-discipline:

> To be born human and not be able to write is to be less than human. Illiteracy is a form of blindness. It brings shame on your teacher, shame on your parents, and shame on yourself. The heart of a child of three stays with him till he is a hundred as the proverb says. Determine to succeed, study with all your might, never forgetting the shame of failure . . . . Cooperate with each other to behave yourselves as you should, check in yourselves any tendencies to be attracted to evil ways, and put all your heart into your brush-work.

> At your desks let there be no useless idle talk, or yawning or stretching, or dozing or picking your nose, or chewing paper, or biting the end of your brush. To imitate the idle is the road to evil habits. Just concentrate whole-heartedly on your writing, giving each character the care it deserves.[11]

There is much more of the same with special enumeration of all the careless or undisciplined ways that the students are admonished to avoid, incidentally giving a pretty graphic picture of the pranks, misdemeanors and bad habits that Japanese schoolboys seem to have in common with their peers all over the world. Apparently, neither the social aspiration of commoners nor hereditary privilege with its pride of rank were sufficient in themselves to inculcate self-discipline.

In the fief schools as well as in schools for commoners, instruction became a highly formalized affair which was intrinsically dull and meaningless, as Dore points out. Without holding the individual's interest, the teachers apparently insisted on writing and reading as media through which the student should learn proper behavior and the right frame of mind. Tedious repetition under conditions in which the student's bearing and attitude were subjected to the most detailed scrutiny and control, were the means used to teach self-discipline. It must remain uncertain how far these educational methods succeeded in inculcating the habits of thought and action that proved highly suitable for the rapid modernization of Japan after 1868. All we really know is that the educational system helped to maintain the ideals of the samurai. One might also say that the teachers had a vested interest in these ideals and that daimyos and Bakufu officials encouraged their educational endeavors, because they considered these ideals suitable supports of domestic stability. If one goes beyond these statements to the conclusion that in the schools of the Tokugawa period students internalized ideals of conduct and hence actually acquired the drive and discipline that were in evidence later on, one is guilty of the same confusion between cultural prescription and psychological impulse noted earlier.[12]

Certainly, Tokugawa education put a high premium on self-discipline, filial piety and an activist way of life. But there is evidence that many samurai students did not take to this education with alacrity. Fief edicts frequently deplored the lack of diligence among samurai students and admonished them to greater effort. Moreover, it is difficult to imagine that the personal militancy of the samurai remained unimpaired under a regime that sought to control all manifestations of aggressive or competitive behavior. The fief schools discouraged all forms of rivalry between different schools and strictly prohibited contests or simulated combat among their pupils, even though the ideology and practice of swordsmanship continued unabated. One result of this double-edged policy was that, as Dore comments, "combat was less and less practiced, and swordsmanship and the use of the lance became increasingly a matter of formal gymnastics, and disciplined choreography." Presumably this applied to those pupils who put dignity, respect for elders, self-discipline and wisdom above the "cult of action." There were others, however, whom circumstances and temperament prompted to make the opposite choice. As *ronin* or masterless samurai they lived a wayward life by the sword at the expense of most other tenets of the samurai ethic. One can gauge the tensions inherent in Japanese culture before the Restoration when one observes that the Tokugawa regime did not abandon its praise of militancy despite its policy of pacification and the apprehensions aroused by the activities of the ronin.

The famous story of the 47 ronin exemplifies many of these themes. At the Shogunal Court a daimyo has drawn his sword and wounded a high Court official, to avenge an insult. As a penalty the daimyo is asked to commit suicide, because by his act he has jeopardized Tokugawa supremacy and the policy of pacification on which it rests. The daimyo's retainers are now without a master; they acknowledge that he had to die, but out of loyalty to him they make every effort to preserve their Lord's fief for the members of his family. This effort fails. For two years the 47 ronin (the original number is larger, but many withdraw) secretly plan to avenge their Lord. After successfully eluding the ubiquitous Tokugawa police, they kill the Court official who had provoked their master. As penalty for this violation of the

Tokugawa peace the Shogun demands that the 47 commit suicide in turn. The conduct of these men exemplifies unconditional loyalty to their master, self-discipline in guarding their secret plans, and complete devotion to the cult of action in the successful consummation of their endeavor. The 47 ronin epitomize the priorities and contradictions of the ideals of Tokugawa culture. They divorce their wives or have their wives and daughters turn to prostitution so that they can fulfil their pledge of loyalty to their master; and they combine this act of upholding the hierarchy of rank with the unconditional commitment to action that the Bakufu simultaneously encouraged and suppressed. The hierarchy of rank is more important than the family while the peace of the Tokugawa is still more important than the hierarchy of rank. Both these priorities are here exemplified by actions which can be turned against others only at the price of turning against oneself in the end.

This true story of the early 18th century instantly became the cultural epitome of the samurai ethic, but in retrospect it reads more like an epitaph than an apotheosis. Its heroes serve their master by their deaths, since they can no longer serve him in their lives. Such symbolic consummation of the cult of self-disciplined action points insistently, albeit by implication, to the discrepancy between this cult and the daily round of a retainer's life that characterized the lives of most samurai under the Tokugawa settlement. One would suppose that many of these men, for whom militancy was the mark of rank, were aware at times of the emptiness of that pretense. While the story of the 47 ronin certainly upheld the ideal, did it not also underscore the pettiness of militancy without war? At any rate, the ideal heroism of these ronin does not explain whether and how such ideals could be harnessed to meet the contingencies of everyday life, which developed precipitously following the Restoration of 1868.[14] In the Japanese case we certainly have an instance of the discrepancy between cultural ideals and behavior; perhaps we can infer—for the decades preceding the Restoration—a growing ambivalence and even a diminished adherence to these ideals. The question is how such evidence and the more tentative inferences based on it can be related, however provisionally, to the intense and disciplined effort of many samurai immediately following the Restoration.

Historical instances are numerous in which discrepancies of this kind lead to a decline of an ideal. Under the Tokugawa regime the peaceful existence of most samurai was increasingly at odds with their militant stance, a condition hardly conducive to the vigor and self-discipline that the samurai displayed during the Meiji Restoration. Here some allowance must be made for the accident of timing: we will never know whether the samurai ethic would have become an empty sham in spite of teaching, official propaganda and increased education of commoners *if* the Western challenge to Japanese independence had come much later. All we know is that this challenge brought into the open a capacity for self-disciplined action that had been jeopardized (and may well have been diminishing) by the discrepancy between ideal and conduct under the Tokugawa regime.

Before 1868 the samurai ethic was maintained in its entirety by the educational system and by the officials of the Bakufu. There is evidence that the militant ideal of self-disciplined and vigorous action could be "domesticated" through the educational system. Dore shows how this ideal was incorporated in the teaching of reading and writing as well as in the "demilitarized" practice of military skills. The spread of Terakoya education and the high level of literacy by the time of Restoration suggest that samurai ideals gradually became ideals for commoners as well.[15] Moreover, the samurai tradition of militancy was kept alive in several ways despite the increasing discrepancies between cultural ideals and behavior. In response to the contrast between high social rank and low economic position the samurai who turned ronin chose to act out the militant aspects of their ethic at the price of neglecting other aspects of its code. For their part, samurai retainers adopted the alternative way of emphasizing rank-consciousness and stylized behavior at the price of turning militancy into "disciplined choreography," a pattern also followed by the samurai whose way of life became hardly distinguishable from that of commoners. One imagines that subjectively samurai of every description adhered to their ideals with that "sensitive pride and the fear of shaming defeat" (Dore) which most experts consider the exemplary motivational pattern of the Japanese people.[16] In this they were greatly aided by the Bakufu officials, who always upheld the ideal of samurai militancy, even though they suppressed the aggressive conduct that was an essential part of this ideal. Thus, before 1868, formal education and official ideology supported ideals some of which it disavowed in practice.

Since after 1868 the samurai implemented their ideal of disciplined action in economic, political and intellectual pursuits, one can infer that the Restoration provided the opportunity to overcome the long-standing, internal contradictions of the Tokugawa regime. Paradoxically, the same qualities that had sustained a quiescent and internally contradictory regime for so long, now found a new outlet. As Dore puts it in a telling summary:

> Sensitive pride and fear of shaming defeat, the strength of which probably led the majority of samurai to avoid competitive situations and certainly prompted most educators and teachers of military skills deliberately to refrain from creating them, also meant that—once competition was declared and the race was on, the self-respecting samurai really did go all out to win.[17]

Thus, the release of pent-up energies was decisive and there is little doubt that it was occasioned not by internal structural changes but by an external event, the arrival of Commodore Perry's ships and the challenge to national preservation that is symbolized. During the critical period from 1853 to 1868 (the so-called Bakumatsu period) the national goals of Japanese society were defined unequivocally, perhaps for the first time, the "ethic" of filial piety, self-discipline and an activist way of life was greatly reinforced by the external threat, and the intense social conflicts that ensued turned primarily on how best to meet the Western challenge.[18]

From the perspective of Japanese development one gains a clearer view of the cultural preconditions of development from tradition to modernity. For our purposes the central fact of Tokugawa Japan is the contradiction between official support of the traditional ideal of militancy and official suppression of warlike actions which accord with that ideal. The Bakufu officials who upheld the ideal of militancy surely did not wish to encourage the outlawry of the ronin, and they may have had misgivings concerning the increasingly empty pretense of samurai-retainers. Yet in effect they encouraged both, and the contrast between official ideology and practice would have undermined the ideological support of the Tokugawa regime in the long run. It is reasonable to suppose that this support was weakening in the decades preceding the Restoration.

Apparently, then, an event external to the society, the sudden jeopardy in which Japan was placed by the Western challenge to her isolation, was responsible in large measure for defining national goals and the redirecting and intensifying actions based on unchanged motivational patterns and unchanged cultural ideals. The Western challenge redefined the situation for large numbers of Japanese, and while it is true that for a time Westernization was "the rage," a wave of Japanization followed in turn, leading to a reaffirmation of cultural ideals and to a reenforcement of filial piety and the sense of hierarchy, which were now compatible with more national unity and economic development than had existed before 1868.

With this interpretation in mind we can turn once again to the problems raised by Max Weber's analysis. That problem consists, as stated earlier, in the hiatus between doctrine and conduct, between the *incentives* implicit in religious ideas and the internalized *impulses* that prompt groups of men to act in the manner Weber defined as "inner-worldly asceticism." An attempt to elucidate this unresolved question by reference to the Japanese development may appear far-fetched. After all, how is it possible to find points of comparison or even analogy between the Western challenge to Japanese isolation and, say, Calvin's or Luther's challenge of Catholic orthodoxy? Yet at an abstract level we deal here with rather similar phenomena. Both cases have to do with the process by which cultural ideals supporting tradition give rise to cultural ideals supporting modernity.

The discrepancy between official ideology and practice in Tokugawa Japan finds its analogue in the pre-Reformation spokesmen of the Catholic church who upheld the traditional faith but condoned religious practices, like the indiscriminate sale of indulgences, at variance with the ideals of that faith. The same spokesmen also condemned and at times suppressed individuals and movements that appeared to challenge the supremacy of the Church. It is common knowledge that the immediate antecedents of the Reformation were only the past phases of a century-long development in which the Church had had to grapple again and again with the doctrinal, pastoral and organizational consequences of the hiatus between faith and secular involvement. It is reasonable to suppose that in the course of this development orthodox spokesmen found themselves time and again in a situation similar to that of Tokugawa officialdom. Whatever the differences in culture and social structure, the task of upholding an orthodox doctrinal position while prohibiting and suppressing actions in consonance with orthodox principles is similar in an abstract sense.[19]

For present purposes it is most relevant to note the probable collective effect. Confronted with a patent discrepancy between official doctrine and sanctioned behavior, a large population—whether of Catholic believers or Japanese samurai— becomes divided into hypocrites and true believers. We know too little about this process, but there is ample evidence from both medieval Europe and Tokugawa Japan that the discrepancy between doctrine and practice was welcomed by some and condemned by others. Some used the occasion as an excuse for moral laxity, others became moral rigorists as a reaction against official dishonesty. The proportions of the population responding in one way or the other may never be known. Perhaps no more can be said in the end than that Catholic Europeans had to live with this discrepancy between doctrine and sanctioned behavior for a much longer period than the population of Tokugawa Japan. Prior to *the* Reformation, the number and intensity of movements for internal reform of the Church probably exceeded the analogous stirring of reform-movements in Tokugawa Japan prior to the Restoration. It is conceivable that this longer history of spiritual and psychological unrest indicates a greater attenuation of the moral code in Europe than in Japan. Speculative as such reasoning is, it suggests that we must look for some massive cause, affecting large numbers, if we are to explain how a considerable part of a population could turn for a significant period from the hypothesized vacillation between laxity and rigorism to self-disciplined action in this world, to inner-worldly asceticism. The venturesome analogue of the Japanese development suggests that this massive cause may well lie in events external to that self-contained world of religious ideas and moral precepts that Weber analyzed with such insight.

What was the context in which the incentives implicit in religious doctrines became linked with the impulses that prompt men to action?[20] In the case of the Lutheran Reformation it is noteworthy that around 1500 Wittenberg was located in a German frontier region, bordering on areas inhabited by people of Slavic descent. The town had 2,500 residents, of whom 550 were liable to pay taxes; composed primarily of artisans and local traders, the community provided little opportunity for the development of an urban patriciate. During the crucial years of Luther's work, Wittenberg had to accommodate between 1,500 and 2,000 students, and Schoeffler shows that under Luther's influence the faculty of the university rapidly became very young indeed. Men in their twenties and thirties predominated while older professors retired or left the university altogether. Surely, Luther was a very powerful and courageous innovator, who attracted students from far and wide, and who succeeded in transforming the bulk of the faculty into a group of loyal collaborators and followers.[21] Thus Luther created some of the community support he enjoyed. But in the larger context, he could do so because Wittenberg provided cultural and political opportunities for his reorientation of established traditions. Located in a linguistic and cultural frontier area, Wittenberg was a natural setting for a cultural and religious appeal based on the vernacular and the original: the translation of the Bible into German, the use of German in religious ceremonies, and beyond this, recourse to the texts of classical antiquity in the original rather than dependence on commentaries. This link between religious reform and a revival of humanistic learning also appealed to other regions and universities lacking in tradition, in striking contrast to areas with more established traditions and older universities where these innovations were bitterly opposed for cultural as well as for religious reasons. Schoeffler examines the signatories of the Augsburg confession (1530) and suggests that they represent ",outposts" of German settlement and areas of relatively late Christianization, which either lacked universities altogether or had universities bereft of the scholarly traditions of that period.

On the Continent the Lutheran Reformation became stabilized through the Articles of Schmalkalden (1537) which distinguish between the coercive, legal authority of the temporal power and the spiritual authority of the church, but then place a certain authority over affairs of the Church in the hands of the prince. His duty is to "diligently further God's glory." To this end he must place his authority in the service of the Church, which at the time meant the right and duty to defend correct doctrine and superintend preaching and worship. Henceforth, acceptance of established, secular authority became an integral part of Lutheran piety—a link which to this day has had repercussions in German society especially. In this instance it is easy to see that to the extent that the incentives implicit in Luther's theological doctrines were internalized, they were internalized in a political context—however difficult it may be to disentangle the religious from the political incentives or to analyze the interweaving of both in a socialization based on Lutheran precepts.

The context of the English Reformation differs greatly from that on the Continent. Schoeffler points to the absence of a religious leadership in any way comparable to that of Luther or Calvin. Initiated under political auspices the English Reformation lacked a great religious ethos. During several decades of the 16th century the government was markedly unstable. Yet each new government gave rise to new, authoritative decisions on Church policy. As a result the English people were exposed to the whole gamut of religious disputes characteristic of the period, an experience which in Schoeffler's judgment created considerable religious anxiety while providing no prospect of a new consensus on religious questions. In this case religious anxiety is attributed to the uncertainties introduced into Church affairs by a vacillating government which has assumed authority over these affairs but proves unable to develop a consistent approach to the organizational and spiritual problems of the Church. Yet each approach to Church policy found its passionate advocates, leading eventually to the formation of sects whose members adhered to their religious convictions all the more stubbornly, the more the authorities continued to vacillate. As Schoeffler puts it:

> The English nation is the only great people, which in all its segments was really led into a state of religious need or anxiety (*Not*). Everyone had to make his own decision among several and eventually among many doctrinal systems and principles of church organization, while the state was in no position to take this decision into its own hands.[22]

Having made such decisions under conditions of special uncertainty the new sectarian communities were anxious to preserve the faith they had had to discover for themselves, and the unity of the congregation which had been forged in the midst of political conflicts and religious disputes. Thus, the political context of the English Reformation helps us to interpret the link between the incentives implicit in religious ideas and the internalization of these religious precepts, which Weber has analyzed in part.

There is no need to examine the manifest dissimilarities between the English Reformation and the Japanese response to the Western challenge. In both instances motivation was intensified along established lines, apparently because the context stimulated a heightened concern with the supreme value of personal salvation or national integrity, respectively. The two cases suggest that the cultural-educational preconditions of economic development can be understood more clearly, if the internal structure of a society is analyzed in relation to its political structure and international setting.

To answer the questions of how cultural patterns that support tradition can give rise to cultural patterns that support modernity, I have explored two different settings. The question is especially difficult to answer because such patterns are accessible to the scholar only so far as they are reflected in documents, and documents which do that tend to be "projections" of a cultural minority. Hence, the meaning of cultural patterns for large numbers remains inevitably speculative. And yet, without some answer to the questions of what these patterns mean, at least to leading strata of a society numbering in the thousands, we cannot expect to understand the cultural preconditions of economic development. This essay has advanced two suggestions in this respect.

One is that the mass effect of cultural patterns can be understood better if their political context is observed. In the Japanese case the evidence points unequivocally to a massive redirection of effort as a response to the Western challenge. The evidence from the Reformation is much more complex. Yet, if it be true as Weber argued that men of that time were very directly concerned with abstract theological doctrines, then it seems just as plausible to suggest that this concern with personal salvation was hard to separate from political controversy at a time when theological and political differences went hand in hand. Political involvement, I suggest, is another side of that devotional piety or innerworldly asceticism that Weber analyzed in Lutheranism and Calvinism, and I believe that the intensification of motives which he emphasized cannot be understood without attention to this aspect.

The other suggestion is more abstract, but perhaps more important. Throughout his work Weber was concerned with the uniqueness of Western civilization, from Greek philosophy and Roman jurisprudence to the Protestant Ethic, capitalist enterprise and modern science. Since his day a few other countries have accomplished a transition to modernity, aided by the preceding developments of Europe and America but also contributing cultural elements of their own. Japan is an outstanding example. But the number of such countries is quite limited, and the question seems warranted whether across all the differences among them this "capacity for development" points to some common element. I noted that both Tokugawa Japan and Catholic Europe were characterized by protracted discrepancies between orthodox doctrine and practical accommodations, giving rise to moral "tokenism" on one hand and moral "rigorism" on the other. The tensions imparted to both cultures as a result may have prepared the ground for the innovating impact of political challenges and religious ideas.

FOOTNOTES

1. No one who has examined some of the personal documents of the period, will want to minimize that anxiety. Especially impressive in this respect is the fear induced in children as documented in Sanford Fleming, *Children and Puritanism* (New Haven: Yale University Press, 1933).

2. Cf. the related points made by Paul Lazarsfeld and Anthony R. Oberschall, "Max Weber and Empirical Social Research," *American Sociological Review,* 30 (1965), pp. 191-93. Cf. also the discussion in Reinhard Bendix, *Max Weber, An Intellectual Portrait* (Garden City, N.Y.: Anchor Books, 1962), Ch. 7.

3. Max Weber, *The Protestant Ethic and the Spirit of Capitalism* (New York: Charles Scribner's Sons, 1958), p. 97. My italics.

4. This is made possible for me by Ronald Dore's volume, *Education in Tokugawa Japan* (Berkeley: University of California Press, 1965). I am indebted to Professor Dore for making the manuscript of the book available to me before publication.

5. The reiteration of the phrase "cultural incentive" in this altered context calls for an additional comment. In his analysis of Calvinist and other Reformed doctrines Weber was not concerned with their explicit moral injunctions but with their implicit effects. The following discussion of Japanese materials is similar in the sense that explicitly the official code called for militancy, while official practice discouraged certain forms of it, and this discrepancy provided the "cultural incentives" of the Tokugawa period.

6. See the data reported by Ronald Dore, "Mobility, Equality and Individuation in Modern Japan" (mimeographed paper presented to Second Conference on Modern Japan, Bermuda, January, 1963). Dore notes that until well into the 20th century it remained customary for a man to declare himself a commoner or aristocrat on every legal document or hotel register.

7. The following summary does not do justice to the richness of Dore's materials, but it attempts to make a contribution by singling out the issues that appear critical in a comparative perspective.

8. In 1703 only 9 per cent of all daimyo fiefs had schools, but the unbroken continuity of the samurai-ethic makes it probable that a significant proportion had private instruction. By 1814 about one half of all daimyo fiefs and almost all of the large fiefs had schools; by the time of the Restoration only the smallest fiefs remained without them.

9. This inference is based on a comparison between Dore's estimate of formal schooling and literacy and Abegglen and Mannari's estimate that all ranks of the aristocracy comprised 460,000 out of 7 million households or about 6.1 per cent of the total population in 1872. Cf. James J. Abegglen and Hiroshi Mannari, "Japanese Business Leaders, 1880-1960" (mimeographed paper presented to the Conference on the State and Economic Enterprise in Modern Japan, Estes Park, Colo.: June, 1963), pp. 9-11. It is of course, speculative to identify the proportion of children from aristocratic households with the proportion of aristocratic households, since this assumes that the number of children per aristocratic household was identical with the national average. But a sizable proportion of Japanese boys with formal education must have come from households of commoners, since aristocratic households could hardly have made up in excess of children what they lacked in total numbers.

10. Quoted in Dore, *Education in Tokugawa Japan, op. cit.,* p. 64.

11. *Ibid.,* p. 323 ff.

12. This confusion is widespread because all cultural values have such *possible* psychological correlates. In the field of psychological drives or patterns, the *post-hoc-ergo-propter-hoc* fallacy is especially hard to avoid, because observation of such drives or patterns invites inquiry into their antecedents, and in most instances it is impossible to document that these antecedents did *not* exist.

13. Dore, *Education, op. cit.,* p. 151.

14. In 1867 payments in rice to the samurai amounted to 34.6 million yen, while in 1876 the value of yearly interest paid on a commutation basis had fallen to 11.5 million. For a relatively short time the Meiji government cushioned this precipitous decline by allocating a sizable portion of its budgets for stipends to dispossessed samurai, as well as by the more intangible method of ideological support for their high rank. But these short-term methods only delayed for a little the stark necessity of going to work.

15. The "demilitarized" teaching of the samurai-ethic probably facilitated its general applicability, especially among commoners. Dore emphasizes that there is hardly any evidence in Tokugawa Japan of assertions that commoners should be barred from the acquisition of literacy, while such assertions were frequent in Europe on the ground that such a skill would make the lower orders unruly. In this sense the adoption of samurai-precepts in the instruction of commoners was a move in the direction of equality despite the rank-consciousness instilled by these precepts.

16. For a telling description of this pattern, illuminated by evidence from Japanese history, cf. Edwin O. Reischauer, *The United States and Japan* (New York: The Viking Press, 1957), pp. 99-177.

17. Dore, *Education, op. cit.,* p. 212.

18. For a masterly exposition of these conflicts over policy and their compatibility with a basic agreement on national goals, see W. G. Beasley, "Introduction," in W. G. Beasley (ed.), *Select Documents—Japanese Foreign Policy, 1853-1868* (London: Oxford University Press, 1955) pp. 1-93.

19. This similarity can be analyzed in several ways. Cf. for example, the analysis of this parallelism in the case of Catholic and Communist orthodoxy in Zbigniew Brzezinski, "Deviation Control: A Study in the Dynamics of Doctrinal Conflict," *American Political Science Review* 56 (1962), pp. 5-22.

20. The following observations are based on the work of Herbert Schoeffler, *Wirkungen der Reformation* (Frankfurt: V. Klostermann, 1960), containing essays originally published in 1932 and 1936. My brief statement cannot do justice to the subtlety of Schoeffler's analysis.

21. Both directly and indirectly Luther had special influence with the Elector Friedrich of Saxony, who used his authority to effect these changes of personnel at the university.

22. *Ibid.,* p. 324.

APPROACHES OF THE JAPANESE INNOVATOR TO CULTURAL AND TECHNICAL CHANGE

John W. Bennett and Robert K. McKnight

European nations experienced modernization as part of a gradual historical development from feudal society through nationhood and the industrial revolution. Nonliterate tribal societies have undergone related changes as a consequence of colonialization and economic exploitation by the West. In most cases change in these societies has taken the form of a haphazard transition, with accompanying disharmonies in rate and scale as measured by the classic European evolution. Non-Western civilized societies, like Japan, commenced their transformation to modern industrial nationhood from stages of relative political and economic complexity, and with varying degrees and kinds of prior association with Western nations.

In the Asian countries the transition from a traditional social order to a modern framework of institutions has tended to engage the interests and emotions of a majority of the intelligentsia: there have been—and this is true of Japan—few "free-floating intellectuals." The educated person, as an academic or professional specialist, has occupied a vital role: he has been called upon to serve his country and its goals (or to attempt to reformulate them), and he has viewed the world through special lenses colored by the needs and problems of the national experience with modernization. Cultural and technical change in these countries has not been simply a practical problem of instituting educational facilities, constructing factories, and organizing bureaucracies. It has involved the intellectual question of how people are to orient their images of themselves in the changing scene, and how the society is to orient itself to the world as a whole.

In other words, many aspects of modernization in those societies that are "catching up" or have "caught up" with Western developments may be treated as ideological problems of individual and social perspective. In this paper we shall be concerned with the innovator and ideologist in one of these societies, Japan, and will consider the position of highly educated Japanese persons in cultural and technical change with respect to their attitudes, values, and social roles.

Modernization Among the Latecomers

An important difference in the historical process of the modernization of Europe and of a country like Japan lies in the fact that in the latter the changes were not so much a matter of social evolution as the products of continuous planning taking place within a few generations. The rapid and *planned* character of modernization in Japan, as in many non-Western civilized nations, has been given an

Bennett/McKnight — *From The Annals*, Vol. 305, (May, 1956), pp. 101-133. Reprinted by permission of The American Academy of Political and Social Science and the authors.

urgent accent by international developments. In Japan the desire to escape colonial or imperial domination—as witness the fate of China—lay behind much of the energy and singleness of purpose which characterized her transformation. In India today, the need to attain modern nationhood as a device to escape economic and military encirclement is equally potent as a stimulus to rapid, efficiently planned transformation. Latin American countries have presented similar profiles. This is not to imply that planning did not accompany some phases of the European transformation, but only that Japanese leaders attempted to exercise strong and continuous rational control over the nation's institutions and their alterations. Modernization thus came to be seen by many Japanese as the result of consciously formulated ends and means and not as a gradual and inevitable evolutionary process.

In view of these differences in the social process of change, it is useful to consider certain broad aspects of the history of modernization as a background for our analysis of basic ideologies. In the case of Western nations, contemporary analyses seem to agree on a definition of three major developmental stages: the first consists of feudal society, with its traditional culture, fixed contractual relationships between classes, and static economy; the second is the stage of dynamic politico-economic expansion, with ideological controversy and great individual mobility; the third is the period of consolidation, with an emphasis upon consumption, greater predictability in career development, and pressures toward conformity (though science may continue its creation of new horizons, and political dynamism, at least between nations, persists).

The directed role of the educated in modernization. These three stages, superficially at least, may be evident in Japan's historical development from Tokugawa feudalism to the contemporary period. However, the *differences* in Japan's changes when compared with those of Western nations are more important for our present discussion. First, as we have noted, the process in Japan was more rapid and under much greater conscious control. Unrestricted individual achievement was less evident, and mobility was generally directed by national purposes or took place within traditional forms of interpersonal relations. The European second, or transitional, state was exceedingly attenuated. In Japan the balance of political power was retained by the elite aristocracy, and the social forces that might have instituted social-relational forms and philosophy along European lines experienced frequent frustration by a national loyalist mass movement efficiently activated via educational and communication facilities by the government. There was less opportunity to escape or to evade the system—for geographical as well as for social-structural and political reasons.

There did not, in this atmosphere, develop an effective philosophy of individual independence and equality, and throughout the entire transition the individual innovator strongly felt his social obligations to his family and to his society. His role within the Japanese social hierarchy, while somewhat less encumbered with ritual and formality, was nevertheless effective in regulating his activities to the purpose of the larger group. It has been the insignificant few rather than the significant many who have broken family ties or have neglected, for intellectualized reasons, their social obligations.

The ideological perspectives of the capable, educated individual have become important aspects of the whole process of modernization, and the intellectual, as he participates in shaping his nation, is continually inspected by his superiors in order to ascertain if he possesses the correct ideological orientation to national goals and purposes. Moreover, the intellectual, in the majority of cases, has accepted rather than rebelled from such engagements with social reality; the supervision was as frequently introspective as externally exercised.

Modernization by example. Finally, greater predictability in social change and increased efficiency in technical change can potentially exist for the nations arriving late in the arena of modern civilization. Western notions about the future of society often have been little more than judicious hunches based on interpretations of history and social trends. Scientific achievements have been marked by experimentation and inefficient trial and error methods. On the other hand the intellectual and the scientist in Japan, particularly the individual with educational experience in the West, have been provided with indicators of the outcome of social innovation and with the formula and blueprints for scientific development. They have had at their disposal the numerous predictions, utopias, and critiques of Western scholars, as well as empirical evidence of confirmation and refutation in the modern histories of European nations.

Thus the educated Japanese person in 1900 felt that he could predict more accurately than the seventeenth-century European his own fate and that of his society simply by looking at examples of Western development.[1] The urgency of the situation precluded actual experimentation, and the Japanese intellectual was in a position to suggest the outcome of certain innovations, thereby increasing his usefulness to the political administrator. In this favorable atmosphere, the highly educated man in Japan has usually accepted as a personal obligation an active interest in social affairs and has often sought an active role in the political machinery of change. The relatively low pay attached to government officialdom, a position in the foreign office, the Diet, or the home ministry has always been counterbalanced by the social rewards and modes of access to unofficial monetary gain afforded the intellectual who successfully attained such a position. His importance to the process of national development has been duly recognized, if not in the pay scale, at least in social prestige and perquisites.

Japanese Hypotheses Concerning Modernization

The personal views of educated Japanese with respect to the issues of modernization and the future of Japan can be found to vary in detail, as they have for the intelligentsia of all nations. We shall not be concerned with individual variation in ideology as such. We are interested in the fact that the conditions of national planning of modernization required the educated classes to subscribe to, or to carry out in their particular roles in the transformation, one or another fairly explicit and public orientation or "hypothesis" concerning the appropriate course of national development. We shall describe these orientations or hypotheses in this paper and present some illustrative data upon how individuals conformed to them, or changed with respect to them. There are three major positions, and we have named them the "conservative hypothesis," the "liberal hypothesis," and the "pragmatic hypothesis."

In brief, the "conservative hypothesis" asserted that the successful modernization of Japan was dependent upon maximal continuity with Japanese cultural tradition. Japanese cultural patterns, according to this hypothesis, have been intimately and ideally adjusted to Japanese historical and environmental conditions. In its extreme version, now rejected, the model for social planning was cast by the prehistoric and mythical founders of the nation, and national success depended upon the proper interpretation of and adherence to this ancient plan.

The "liberal hypothesis," on the other hand, asserted that successful modernization depended upon the institution of changes in Japanese society according to Western models of social development. Thus, the "natural" evolution of society as exemplified by European historical development was accepted by Japanese of this persuasion as the model for the Japanese transformations as well.

The "pragmatic hypothesis" asserted that successful development depended upon the resolution of specific and immediate situational problems and that more global attitudes and long-term platforms of change which derived from systematic cultural models were inadequate to meet the complex needs of modern Japanese civilization.

It should be stipulated that by using the terms "conservative" and "liberal" in designating hypotheses about national development we *do* imply certain general correlations with political ideologies and trends similarly designated in Japanese society. However, the relationship is not complete. For example, persons representing many varieties of political action might assume the "liberal hypothesis" as basic to their ideology. Japanese Christians, socialists, pro-Western businessmen, or any persons who accept a Western cultural and institutional model for national development have generally made such an assumption. Questions about the precise relationship of those who adopt one or another hypothesis to Japanese political trends and movements will be discussed in a section to follow, when we will deal with "conservatives," "liberals," and "pragmatists" as persons confronted with particular political situations and trends.

Attitudes and Roles:
Culture Change and Technical Change

With this background, we can now turn to a consideration of the attitudes and roles of the Japanese innovator with respect to technical and cultural change. We have suggested in the previous discussion that practically all of these innovators, whether they have accepted the "conservative," "liberal," or "pragmatic" hypothesis, have approved of the modernization of Japanese institutions and organization. That is, they have approved of what has generally been referred to in Western writings as "technical change." However, they frequently differ in their perception of the relationship between technical change and the broader culture, or the extent to which the two processes of technical and cultural change are interdependent and demand co-ordination and control.

"Technology" and "culture" do not, of course, yield easily to clear-cut distinction. Actually, technical changes almost always imply or produce culture changes as well, or, given a broad definition of the term "culture," the two processes become indistinguishable. Our purpose in this paper is not to distinguish between the *processes* of technical and cultural change, but rather to show that Japanese innovators have differed among themselves in their conception of the relationship of technical change to the whole culture in which it takes place.

Thus, in general, we find that the majority of the Japanese intelligentsia, excepting an insignificant fringe of fanatic traditionalists who advocate a return to earlier and simpler forms of civilization, have approved of technical revisions of Japanese organizations, industrialization, the creation of bureaucracies, mass education, and the like. It has been rather the influence or relevance of these "modernizations" with respect to the broad cultural order that has generated Japanese ideological and political controversy and factional activity.

The three hypotheses—"conservative," "liberal," and "pragmatic"—may be viewed as basic positions taken by Japanese intelligentsia relative to Japanese national development. On the basis of the individual's assumption of one or the other of these hypotheses we can make rough guesses about his political orientation to Western culture and his concrete conceptualization of technical change, as well as some estimate of his contribution to national development. We find, however, that individuals sometimes do not adhere to the logical corollaries of their basic assumptions about national development. Rather, we find a certain amount of contradiction between ideologies and ideals and actual behavior; tendencies to compromise with reality; or in some instances to compartmentalize or leave unresolved contradictions between ideals and behavior. All this may now be discussed.

The Conservative Hypothesis

In general, Japanese intellectuals who have assumed the "conservative hypothesis" have tended to resist the introduction of Western cultural values and social behavioral patterns and have viewed technical change as a separate or independent process which ought to take place without important modification of the cultural base. Modernization, in this view, is accomplished for the greater glory and power of Japan. Innovators of this "conservative" orientation have been influential in furnishing the financial means and political authority by which national goals of modernization were accomplished. In addition, the traditional ideals of "conservatives"—loyalty, power, and national glory, integrated with a tight hierarchical social system—have increased national solidarity behind the development program.

The precedent for this "conservative" orientation was established by the intelligentsia of the early modern period. Among certain aristocratic samurai leaders of the Tokugawa regime in the early nineteenth century and among the leaders of the early Meiji Restoration period (1870–90) this view predominated and led to many reforms and reorganizations derived from Western models, but introduced without any direct violation of the conventional social system and hierarchy of control. For example, in the promulgation of the Meiji Constitution, reforms and changes were "granted" to the Japanese people in "benevolent" acts which were compatible with the *noblesse oblige* pattern of aristocratic social consciousness which had long existed in the Japanese value system. These reforms themselves did not, by any direct or obvious consequence, interrupt the continuity of aristocratic social and political leadership.

However, the pursuit of national goals in modernization, technological advance, governmental reorganization, and the like led to many indirect or unpredicted consequences, and frequently led to the practical necessity to accept more than just Western techniques of organization, production, and other "noncultural" aspects. That is, the course of modernization, even though dominated and financed by leaders who attempted to adhere to the "conservative hypothesis," did lead to the influx of many cultural aspects of Western life. Faced with the necessity to accept more of the West than its technology alone, if national goals were to be accomplished, a few "conservatives" did an about-face on the issue and advocated a return to the earlier, simpler Japanese civilization. In the early years one line of ideological divergence among "conservatives" could be delineated between fanatic reactionaries educated in the tradition of Chinese classical learning and those more receptive to the West who derived their standards from the new Western studies. Some of the reactionary "conservatives" became behind-the-scenes leaders of fanatic youth groups who were responsible for assassinations of liberals and violence against Westerners in the early Meiji period; others, more passive in their behavior, isolated themselves from the "shameful" contemporary scene and delved further into studies of Chinese classics, finding a few intellectual followers and a quiet spot in the academic world for their activities. The division between reactionaries and those more receptive to the West also centered upon current political issues. Thus, those intellectuals who remained loyal to the displaced Tokugawa regime were largely removed from public office and assumed the role of reactionaries actively or passively opposed to the new group of young samurai leaders who, for practical as well as ideological reasons, had reinstituted the Emperor to a position of increased political significance.

In any event, conservative leaders in active administrative posts in the new Meiji regime did not, generally, take such a reactionary view of the encroachment of Western culture. Some modified their basic "conservative hypothesis" to accommodate an active receptivity to Western cultural influence. Others modified the hypothesis in a pragmatic direction of compromise and adjustment with the Western trends. Relative to those who assumed the "conservative hypothesis," therefore, we may introduce in addition to the "conservative" political position outlined above, two orientational types: the "conservative-pragmatic" and the "conservative-receptive."

Conservative-pragmatic orientation. Among the conservative-pragmatic group were many educators and political administrators who realized the necessity to reward technical ability and skill as well as social position in awarding educational scholarships and in assigning positions of importance in the rising bureaucracies. For example, the conservative-pragmatic influence is evident in the stringent examinations which have characterized the Japanese educational system and which have modified, though not eliminated, the traditional approach to social reward as a function of inherited position in the social hierarchy. There was, in the early period, a drastic shortage of trained persons capable of instituting the technological and organizational changes called for in the modernization program. In the face of this shortage "conservatives," as well as those with more liberal views, recognized the need to exploit the widest possible sources of potentially capable young scholars and professionals. Later, as national needs were met more fully, the criteria for social and professional recognition came again to be defined more in terms of social backgrounds.

Again conservative-pragmatic influence has been evident in the tolerance of Western religious missions to Japan. Religious tolerance as such is a value which can find support as well as negation in historical Japanese political action. However, tolerance of Christianity by conservative-pragmatic leaders has had the effect of currying favor and recognition among dominant Western powers and has been a necessary practical policy.

Conservative-receptive orientation. There were also those "conservatives" who recognized many familiar features in Western moral doctrine concerning persistent endeavor and frugality which not only found considerable support in traditional Japanese values but also seemed appropriate to the difficult tasks that faced the Japanese in the modernization of their nation. Not a small number of "conservatives" adopted Christiantity as their religion and were actively receptive to Western patterns of moral thought and action. A Puritan religious orientation, rivaling its classic counterpart in the West in severity of moral sanctions, was not uncommon among conservative-receptive leaders in the early period of Japanese modern history.

Even in the area of broader cultural values, early as well as recent conservative intellectuals could, if they looked for them, find considerable justification for equating Japanese values with those of the West. For example, Viscount Shibusawa, prominent in big business in Japan and abroad, who was "conservative" and antiforeign in his youth but more receptive as he accumulated experience with Westerners, provided an impressive list of traits which he perceived to be common to American and Japanese character (note, however, *absence* of traits suggesting "liberal" values such as equality, individuality, and individual gain, in contrast to emphasis on traits suggesting subservience to the larger society): "justice, humanity, fair play, the square deal, self-sacrifice, loyalty, philanthropy, chivalry, co-operation, unity, patriotism, public-spiritedness, orderliness, and respect for law." Recently a postwar "conservative" student was interviewed in America and was found to be favorably impressed by similarities which he noted between Japanese and American systems of denoting social status.

Other variations of the conservative-receptive orientation can be observed. In general, this particular orientation may be characterized by many conflicts and tensions. Precisely what can be accepted from the West while still maintaining a basic conformity to Japanese cultural tradition—or how are Western and Japanese ideals to be integrated into a single, successful system of thought and action? These are problems which some met simply by ideological compartmentalization, retaining, for example, a conservative orientation in personal life and habits while advocating and following a more receptive path in the public administration of professional or political duties. For some—Viscount Shibusawa, for example—the solution lay in part in attempting to divorce personal actions from any cultural context in the pursuit of professional goals which, nonetheless, were seen as contributions to national development. In fact, the historical trend in the direction of "pragmatism," or a tendency to act on the basis of short-term, practical decisions or situational demands, in part finds its genesis in conflicts between conservative motives to preserve the continuity of Japanese culture and generalized receptivity to Western cultural influence.

The Liberal Hypothesis

Even before Japan ended her century and a half of political isolation there were a few Japanese intellectuals who assumed the superiority of Western life and institutions and thereby set the precedent for the later "liberal hypothesis" concerning the needs for modernization in Japan. The position taken by those who have adopted the "liberal hypothesis" has been that sociocultural aspects of Western life must be introduced along with technological modernization. Compared with the "conservatives, " however, the "liberals" have had far less opportunity to wield the political power necessary to institute their programs of modernization and social reform. Those among them who based their models for reform completely upon Western culture seldom even gained much public attention— except as radical extremists or political criminals. Thus, like the extreme "conservatives" who turned their backs on contemporary trends in Japan, the extreme "liberals," the syndicalists, the Communists, and those who had too completely modeled their life styles and preferences on Western standards have generally been isolated from active, or at least public, influence in their society—though not generally by their own choice. In some instances their fate was more violent. Arinori Mori, a pro-American statesman, was sent by the conservative

Meiji regime as a highly successful minister to the United States, but not long after his return to Japan he was assassinated by a conservative fanatic. Social isolation has been the potential fate of any Japanese overseas scholar with liberal ideals who remained too long and became too well acclimated in a foreign, particularly an American, environment.

Prior to about 1890, the character of Japanese national development was marked by indiscriminate copying of Western ideas and modes. Both liberals and conservatives could dream of successfully instituting social models in the new era of modernization. But the balance of political and military authority throughout the period favored conservative leaders who drew upon national tradition for their ideologies, and before the end of the century the conservative trend was clearly established in the national development program. Thus, from this time on the typical political position of those who assumed the "liberal hypothesis" was one of cautious tact and gradualism in reform. More specifically, "liberals" of this later period generally sought to demonstrate not only their own loyalty to Japan, but also that the Western models which they advocated were somehow compatible with Japanese cultural tradition. The Japanese historian Okakura, a conservative, wrote in 1904 that many leaders of liberal parties of that late Meiji time—the Unionists, for example—drew their models from Western society but were the first to note similarities between Western democratic ideals and Confucian political theory. Western historians observing the same period in Japan have noticed that few thoroughly pro-Western liberals achieved any significance and that "liberal" movements all seemed to have ideological roots in the historical tradition of Japan. By about 1900, therefore, the "liberal" intellectual, whether motivated by Japanese loyalty or by practical reasons, generally found it necessary to modify the "liberal hypothesis" to comply in some fashion with popular ideology or with Japanese cultural patterns.

Liberal-pragmatic position. The successful liberal innovator, that is, the individual who was not forced into oblivion, was, in this sense, a "liberal pragmatist." In emphasizing similarity between Western and Japanese culture, the liberal-pragmatic position bears considerable resemblance to the conservative-receptive orientation. However, the differences are not difficult to detect. The most noticeable common factor in the biographies of Japanese "liberals" is an adolescent experience of emotional rebellion directed toward the culturally defined centers of authority or the social order in general. Significantly, the ranks of radical liberals in Japan thin considerably with age and with adult concern for security and professional success. General social pressure and authority retained in conservative cliques which dominate many professions require compromise or public demonstration of conformity from the ambitious, educated man in Japan. However, throughout their lives, most Japanese intellectuals who have at one time accepted the "liberal hypothesis" tend to be introspectively aware of their actions and attitudes. Many are keenly conscious of the cultural relevance of their behaviors— they know when they are acting like typical Japanese, in contrast to equalitarian and individualistic ideals (for example, in assuming a submissive role toward one defined as superior in the social hierarchy). In contrast, the conservative intellectual seems only rarely to reflect on the "Japaneseness" of his habitual behavior.

Liberal pragmatists, while they have not often achieved positions of political significance, have been successful in many fields. Ryunosuke Akutagawa, whose writings were incorporated in the movie *Rashomon,* achieved considerable literary acclaim as a satirist of Japanese culture during the brief liberal fling which Japan experienced in the 1920's. At an earlier date, Yukichi Fukuzawa, the famous Japanese educator-liberal, maintained a strict policy of aloofness from positions of political authority and public controversy.[2] Cognizant of the conservative trends in Japanese national development, he hoped for and gained the opportunity to promote his liberal views through the promotion of higher education, thereby contributing directly to the program of national development and indirectly to the growth of liberal Western ideology. In this pattern, many "liberal" intellectuals, for example Fukuzawa, unobstrusively taught Western liberal ideals, in the guise of "European" or "American" rather than personal ideologies.

Liberals in the postwar years. In the postwar years the scene changed considerably for "liberal" intellectuals. Many who had been stigmatized and isolated for their prewar and wartime liberalism were placed in positions of administrative and political authority and were made responsible for the field work of the occupation in supervising and instituting Western-style reforms.

Many of the liberals, faced with administrative duties, realized the difficulty, for cultural as well as economic and demographic reasons, of rapidly instituting Western models. They found it necessary frequently to compromise or to use Japanese cultural forms for the sake of expediency and communication with the less tutored and less idealistic public. In the course of events many changed in personal orientation toward the liberal-pragmatic position; others became out-and-out pragmatists, simply fulfilling the specific functions of their role in the administrative bureaucracy; and some divorced themselves from administrative duties and political controversy in order to preserve the integrity of their liberal orientations.

During the postwar years a number of liberal scholars have modified their basic "liberal hypothesis" in still another direction. Among Japanese scholars who have had firsthand experience with Western peoples, a few have returned to Japan quite disillusioned with the West. Many of the disillusioned have seemed to move in the pragmatic direction, and observe, for example, that many aspects of Japanese tradition are more suitable than Western cultural forms to Japanese conditions. Others, however, have adopted what we may term the "liberal-resistive" position, and have viewed the over-all trends of civilization in Japan as well as in the nations of the West as destructive of the finer qualities of human meaning and experience. Taking a view which has been articulated by a number of Western critics of Western civilization (for example, Fromm and Mannheim), they have initiated a personal quest for "higher goals" and humanitarian ideals integrated with the civilized order to serve as models for personal and social reform.

The Pragmatic Hypothesis

We have suggested a general historic trend toward pragmatism, or the assumption of the "pragmatic hypothesis" on the part of Japanese innovators—a tendency, that is, to respond to the needs of particular or immediate situations rather than to one or another rigid cultural model in administrating the national program of modernization. Up to this point we have viewed the pragmatic orientation in political thinking as an outgrowth of experience on the part of conservatives and liberals with practical situations of professional activity or political administration in their own culture. It is probable that most Japanese youth in pursuing a higher education have at one time assumed either the "conservative" or "liberal" hypothesis as an ideal in their personal orientation. However, for some the assumption of one or the other of these culturally determined hypotheses has been relatively insignificant. Thus a graduate engineer studying in America expressed his lack of concern for political and cultural issues by saying that it made little difference to him whether the political order in Japan were Communistic, democratic, or nationalistic—as an electrical engineer he felt assured that his services would always be in demand. Basically he felt obliged to serve Japanese national ends, but he was singularly unconcerned about the political nature of these ends.

The genesis of the "pragmatic hypothesis" as a basic orientation may be traced, it is felt, to at least two sources. First, the parents of many of the current generation of educated youth in Japan were either conservatives or liberals who experienced a compromise of their basic assumptions in the pragmatic direction. Therefore it is possible that pragmatism became ideologically central for some of their offspring. Typically, characterizations of the father by students who adopted the "pragmatic hypothesis" portrayed them to be more involved with business obligations than with political conditions or even family needs. Fathers were admired for their persistence in practical and professional activity.

A second source of pragmatism as a basic orientation has been the downfall of Japan herself as a cultural model. Stoetzel,[3] observing a much wider sample of Japanese youth than the highly educated alone, has pointed to the political apathy that characterizes large numbers of postwar youth who apparently have rejected the idea of placing faith in any cultural model after the defeat of Japan. Thus although among earlier intellectuals pragmatism was the outcome of compromise or rational adjustment which permitted them to meet the complex needs of Japanese modernization with more versatility, in the current generation pragmatism may become a basic life orientation and may, in some cases, take the form of political lassitude or apathy.

Difficulties of political detachment. However, "pure" pragmatism with regard to political or cultural models among intellectuals has not been an easy course to steer even though it has served many conservatives and liberals alike as a means of adjustment. Political detachment, or a policy of non-affiliation with particular political ideological groups has limited professional and social acceptance. In the long run the intellectual in Japan has usually been called upon to commit himself, at least publicly, to one or another ideological orientation. This was of course true in the pre-war years of intense nationalism and is increasingly the case in the postwar period as Japan's destiny becomes involved with the issues of the cold war, and as advocates of the older order of Japanese nationalism emerge with greater confidence in opposition to recent liberal currents.

In Western nations the intellectual can commonly speculate with some detachment about the probable course of civilization and adopt a "free-floating" attitude toward national and cultural identifications. For the Japanese intellectual similar speculation generally takes the form of a personal ideological commitment with explicit cultural allegiances. The highly educated individual has been constantly drawn into political controversy on this or that practical problem of national development. Emotional involvement, rather than detachment, has been the rule, diminishing the likelihood for political apathy and "pure" pragmatism. In many instances, it has proved detrimental to objectivity in intellectual and innovative endeavor as well.

Conclusions

Some acculturation studies, as an outcome perhaps of anthropological preoccupation with small tribal cultures, suggest that regularities in culture change can be detected and categorized on the basis of specific cultural differences between the receptor society and the source society. The studies have tended to concentrate on a few specific items of technical skill, material property, or ideology which have found their way to a small community, and to show the influence of these as a direct consequence of their inherent difference from and disintegrative effect on the traditional culture.

In studying innovation in a complex society such as Japan we are struck with some immediate differences: the durability of the cultural base and the ability of conservative leaders to make native cultural ends compatible with a variety of new techniques, ideas, and world views. While westernization in a small, compact tribal community may have an intense and destructive impact on the pre-existing cultural order, in Japan the force of national culture itself, exerted through traditional as well as modern means of social control, appears to have contributed to the extraordinary rapidity of modernization.

In addition, the study of specific changes and influences of new techniques in a small society is an easier task than assessing the influence of new techniques and ideals in a large, complex society. In the latter case, regularity and predictability appear to derive as much from the character of the ideologies and political purposes which influence the adoption of new ideas and techniques as from the effects of the innovations themselves. That is, the intersection of new and old at the level of personal histories of ideologues, political platforms, interest groupings, and the like seems to be as informative for the student of acculturation as the diffusion of specific new techniques and ideologies.

Of course the two approaches—according to the influences of the innovations themselves or according to the motives of those responsible for innovation—form a problem matrix which is difficult to analyze. For example, in Japan it is generally possible to describe the conservative rationale for adopting specific technical innovations. But once adopted, many such innovations had effects beyond those which were proposed by the planners. Mass education led in part to a breakdown of faith in the ritual and lore which formed the essence of Japanese tradition. Tolerance of Western missions, while serving conservative ends as a means to curry favor among powerful Western nations, contributed to the spread of Western ideologies and social-relational patterns which have sometimes been contradictory to traditional techniques of social control. Overseas education, a conservative policy, contributed to the ranks of those who have adopted Western cultural models for reform in ideals and customs.

More generally, the whole conservative platform of modernization contributed to the growth of a cultural medium in which people—especially the highly educated—could assume purposes counter to conservative goals, generally in the direction of pro-Western liberalism. In turn, these proponents of liberal reforms contributed to cultural change through their own innovations: translations of Western books; their own writings and teaching; and, in some periods, direct political action. Thus both the impact of specific innovations and the ideological or political motivations of the innovators contribute to an explanation of the dynamics of cultural and technical change in a complex society.

FOOTNOTES

1. The Japanese government program of foreign education for Japanese scholars was developed with this view in mind, so that the basic reference here is the Imperial Oath of 1868 in which Japanese scholars were advised that "Knowledge shall be sought for all over the world, and thus shall be strengthened the foundations of the Imperial Polity."—Translated by Robert

O. Ballou, *Shinto: the Unconquered Enemy* (New York: Viking Press, 1945), p. 164.

2. *The Autobiography of Fukuzawa Yukichi* (Tokyo: Hokuseido Press, 1948) is a mine of information on "liberal-pragmatic" tendencies. Fukuzawa's entire career may be understood as that of a liberal who avoided all incriminating activities and concentrated upon the construction of institutional form for hoped-for liberal consequences.

3. J. Stoetzel, *Without the Chrysanthemum and the Sword* (New York: UNESCO and Columbia University Press, 1955), pp. 214–24.

JAPAN AS A MODEL OF ECONOMIC DEVELOPMENT

R. P. Dore

The often-made distinction between endogenous or autonomous industrialisation and imitative or induced industrialisation is really one of degree. On a strict definition, England offers the only pure type of the former; it is the only country whose industrialisation was not accompanied by any sense of 'catching up with' an admired foreign model; where invention was more important than imitation in the early stages, where political change was largely consequent on economic change rather than vice versa, and where state initiative and direction played a negligible part in the industrial transformation. The underdeveloped countries of today quite clearly belong at the opposite end of these continua, their intellectuals' consciousness of backwardness is acute, the state's role is bound to be very important, and so on. But among the highly industrialised nations of the modern world, the only country which falls equally clearly at the 'induced' or 'imitative' end of the scale is Japan. Is it possible that Japan, as the first and so far the most successful example of directed, catching-up development (more successful by most economic indicators than her closest rival, the Soviet Union) can provide a model of how to do it?

There is a sense, of course, in which no model can be of much use. As Raymond Aron has recently reminded us,[1] 'every example of growth has its own unique history, which unfolds at a given period with the scientific knowledge and technology offered by that period.' It is not only that the new industrial countries have the advantages stressed in the Gerschenkron model[2]—of not having to start with the inefficient steam engine and the crude blast furnace. There are more dubious advantages too. Modern medicine and public health techniques mean that demographic trends, a crucial factor in the economic equation, can never be the same for, say modern India as they were for nineteenth century Japan.

Nor is it only in a technological sense that the world moves on. The leaders of Meiji Japan did not have Moscow radio breathing down their necks, and it was not until 1922 that Japan had to send delegates to ILO conferences to be embarrassed by accusations that Japanese workers were exploited. That nebulous thing called the "movement of world public opinion," for all its intangibility, is a real factor. It means that the governments of underdeveloped countries today must do things to maintain a semblance of respectability in the eyes of their foreign critics and a semblance of legitimacy vis-a-vis their own population which no nineteenth century government was ever called upon to do. Even the most dictatorial of governments today makes some formal gesture of submitting itself to the test of electoral opinion. It is a very rare politician indeed who declares publicly that full employment is undesirable or that the poor should be made to starve in order to encourage the others. The Japanese started their development drive at a time when

Dore — *Reprinted by permission from the *European Journal of Sociology*, V (1964), 138-154.

even absolutism had not entirely lost its international respectability; the internal opposition demanding a constitution with an elected parliament did not draw such overwhelming moral force from an international consensus that its demands were irresistible. It could be ignored or bargained with for 15 years, and eventually fobbed off in 1889 with a constitution which only marginally circumscribed the authority of the oligarchy. Japanese leaders in the 70's could choose whether or not to make compulsory education a goat of their policy; it was by no means axiomatic that universal education was something every developing country had to have. It was not until 1911 that Japan had her first reluctant factory act, and not until the twenties that there was a beginning of welfare services. Modern leaders of developing countries have a much narrower range of choice, and indeed the greater their devotion to development as a means to popular welfare and the greater their reliance on popular support, the stronger the pressure to accept high welfare charges on the national budget at the expense of the kind of investment that would lead directly to an increase in productive capacity. In so far as high rates of economic growth were achieved by Japan, as by Russia, only because their governments could be ruthless in withdrawing funds from consumption, such a pattern of development is beyond the realm of feasibility as a model for developing countries.

In one more respect the world has changed. Japan industrialized before the conscience, or the sense of enlightened long-term self-interest, of the rich countries was canalized into modern programmes of economic aid. She used very little foreign capital. A modern underdeveloped country which plays its cards right need not be so abstemious.

These are respects in which no historical model is likely to be directly applicable to any later situation. There are certain other features specific to the Japanese case which limits its particular applicability. Japan was in some respects already much more favourably endowed with the "preconditions for growth" when the political decision to industrialise was taken than most of the underdeveloped countries today.[3] In the more strictly economic field there was already a considerable development of internal commerce, of banking and exchange techniques, and some considerable accumulation of capital in private hands. The techniques of agriculture and handicrafts were fairly sophisticated. Perhaps the most important of these economic features, however, was the highly rationalised and routinised system of taxing agriculture developed by the feudal authorities in their fiefs which it was a simple matter for the new government to centralise and standardise and thus, without new and unpopular impositions, put itself in command of the major part of the surplus yielded by the traditional economy and use it for industrial development.

Another of Japan's initial advantages is less easily traced through all its concrete consequences. The development of education in the late eighteenth and early nineteenth centuries was such that by 1870 probably more than forty per cent of boys and ten per cent of girls were getting some kind of formal schooling. Perhaps about half of the total population might have been to some degree literate. At the same time that five per cent upper crust of samurai from whom the leaders of the Restoration government were to be recruited had been subjected to a much more prolonged training in the Confucian classics; a training which at its best bred a considerable sophistication in the techniques and morality of authoritarian rule, at least a well-developed sense of the dichotomy between public and private interest and of the immorality of the corrupt confusion of the two.

So, in the first place no empirical model is likely to be very useful, and in the second place the Japanese model is not likely to be appropriate to societies with different initial conditions. Altogether, it would seem, underdeveloped countries had better take their lessons from history as they are digested through the theoretical models of the Rostows and Harrods, or the rule-of-thumb anti-models of the Hirschmanns and Lewises of this world. It is still worth looking at Japan, however, to see if there are features of her development which are generalisable and capable of being incorporated into a theoretical model or a rule-of-thumb guide book. Economists have isolated several such features;[4] the role of the state in providing the infra-structure of communications and banking, the increase in productivity of agriculture as a means of expanding the surplus and providing funds for modern industry, the resilience of other traditional sectors besides agriculture, the role of the government in maintaining effective demand, and so on. Here I wish to consider two aspects of the patterns of motivation and interpersonal relations which have helped to determine these economic phenomena—the role of nationalism and the authoritarian structure of primary groups.

There are few more sweeping and implausible generalisations about economic development than Rostow's to the effect that what he calls a 'reactive nationalism' has been a major stimulant in every case including England.[5] But Japan at least is an example which fits his scheme very well. Let us consider in turn, firstly, the initial given conditions which contributed to the strength of Japanese nationalism; secondly, the role of government policy in developing nationalist sentiment; and thirdly, the effect of that nationalism on economic development. For the purposes of this discussion, nationalism and nationalist sentiment are equated. That is to say, the terms are used to describe not an ideology, but a consciousness on the part of individuals of their membership of the national community, an emotional attachment on their part to leaders and symbols of the nation, and a willingness to sacrifice individual interest in order to further what are considered to be the interests of the nation as a whole. On this definition the strength of nationalism in a nation is a summation (weighted according to the purpose of the inquiry) of its strength in individual consciousnesses. And any attempt to take an empirical measure of the strength of nationalism in an individual would have to try to determine the extent to which an awareness of his membership of the nation plays a part in the motives of his behaviour—how often, for instance, and how readily, he gets excited about his national team's performance in Olympic Games, buys national savings bonds, feels anger or shame at foreigners' disparagements of his country, and so on.

The initial conditions which made this sense of community easy to create in nineteenth century Japan are not hard to identify. Ethnic, linguistic and religious uniformity gave the population a homogeneity which few of the developing countries of today can match. And internal homogeneity was combined with external differentiation. The geographical boundaries of the Japanese state were clear and sharp and coincided with the boundaries of the ethnic and linguistic community. Japan shared Confucianism with China and Buddhism with other Asian countries, but there were no channels of personal communication with Confucianists and Buddhists in these countries to turn this similarity into a desire for unity; consequently, there was no feasible basis for anything like Pan-Africanism or Pan-Arabism which might diffuse the focus of loyalty. The sense of belongingness could all be directed towards the Japanese state.

Secondly, some five per cent of the male population had had an education which usually included some instruction in the history of Japan.[6] This both in itself created a sense of the national community as an historical actor on the international scene and gave depth of meaning to the existing symbols of Japanese identity and separateness—the Emperor, scion of a line "unbroken for ages eternal coeval with Heaven and Earth" (as the official English translations of Imperial Rescripts used to say) and the forms of worship at Shinto shrines which represented peculiarly Japanese ways of worshipping gods who were peculiarly the protectors of the Japanese people.

Thirdly, the fact that education had largely been a Chinese education, predicated on deference to the philosophy and morality of Chinese sages, had in its own backhanded way enhanced the student's sense of this Japaneseness. By being constantly made aware of the existence of an alien country he was *ipso facto* reminded of the otherness of his own, an effect which a more indigenously insular type of education would not have had.[7]

Fourthly, very similar effects were produced by Western contacts, but on a magnified scale. Because of the deliberate seclusion policy which had kept Japan isolated since the seventeenth century, personal contact with Westerners, with Western artifacts and with Western ideas came very suddenly and in full volume to the Japanese; not as a trickle but as a flood, and with a correspondingly more dramatic impact.

Of more lasting importance was the fact that the Westernisation of Japanese intellectual and cultural life had the paradoxical effect of heightening the Japanese' sense of their separateness. The method by which the country was to be modernised was, in the words of the new Government's Charter Oath of 1868, by 'seeking knowledge throughout the world.' And as the drive to modernise got under way more and more Japanese had to learn foreign languages, visit foreign countries as students and observers, or learn from the foreigners brought to Japan as teachers and advisers.[8] This increased contact with things foreign served to enhance their awareness of the separateness of things native, the more so perhaps because of the pattern of personal relations which typically obtained between Japanese and foreigners. The Japanese soon discovered that if they were to treat as equals with foreigners they simply had to accept the foreigner's equation of 'western' with 'civilised' and 'Japanese' with 'barbarian.' It was they who had to adapt, not only in intellectual matters but also in the etiquette of social intercourse. And so they learned to write polite English letters, to cramp their feet into tight leather boxes, to shake hands and to forego the pleasure of picking their teeth at meals. Their adaptation was not always entirely successful; even if it was, some foreigners sneered at their 'veneer' of Western polish as merely presumptuous. Hence a good proportion of the intellectual and political elite had the frequent experience of meeting with rebuffs and personal embarrassments which reminded them in an acute because humiliating way of their non-Western Japaneseness.

It was, perhaps, partly this difficulty of ever gaining a personal sense of belonging to the Western intellectual community which kept alive until recent times a sense of the alienness of Western intellectual culture, long after it had in fact been fully assimilated and it became possible for Japanese to receive a Western education in Japanese universities entirely through the medium of the Japanese language, and entirely at the hands of Japanese teachers. The development of a special brand of translationese helped in this. Even today it is rare for the translator of an academic work to seek to give the illusion that the work might originally have been written in the Japanese language. Translations are expected to sound foreign. Similarly, most Japanese universities, have, not a history department, but departments of Western, of Japanese, and of Chinese history. Philosophers teach the history of Western, or of Oriental philosophy. Artists do either Western painting, or Japanese painting.

The assimilation of Western material culture has followed a similar pattern. The label 'Western' is still firmly attached to most importations. Houses have rooms and 'Western rooms'; one wears a 'kimono' or Western clothes'; one has rice with one's meals or eats 'Western food.' The loan-words which have come with these products are written with a special script. 'Table', and 'base-ball,' 'strip-show,' 'handerchief,' stand out in a Japanese written sentence with more alien prominence than an italicized word in English. The point is, perhaps, that these importations have competed and coexisted with the native material and aesthetic culture, not replaced it. Japanese domestic architecture, Japanese foods and wines and leisure pursuits, are still highly valued. They were of sufficient intrinsic quality to survive the Western impact, and not just as symbols of backwardness but as an integral part of the daily life of the richest sections of the community. An economist recently found in an analysis of family budgets that the two items of expenditure which showed the highest income elasticity of demand, the desired luxury goods *par excellence,* were cameras and silk *kimono* material.[9] There is probably more that is consciously Japanese in the daily life of the Japanese middle class than there is even that is consciously Indian in the lives of the Indian middle class, and the contrast with most African countries must be even greater. This persistence of valued traditional elements helped to foster national consciousness in two senses; by serving as symbols of pride in national traditions, and by keeping alive a sense of the alienness even of fully assimilated Western importations.

The initial impact of the West in the nineteenth century was, of course, all the more effective as a stimulant of nationalism because of the threat of colonisation which it carried. Westerners were not just different from Japanese; they were dangerous, and Japanese were not just brothers, they were brothers who needed to capitalise on their brotherhood in order to preserve themselves. If a part of nationalism, in the definition I suggested, is the willingness to sacrifice private interests in the pursuit of national interests, the Western threat had the effect of defining the national interest with unmistakable clarity in a way which admitted no possibility of disagreement. In the preservation of independence there was a dramatic aim to which private interests could be subordinated.

These, then were some of the initial given conditions which helped to make nationalism in Japan stronger than it is ever likely to become in most of the developing countries today. The second question is: what did the political leaders of Japan do to preserve or strengthen this nationalism by artifice or by accident? There is no doubt that the leaders of Japan in the Meiji period and since were very anxiously concerned to find means of strengthening nationalist sentiment, and they found a good number. The conscription system, introduced in 1872, was very deliberately used, especially after the issue of the Imperial Rescript to Soldiers and Sailors in 1882, as a means of education in patriotism.[10] Of even more universal effect was the attempt, beginning in the late 80's, to add to the atmosphere of awe and mystery surrounding the Emperor as a symbol of the antiquity of the Japanese state and of its uniquely divine origins. After 1890 it was always unwise to cast doubt on the myth of the Emperor's descent from the sun-goddess. With the tightening of the straight-jacket of nationalist orthodoxy as the army gained control in the years after 1930 it became not merely unwise, but positively suicidal. A related measure was the invention of State-Shinto; the creation out of elements of popular beliefs and Court traditions of a new cult of patriotism with a whole set of rituals enforced on school children, and in war time on the general citizenry as well. Although these rituals were conducted with religious solemnity and were overtly predicated on the existence of supernatural protectors of the Japanese people, they were, it was claimed, 'civic rituals' which the State could require everyone to attend, irrespective of whether, in their 'personal faiths,' they were Christians, agnostics or Buddhists.[11]

Perhaps more important, because of greater cognitive content, was the use made of school education. The teaching of history as a means of glorifying national traditions is of course a common, if not universal, device. More unusual was the "ethics course" which taught, in part patriotism and the civic virtues, but also the morality of personal relations.[12] The core of the ethics teaching was provided by what was called the "Japanese family system," the ideal pattern of family relations which was largely derived from Confucian sources but which was claimed to be a uniquely Japanese product.[13] And its unique Japaneseness was constantly stressed. Hence when the little boy was inspired by the pictures in his ethics text book to bow neatly and squarely before his parents every morning and give them the prescribed formal greeting he was conscious, not simply of being a good boy, but of being a good Japanese boy, superior in virtue to the lesser breeds without the law.

There was another feature of the educational system which served to strengthen nationalism, an effect which was not perhaps quite so much the result of conscious design. In order the better to use the schools to breed patriotic citizens the Government assumed a monopoly over text-book manufacture in 1903. Since there was almost no development of private elementary schooling for the upper classes, the result was an almost total uniformity of education experience in the first six school years of the life of every Japanese child. By 1940 this had produced a homogeneity of popular intellectual culture which has probably never been equalled in any society of 70 million people. Every Japanese knew about the same heroes of Japanese history, about Benjamin Franklin's kite and his public spirit and Lincoln's patriotism, and about the mixture of fortitude and enterprise of some obscure Welsh bridge-builder celebrated only in the pages of Samuel Smiles. The result was the market researcher's dream—and the government propagandist's—an audience sufficiently homogeneous in attitudes and interests that there was a minimal risk of the approach which appeals to one section of the population alienating another.

One other aspect of government policy should be mentioned among the factors which preserved and strengthened nationalism. We have seen how in the 1860's and 1870's the threat of colonisation provided one dominant and clearly defined national purpose to which all individual purposes should be subordinated. Throughout almost the whole of the subsequent period, some such national objective has been constantly kept in the forefront of people's minds, dominating the head-lines in the newspapers and providing a staple topic of conversation in barber shops and bath houses, in business men's clubs and in the lobbies of village council chambers. The essential ingredients of such an objective were two; that it should be unifying (that, in other words, it was considered to be in the interest of every Japanese because it was in the interest of Japan as a transcendental entity), and secondly, that it was an objective which in some way put Japan into a competitive relationship with other powers. As soon as the colonisation threat had been removed, the objective was the amendment of the unequal treaties which gave foreigners extraterritorial rights in Japan. As soon as that was solved there came the war with China over Korea and Formosa. After the end of the China war, the next

10 years were dominated by the struggle with Russia for control of Korea. Success in the Russo-Japanese war gave Japan pretentions to Great Power status. Thereafter the objective was to affirm that status in the eyes of a world reluctant to grant it—to achieve full international equality. It was a less clearly defined objective than before, but its salient importance can be seen from the prominence given in the press to the evidence of Japan's failure to achieve it. The snubs at Versailles, the abrogation of the Anglo-Japanese alliance, most of all the Congressional acts to exclude Japanese immigrants from the United States, were lovingly dwelt on as humiliating reminders that something had to be done. After 1930, this objective was redefined into an attempt to force grudgingly from the Western powers the recognition of Japan's equality which would not be willingly given, to find for Japan a place in the sun by dominating Asia and throwing out the white man. After 1945 this was again reformulated as an attempt, in General MacArthur's words, to regain a place of honour in the comity of nations by demonstrating how thorough and sincere could be Japan's conversion to democracy.

Japan's admission to O.E.C.D. in 1963 marked the formal achievement of this objective, the disappearance of the last remaining symbols of second-class citizenship. But just as 'need achievement' in the individual always provides new peaks to climb as soon as the old ones are conquered, so the predisposition to work for national goals throws up its own succession of objectives. The major current national endeavour is to manage the 1964 Olympic Games in a way that will excite the admiration of the world. It has been difficult for the last two years to find an issue of a national newspaper which does not make some reference to the preparations for this event, often with expressions of anxiety lest Japan should fail to make a good impression.[14] A second national objective has been in the process of formulation in the last few years. Around 1960 the awareness began to spread among the Japanese that their economy was expanding at a faster rate than that of any other industrial country. Favourable foreign appraisals of Japan's economic performance were given prominent attention[15] and have provided the basis for a new sense of national pride—in the superior ingenuity and dynamism of Japanese businessmen, in the success of Government planning, and in the energy and skill of Japanese workers. It also provided a new objective: to keep Japan ahead in the growth-rate stakes; to produce more and more transistorised television sets and racing motorbikes to evoke the admiration of the outside world. Perhaps in no other country is one likely to find the leading news story of a national newspaper selling four million copies devoted to a press conference given by the Head of the Economic Planning Agency and carrying the banner headline 'Next year's growth rate 5.6%.'

These then have been some additional factors, largely the result of human design, which combined with the favourable set of initial given factors to intensify the strength of Japanese national sentiment. The final question is: so what? What contribution did this nationalism make to Japanese economic growth?

The most obvious answer is also probably the most important. The willingness to subordinate individual interests to the national interest really was present in enough individuals to make it possible for the State to exact in taxes the funds necessary for the protection, subsidisation or direct investment which helped to get industry on its feet. That willingness, of course, was always greatest when Japan was actually in a war, but then for a good part of her modern history she has continually been either in, or preparing for war. And always, whether it was the development of rail and sea transport and communications in the 1870's, the founding of the first steel mill at the end of the century or the build-up of the aviation industry in the thirties, these economic activities were justified in terms of the dominant national objective of the time. It was always a means to a national end. The favourite policy slogan of the 1870's was 'Enrich the country, strengthen the army.' The absence of connecting particles left this open to a variety of interpretations. For most Japanese it meant 'enrich the country *in order* to strengthen the army.'

The economists can trace numerous ways in which the economy has grown on war. Rosovsky has recently analysed the large role played by direct military expenditure in domestic capital formation throughout the period 1870 to 1945, and the crucial role of government expenditure in maintaining pressure for economic change.[16] A recent survey of postwar economic growth attributes a good deal of the credit for its rapidity to government investment during the 30s and 40s in equipment and especially in technical education.[17]

The Japanese economy has thrived on war and the prospect of war. This is one of the unfortunate weak points of the Rostow theory of how economies grow. Nationalism, he claims, is the spur. But nationalism can be abused. Instead of turning inwards to internal development it can turn outwards to external aggression and so cease to have beneficent economic effects in that it simply diverts and wastes resources. The equation is simple and morally satisfying. Nationalism turned inwards is good in the sight of the Lord and the State Department and also good for economic development. Nationalism turned outwards is not only wicked but also bad for economic development.[18] It is unfortunate that the real world is not so simple. The Japanese case suggests that even granted the waste of resources, the appeal to patriotism in the pursuit of military objectives can so enhance the government's ability to mobilise for investment resources which would otherwise be privately consumed that the ultimate net effect, even on levels of domestic consumption, is favourable. One can be quite certain that the Japanese rate of growth in *per capita* national income between 1870 and 1945 would have been much slower without the military stimulus; one can be equally certain that the accumulation of capital (including equipment and skills and institutional infra- structure) ready to be converted to peaceful production after the virtual cessation of military waste in 1945 produced a subsequent rise in living levels much more rapid than would otherwise have been possible; one could even plausibly argue that there was a rise in the levels of living of ordinary Japanese between 1870 and 1945 which would not have been possible without armaments expenditure. (Though here the direct economic pay-off of Japan's wars is also relevant. She received indemnities and gained colonies, for she was operating at a time when local international buccaneering was still possible.)

There are at least two other aspects of the relation of nationalism to economic growth that are worth mentioning. Firstly, one feature of Japanese government policy in the nineteenth century which has often been admired is the fact that, right at the beginning of the programme of development, the government established a scheme of universal compulsory elementary education. It took about two and a half decades to put fully into effect, but nevertheless, given nineteenth century values and assumptions, it can stand as an example of enlightened and progressive policies which in the long run probably contributed a good deal to economic growth. And note too that policy took the 'egalitarian' popular approach rather than the 'elitist' approach of concentration on secondary education; there was very little diversion of resources either public or private into secondary education until the spread of elementary education was almost complete. What was it that made Japanese leaders behave in this way, in a manner so different from most other governments, even those which have had some partial success in modernisation, such as those of Turkey and Mexico? There are several parts to the answer, but at least one of them is that national sentiment was so strong, and the sense of a shared unique culture was so strong, that the Japanese leaders shared an assumption of common Japaneseness with the poorest Japanese peasant far greater than the Ottoman Turk could ever feel for an Anatolian peasant, or a Mexico City bureaucrat for an half-Indian peasant of the Mexican interior.

A second question is: how far did nationalism enter into the motives of those Japanese entrepreneurs who were responsible for developing the private sector of the economy? A good deal of attention has been given to the so-called "community-centered entrepreneur"[19] and his role in Japanese development—men such as Shibusawa who supposedly risked a fortune to start a fertiliser company in a way which was not economically rational but largely dictated by a conviction that his country needed fertiliser. The argument is that whereas in Western capitalism the entrepreneur is driven on by the desire to maximise his profits, according to the Marxian model, to do this, seek expression of his rationalising instincts and ward off fears of his damnation in the Weberian model, to express his creative ingenuity or to excel his status-deprived father according to whether one follows Schumpeter or Hagen; in the Japanese case there was an additional motive of considerable power: to make one's country strong and to make it modern enough to bear comparison with anybody else's country.

It is difficult to know how much causal significance to attribute to this motive. Japanese entrepreneurs did not exactly die in poverty.[20] This much at least can be said. One need not even postulate a selfless sense of public service to accept the force of this motive. Patriotism was not simply a matter of private motives, it was also a matter of explicit public ethics. Most of the boldest of nineteenth century entrepreneurs were ex-samurai, and even those who were not had absorbed a good deal of the samurai ethic which affected to despise individualistic self-seeking and made service of the fief, the family and the nation the only laudable aspiration. Consequently the only way to gain honour among one's fellows was by, in at least some respects, conforming to that ethic. Most men want honour as well as money and power. But whereas in, say, the nineteenth century United States, one could gain honour simply by the mere fact of making money, by having maximised one's profit more successfully than anyone else—in nineteenth century Japan this was not enough. The man of honour might well hesitate to go into the soft drink business when his country's need was for fertiliser. He might well risk a considerable fortune to introduce a new spinning technique in part because he had visions of a medal and a letter of commendation from the Emperor which would certify to the whole world the public purity of his motives. (The Japanese sanctioned the patriotic motive with a complex system of awards and honours for service to the nation through industry long before the world had heard of Mr. Stakhanov.) The ethic made so explicit by these and other means undoubtedly did have some restraining effect. Motives are always mixed, but patriotism must very often have been one ingredient in the entrepreneurial mixture; and, of course, the bigger the tycoon, the more prominent his activities, the more he was called on to make speeches on the ethics of the patriotic business man, the richer he got and the more he could afford to lose, the greater was the restraint that the official ideology imposed on him.

So much for nationalism. The second theme, the relevance of the authoritarian structure of group relations to economic growth, can be only briefly illustrated, firstly in agriculture and secondly in industry.

Until about 1920 Japanese villages in general were still largely feudal in the loose sense that we think of the Russian countryside as feudal until the end of the nineteenth century. Landlords exercised a paternal control over the private lives of their tenants, received exaggerated forms of deference from them and so on. It so happened that a fair proportion of these landlords were progressive farmers with some interest in making two blades of grass grow where only one grew before. Seed Exchange Societies and Agricultural Associations developed fairly rapidly in the last half of the nineteenth century, partly on the initiative of the central government, but partly also on the initiative of the landlords who dominated these organisations. From their strategic position in the village these landlords were often able to order their tenants to adopt the new seeds, new methods and new fertilisers which raised Japanese agricultural productivity by a considerable margin and helped to prepare the way for industrial growth. There is good reason to believe that had Japan had a land reform which destroyed the power of the landlords and attempted from the very beginning to establish new channels of communication for the extension of agricultural improvements through democratically organised egalitarian associations, the results would have been much less impressive. (This is almost certainly not the case, however, after 1920 and perhaps not even after 1910. By that time more landlords had become mere rentiers and growing political consciousness had made the tenants disaffected, thus destroying these channels of communication or weakening their value as a means of agricultural extension.)

It is less easy to generalise about industrial organisation. Whereas small-scale industry has continued to retain traditional kinds of master-servant relations almost to the present day, employment practices in large-scale industry in the early period of industrialisation were as impersonally ruthless as one would be likely to find anywhere. The result was a good deal of industrial unrest and violence and eventually, from about the time of the first world war, the gradual consolidation of a trade union movement. The response was not simply repressive, but an attempt, partly under private and partly under official sponsorship, to develop a new pattern of employment relations—the old patterns of personal face-to-face paternalism reinstitutionalised on a large and impersonal scale. Thus was created the system of personnel management described by Abegglen in his book *The Japanese Factory*.[21] Its essential condition is a low level of labour mobility, the general assumption being that one enters the firm of one's choice straight from school and expects to stay with it for the rest of one's working life. This permits a middle-class type of seniority wage system with arrangements to tailor income according to family need impossible in an English type of wage-for-the-job system. With it goes a system of incentive payments which reward diligence and loyalty as much as skill, and a very firm emphasis on status differentials and on the authority of management which the recent growth of trade unions has not done a very great deal to modify. Even trade unions are nearly always enterprise unions and as such can tend to intensify, rather than weaken, the worker's sense of belongingness to his firm even though they may fight hard, and call successful strikes, to force wage increases. In many ways it is a benign system, especially if one likes the idea of gathering for morning assembly to sing the "old firm song" every morning. But benignity apart, there are good grounds for thinking that it is a system which has promoted economic growth. Its seems to promote high industrial morale and a high level of diligence and skill, if only because the job security and the closer matching of a man's income to the curve of his financial responsibilities reduces anxiety, and the expectation of life-long service promotes identification with the firm and its success. Likewise, the fact that the firm assumes the responsibility to find work for redundant men, together with the fact that wages are not closely related to actual work, means that there are very few restrictive practices and little resistance to technological innovation.

This sounds, of course, like that world where every man knows his place which is the dream of the conservative middle classes of Europe. The fact is that the Japanese middle class worked hard and planned intelligently to produce this world, something which the European middle classes have not been foresighted enough to do. One ingredient in this foresight was the lingering sense of the moral responsibilities of authority which derived from the Confucian education the samurai had received in the Tokugawa period, and which still retained some force in the motives of the more morally sensitive of Japanese statesmen and businessmen. Another ingredient was the very nationalism discussed above. It was not just that the employer was made conscious of his workers as fellow Japanese, and not simply as animal power or a source of purchasable skill; there was also a more direct connection in that the ideology of the 'Japanese family system,' and its analogous application to the state—the extended family of all Japanese of which the Emperor was the patriarchal head—reinforced and validated the industrial ideology of the 'enterprise family.' The essential instrument in shaping the attitudes—in both employers and employees—which made this system possible was the school ethics course with its emphasis on the Japanese family system and on the beauties of those twin core virtues of loyalty and filial piety, justified and requited by the benevolent paternalism of authority.

Since 1945 Japanese schools have ceased to provide this essential ingredient for the reproduction of pre-war Japanese society. It remains a matter of interesting speculation whether the inertia of the industrial institutions themselves can continue to hold a less submissively malleable generation within the same mould. And this is part of a more general question. Are the characteristics described above—nationalism and paternalism—characteristics only of Japan's method of reaching the stage of high industrialism, or lasting characteristics of the Japanese version of industrial society?

Veblen, writing in 1915, had no doubt that these were characteristics of the process, not of the end result.[22] Japan, he said, was entering a critical stage of maximum military power because she combined modern technology with the power of authoritarian direction and irrational fighting loyalty provided by a feudal social structure and the *'opera bouffe* mythology' surrounding the Emperor. In a generation or two the growth of rationality and individualism, *inevitable* as a result of industrialisation, would destroy that feudalism. So far events have proved him partially right. The *opera bouffe* mythology has gone. But granted a growth of rationality, granted the gradual erosion of feudal authority in the village and its eventual destruction by land reform, it is not all clear that there has been the same inevitable trend towards individualism. There is still (*vide* discussion of the Olympic Games above) a considerable capacity for enthusiasm about collective national goals. And Japanese workers can still develop a strong sense of loyal identification with their firm, allied to a satisfied acceptance of their own subordinate position within it. Veblen's predictions will have to be re-read another generation or more hence.

It is time to return to our starting point and ask the question: do these social background elements in Japan's economic growth make any contributions to a prescriptive model which can provide policy 'lessons' for the world's underdeveloped countries today? Nationalism, it is clear, can be an effective stimulant of growth. Indeed, China, Israel, India, Egypt, and Cuba are only a few of the countries which have discovered for themselves in recent years the economic value of the imminent threat of a defensive war. An imminent war which never comes, however, is bound to lose its psychological efficacy. Japan sustained the war atmosphere over a long period by switching the national objectives from defense to expansion. One hopes that the possibilities of local aggression are now so much more limited that she is likely to have few imitators. In any case, the Japanese example provides no evidence at all that nationalist sentiment can be harnessed directly to the goal of economic growth as an end in itself—until, that is, the last few years. Even in the case of the recent national drive for rapid growth it is growth as a symbol of national excellence, rather than economic growth as a means to higher living levels, which mobilises *nationalist* sentiment (as also seems to be the case in modern Russia and even more in China where economic goals are frequently expressed in such terms as 'surpassing England in coal production by 1960'). Moreover it seems that Japan was so unusually endowed with the conditions which made strong nationalist sentiment easy to create that it is doubtful if many other nations could develop it to the same pitch of intensity.

The same scepticism seems justified about the value of using traditional patterns of authority. The moral would run: don't destroy your existing authority patterns in primary groups until you are sure that newer more egalitarian forms are likely to be as effective in promoting innovation and industrial efficiency as the old. But this too is likely to be irrelevant advice; because traditional authority patterns have often been destroyed by colonialism or by independence struggles in any case; because the ideological pressure for change is in any country greater today than it was in nineteenth century Japan, and because not many countries have anything like Japan's Confucian background to draw on for the ideological formula in which to preserve those traditional patterns.

Finally, even if the Japanese model were not in this respect irrelevant to the situation of most modern underdeveloped countries; even if it were feasible to follow Japan's example, it is doubtful if any nation seeking economic growth as a means to popular welfare would be advised to do so. Japan began to reap really substantial advantages in higher living levels from her advanced industrial capacity only after the total collapse of the military ambitions which both fed and were bred by intense nationalist sentiment, and only after the destruction of the Army which rode on the crest of those sentiments to gain complete control of the Japanese state. It is one of the paradoxes of economic indicators that *per capita* national income rises faster if more lives are lost in the process. And in reckoning the cost of Japan's advance, one has to include the death and destruction wrought not only on her own population but also on those of her neighbours and opponents. There are also invisibles in the cost side of the equation, such as the effect on the personalities of a generation of Japanese brought up on the ideology of an irrational Japanese racism in the immediate pre-war period when nationalist sentiment reached its most virulent form. Economic growth can sometimes be bought at a higher price than it is worth.

FOOTNOTES

1. Raymond Aron, *Dix-huit lecons sur la societe industrielle* (1962), p. 202.

2. Alexander Gerschenkron, "Economic backwardness in historial perspective," in Bert F. Hoselitz, ed., *The Progress of the Underdeveloped Areas* (1952).

3. For a recent discussion of these features, see H. Rosovsky, *Capital Formation in Japan* (1961), chapter IV, and E. S. Crawcour, "Japan's economy on the eve of modernisation," an unpublished paper to appear in a volume on Japanese economic development edited by W. W. Lockwood and published by the University of Princeton Press.

4. See the concluding chapters of W. W. Lockwood, *The Economic Development of Japan* (1954), and for an excellent brief analysis comparing Japan to other examples of industrialisation, Rosovsky, *loc. cit.*

5. W. W. Rostow, *The Stages of Economic Growth* (1961), p. 34.

6. W. G. Beasley and Carmen Blacker, "Japanese historical writing in the Tokugawa period," in W. G. Beasley and E. G. Pulleyblank, eds., *Historians of China and Japan* (1961).

7. See W. W. Lockwood, "Japan's response to the West: the contrast with China," *World Politics,* IX, (1956).

8. G. B. Sansom, in *The Western World and Japan* (1951), gives an excellent account of the initial impact.

9. H. Rosovsky, " The indigenous components in the modern Japanese economy," *Economic Development and Cultural Change,* IX (1961), p. 495.

10. For this rescript see E. Benedict, *The Chrysanthemum and the Sword* (New York 1946), p. 211.

11. For these aspects of Japanese nationalism, see D. C. Holtom, *Modern Japan and Shinto Nationalism,* rev. ed. (1947), and D. M. Brown, *Nationalism in Japan* (1955).

12. An idea of the content of this course may be gained from R. K. Hall, *Shushin, the ethics of a defeated nation* (1949).

13. For an example of the Japanese doctrines on the subject, see N. Hozumi, *Ancestor Worship and the Japanese Law,* 4th rev. ed. (1948).

14. Choosing at random the May 1963 index for the Mainichi newspaper, one finds no fewer than 61 references to the Olympic Games. They are eventually due to take place in October 1964.

15. For example, a translation of the pamphlet published by the staff of the London *Economist, Consider Japan,* has enjoyed very wide sales in Japan.

16. *Capital Formation in Japan,* esp. ch. II and p. 88.

17. *Economist* [London], *op. cit.* (1963).

18. W. W. Rostow, *op. cit.* pp. 29-31, 112-121.

19. G. Ranis, "The community-centered entrepreneur in Japanese development" *Explorations in Entrepreneurial History,* VIII, and J. Hirschmeier, "Shibusawa and modern business enterprise," unpublished paper to appear in a volume on Japanese economic development to be edited by W. W. Lockwood and published by Princeton University Press.

20. Professor Maruyama quotes the following passage from a turn-of-the-century novel, Soseki's, "Since Then." It is a conversation between a young man and his sister-in-law.

And what did Father find to scold you about today?

That's hardly the point. He always finds something. What really did surprise me, though, was to hear that Father has been serving the nation. He told me that from the age of eighteen until today he has never ceased serving the country to the best of his ability.

I suppose that's why he's made such a success.

Yes, if one can make as much money as Father has by serving the nation, I wouldn't mind serving it myself.

This kind of irony was, however, a scarce commodity in pre-war Japan. Maruyama comments that the Father here portrayed "can be regarded as the typical Japanese capitalist [. . .] it was precisely when the success motive joined with nationalism that modern Japan was able to embark on its 'rush towards progress'." Masao Maruyama, *Thought and Behavior in Modern Japanese Politics* (1963), p. 7.

21. J. C. Abegglen, *The Japanese Factory,* 1958.

22. Th. Veblen, "The opportunity of Japan", reprinted in *Essays in Our Changing Order* (1934).